ISBN 1-56991-111-8

American Correctional Associa
4380 Forbes Blvd.
Lanham, Maryland 20706-4
www.corrections.com/aca
1-800-222-5646

CONTRIBUTORS

Michael Bamberg, PhD, Clark University, Worcester, MA, United States

Chris Barker, PhD, University College London, London, United Kingdom

Kathy Boudin, EdD, Columbia University, New York, NY, United States

Katherine Bradbury, PhD, Southampton University, Southampton,
United Kingdom

Paul M. Camic, PhD, University College London, London, United Kingdom,
and Canterbury Christ Church University, Tunbridge Wells, United Kingdom

Andrew Causey, PhD, Columbia College Chicago, Chicago, IL,
United States

Adele Clarke, PhD, University of California, San Francisco, San Francisco,
CA, United States

Kathleen M. Collins, PhD Candidate, University of Massachusetts Boston,
Boston, MA, United States

Sebastian J. Crutch, PhD, University College London, London,
United Kingdom

Megumi Fieldsend, PhD, Birkbeck University of London, London,
United Kingdom

Michelle Fine, PhD, City University of New York, New York, NY,
United States

Carrie Friese, PhD, London School of Economics, London, United Kingdom

Colin Griffiths, PhD, Trinity College Dublin, Dublin, Ireland

Ann Dorrit Guassora, MD, PhD, University of Copenhagen, Copenhagen,
Denmark

Emma Harding, PhD, University College London, London, United Kingdom

Heidi M. Levitt, PhD, University of Massachusetts Boston, Boston, MA,
United States

Kirsti Malterud, MD, PhD, University of Copenhagen, Copenhagen, Denmark; NORCE Norwegian Research Centre and University of Bergen, Bergen, Norway

Leanne Morrison, PhD, Southampton University, Southampton, United Kingdom

Michael Murray, PhD, Keele University, Newcastle-under-Lyme, United Kingdom

Nancy Pistrang, PhD, University College London, London, United Kingdom

Jonathan Potter, PhD, Rutgers, The State University of New Jersey, New Brunswick, NJ, United States

Volkert Siersma, PhD, University of Copenhagen, Copenhagen, Denmark

Jonathan A. Smith, PhD, Birkbeck University of London, London, United Kingdom

Mary Pat Sullivan, PhD, Nipissing University, North Bay, ON, Canada

María Elena Torre, PhD, City University of New York, New York, NY, United States

Rachel Washburn, PhD, Loyola Marymount University, Los Angeles, CA, United States

Cheryl Wilkins, MS, Columbia University, New York, NY, United States

Lucy Yardley, PhD, University of Bristol, Bristol, United Kingdom; Southampton University, Southampton, United Kingdom

Keir X. X. Yong, PhD, University College London, London, United Kingdom

PREFACE

Paul M. Camic

A warm welcome to the second edition of *Qualitative Research in Psychology: Expanding Perspectives in Methodology and Design* nearly 20 years after it appeared as the American Psychological Association's (APA's) first textbook of qualitative methods (Camic et al., 2003). At the time, APA was skeptical but supportive; neither the publisher nor the editors had any inkling it would become an APA "best seller" and be read by thousands of people worldwide. The second edition has been completely revised and is closer to being an entirely different volume than a usual second edition and includes contributions from Canada, Denmark, Ireland, Norway, the United Kingdom, and the United States.[1]

Chapter 1 (Camic) compares, contrasts, and suggests integration between qualitative and quantitative approaches to research, and in Chapter 2, Barker and Pistrang, drawing on pragmatism and pluralism, offer the new researcher much-needed guidance in choosing a qualitative method. Bamberg (Chapter 3) broadly discusses narrative psychology as a way to make bridges and connections to other qualitative methods and conceptually offers readers a way to consider many qualitative approaches as involving a form of narrative.

New authors and chapters have been added to the second edition on emerging methodologies, such as interpretive phenomenological analysis (Smith & Fieldsend, Chapter 8), situational analysis (Washburn, Clarke, & Friese, Chapter 9), visual grounded theory (Griffiths, Chapter 10), line drawing in focused ethnography (Causey, Chapter 11), and using qualitative research for intervention development and evaluation (Yardley, Bradbury, & Morrison, Chapter 13). Malterud, Siersma, and Guassora present a new approach to consider sample

---

[1]All client names and identities have been disguised in the chapters that include case studies.

size across qualitative methods (Chapter 4), and Collins and Levitt introduce qualitative meta-analysis in Chapter 14. Other chapters, on critical participatory action research (Fine, Torre, Boudin, & Wilkins, Chapter 5), narrative data and analysis (Murray, Chapter 6), and discursive psychology (Potter, Chapter 7), have been significantly revised to reflect the changes in these dynamic areas of psychological research.

Two chapters address different approaches to mixed methods. Fine et al. (Chapter 5), with critical participatory action research, use a collaborative approach to study design and methods selection involving different qualitative methods (interviews and focus groups), along with cost–benefit and reincarceration analyses. Harding, Sullivan, Crutch, and Yong (Chapter 12) describe a qualitative case study and focused ethnography used together with neuropsychological and physiological data. Both of these chapters offer pragmatic and pluralistic approaches to combining methods while retaining clear qualitative contributions.

I first became interested in qualitative methods as an undergraduate at Clark University in Massachusetts, a place that allowed me to explore ideas; challenge assumptions; and engage in the social, political, and environmental issues of the times in an intellectually stimulating and supportive atmosphere. It wasn't in a psychology class where I was introduced to qualitative inquiry, however, but in an advanced course in social geography as part of the environmental studies program. My junior-year project was to interview different users of University Park, a public park area bordering the campus. After developing a research plan and designing an interview schedule with the help of a graduate teaching assistant, I set off interviewing anyone I saw in the park over a 2-month period. My participants included older, local residents, mostly of Irish or Puerto Rican heritage; university students; teenagers, some of whom told me proudly that they belonged to various gangs; a few homeless people; and scattered others. I was surprised to discover the varied uses and meanings people gave to this park, which, quite frankly, I had only seen as comprising typical physical qualities common to many medium-sized urban parks: trees, grass, a pond, trails, some litter, and feeling a little dangerous after dark. It had not occurred to me *why and how* people used the park, and I was surprised to discover how valuable it was to many users: A somewhat "grubby" city park was actually valued by local residents. I needed to go a long way in my own reflective practice to be aware of my suburban, White, lower middle-class influences to understand the meaning this 2-acre piece of land had to Main Street South neighbors who were of different ethnicities, ages, abilities, and educational levels. Although too late in my university education to change majors, it was that experience, in addition to being a peer counselor to the campus gay alliance and volunteering as a tutor in Worcester Public Schools, that led me to psychology and eventually to qualitative research.

Next stop was a 2-year master's degree at Tufts University, where quantitative methods and positivism were the norms but where hints of qualitative "resisters" existed. It was 6 years before matriculating at Tufts, where I was learning to administer and interpret psychometric tests, that a lawsuit was first brought by African American parents against the San Francisco United School District Board of Education challenging its use of culturally biased IQ tests that labeled Black students as "retarded" and placed them in special education classes at disproportionately higher levels than their Caucasian peers (*Larry P. v. Riles,* 1979). At the time, the faculty member teaching the course did not acknowledge the issue of cultural bias in psychometric testing, nor had I yet to hear of it. When I was in a clinical placement testing African American and Chinese American children, many of their scores were lower, and some were diagnosed as "retarded," which shocked me because my conversations with them revealed a very different perspective of their abilities. The standardized quantitative data placed them in a particular diagnostic category that could have profound, possibly lifelong effects on their lives. The dilemma of psychometric scores being so different from my clinical interviewing lit another spark, leading me to further question the primacy of a positivist epistemological perspective that overly valued standardized scores and ignored self-reports of lived experience.

A few years later at Loyola University in Chicago, I had a great awakening moment taking a full semester elective course in qualitative research methods taught by Professor Steven I. Miller. Together with his guidance and six highly enthusiastic and supportive PhD students, we explored the ontological and epistemological foundations of psychological research and then delved into specific qualitative methods, beginning with the constant-comparative method developed by Bernie Glaser and Anselm Strauss just 15 years before at the University of California–San Francisco (Glaser & Strauss, 1967). My quasi-experimental PhD dissertation on male sexual dysfunction (as it was called then) was to take on an unexpected qualitative component, but this component, which was arguably the most interesting aspect of the study, was rejected by the journal that eventually published the study labeling it as "not being scientific" (Camic, 1983). Although times have changed and qualitative research is now widely published, mixed-methods research often remains a difficult sell to journals with lowered page limits and skeptical reviewers.

For most of my professional career, I would probably define myself as a pragmatist regarding ontological, epistemological, and methodological perspectives and paradigms—pragmatic in the sense that humans, and not the gods, created research methods and the "rules" governing them, and these can be altered if transparent rationales are provided and methodological integrity is maintained. I see few reasons why methodologies cannot be "mixed," and, while respecting epistemological differences, let them not dictate our research questions nor limit our curiosity. Having supervised students and taught research methods for the better part of 35 years in both the United States and United Kingdom to psychology, medical, and dance and art therapy students, if there is one takeaway I have learned it is this: The research *questions* matter most. Let the various methodologies serve the questions that society, stakeholders (e.g., those who health care services care for), and we, as researchers, have. Be aware of ontological assumptions and epistemological variations, but don't make them the red lines never to be crossed or questioned.

As incongruous as this might sound, have fun with this book and with qualitative approaches to research. Qualitative inquiry allows one to see the world differently—not with rose-colored glasses, but with wide-spectrum binoculars that may make you uncomfortable at times as they encourage and allow different ways to explore.

Let me conclude by quoting from the first stanza of *Ithaka* by the Greek-Egyptian poet C. P. Cavafy, one of my favorite poets who always seems to get it right:

> *As you set out for Ithaka*
> *hope the voyage is a long one,*
> *full of adventure, full of discovery.*
> *Laistrygonians and Cyclops,*
> *angry Poseidon—don't be afraid of them:*
> *you'll never find things like that on your way*
> *as long as you keep your thoughts raised high,*
> *as long as a rare excitement*
> *stirs your spirit and your body.*
> *Laistrygonians and Cyclops,*
> *wild Poseidon—you won't encounter them*
> *unless you bring them along inside your soul,*
> *unless your soul sets them up in front of you.*
>
> —(1975, pp. 36–37; Reprinted with permission
> from Princeton University Press)

ACKNOWLEDGMENTS

I would like to thank the many contributors to this book for their enthusiasm about participating in the second edition; their far-reaching knowledge and experiences across a range of qualitative and mixed-methods have made the book what it is. It has been an honor and pleasure to work with all of you. Second, thanks go to my nearly 4 decades of master's and doctoral students at universities in the United States and United Kingdom for their enthusiasm, challenging questions, engagement, critical thinking, and camaraderie. For those of you who have become coauthors with me on dozens of publications, thank you for being part of the journey and for contributing to my continual learning; I hope I've helped you in your own journeys. To my colleagues at the Dementia Research Centre at University College London and the Salomons Institute for Applied Psychology of Canterbury Christ Church University, huge thanks for providing me with welcoming and truly supportive research and scholarly environments.

A special thank-you to the hundreds of research participants I have had the privilege to work with over the years. You have contributed in so many ways and I cannot thank you enough. To my colleagues at APA for taking the plunge back in the early 2000s with the first edition; to Linda McCarter, senior acquisitions editor at APA Books, for inviting me back, many heartfelt thanks; and to Katherine Lenz, reference project editor at APA Books, for your kindness, humor, professionalism, and superb editorial skills; this is a better textbook because of your efforts. And to my husband of 27 years, Lawrence Wilson—English teacher, poet, singer, printmaker, ceramicist—who has supported me with edits, spell checks in U.S. and U.K. English, challenging discussions, questions, fabulous cooking, and love. None of this would have happened without you.

—Rye, East Sussex, United Kingdom

REFERENCES

Camic, P. M. (1983). Differentiating organic and psychogenic erectile dysfunction with the Millon Behavioral Health Inventory. *Sexuality and Disability, 6*(3–4), 145–149. https://doi.org/10.1007/BF01136071

Camic, P. M., Rhodes, J. E., & Yardley, L. (Eds.). (2003). *Qualitative research in psychology: Expanding perspectives in methodology and design.* American Psychological Association. https://doi.org/10.1037/10595-000

Cavafy, C. P. (1975). *C. P. Cavafy: Collected poems.* Princeton University Press.

Glaser, B. G., & Strauss, A. L. (1967). *The discovery of grounded theory: Strategies for qualitative research.* Aldine.

Larry P. v. Riles, 495 F. Supp. 926 (N.D. Calif. 1979). https://law.justia.com/cases/federal/district-courts/FSupp/495/926/2007878/

LAYING THE FOUNDATIONS: THE PLURALISTIC APPROACHES OF QUALITATIVE INQUIRY

1

Going Around the Bend and Back

Qualitative Inquiry in Psychological Research

Paul M. Camic

If you go "around the bend," it's thought that you might be very confused, mixed up about things, or even feeling a little crazy; this has been my experience of how challenging it can sometimes feel to learn—and to teach—qualitative methods. From what I came across as both an undergraduate and a doctoral student, and later as an early career researcher and clinician, the excitement of qualitative possibilities in research occasionally felt impenetrable under the lexicon of qualitative terminology, like being lost in a fog of jargon that seemed disconnected from what I already knew about the scientific method, positive epistemology, and statistical analysis. It was, at times, a very long bend in the road, making it unclear where one was going to end up. Recent doctoral students have also sometimes echoed my earlier experiences during discussions about the density of "epistemological positions," impenetrability of "competing paradigms," or the mystery of "emerging themes," for example, which to them has felt like some sort of loyalty test or political party broadcast. This has not been helped by some qualitative researchers and theoreticians who have created an "us versus them" environment, akin to a formidable 1960s Berlin Wall–style structure of concepts, ideas, methods, and analytic processes that never allowed the bend to straighten out and come to an intersection where it could connect with other roads that might offer possibilities to integrate different paradigms, epistemologies, methodologies, and their resulting research designs. The sometimes off-putting language of differing ontological beliefs and epistemological positions, occasionally seeming defensive, has not always done

https://doi.org/10.1037/0000252-001
Qualitative Research in Psychology: Expanding Perspectives in Methodology and Design, Second Edition, P. M. Camic (Editor)

qualitative research in psychology any favors, although it is understandable that the field has needed to differentiate itself from the Goliath of quantitative research (Hamilton, 1994).

More recently Rennie (2012) identified the lack of a unifying qualitative methodology contributing to the relative marginalization of qualitative inquiry within psychology. For qualitative methods to have more credibility, he suggested that all qualitative research is hermeneutical and through the use of the hermeneutic circle method, the "activity of educing and articulating the meaning of a text through abduction, theorematic deduction and induction . . . enables demonstration, achieved rhetorically, of the validity of the understandings of the text under study" (p. 385). His attempts at developing a coherent qualitative methodology that might unify many if not all qualitative methods is an important development in psychological science.

The present volume views qualitative designs and methods as both independent approaches to research that stand on their own and that act as companions to other qualitative (Fine et al., Chapter 5) and quantitative (Harding et al., Chapter 12) methods, while also being key components for intervention development and evaluation (Yardley et al., Chapter 13). The book is intended to help guide you around the bend but also take you back to a place where some form of integration among epistemological perspectives, different paradigms, types of research questions, data collection processes, analytic tools, and writing discussion sections might seem feasible—and possible. From my perspective, going around the bend and back means connecting up qualitative research to the wider psychological, social science, and health sciences communities and to the problems they are trying to solve. It means pragmatism over ideology and encourages qualitative inquiry to be used alongside different methodological and paradigmatic traditions to answer different and sometimes complementary research questions (for an expanded discussion of pragmatism in psychological research and in research practice, respectively, see Rennie, 2000; and Yardley & Bishop, 2007). Qualitative research is not a unified field, and forms of data collection, goals of research, and types of data analysis can vary widely (Madill & Gough, 2008), making it a far more pluralistic approach than is sometimes recognized (see Barker & Pistrang, Chapter 2).

Qualitative inquiry in psychology has had a distinguished, albeit somewhat hidden, history among North American psychologists until relatively recently, when it has gradually entered the curriculum of a number of undergraduate and graduate psychology departments. Although it has tended to be more widely accepted in Europe, as demonstrated by undergraduate and postgraduate course offerings and by research output, the American Psychological Association (APA) has shown increased interest and support through the addition of a qualitative section to its methodology division and renaming it "Division 5: Quantitative and Qualitative Methods" (APA, n.d.) and by developing new journal reporting guidelines on qualitative, mixed-methods, and qualitative meta-analysis (Levitt et al., 2018). In Asia, the launch of the Asian Qualitative Research Association in 2015 brought together hundreds of researchers from different disciplines; it has now grown to several thousand members. Qualitative research in Africa remains more limited, likely because of the restricted financial resources and the lack of interest in these methods by policy makers and government funders (Dzvimbo, 2006), yet there is a growing and dynamic community of researchers in many countries across different disciplines (Barnes, 2012) that are making substantial contributions to an African-centric perspective, researched and written by Africans and not by visiting Europeans and North Americans looking in from afar.

(TRYING TO) MAKE SENSE OF COMPLEXITY

In the classic children's book *The Phantom Tollbooth*, Norton Juster tells the story of two brothers, King Azaz and the Mathemagician, who inherited their father's kingdom of Wisdom. They were by nature very suspicious and jealous. Each one tried to outdo the other. King Azaz insisted that words were far more significant than numbers and hence that his kingdom was truly the greater, and the Mathemagician claimed that numbers were much more important than words and hence that his kingdom was supreme. They discussed and debated and raved and ranted until they were on the verge of blows when it was decided to submit the question to arbitration by the princesses Rhyme and Reason. After days of careful consideration in which all the evidence was weighted and all the witnesses heard, they made their decision:

> Words and numbers are of equal value, for, in the cloak of knowledge, one is warp and the other woof. It is no more important to count the sands than it is to name the stars. Therefore, let both kingdoms live in peace. (Juster, 1965, pp. 74–75)

Unfortunately, Rhyme and Reason's exquisite logic fell on deaf ears. The princesses were banished from the kingdom, and the full breadth of knowledge remained elusive for many years. Until the past 10 years or so, a similar fate appears to have beset the kingdom of psychology, where quantitative and qualitative methodologists have met each other with resistance and skepticism. Yet promising new developments have seen, if not parity, an acceptance and a welcoming of methodological diversity in psychology, medicine, gerontology, and related fields (e.g., Cooper, 2012; Kitto et al., 2008; Levitt et al., 2018; Schoenberg & McAuley, 2007). Since the publication of the first edition of this book in 2003, attempts at finding common ground are prevailing and qualitative approaches to understanding the human experience are no longer being relegated to an ancillary role (e.g., Cooper et al., 2012). One could argue that an overreliance of psychology on positivist epistemology, which asserts that there are universal truths or laws to be discovered and quantitatively measured, has hampered inventiveness, restricting the very nature of the questions that have been asked and the sources of data that have been considered legitimate. As in *The Phantom Tollbooth*, wherein the princesses were ultimately rescued and their recommendations heeded, momentum from different fields within psychology and related disciplines are now incorporating qualitative methods into a range of research areas. Like the first edition, my hope is that this volume helps to continue the momentum by encouraging psychological researchers to value the kinds of questions qualitative methods can answer, to further consider a pragmatic approach to paradigm integration, and to bring about greater methodological inclusiveness and appreciation of the range and depth of qualitative approaches to psychological and social research.

BACKGROUND: THE FUNDAMENTAL QUESTIONS

In his attempt to rescue Rhyme and Reason, the protagonist in *The Phantom Tollbooth*, Milo, journeys through the kingdom of numbers, Digitopolis. There, a man who poses a series of problems, including one about a 68-foot-long beaver, confronts him:

> "That's absurd," objected Milo, whose head was spinning from all the numbers and questions. "That may be true," he acknowledged, "but it's completely accurate, and as long as the answer is right, who cares if the question is wrong? If you want sense, you'll have to make it yourself." (Juster, 1965, p. 175)

Historically, psychologists, perhaps more than other social scientists, have been prone to privileging methods and procedures over research questions (Camic et al., 2003; Gergen, 1985). Putting the methodological cart before the horse of a research question can constrain our full understanding of psychological processes by limiting the kinds of questions we can ask as researchers. Moreover, basic ontological, epistemological, and methodological questions, such as "What is real?" "Who knows what is real?" and "How do you know what is real?," respectively, are critical considerations that underpin planning psychological research and push researchers to challenge their assumptions about values, knowledge, and "acceptable" data. Pluralistic psychological research goes beyond positivism, which implicitly privileges experimental approaches to knowledge. In deciding what is real, and for whom it is real, a pluralistic approach to research might encourage both skepticism and innovation, be a little subversive, and take on new topics and questions, but remain rigorous, thorough, and useful. Shweder (1996), in an important essay about the differences between *quanta* and *qualia*, suggests that we "put our metaphysical cards on the table (our assumptions about the underlying nature of social reality)" (p. 175), thereby revealing what each of us thinks research is all about.

Those "cards" vary, of course, among the contributors to this volume. What is perhaps a common core to all the chapters, however, is discarding the notion that what separates quantitative and qualitative approaches to research is whether to count or not count, measure or not measure, sample or not sample, administer a questionnaire or conduct an interview. Because all social science research counts and measures in some way or another, a pluralistic approach considers *what* to count and measure and what one discovers when doing so (Shweder, 1996, p. 179). Stated another way, the questions become "to count and/or to discover the name," "to measure and/or to listen and observe," or "to administer a questionnaire and/or talk with someone." Qualitative research interrogates whether an objective conception of reality can truly exist and suggests that other forms of investigation are necessary to increase our understanding of the phenomena we are studying. Writing several decades ago, the Austrian sociologist and phenomenologist Alfred Schütz (1962), seeking to bridge the gap between different forms of inquiry, wrote, "the principles of controlled inference and verification by fellow scientists and the theoretical ideals of unity, simplicity, universality and precision prevail" for all empirical sciences, be they social or natural sciences (p. 49). He argued for an appreciation of pluralistic approaches to research that included valuing different research questions and methodologies that are independent of the natural (e.g., biological, physical) sciences and more relevant to studying the lived social and psychological world of people. Logic is important for all research, he contended, but the logic of the natural sciences can lead to a "monopolistic imperialism" that disregards other types of problems worthy of study.

"What is real?" evokes the issue that divided the brothers in the Kingdom of Wisdom. Stated another way, one might ask, "What is valuable?" As a profession, psychology has historically decided that numbers are more real—and more valuable—than words and responses on paper-and-pencil tests more real (and valid and valuable) than interviews, conversations, and other complex forms of representation. However, "How do you know what is real?" is perhaps the question that best defines empiricism and provides a substantial foundation for a qualitative psychology. Of course, we all know what is real—but our realities may be different, depending on our cultural and socioeconomic backgrounds, language abilities, gender, race, ethnicity, sexual orientation, and age. This was particularly evident in the 2020 American election, when the sense of very different lived realities were strongly articulated. Each of us—and certainly each and every research participant in our respective studies—possesses "an alternative symbolic universe (which) poses a threat because its existence demonstrates empirically that one's own universe is less than inevitable" (Berger & Luckmann, 1966, p. 108). However, to make psychology more than empirical—to make it scientific—many of our research paradigms and methods discount the existence of an alternative symbolic universe where methods might be "mixed" (Tashakkori & Teddlie, 2010) and paradigms integrated (Madill & Gough, 2008) to answer different types of questions and explore issues more broadly and deeply (see Chapters 5 and 12, this volume).

Among other problems, the assumption that it is primarily scientists who know what is real becomes a denial of the experience of research participants as a valid source of knowledge. This is really not an issue for biologists or chemists because their "subject" may be a diseased cell or a chemical interaction. When doing research involving people, a de facto hermeneutic relationship, where meaning is intersubjectivity created, develops in that the researcher and the participant are affected by each other and modify their responses, behaviors, and perceptions based on that interaction—and of course on events and histories before the interaction. This is the case whether one uses an interview or a psychometric instrument to collect data. Yet in most of psychological research, the psychologist-scientist controls the definition of reality and "the threat to the social definitions of reality is neutralized by assigning an inferior ontological status, and thereby not to be taken seriously cognitive status, to all definitions existing outside the social universe" (Berger & Luckmann, 1966, p. 115). For example, what happens in a laboratory where a controlled social experiment takes place has had more value in psychological research than speaking with people in their own environments (see Chapter 12, this volume). Representations of research that exist outside of positivism and the experimental method in psychology, while gaining significant recognition and appreciation (e.g., Levitt et al., 2018), can still be looked on as inferior and are not taken as seriously by some journals, funding sources, doctoral dissertation committees, and psychology faculty (Roberts & Castell, 2016).

Related to this issue is the question of "Who is to judge what is real?" In *The Phantom Tollbooth*, Rhyme and Reason, as a collaborative pair, were the judges of what was real. They carefully evaluated the worth and importance of words and numbers within the context of their society and could see that both brothers' perceptions of number and narrative had merit. For psychological research, the same also needs to hold true—both qualitative and quantitative approaches have value and neither should be privileged, but both should be evaluated by criteria relevant to each approach. In judging qualitative research, criteria related to methodological integrity, fidelity to the subject matter, utility in reaching goals, transferability (Levitt et al., 2018), unity, simplicity, and precision (Schütz, 1962), as well as questions about who controls the data and from whose perspective the data are interpreted (Jennings et al., 2018), taken together, form a solid evaluative foundation.

I would also add another consideration, is the research valuable and to whom? Value is often held by the grant makers, admissions committees, journal editors, and traditions of a discipline—powerful voices indeed. But what about the value of research to stakeholders, those people receiving health care services, caregivers, policy makers, community residents, and the general public? Not only for qualitative researchers but an important question for all engaged in research to consider is this: Has the research question and resulting method(s) taken into consideration the interests, priorities, opinions, and experiences of those we are researching? Consulting the population we are planning to engage in research at a very early stage in its development can lead to new insights, different priorities, and a joined sense of the value of a particular study (Boivin et al., 2018). There is room in a pluralistic approach to paradigms to be more flexible and accommodating to a wider range of voices and perspectives without compromising quality, methodological integrity, trustworthiness, or transferability.

METHODOLOGICAL INTEGRITY: DECIDING WHAT IS GOOD QUALITATIVE RESEARCH

Although this is a textbook about qualitative methods, it is important to briefly critique and contrast three concepts that are often cited as foundations of quantitative methods and, by frequent implication, all psychological research: validity, objectivity, and reliability. It is likely these terms would be first encountered in an undergraduate course on research methods. They are most often associated with quantitative approaches to research but regularly qualitative methods are also, problematically, assessed by these criteria. They relate to the degree of control that each purports to be necessary within a research project. Historically, this often amounts to whether the research takes place in a naturalistic context or in a regulated laboratory-like or quasi-experimental setting (Hoshmand, 1999; McGartland & Polgar, 1994). There are several problems with this conceptualization, which dichotomizes and oversimplifies the issue of validity, and with setting criteria that all psychological research must demonstrate objectivity and generalizability, thus creating artificial boundaries and falsities. A quick exploration is needed. First, this conceptualization begs the definition of "naturalistic," a possibly outdated term because there is nothing naturalistic about a psychiatric hospital, outpatient counseling service, chronic pain clinic, cancer treatment program, art museum, large corporation, music hall, or school—all examples of settings in which psychological research has taken place. Second, there is little that is naturalistic about the actions of observing, interviewing, or testing someone. Third, elevating the laboratory and the experimental method onto a "pure" and objective plane where the values and biases of the researcher are supposedly left at the door and where statistical control ensures validity and objectivity is highly problematic. Fourth, "objectivity," like generalizability, is a highly contested construct (Hager, 1982; Mitroff, 1972; Smaling, 1992). No experiment, no research question, and certainly no interpretation of data can possibly be truly objective. Likewise, to assess all psychological research results as to their generalizability to a wider population ignores the nuances of context and presupposes that only studies with very large sample sizes are valid, and, by default, only quantifiable information is "real" (and valuable). The types of problems we are interested in, the questions we ask, the kind of data we collect, and the analyses we undertake all emanate from some context, be it racial, socioeconomic, political, cultural, geographic, or personal. Qualitative research is particularly suited to appreciate and understand contextual aspects of stories, place, language, situation, race, gender, and lived experience.

Moving beyond the historical use of terms such as validity, objectivity, and generalizability, APA qualitative researchers have conceptualized new ways to determine (and improve) methodological integrity across different qualitative methods, for use by researchers, supervisory panels, ethics committees, dissertation examiners, and journal editors (Levitt et al., 2018):

> The (Division 5) Task Force recommends the concept of methodological integrity and recommends its evaluation via its two composite processes: (a) fidelity to the subject matter, which is the process by which researchers develop and maintain allegiance to the phenomenon under study as it is conceived within their tradition of inquiry, and (b) utility in achieving research goals, which is the process by which researchers select procedures to generate insightful findings that usefully answer their research questions. (p. 2)

The process of determining methodological integrity bypasses the artificial boundaries and falsities of validity, objectivity, and generalizability to study the human experience as Schütz (1962) and Rhyme and Reason urge, by bringing more information and experience—about ourselves as researchers and the people we study as participants—under the cloak of knowledge. A "higher power" has not provided us with psychological methods, they are not sacrosanct, and therefore should be critically assessed and reflected upon for the assumptions they bring to each research situation and the corresponding research questions.

Knowing that methods have the effect of constraining what one looks for and that "nothing is as selective as perception" (Eisner, 2003), Barker and Pistrang (Chapter 2, this volume) argue that all forms of inquiry, like all forms of representation, have their own advantages, limitations, and biases. They approach how to choose a qualitative method from a pluralist and pragmatist perspective and contend that *"pluralism* means celebrating variety—in this case, variety in research approaches—and *pragmatism* means doing what works—in this case, choosing the method that works best for the research question that you are attempting to address" (p. 27). To this end, they suggest strategies for evaluating and selecting the most appropriate qualitative method. Rather than arguing the merits of any particular approach, they take a more pluralistic strategy. Because different methods pose different, as well as complementary, strengths and weaknesses, Barker and Pistrang suggest considering a wide range of qualitative methods at an early stage of the research process, all of which fit well with concept of methodological integrity (Levitt et al., 2018).

The outcome of the research must be demonstrably shaped by the process of eliciting data, whether this is achieved by means of experimental hypothesis testing, participant input, or inductive theory building. To qualify as good-quality research, rather than casual description or uninformed interpretation, the researcher(s) must also display thoroughness; expertise in the application of the method selected; and awareness of the relevant theoretical, historical, sociocultural, and interpersonal context of the research. To demonstrate the preceding qualities, the methods used and conclusions drawn must be clearly described and carefully justified. A final pragmatic criterion for good research is that it should be meaningful and useful to at least some people, for some purposes—ideally, outside of academia. Good questions to ask in the planning stages of any research project in psychology are "How might this research have impact? What outputs—aside from a journal citation—might the research produce?" (e.g., in Chapter 5 of this volume, Fine et al. describe outputs from participatory action research).

All research, be it qualitative, mixed methods, or quantitative, seeks to tell a story to an audience. The antagonist of the story might be a public health crisis such as the emergence of HIV/AIDS or, more recently, COVID-19. A mental health problem such as rate of major depression among American adolescents or a worldwide disease like young (or early) onset dementia might equally fill this role. Profound social inequality, racism, ageism, sexism, and homophobia can all audition, and it would be a hard call to reject any of them. Protagonists could be a new medication, psychosocial intervention or a combination of social components, specific activity and location, such as a museum or art gallery (e.g., Camic & Chatterjee, 2013) to help reduce social isolation in older people, provide new ways to think about dementia care, or help people with severe and enduring mental health problems. The audience could be a varied one—other academics, policy makers, health care planners, private insurance companies, community activists, grant funders—each with their own interests and stories to tell. I would argue that narrative in qualitative research occurs across all qualitative methodologies and, as Bamberg attests in Chapter 3 of this volume, "giving narrative . . . a prominent place within the overall frame of doing qualitative inquiry requires . . . [determining with] more clarity which aspects of our engagement with qualitative methodologies" are most valued and "which aspects of narrative inquiry do we deem particularly relevant in our overall qualitative approach, and which 'definitions' of narrative do we embrace as productive in pursuit of more specific research questions" (p. 51). Although I am sure this will be contentious, building a narrative qualitative psychology as an overarching cohesive framework for qualitative inquiry could provide a powerful dialogic tool to engage participants, creators of research, and its consumers and has relevance across methods discussed in the following chapters.

One issue that often frustrates and confounds those new to qualitative research is deciding on the sample size of one's project. For example, obtaining a precise sample size is crucially relevant to statistical power but has minimal relevance to many qualitative methods. As a consequence, it is challenging to specify clear-cut common procedures for ensuring validity across all qualitative methods. Although still frequently used, checklists for evaluating the quality of qualitative studies have been shown to have significant limitations (Barbour, 2001), and their value is questionable. In Chapter 4, Malterud et al. introduce a novel approach examining sample size and suggest shared methodological principles for estimating an adequate number and type of units, events, or participants across qualitative methods. As Yardley (2000) attested, there are higher order criteria that are relevant to all forms of rigorous empirical research, whether qualitative or quantitative, and can be satisfied in very different ways by each different piece of research (Yardley, 2000). First, to qualify as empirical—in some way corresponding to what is real—research must be shown to be well-grounded in some kind of data.

John Dewey (1934), a pioneer of psychology and "pragmatic" philosophy, suggested that all inquiry and evaluation, whether scientific, moral, or common-sense, is ultimately concerned with the question of what things are good for. This question is undoubtedly of central importance to our inquiry into how the methods that are used by psychologists might profitably be expanded by the adoption of qualitative methods. Because we have suggested that qualitative methods may offer different and complementary benefits and insights from the quantitative methods used by psychologists, the following section considers what qualitative methods are particularly good for, illustrating these merits by reference to the wide range of very different approaches to qualitative research presented in the second section of this book.

HOW CAN QUALITATIVE RESEARCH HELP US TO UNDERSTAND THE WORLD AROUND US?

In keeping with the tradition of qualitative research, to address this question, a personal, selective interpretation is offered of some of the themes that recur across several methods. However, this analysis is far from exhaustive or definitive but is hoped to be a solid introduction to well-known methods and innovative approaches within qualitative research in psychology, allied health sciences, and social sciences.

Exploration and Theory Development

A valuable use for qualitative research, of which most quantitative researchers are aware, is as a tool for exploring a topic or problem that has not previously been researched. The logic of experimental or questionnaire research demands that the relevant variables are predefined and outcomes predicted a priori on the basis of theory. In contrast, more inductive methods, such as situational analysis (Washburn et al., Chapter 9), visual grounded theory (Griffiths, Chapter 10), and focused ethnography (Causey, Chapter 11), encourage the researcher to approach a topic without firm preconceptions about what variables will be important or how they will be related and to gradually build a theory to explain the data that are collected. Similarly, the interpretive phenomenological analysis method (Smith & Fieldsend, Chapter 8) is a method for discovering psychological meanings by identifying the essential psychological constituents or structure of an interviewee's description of an experience. However, qualitative researchers do not view such exploration as an attempt to produce an "objective" description of a phenomenon because they assign a vital role to the researcher in constructing the analytical interpretation, whether through imaginative transcendence of "taken-for-granted" meanings (Giorgi, 1970) or by applying disciplinary knowledge and theoretical sensitivity to the topic (Henwood & Pidgeon, 1994).

Situated Analysis

As the authors in the first section of this text point out, it is impossible to seek to maximize simultaneously both external validity (representativeness of real-world contexts) and internal validity (precision and control). Although it is misleading to make an absolute distinction between "naturalistic" and "scientific" research, it is clear that experimental research usually requires a degree of artificial manipulation or control of the key variables, whereas qualitative research typically seeks to maximize the ecological validity of the data by gathering it in real-world contexts. This latter approach permits analysis of the way in which these real-world contexts affect the phenomenon under investigation. Chapter 9 (Washburn et al.) introduces situational analysis, a methodology that produces relational, ecological, and situated understandings of meaning and inquiry of a situation as a key unit of analysis rather than focusing on individual participants, which is done by nearly all other qualitative methods. It employs several types of situational maps to better understand the dynamics and complexities of an issue, locating it more broadly in a particular context such as, for example, medical care decision making during a pandemic, the role of mental health diagnoses in a private health care system, and where rare forms of dementia fit into international and national dementia care strategies.

On a more individual level, awareness of the fundamental influence of social context on what people say has led discourse analysts (see Potter, Chapter 7) to focus their attention on naturally occurring talk because the discursive resources and strategies people use are often quite different in everyday conversation than when speaking to a research interviewer. To gain a further understanding of the influence of context, some researchers find it helpful to immerse themselves for a prolonged period in the personal, sociocultural, or historical context of the topic they are studying (Causey, Chapter 11; Harding et al., Chapter 12).

Holistic Analysis of Complex, Dynamic, and Exceptional Phenomena

Qualities are emergent properties arising from the configuration of elements in a whole. Hence, qualitative research is necessarily holistic; microanalysis of parts is always undertaken in the context of a larger whole. For example, the discussion of how applied ethnography can be integrated into psychological research provided by Causey in Chapter 11 involves the innovative use of line drawing as an investigative method. He describes how scrutinous drawing can be employed to "focus on using of the act of drawing as a process of perception" (p. 220) rather than to focus on the picture created. Using a mixed-methods approach, Harding et al. (Chapter 12) analyzes in detail a day in the life of people with dementia-related visual impairment living within a home environment using focused ethnography, interviews, and neuropsychological testing to explore how the challenges in these intersecting environments are navigated in real time and in the social and relational context in which they occur, while also exploring how a variety of data sources might contribute to this understanding.

Using mixed methods is not straightforward, however. Qualitative methods can be treated as subsidiaries to quantitative work, an approach that is unable to maximize the potential of both methods (Marecek, 2003). Moreover, quantitative and qualitative methods often are premised on divergent epistemological bases and may produce contradictory sets of outcomes. Nevertheless, inclusion within a single study of both qualitative and quantitative methods can be helped by developing more pragmatic, integrative paradigms (Yardley & Bishop, 2007) justified on the grounds that interlacing methods, even when they yield disparate findings, enrich our understanding of human behavior (Rabinowitz & Weseen, 2001). By touching on different aspects of the same phenomena, two (or more) methodological approaches yield a more complete story. Additionally, besides being able to stand on their own as independent methods, qualitative approaches can be part of a "stepped approach" to understanding a particular problem or issue, occurring before a larger scale quantitative study or as a poststudy analysis to discover more about how and why an intervention or activity worked well or failed to have an impact, among other pertinent questions. Qualitative approaches are exceptionally compatible with the development stage of planned behavior change interventions. As discussed by Yardley et al. in Chapter 13, "qualitative approaches to exploring and analyzing experiences of behavior change interventions are particularly well suited to understanding the complexity of such interventions" (p. 263) by being used in feasibility trials to detect components of intervention protocols that need to be better understood.

In qualitative research, collection of very detailed data about just a few examples of a phenomenon—even a single case, as can occur within interpretive phenomenological analysis (Chapter 8)—permits analysis of multiple aspects of a topic. A period of observation or series of interviews typically yields an intimidatingly vast repository of data about a multitude of interacting elements and aspects of the topic studied. Inevitably, qualitative researchers must be selective in their analysis, but freedom from the restrictive constraints of meeting statistical assumptions (McGrath & Johnson, 2003) permits consideration of fine distinctions, exceptions, and complex patterns of interrelationships. Qualitative data also allow researchers to develop multilayered interpretations by returning to the data to carry out multiple analyses of different aspects of the topics, which can be contextualized by the other analyses (Barker & Pistrang, Chapter 2). For example, Griffiths (Chapter 10) analyzes video recordings of nonverbal and verbal interaction to develop *attuning*, a theory of interaction of people with severe and multiple disabilities and their caregivers "whereby communication partners move symmetrically or asymmetrically towards or away from each cognitively and emotionally" (Griffiths & Smith, 2016, p. 130). Video and grounded theory are used to present "a method of qualitative inquiry that enables an understanding of how individuals behave by not only delving into their verbal texts but also by considering visual as well as aural forms of data" (Griffiths, Chapter 10, this volume, p. 188). The narratives that Griffiths explores are the often ignored nonverbal narratives "characterized by behaviors that are seen as fleeting, small, and unimportant." The use of video and video analysis in qualitative psychological research is an expanding frontier that allows diverse ways to obtain data and perform different types of analysis, including micro-analysis to examine deviation, inconsistency, and omission.

Whereas in quantitative research inconsistency is treated as error and nonresponse as missing data, in discourse analysis (Potter, Chapter 7) and psychoanalytical analysis (Kvale, 1996), for example, the internal contradictions, pauses, and absences in people's talk are valuable pointers to important areas of tension, difficulty, or conflict; deviations from typical or "normal" behavior provide particularly useful information about cultural norms and the reasons for and consequences of transgressing these. The dynamic complexity added by the dimension of temporal change is also fundamental to many forms of qualitative research. Murray (Chapter 6) explains how people's narratives embody the dynamics of their identity by simultaneously shaping the past and projecting into the future; hence, narrative analysis provides an intrinsically chronological perspective on the lives of narrators.

Analysis of Subjective Meaning

One way of thinking about the difference—and complementarity—between quantitative and qualitative research is to consider quantitative research as the process of producing a map of a place and qualitative research as the process of producing a video of that place. A map is extremely useful; it conveys with economy and precision the location of a place and its relationship to other places in terms of proximity and direction. However, even the most detailed map is unable to convey an understanding of what it is like to be at that place. In contrast, a video conveys in vivid detail the constantly changing perspective of the observer. Although this perspective is selective and could not easily be used for navigation, it is able to communicate something of the subjective experience of being there. This capacity of qualitative research to gain partial access to the subjective perspectives of others therefore makes it an ideal method for research into subjective meaning, whether this consists of abstracting the psychological core of an experience (Smith & Fieldsend, Chapter 8); "studying how psychological issues and objects are constructed, understood, and conveyed in the many interactions across public displays, constructions, and orientations of people" (Potter, Chapter 7); or using video analysis and grounded theory to understand the subjective experience, feelings, and communication of those with extremely limited cognitive ability (Clare et al., 2020; Griffiths, Chapter 10, this volume).

Although subjectivity has often been associated with bias that must be contained and reduced, Gough and Madill (2012) suggested that researchers consider "the benefits of a more . . . reflexive scientific attitude" that involve accommodating participant subjectivity and reflexively working with researcher subjectivity, where relevant to the theories, research question, and methodology being used in a particular study. Their multiple suggestions allow numerous ways for researchers to consider subjectivity as a dynamic part of research and is an exciting development that can better incorporate it "as a valuable resource that can be tapped to illuminate both the phenomenon under investigation and to situate research design and practices more generally" (p. 382).

Just as making a video is not a matter of random or neutral recording but rather of aesthetically framing a sequence of scenes to convey a particular impression to a viewer, the analysis of subjective meaning contains aesthetic and interpersonal dimensions (Washburn et al., Chapter 9) that are largely absent—if not excluded—from the process of quantitative research.

Relational Analysis and Reflexivity

Undertaking situated, holistic analysis of meaning does not simply entail considering multiple aspects of a phenomenon and contextual influences; rather, it implies a fundamentally relational approach to the topic and to research itself. Qualitative research therefore requires an appreciation of the relationships of all participants in the research with each other and with the wider society in which they are embedded. For example, Miller et al. (2003) explained how ethnography always entails at least double vision because the process of trying to understand another culture inevitably involves contrasting it with one's own culture so that insight is gained simultaneously into the taken-for-granted assumptions and interpretive frameworks of both cultures. Likewise, Causey (Chapter 11) and Harding et al. (Chapter 12) draw on forms of ethnography, along with other methods, to examine and challenge the ways we understand the culture of going psychological research and the culture of those living with a dementia, respectively.

Discourse analysis, another form of qualitative research, is founded on relational analysis. Discourse can be analyzed relationally in several ways (e.g., Wetherell et al., 2000). First, the intrinsically relational nature of linguistic meaning can be a focus for study; for example, how terms such as *migrant* or *male* take their meaning from their relation to the terms *citizen* and *female*. Second, discourse can be analyzed as dialogue or social interaction. Discursive psychology (Potter, Chapter 7) examines the ways in which meanings and effects are coproduced in interactions, playing close attention to how this process of coconstruction is influenced by the context of the setting in which the dialogue takes place. For example, in a country that has a historically negative view of socialism or is invested in painting any form of socialism as dangerous without attention to the vast differences across socialistic approaches to government, an account of a country's political leader promoting a private, high-cost health care system could take the meaning and have the effect of an excuse to avoid exploring who does not benefit from such a system if offered in the context of the discourse that "universal health care for all is socialism." If those who see universal health care as "socialistic" politely sympathized with the leader, they help to construct the political leader as blameless. A third implicit context for all discourse is the wider sociocultural and rhetorical context in which such coconstructions take place. For example, the account is more likely to be successful in constructing such political leaders as blameless if they are relatively powerful, or a core group member, than if they are low-status outsiders—and if the account can draw on effective rhetorical resources (e.g., humorously depicting the people who cannot afford to pay health care premiums as feckless and criticism of the leader as unfair and undemocratic).

Murray (Chapter 6) notes that the influence of sociocultural context on apparently personal narratives is so profound that it shapes our identity and consciousness, furnishing the roles and plotlines that we use to live in a way that makes coherent sense to ourselves and to those with whom we interact. For example, exemplifying a critical participatory action research (CPAR) perspective, a collective of female researchers and inmates at a New York state prison and local universities (Fine et al., Chapter 5) look back over a 25-year period and show how inmates' narratives depicting themselves as dual personalities—the "old, bad" and "new, transformed" selves—did not simply reproduce negative social stereotypes of criminals but facilitated the development of a reflective agency that allowed the women to condemn the crimes they had committed in the past while articulating a positive identity for the present and future. Fine et al. (Chapter 5) highlight CPAR elements:

> the research is deeply rooted in community; designed by collectives of academics and community members; centers on the perspectives of those most impacted; integrates evidence from history, statistics, and narratives; and results in publishing and disseminating 'products' that are scholarly, policy-oriented, and accessible to the local community. (p. 98)

Awareness of the constructive nature of talk is most explicit in forms of discourse analysis but has much wider relevance. All psychological studies involve humans who are speaking and acting in a social and linguistic context, and so qualitative researchers whose interest is not solely in language nevertheless find it useful to consider the sociolinguistic processes influencing the talk and action they are studying. For example, enriching a grounded theory study with consideration of different interpretative perspectives on the themes that had emerged, including perspectives that analyzed these themes as discursive practices (Henwood & Pidgeon, 2003), allowed researchers to consider participants' statements about "valuing trees" not simply as expressing personal opinions about vegetation but as tapping into and constructing systems of symbolic and social value in which trees were associated with life and health.

For many qualitative researchers, awareness of sociocultural context and interpersonal relations necessarily extends to a reflexive consideration of the role of the researcher, the relationship between researcher and participants, and the influence of the researcher on the research process (Fine et al., Chapter 5; Gilligan et al., 2003). This requires researchers to attend to their own responses to the interviewee's narrative—partly to ensure that the voice of the interviewee is not distorted or submerged by the emotional response of the researcher, but also because, as in psychoanalysis, the analyst's reactions provide a valuable empathic link to the subjective experience of the interviewee. Kvale (2003) highlighted additional features of the psychoanalytical relationship from which researchers might profit, suggesting that the close, embodied interaction between analyst and patient fosters intuitive and bodily modes of knowing and provides a wealth of information that is absent from the "psychology of strangers" constructed from single "snapshot" encounters with research participants. Both Kvale (2003) and Murray (Chapter 6, this volume) welcome the opportunity provided by narrative and interview methods for interviewees to exert control and influence, setting the agenda and entering into dialogue with the interviewer to reject interpretations that do not make sense to them.

As this section has made clear, qualitative research methods can be extraordinarily useful, providing unique access into our understanding of the human experience. In a sense, the chapters in this volume enable psychologists to circle above the patchworked landscape of various qualitative approaches, noting their different hues and shared boundaries. It is only when researchers are on the ground and meaningfully using the methods, however, that they can fully experience their texture, affordances, and constraints. Moving from the negative stereotypes of qualitative research to a more balanced approach has begun in North America and elsewhere. As students are exposed to qualitative methods alongside quantitative methods, my experience has been that they better appreciate the relative strengths and limits of both approaches. To this end, it is exciting to see psychology departments continuing to incorporate qualitative methods courses that provide the same meticulous level of detail as the courses that are typically offered in quantitative methods. The final section of this chapter offers encouragement to academic psychology to take up this challenge and provide more teaching resources in qualitative methods.

The Temporal in Qualitative Research

Much of the data collection for qualitative research in psychology has taken place at one point in time. A research participant's experience or understanding of a personal event, circumstance, situation, discourse, or perspective is too often collected as a data source during one interview or observation. There have been exceptions, of course, and they are worth noting. Narrative analysis (Chapter 6) seeks to understand stories over time; ethnography and applied ethnography (Chapters 11 and 12) look at long-term and briefer time periods, respectively; and participatory action research (Chapter 5), by its design as an action-oriented methodology, always collects data over time. Situational analysis (Chapter 9) examines complex phenomena that exist in a dynamic context that develops over time. All of these methodologies explore change over time.

In going forward, one area in which qualitative analysis can be developed and expanded is in its use as a longitudinal methodology. Collecting information from one participant at a given point in time is often the bulk of doctoral level data as well as many published works using qualitative methodologies (e.g., interpretive phenomenological analysis, discourse analysis, thematic analysis, conversational analysis, grounded theory). To further advance qualitative inquiry and to deepen our understanding of change—about an issue, topic, area, or phenomenon—using multiple data collection points over a period of time would enhance our knowledge and provide a wealth of more nuanced information. Admittedly, this would in itself would be more time-consuming for hard-pressed students and established researchers and create cost and accessibility implications. Yet longitudinal qualitative research also permits more options to better explore the concept of change; describe and analyze the dynamics of interpersonal interaction; provide research participants more opportunity to reflect, review, and summarize in a different way than the imposed limitations of a one-off research encounter; and better explore the concept of change (e.g., Carduff et al., 2015; Holland et al., 2006; Morrow & Crivello, 2015; Neale, 2018). Harding et al. (Chapter 12) provide an example of different types of data collected over the course of 1 day rather than the usual 1- to 2-hour period seen in many qualitative reports. Focused ethnography also offers an approach to longitudinal research that is applicable to some areas of psychology (Simonds et al., 2012).

Ethics in Qualitative Research

Ethical decision making across all health, social, and psychological research is an essential component of a successful project. It should not be a secondary consideration but one that is central to the research question, recruitment decisions, choice of methods, data collection processes, analysis, and dissemination. Although APA's *Ethical Principles of Psychologists and Code of Conduct* (2017) and the British Psychological Society's *Code of Human Research Ethics* (2014), for example, thoroughly address the basics of research ethics, neither document provides sufficient guidance for qualitative researchers. For both new and seasoned researchers, there are, however, additional resources that can provide useful information about some of the key ethical issues to consider when conducting qualitative research (e.g., Sanjari et al., 2014). Some of these issues are methodology-specific, whereas others go across most, if not all, qualitative research. Each chapter in this book addresses ethics as related to its respective topic area, but overarching issues to consider are addressed in this section.

Compared with quantitative research, the qualitative researcher will take on different roles depending on the methodology used, but cutting across all qualitative research is the importance of the reflective research practitioner (Mortari, 2015). Qualitative researchers are in powerful positions when interacting with research participants. They are interpreting the lives, words, experiences, actions, and opinions of other people who will sometimes be vulnerable, at risk, societal outsiders, and with limited abilities and resources. Understanding the dynamics of an inherently unequal relationship can result in a higher quality, more equitable project that comes closer to capturing what the research has set out to do. It's not that quantitative researchers are not reflective, but in qualitative research, reflective practice is essential to the conduct of the research and for that reason it is also part of good ethical practice. Most people reading this book, and particularly psychologists, would have likely encountered quantitative methods in the past. This may have created a worldview of how research and science should be structured and understood (e.g., Cooper et al., 2012), and at first glance qualitative approaches may seem unscientific because they do not use statistical analysis and often have small sample sizes. Yet because qualitative research asks different types of questions than quantitative research, it needs to use different tools to ensure quality, rigor, and trustworthiness, all part of ethical practice. Because qualitative approaches rely on subjectivity and the close involvement of the researcher at every stage of the research (Tracy, 2010), reflexivity becomes an important facilitative and analytic tool. Reflexivity involves a

> continuing mental process consisting of intentional thinking and critical analysis of knowledge and experience, directed towards attaining a deep understanding of the meanings people ascribe to their assumptions about human behaviours and experiences, and about the world. (Goldblatt & Band-Winterstein, 2016, p. 101)

Students can be helped to develop reflective practice through discussions with teachers and supervisors but can also be assisted by other students.

Similarly, a seasoned research team's engagement in reflective practice helps bring to light the assumptions each member brings to the research and how the team understands and interprets the material they encounter across the entire research process.

Another important issue to consider is the researcher's interaction with a research participant. Unless previously collected data, such as historical or archival materials, are exclusively being used in a project, the researcher will be directly engaging with human participants, often asking highly personal and probing questions in a one-on-one meeting or group format. Consideration needs to be given to question development and the potential assumptions underlying each question. A few examples may be helpful here. When interviewing a person with a learning disability (LD), "What assumptions and knowledge does the interviewer hold about LD?" "How do they understand the construction of LD as a diagnostic category of people who will have a range of abilities?" "In what environments and situations has the researcher previously encountered people with LD?" And if someone being interviewed is Black, a lesbian, or holds highly conservative religious views, "What are the researcher's personal understandings, experiences, and thoughts about these groups of people?" It's not so much a matter of "right" or "wrong" opinions or trying to be "politically correct" that is an ethical concern, but that unexplored and unexamined, personally held assumptions may well alter the questions we ask and influence our analyses. Likewise, a Hispanic researcher interviewing people from a Hispanic community group will also need to critically reflect on their held assumptions about the people, neighborhood, and situation involved in their research. A White liberal university student interviewing an anti-abortion activist, as another example, will need to think long and hard about what they are bringing to the research relationship before developing their interview questions and undertaking their analyses. These issues are part of an ethical reflective practice and are a cornerstone in the development of a successful qualitative project.

The issue of confidentiality is important to all research involving human participants, but within many qualitative projects, there are additional considerations. Transcripts of interviews (Chapters 5–9); text from historical and other written records, including social media; and visual information such as photographs, videos (Chapters 10 and 12), and drawings (Chapter 11) are all sources of highly detailed accounts of people's lives. Transcripts and other texts will need careful scrutiny to make sure personally identifying information is removed or, if it is essential to include, to make participants clearly aware of this during the recruitment phase of the project and to use these data only with carefully informed, written consent. Using visual data that identifies or potentially identifies participants will require specific approval by ethics committees along with written consent from participants making them clearly aware of what will be visually captured and how it will be used (e.g., dissertation, conference slides, journal publication, community engagement). In an increasingly visually oriented world, it becomes more likely that visual data will appear alongside written data and the implications for advancing qualitative research are tremendous, but this should never be done without participants being fully aware. Researchers should also consider whether visual information that does not reveal the identity of people (e.g., side or rear head-shot views, views of hands and arms, blurred faces) will be sufficient and dramatically reduce confidentiality risks.

Protecting the confidentiality and unanimity of research participants—and those around them—within specific research settings (e.g., clinic, school, neighborhood, rural community, business) where data were obtained can prove challenging. Sometimes referred to as deductive disclosure, research participants who have consented may unwittingly convey characteristics of others that can lead to their identification, causing strains and difficulties with other people not involved directly in the research. Kaiser (2009) provided a reenvisioning of the consent process that considers an "alternative approach to reduce the uncertainty of detailed data that might lead to deductive disclosure" (p. 7). She accomplished this by involving research participants as part of the "audience" that the research may affect and inviting them, postinterview, to complete a confidentiality form further specifying what information they accept to be released and what details from the interview they wished to alter to protect their and others' confidentiality.

TEACHING QUALITATIVE RESEARCH

At the time the first edition of this book was published in 2003, few psychology departments in North America or Europe taught qualitative research as a regular part of their curriculum in research methods. Nearly 20 years later, a good deal of progress has been made in teaching qualitative research methods and in supervising theses and dissertations using qualitative methodologies. In North America, APA's Division 5: Quantitative and Qualitative Methods (American Psychological Association, n.d.) offers sample syllabi in qualitative methods, and in the United Kingdom, the accreditation section of the British Psychological Society (2017) requires all undergraduate degree programs in psychology to offer qualitative methods teaching, although "many programs still providing little more than tokenistic engagement with qualitative methods" (Gibson & Sullivan, 2018, p. 197). Qualitative methods are not routinely taught in every UK PhD program in psychology, but they are taught in nearly all doctoral programs in clinical psychology. Ignoring methodology that does not fall under the umbrella of positivism is the most significant barrier that impedes new generations of psychologists from understanding and appreciating different ways to examine the phenomena most often studied by psychology. At the undergraduate and graduate levels, room can still be made in the curriculum to incorporate the study of different paradigms and research traditions. The result of this curriculum expansion will be a richer and more substantially encompassing profession that is better able to respond to the increasing complex questions of our times.

Starting at the undergraduate level, an introductory research methods class could begin with an examination of the assumptions of positivist, postpositivist, constructivist, and interpretive paradigms and introduce qualitative methodologies, as discussed in Chapter 2. Using the tenets of problem-based learning, a specific problem (e.g., assessing psychotherapy outcome, determining well-being across stages of dementias, evaluating psychology trauma services) could be used to engage the class in discussion about how best to research these situations. Each paradigm could be treated as a separate "case" that students could decipher and debate. From this comparative beginning, the class could then go on to discover some of the research methods emanating from each paradigm. This would entail examining the questions that each method can and cannot answer. Rather than teaching just one methodological paradigm or epistemological position, this approach encourages students to think more critically about why and how one specific method is chosen over another. This pedagogical approach also encourages students to think about the questions to ask before considering the design and method(s) of the study. A further advanced, optional course in qualitative methods could be another offering in the final year of study.

In graduate education, one master's level course could provide more in-depth information about several of the qualitative methods presented in Chapters 5 to 12 and allow students to obtain some hands-on experience in data collection and analysis in one or two of those methods. At the doctoral level, a two-course sequence that integrates quantitative and qualitative methods could begin a student's research training, followed by two additional research methods classes focused on more advanced methods of design and analysis, in either qualitative or quantitative approaches. Chapters 13 and 14 would work well for students at an advanced stage in their doctoral studies. A capstone research seminar could act as an integrative final experience where student projects are presented and discussed across qualitative and quantitative designs. Helping graduate students develop an integrative perspective about research methods gives them a wider range of intellectual tools and, along with some of the wisdom of princesses Rhyme and Reason, realize the limitations of adhering to a methodological hierarchy that prevents a richer understanding of human beings.

REFERENCES

American Psychological Association. (2017). *Ethical principles of psychologists and code of conduct* (2002, amended effective June 1, 2010, and January 1, 2017). https://www.apa.org/ethics/code/index.aspx

American Psychological Association. (n.d.). *Division 5: Quantitative and qualitative methods.* https://www.apadivisions.org/division-5

Barbour, R. S. (2001). Checklists for improving rigour in qualitative research: A case of the tail wagging the dog? *British Medical Journal, 322*(7294), 1115–1117. https://doi.org/10.1136/bmj.322.7294.1115

Barnes, B. R. (2012). Using mixed methods research in South African psychological research. *South African Journal of Psychology, 42*(4), 463–475. https://doi.org/10.1177/008124631204200402

Berger, P. L., & Luckmann, T. (1966). *The social construction of reality*. Doubleday.

Boivin, A., Richards, T., Forsythe, L., Grégoire, A., L'Espérance, A., Abelson, J., & Carman, K. L. (2018). Evaluating patient and public involvement in research. *BMJ, 363*, k5147. https://doi.org/10.1136/bmj.k5147

British Psychological Society. (2014). *Code of human research ethics* (2nd ed.). https://www.bps.org.uk/news-and-policy/bps-code-human-research-ethics-2nd-edition-2014

British Psychological Society. (2017). *Supplementary guidance for research and research methods on Society accredited undergraduate and conversion programmes.*

Camic, P. M., & Chatterjee, H. J. (2013). Museums and art galleries as partners for public health interventions. *Perspectives in Public Health, 133*(1), 66–71. https://doi.org/10.1177/1757913912468523

Camic, P. M., Rhodes, J. E., & Yardley, L. (Eds.). (2003). *Qualitative research in psychology: Expanding perspectives in methodology and design*. American Psychological Association. https://doi.org/10.1037/10595-000

Carduff, E., Murray, S. A., & Kendall, M. (2015). Methodological developments in qualitative longitudinal research: The advantages and challenges of regular telephone contact with participants in a qualitative longitudinal interview study. *BMC Research Notes, 8*(1), 142. https://doi.org/10.1186/s13104-015-1107-y

Clare, A., Camic, P. M., Crutch, S. J., West, J., Harding, E., & Brotherhood, E. (2020). Using music to develop a multisensory communicative environment for people with late-stage dementia. *The Gerontologist, 60*(6), 1115–1125. https://doi.org/10.1093/geront/gnz169

Cooper, H. (2012). Introduction: Objectives of psychological research and their relations to research methods. In H. Cooper, P. M. Camic, D. L. Long, A. T. Panter, D. Rindskopf, & K. J. Sher (Eds.), *APA handbook of research methods in psychology: Vol. 1. Foundations, planning, measures, and psychometrics* (pp. xxiii–xliv). American Psychological Association.

Cooper, H., Camic, P. M., Long, D. L., Panter, A. T., Rindskopf, D., & Sher, K. J. (Eds.). (2012). *APA handbook of research methods in psychology: Vol. 2. Research designs: Quantitative, qualitative, neuropsychological, and biological*. American Psychological Association. https://doi.org/10.1037/13620-000

Dewey, J. (1934). *Art as experience*. Perigee.

Dzvimbo, K. P. (2006). Qualitative research in African education: Notes and comments from southern and eastern Africa. *International Journal of Qualitative Studies in Education: QSE, 7*(3), 197–205. https://doi.org/10.1080/0951839940070302

Eisner, E. (2003). On the art and science of qualitative research in psychology. In P. M. Camic, J. E. Rhodes, & L. Yardley (Eds.), *Qualitative research in psychology: Expanding perspectives in methodology and design* (pp. 17–29). American Psychological Association. https://doi.org/10.1037/10595-002

Gergen, K. J. (1985). The social constructionist movement in modern psychology. *American Psychologist, 40*(3), 266–275. https://doi.org/10.1037/0003-066X.40.3.266

Gibson, S., & Sullivan, C. (2018). A changing culture? Qualitative methods teaching in U.K. psychology. *Qualitative Psychology, 5*(2), 197–206. https://doi.org/10.1037/qup0000100

Gilligan, C., Spencer, R., Weinberg, M. K., & Bertsch, T. (2003). On the listening guide: A voice-centered relational model. In P. M. Camic, J. E. Rhodes, & L. Yardley (Eds.), *Qualitative research in psychology: Expanding perspectives in methodology and design* (pp. 157–172). American Psychological Association. https://doi.org/10.1037/10595-009

Giorgi, A. (1970). *Psychology as a human science*. Harper & Row.

Goldblatt, H., & Band-Winterstein, T. (2016). From understanding to insight: Using reflexivity to promote students' learning of qualitative research. *Reflective Practice, 17*(2), 100–113. https://doi.org/10.1080/14623943.2015.1134471

Gough, B., & Madill, A. (2012). Subjectivity in psychological science: From problem to prospect. *Psychological Methods, 17*(3), 374–384. https://doi.org/10.1037/a0029313

Griffiths, C., & Smith, M. (2016). Attuning: A communication process between people with severe and profound intellectual disability and their interaction partners. *Journal of Applied Research in Intellectual Disabilities, 29*(2), 124–138. https://doi.org/10.1111/jar.12162

Hager, M. G. (1982). The myth of objectivity. *American Psychologist, 37*(5), 576–579. https://doi.org/10.1037/0003-066X.37.5.576

Hamilton, D. (1994). Traditions, preferences and postures in applied qualitative research. In N. K. Denzin & Y. S. Lincoln (Eds.), *Handbook of qualitative research* (pp. 60–69). Sage Publications.

Henwood, K., & Pidgeon, N. (1994). Beyond the qualitative paradigm: A framework for introducing diversity within qualitative psychology. *Journal of Community & Applied Social Psychology, 4*(4), 225–238. https://doi.org/10.1002/casp.2450040403

Henwood, K., & Pidgeon, N. (2003). Grounded theory in psychological research. In P. M. Camic, J. E. Rhodes, & L. Yardley (Eds.), *Qualitative research in psychology: Expanding perspectives in methodology and design* (pp. 131–155). American Psychological Association. https://doi.org/10.1037/10595-008

Holland, J., Thomson, R., & Henderson, S. (2006). *Qualitative longitudinal research: A discussion paper.* London Southbank University: Families & Social Capital ESRC Research Group. https://www.lsbu.ac.uk/__data/assets/pdf_file/0019/9370/qualitative-longitudinal-research-families-working-paper.pdf

Hoshmand, L. T. (1999). Locating the qualitative research genre. In M. Kopala & L. A. Suzuki (Eds.), *Using qualitative methods in psychology* (pp. 15–24). Sage Publications. https://doi.org/10.4135/9781452225487.n2

Jennings, H., Slade, M., Bates, P., Munday, E., & Toney, R. (2018). Best practice framework for Patient and Public Involvement (PPI) in collaborative data analysis of qualitative mental health research: Methodology development and refinement. *BMC Psychiatry, 18*(1), 213. https://doi.org/10.1186/s12888-018-1794-8

Juster, N. (1965). *The phantom tollbooth.* Random House.

Kaiser, K. (2009). Protecting respondent confidentiality in qualitative research. *Qualitative Health Research, 19*(11), 1632–1641. https://doi.org/10.1177/1049732309350879

Kitto, S. C., Chesters, J., & Grbich, C. (2008). Quality in qualitative research. *The Medical Journal of Australia, 188*(4), 243–246. https://doi.org/10.5694/j.1326-5377.2008.tb01595.x

Kvale, S. (1996). *InterViews: An introduction to qualitative research interviewing.* Sage Publications.

Kvale, S. (2003). The psychoanalytic interview as inspiration for qualitative research. In P. M. Camic, J. E. Rhodes, & L. Yardley (Eds.), *Qualitative research in psychology: Expanding perspectives in methodology and design* (pp. 275–297). American Psychological Association. https://doi.org/10.1037/10595-014

Levitt, H. M., Bamberg, M., Creswell, J. W., Frost, D. M., Josselson, R., & Suárez-Orozco, C. (2018). Journal article reporting standards for qualitative primary, qualitative meta-analytic, and mixed methods research in psychology: The APA Publications and Communications Board task force report. *American Psychologist, 73*(1), 26–46. https://doi.org/10.1037/amp0000151

Madill, A., & Gough, B. (2008). Qualitative research and its place in psychological science. *Psychological Methods, 13*(3), 254–271. https://doi.org/10.1037/a0013220

Marecek, J. (2003). Dancing through minefields: Toward a qualitative stance in psychology. In P. M. Camic, J. E. Rhodes, & L. Yardley (Eds.), *Qualitative research in psychology: Expanding perspectives in methodology and design* (pp. 49–69). American Psychological Association. https://doi.org/10.1037/10595-004

McGartland, M., & Polgar, S. (1994). Paradigm collapse in psychology: The necessity for a "two" methods approach. *Australian Psychologist, 29*(1), 21–28. https://doi.org/10.1080/00050069408257314

McGrath, J. E., & Johnson, B. A. (2003). Methodology makes meaning: How both qualitative and quantitative paradigms shape evidence and its interpretations. In P. M. Camic, J. E. Rhodes, & L. Yardley (Eds.), *Qualitative research in psychology: Expanding perspectives in methodology and design* (pp. 31–48). American Psychological Association. https://doi.org/10.1037/10595-003

Miller, P. J., Hengst, J. A., & Wang, S. (2003). Ethnographic methods: From developmental cultural psychology. In P. M. Camic, J. E. Rhodes, & L. Yardley (Eds.), *Qualitative research in psychology: Expanding perspectives in methodology and design* (pp. 219–242). American Psychological Association. https://doi.org/10.1037/10595-012

Mitroff, I. I. (1972). The myth of objectivity OR why science needs a new psychology of science. *Management Science, 18*(10), B-613–B-618. https://doi.org/10.1287/mnsc.18.10.B613

Morrow, V., & Crivello, G. (2015). What is the value of qualitative longitudinal research with children and young people for international development? *International Journal of Social Research Methodology, 18*(3), 267–280. https://doi.org/10.1080/13645579.2015.1017903

Mortari, L. (2015). Reflexivity in research practice: An overview of different perspectives. *International Journal of Qualitative Research, 14*(5). Advance online publication. https://doi.org/10.1177/1609406915618045

Neale, B. (2018). *What is qualitative longitudinal research?* Bloomsbury Academic.

Rabinowitz, V. C., & Weseen, S. (2001). Power, politics, and the qualitative/quantitative debates in psychology. In D. L. Tolman & B.-M. Miller (Eds.), *From subjects to subjectivities: A handbook of interpretive and participatory methods* (pp. 12–28). New York University Press.

Rennie, D. L. (2000). Grounded theory methodology as methodical hermeneutics: Reconciling realism and relativism. *Theory & Psychology, 10*(4), 481–501. https://doi.org/10.1177/0959354300104003

Rennie, D. L. (2012). Qualitative research as methodical hermeneutics. *Psychological Methods, 17*(3), 385–398. https://doi.org/10.1037/a0029250

Roberts, L. D., & Castell, E. (2016). "Having to shift everything we've learned to the side": Expanding research methods taught in psychology to incorporate qualitative methods. *Frontiers in Psychology, 7*, 688. https://doi.org/10.3389/fpsyg.2016.00688

Sanjari, M., Bahramnezhad, F., Fomani, F. K., Shoghi, M., & Cheraghi, M. A. (2014). Ethical challenges of researchers in qualitative studies: The necessity to develop a specific guideline. *Journal of Medical Ethics and History of Medicine, 7*, 14.

Schoenberg, N. E., & McAuley, W. J. (2007). Promoting qualitative research. *The Gerontologist, 47*(5), 576–577. https://doi.org/10.1093/geront/47.5.576

Schütz, A. (1962). *Collected papers 1: The problem of social reality*. Martinus Nijoff.

Shweder, R. A. (1996). Quanta and qualia: What is the "object" of ethnographic research? In R. Jessor, A. Colby, & R. A. Shweder (Eds.), *Ethnography and human development: Context and meaning in social inquiry* (pp. 175–182). University of Chicago Press.

Simonds, L. M., Camic, P. M., & Causey, A. (2012). Using focused ethnography in psychological research. In H. Cooper, P. M. Camic, D. L. Long, A. T. Panter, D. Rindskopf, & K. J. Sher (Eds.), *APA handbook of research methods in psychology: Vol. 2. Research designs: Quantitative, qualitative, neuropsychological, and biological* (pp. 157–170). American Psychological Association. https://doi.org/10.1037/13620-010

Smaling, A. (1992). Varieties of methodological intersubjectivity: The relations with qualitative and quantitative research, and with objectivity. *Quality & Quantity: International Journal of Methodology, 26*(2), 169–180. https://doi.org/10.1007/BF02273552

Tashakkori, A., & Teddlie, C. (2010). *SAGE handbook of mixed methods in social and behavioral research* (2nd ed.). Sage Publications. https://doi.org/10.4135/9781506335193

Tracy, S. J. (2010). Qualitative quality: Eight "Big-Tent" criteria for excellent qualitative research. *Qualitative Inquiry, 16*(10), 837–851. https://doi.org/10.1177/1077800410383121

Wetherell, M., Taylor, S., & Yates, S. J. (2000). *Discourse as data: A guide for analysis.* Sage.

Yardley, L. (2000). Dilemmas in qualitative health research. *Psychology & Health, 15*(2), 215–228. https://doi.org/10.1080/08870440008400302

Yardley, L., & Bishop, F. (2007). Mixing qualitative and quantitative methods: A pragmatic approach. In C. Willig & W. Stainton-Rogers (Eds.), *Handbook of qualitative research methods in psychology* (pp. 352–370). Sage Publications.

Choosing a Qualitative Method

A Pragmatic, Pluralistic Perspective

Chris Barker and Nancy Pistrang

"Which qualitative method should I use?" Researchers planning a qualitative study will often ask themselves, or ask their advisors or colleagues, this key question. On the surface, it may seem a simple one, but it has all sorts of implications and ramifications. This chapter is intended to help qualitative researchers navigate these sometimes treacherous waters. It develops the discussion in our previous publications (Barker et al., 2016; Pistrang & Barker, 2010, 2012). We hope that it will serve as a guide to researchers, particularly those new to qualitative research, to help you understand what exactly is on offer, and what the implications are of each of the methodological choices that you could make. It is intended to serve as a lead-in to subsequent chapters in this volume, which explore particular approaches in depth.

We approach the choice of methods from a pluralist and pragmatist perspective. We explain these terms later in the chapter, but in brief, *pluralism* means celebrating variety—in this case, variety in research approaches—and *pragmatism* means doing what works—in this case, choosing the method that works best for the research question that you are attempting to address. Our main argument is that no one qualitative method is best overall, all have their relative strengths and weaknesses, and the task of the researcher is to choose the method that best fits the question under investigation. As we have previously argued (e.g., Barker et al., 2016), research should ideally be question-driven, not method-driven.

https://doi.org/10.1037/0000252-002
Qualitative Research in Psychology: Expanding Perspectives in Methodology and Design,
Second Edition, P. M. Camic (Editor)

This chapter explores the implications of pluralism and pragmatism for choosing methods. It starts with an introductory section setting out the conceptual background to the choice of methods. After that, we examine some of the main approaches to qualitative research, which we classify into four main families. The final section uses a running example to show how each of these choices might pan out in practice. But first, in the spirit of qualitative research, we include a brief reflexivity section setting out our own background leanings.

REFLEXIVITY

Given that one's own standpoint affects how one makes sense of the world, it is only right to let readers know where the researcher is coming from, so they can take this information into account when assessing the trustworthiness of the findings. Most qualitative approaches emphasize that reflexivity lies at the heart of qualitative research: Conducting research is an interpersonal activity that affects, and is affected by, both researcher and researched. *Reflexivity* can be formally defined as "how the researcher and intersubjective elements impact on and transform research" (Finlay, 2003, p.4).

So, even though this chapter is exposition rather than research, we will set out our own position so that readers can have a sense of what informs the ideas behind it. We are both White, British, research-oriented clinical psychologists in our late careers. We have long advocated a methodological pluralistic stance in research (e.g., Barker & Pistrang, 2005, 2012; Barker et al., 2016). Accordingly, we conduct both quantitative and qualitative research, the latter using several approaches. However, our stance is broadly phenomenological—we seek to understand participants' experiences and how they make sense of the world. We often collaborate with each other on our research publications, which are mostly about psychological helping and support. (We also collaborate on other things in life too.)

Having said that, we do not believe that a researcher's background must inevitably influence their findings. Just as skilled therapists are trained to empathize with clients from a range of backgrounds, so skilled researchers are able to set aside their own presuppositions and personal leanings (a process known as *bracketing*; Ahern, 1999; Fischer, 2009; Gearing, 2004) to attend deeply to what their participants are telling them and to conduct their analyses fairly, without bias.

WHY ADOPT A QUALITATIVE APPROACH?

The Growing Prominence of Qualitative Research in Psychology

The discipline of psychology was a latecomer to qualitative research. Although it has long been a central part of other related disciplines, particularly anthropology and sociology, it was until fairly recently rarely to be found within orthodox psychology departments in the English-speaking world. When the two of us were both graduate students, at UCLA in the 1970s, research methods teaching consisted entirely of quantitative methods and statistics (and very good it was too). Qualitative approaches, however, were simply not mentioned.

However, as Wertz (2014) pointed out, some landmark studies in psychology used qualitative methods, even if they were not explicitly labeled as such. The work of Piaget is one major example; Festinger and Zimbardo are others.

The picture began to change from the 1980s onward. Some historical landmarks are Gergen's (1985) *American Psychologist* paper on social constructionism, Potter and Wetherell's (1987) book on discourse analysis, papers by Rennie et al. (1988) and by Henwood and Pidgeon (1992) on grounded theory, Richardson's (1996) handbook of qualitative methods published by the British Psychological Society, and of course the first edition of the present American Psychological Association (APA) volume (Camic et al., 2003). One recent indicator of the enhanced status of qualitative research is that the APA's journal article reporting standards give equal prominence to qualitative and quantitative approaches (Levitt et al., 2018). However, in terms of journal article publication, qualitative research still seems somewhat ghettoized: It tends to be published in specialist journals, but the discipline's flagship journals are still broadly quantitative.

We have published three editions of our clinical psychology research methods textbook at approximately 10-year intervals. The book attempts to embody a pluralistic spirit—in particular, to be even-handed between qualitative and quantitative approaches. In the first edition (Barker et al., 1994), that approach felt novel and somewhat daring; in the second (Barker et al., 2002), qualitative research was rapidly becoming more accepted, and by the time of the third, in 2016, there was an extensive qualitative and mixed-methods psychology literature to draw upon.

Advantages and Disadvantages of Qualitative Approaches

Before choosing a particular qualitative research approach, it is good to step back and ask yourself why you want to do qualitative research in the first place. Each of the two broad classes of research approaches—qualitative and quantitative—have their characteristic strengths and weaknesses (see the summary in Table 2.1).

The key advantage of qualitative approaches is that they are able to paint a vivid, subtle, and complex picture of the topic under investigation: to enable what Geertz (1973, p. 6) called "thick description." To give a simplified example, suppose that you are investigating self-esteem in adolescence. The quantitative approach would be to administer a standardized measure, say the Rosenberg Self-Esteem Scale (Rosenberg, 1965), which yields a score from 0 to 30. Say a particular adolescent has a score of 18. If you actually ask her how she feels about herself, she will say something like "I mostly feel good about myself, but I really don't like how my ears stick out, I'm no good at sports, and my teacher says I talk too much, which I find upsetting. However, I've got a lot of friends, and most of the time I'm happy." Even this brief snippet conveys

TABLE 2.1. Advantages and Disadvantages of Quantitative and Qualitative Research Approaches

	Quantitative	Qualitative
Advantages	Enables precise description	Allows a rich description
	Enables comparison	Avoids oversimplification
	Can use inferential statistics	Good for hypothesis generation and discovery-oriented research, particularly in underresearched areas
	Can use psychometric theory	
	Fits with hypothetico-deductive model of science	
		More likely to find unexpected results—serendipity
		Fits with naturalistic models of enquiry
		Gives more freedom to participants
		Gives voice to marginalized groups
		Accounts more readable—data are vivid and easy to grasp
Disadvantages	Does not capture subtleties of experience	Hard to make comparisons
	May give a false sense of precision	More prone to researcher influence
	Can be irritating or constraining to participants	

considerable information, enabling you to know the young person in a way that the Rosenberg score does not. However, how you go about analyzing such qualitative data, and how you make comparisons with other adolescents' accounts, is not readily apparent.

Other advantages of qualitative approaches are that they

- are well suited to exploratory, discovery-oriented, hypothesis-generating research, particularly in areas where little previous research has been done.

- have the potential for serendipitous findings—things that you were not expecting.

- are able to "give voice" to members of marginalized populations: There is a direct connection between the participant and the reader, since the participants' words are quoted directly in the write-up of the research.

- give more freedom and are generally more congenial to participants, in contrast to, for example, the constraints of fixed-answer rating scales.

- produce more readable accounts: The data are vivid and easy to grasp.

- fit with naturalistic models of enquiry (discussed later in the chapter).

However, qualitative approaches are less well suited to making comparisons across participants or between groups, and they are arguably more prone to researcher influence than quantitative methods because there is greater scope for researcher judgment. They are also less suited to a hypothesis-testing approach.

Some beginning researchers choose a qualitative approach on the grounds that it initially appears to be less hard work than quantitative approaches because there is no statistical analysis needed. This is rarely the case. Analyzing qualitative data properly is a time-consuming and demanding process.

The final consideration is about your personal cognitive leanings. Some researchers feel more comfortable with words rather than numbers (and some vice versa). If you find statistics highly challenging, then it may be a good idea to avoid conducting quantitative research. However, it is still important for all psychologists to at least be able to read and understand both qualitative and quantitative research, so some practical experience in the quantitative approach is usually beneficial.

Ethical Considerations

Before embarking on any qualitative study, the researcher needs to address the central ethical principles common to all psychological research: informed consent, avoidance of harm, privacy, and confidentiality (Barker et al., 2016). These may have heightened prominence in qualitative research, especially when the study focuses in depth on sensitive personal topics. In this case, particular care is needed to safeguard participants, both during and after the study.

Some Conceptual and Philosophical Background

Before describing our framework for thinking about different approaches to qualitative research, we attempt to acquaint readers with some philosophical background concepts that underpin the choice of methods—most importantly, realism versus constructionism, positivism, and phenomenology. We also explicate the animating concerns of the present chapter: pluralism and pragmatism.

Much of this material comes under the heading of *epistemology*, that is, the study of what constitutes knowledge. The question of how one gains understanding is obviously fundamental to the whole research enterprise. How does one know what will cure cancer—chemotherapy or crystal healing? Or what causes or alleviates, anxiety—medication, mindfulness, psychological therapy? It is important for qualitative researchers to reflect on these epistemological concepts. The more you are able to understand the conceptual foundations of the approaches you are considering, the better you will be able to choose between alternatives. A basic knowledge of epistemology also helps you to understand the controversies in the field, which often stem from differences in epistemological positions and often result in philosophical name-calling (e.g., researchers labeling other researchers as "positivist" or "naive realist"). We will attempt to acquaint readers with the implications of such labels.

However, in our opinion, epistemology is a medicine on which one can easily overdose. Much epistemological writing is impenetrable to nonphilosophers and ultimately only of value to other philosophers. Our pragmatist position counsels researchers against getting too hung up on epistemological concerns and to pay more attention to what each method is actually achieving. If you have limited patience with philosophical discourse, this whole section is skippable on first reading. You could possibly fast forward to the next major section, on families of qualitative research, which is more practically oriented, or you could just look up the particular approaches that you are considering adopting, and then return to this section if there is something that you do not understand or want to learn more about.

We will therefore attempt to summarize the main philosophical issues here. We first look at pluralism and pragmatism, and then address issues raised by the contrasting approaches of realism and constructivism.

Pluralism

Pluralism, which denotes the valuing and encouragement of variety, is a fundamental notion that can be applied to a wide range of activities. There are many types of pluralism—notably political, cultural, and religious pluralism. For example, political pluralism refers to nation-states wherein a diversity of opinions can be expressed and taken into account (Inazu, 2016), in contrast to autocratic governments or one-party states that are intolerant of criticism or contrary opinions. (Perhaps you can think of your own examples when you read this; at the time of writing, there is no shortage of them on the world stage.) Similarly, some societies are culturally pluralistic, whereas others are intolerant of minority groups because of racism, xenophobia, prejudice, or stereotyping. Finally, some societies embrace religious pluralism, whereas others are theocratic states where only a single religion (or none at all) is permitted.

As can be inferred from the preceding comments, we are in favor of pluralism. However, it is not unproblematic. Its critics fear that it may lead to divided loyalties because individuals may hold allegiance both to their own subgroup and to the wider society. It has also been criticized as being *relativistic*—in other words, that a pluralistic society has no fixed values, which can lead to moral anarchy. The counterargument is that a society can have agreement on a set of superordinate values, limiting what constitutes unacceptable variety (Inazu, 2016). For example, adherence to fundamental human rights can override some unacceptable cultural or religious practices, such as denying education to girls and women.

These considerations are paralleled in the application of pluralism to research methods. Known as *methodological pluralism*, it is the celebration of the variety of research methods—the belief that "no single method is inherently superior to any other: all methods have their relative advantages and disadvantages" (Barker et al., 2016, p. 243). The seminal text is Fiske and Shweder's (1986) edited volume on metatheory in social science, which has an extended discussion of the issues raised by a pluralistic approach. Methodological pluralism is an antidote to the "paradigm wars" that broke out in the 1990s, when proponents of different approaches had acrimonious debates about the superiority of their particular pet approach (Oakley, 1999).

The implication of a pluralistic stance is that the researcher has a toolkit containing a number of methods and chooses the one that is most appropriate for answering the question under investigation. Researchers may also use more than one approach, either within a single study or over a research program (known as a *mixed-methods* approach or as *triangulation* of perspectives).

Like pluralism in general, methodological pluralism has been subject to the criticism that it can lead to anarchy because it seems to imply a loosening of standards. The counterargument is that one can apply specific quality standards tailored to different methods or genres of research while also having some core values that cut across all genres, such as transparency of methods (see Barker & Pistrang, 2005, for an elaboration of this approach).

Some authors also argue that certain methods are more congenial to certain research fields. For instance, some community psychologists and feminist psychologists advocate the particular virtues of qualitative research (e.g., Banyard & Miller, 1998; Carlson, 1972) on the grounds that these are more empowering to participants and that quantitative research is underpinned by patriarchal values of measurement and control. However, it is possible to conduct quantitative research in a manner consistent with feminist values; see Hughes and Cohen's (2010) article, nicely titled "Feminists Really Do Count," and also Peplau and Conrad (1989).

Pragmatism

Pragmatism is the belief that research methods are best selected for their practical value in addressing the particular question you are addressing. It is encapsulated in the slogan "if it works, use it!"

Pragmatism is allied to the pluralistic approach, in that it again implies that research should be question-driven, not method-driven—that you choose the appropriate method to fit the question you are asking. This doctrine of "appropriate methodology" is analogous to that of "appropriate technology" in development economics (Ghosh, 1984), which emphasizes finding empowering, low-tech solutions that best address the problem at hand. So it is with research methods: You ask yourself what is the simplest method that will answer the question you are posing and give primacy to practical value rather than theoretical niceties. The final section of this chapter gives some illustrations of how this works out, using a running example to illustrate which questions different qualitative methods are appropriate for.

Epistemological Positions

Realism

One central distinction in epistemology is that between realism and constructivism. This is sometimes treated as a binary distinction, but, as with many other binary distinctions, the situation is more complicated than a simple dichotomy.

The term *realism* refers to the position that there exists an objective reality and that it is the goal of the investigator to know that reality. Science then progresses by having an increasingly accurate model of the world. For instance, in the mid-19th century, malaria was thought to be caused by bad air (which is what the word *malaria* is derived from in Italian), but later investigations discovered that it was caused by mosquitoes (Centers for Disease Control and Prevention, 2019). Thus, a false theory was superseded by an accurate one.

However, few researchers subscribe to a strict realist position. More common is a position of *critical realism*, which accepts that there is an objective reality but concedes that it is never completely knowable—that our investigations inevitably yield only an approximation to reality.

Positivism

Allied to the realist position is the doctrine known as *positivism*. This was first propounded by Auguste Comte in the 19th century. Comte sought to model the social sciences on the natural sciences, particularly physics (which during that century was making enormous forward strides in understanding the properties of heat, light, sound, and particularly electricity). Positivism (which has nothing to do with positive psychology) is a loose set of beliefs but can be reduced to three propositions:

1. That scientific attention should be restricted to observable facts, that is, behavior, and that "inferred constructs," such as thoughts and feelings, have no place in science. This is a version of *empiricism* (the belief that all knowledge is derived from sensory experience).

2. That the methods of the physical sciences (e.g., numerical measurement, separation into independent and dependent variables, and investigation of general laws) should also be applied to the social sciences.

3. That science is objective and value free.

Adopted fully, this is an extreme position that leads to a sterile discipline in which one cannot talk about thoughts and feelings; instead, one speaks of verbal behavior. Furthermore, limiting oneself to quantitative measures can, as discussed earlier, lead to superficial understandings. For example, researching the topic of back pain, strict positivists would limit themselves to measuring pain behaviors, such as nerve signals, avoidance, and verbal complaints of pain, but not explore how the pain actually felt to the participants. Furthermore, the positivist ideal of a value-free science does not hold up to close examination (Douglas, 2009). Scientists are all too human, and their values inevitably influence the kinds of studies they conduct and the conclusions that they draw from them. Furthermore, as Humphreys and Piot (2012) argued, scientists may confuse facts with opinions, believing that their expertise in producing evidence gives them a privileged status in promoting policy.

In our view, positivism is more of a rhetorical straw person—a convenient caricature for constructivist researchers to oppose. Much ink has been used up by qualitative researchers denouncing its errors. However, it appears that the heat is now dying out of the positivist–constructivist debate, and a resolution of apparently opposing positions seems to be emerging (see the subsequent section on synthesis).

Constructivism

Constructivism (sometimes known as naturalistic inquiry), on the other hand, maintains that what is considered reality is not a fixed entity but is socially constructed. In other words, people make their own realities. How one perceives a conversation, for example, will differ if you are a linguist, a therapist, a nonnative English speaker, an adolescent, or according to what your ethnic or cultural background is. The aim of research then becomes one of understanding how different people perceive the world and arrive at their understanding of it. Furthermore, research is seen as a process of coconstruction of reality: participants' accounts are dependent on, and can be influenced by, the researcher's values, social position, and prior knowledge. This view of research then leads to a consideration of *reflexivity*, which addresses the influence of the researcher on the researched and vice versa (Finlay, 2003).

Phenomenology

Allied to the constructivist position is that of *phenomenology*. This is a philosophical approach about which much has been written since the 1930s. Put simply, phenomenology is concerned with the person's inner experiencing— what individual perceives as they try to make sense of the world. In this respect, it differs sharply from the positivist approach. Again, say the topic of investigation is back pain, then the phenomenological researcher wants to know, for example, what pain feels like to the individual, how they experience both mild and severe pain, what thoughts and feelings they have while they are experiencing pain, and how their behavior is affected.

A phenomenological stance underlies much qualitative research, particularly that which uses qualitative interviews as the main data collection method.

Towards a Synthesis

The philosophical idea of the *dialectic* maintains that ideas progress in three phases: thesis, antithesis, and synthesis. The thesis is the original idea; then follows the reaction to it, the antithesis; and finally, a joining together, the synthesis. In the present case, realism is the thesis, constructivism the antithesis, and the synthesis, which lies somewhere in the middle ground, is currently emerging.

Few researchers identify themselves as totally realist. As the cognitive psychologist Steven Pinker (2014) remarked,

> Even scientists . . . are a bit post-modern. We recognize that . . . the world doesn't just reveal itself to us, that we understand the world through our theories and constructs, and that our ways of understanding the world must be constantly scrutinized for hidden biases. (p. 37)

Similarly, few researchers subscribe to a strictly constructivist viewpoint. No sane person would deny the existence of reality, particularly unpleasant reality, such as rape and murder, racism and xenophobia, and economic exploitation and oppression. In the political climate at the time of this writing, awash with lies and fake news, distinguishing truth from falsehood seems more important than ever. What is valuable about the constructivist perspective is its emphasis on examining how people come to make sense of the world they inhabit.

Qualitative research can be conducted from both a realist and a constructivist position. Suppose that the researcher is interested in studying the current political hot potato of attitudes toward immigration. A realist perspective assumes that each individual participant has a set of beliefs, which it is the researcher's task to ascertain, with minimal distortion. A constructivist perspective, on the other hand, is more interested in how these beliefs come to be formed and articulated, including how the researcher influences what participants may or may not say to them. Both of these stances represent valuable ways to conduct research; they are simply addressing different aspects of the phenomenon.

It is also worth noting that quantitative research, although mostly done from a realist—usually a critical realist—position, can also be carried out within a constructivist position. The classic example is research based on personal construct theory, which uses sophisticated quantitative methods (repertory grids) to examine the structure of attitudes at an individual level (e.g., Winter, 2003).

CHOOSING A QUALITATIVE RESEARCH METHOD

Families of Qualitative Approaches

There are many approaches to qualitative research. Subsequent chapters in the current volume present the major ones, but space constraints resulted in the exclusion of others. The question then arises of how to choose between them all. Following Pistrang and Barker (2012), we will attempt to clarify the issues involved by using a taxonomy—that is, a classification system—that groups the main qualitative approaches into four families (see also Table 2.2):

1. *Thematic analysis approaches*, which aim to identify and describe the central ideas (usually called *themes* or *categories*) in a set of participants' accounts.

2. *Narrative approaches*, which aim to identify the storied nature of accounts—how events unfold over time.

3. *Language-based approaches*, which attend to the detail of the language used and how writers or speakers achieve their ends.

4. *Ethnographic approaches*, which aim to understand the wider cultural system, and are characterized by extensive fieldwork.

The choice of approach then becomes a two-stage one: First, which overall family of approaches best matches the general thrust of your research question, and second, which particular approach within the family best fits your particular research question and way of working. Because there are so many

TABLE 2.2. Taxonomy of Families of Qualitative Approaches

Family	Question addressed	Approach
Thematic analysis	The central ideas (called themes or categories) in a set of participants' accounts	Content analysis Framework approach Grounded theory Empirical phenomenology Interpretative phenomenological analysis Generic thematic analysis
Narrative approaches	The storied or chronological aspects of participants' accounts	Narrative analysis Life history approaches
Language-based approaches	How the language used in descriptions or interactions achieves its ends	Discourse analysis Conversation analysis Process analysis
Ethnographic approaches	The wider cultural or social system	Ethnography Focused ethnography

approaches, the present exposition needs to be selective and brief, but we hope that the general principles will become apparent.

This section presents the basic theoretical ideas behind each of the different approaches; the following one will use a running example to clarify the issues in practice.

Family 1: Thematic Analysis Approaches

The key feature of thematic analysis approaches, as is obvious from their label, is that they aim to identify common themes in the data within and across research participants. Thematic analysis studies often draw on data from semi-structured interviews and are particularly suited to research questions concerning the variety of participants' thoughts and feelings about a particular topic.

For example, Baruch et al. (2018) studied how family members support a relative (e.g., partner or sibling) with bipolar disorder. The first author interviewed 18 participants and found six themes capturing the main aspects of their experiences, such as "Not knowing; like being in a minefield" and "Walking on eggshells."

The mechanics and procedures differ across the approaches within this family, although there is considerable overlap. There are two underlying dimensions. The first is how structured the method is. Some, such as the framework approach (described later), are highly structured, whereas others, such as empirical phenomenology, are less so. This structure dimension is inversely correlated with the second dimension, how interpretive the approach is. The more structured ones tend to be less interpretative and thus make fewer inferences from the data, whereas the less structured ones tend to be more highly interpretive.

Content Analysis. The first member of the family, content analysis (Joffe & Yardley, 2003; Krippendorff, 2013), is not really a qualitative method at all, but we are including it here for heuristic illustration. It lies on the boundary between quantitative and qualitative approaches—its input (i.e., the raw data) is qualitative, but its output (i.e., the results) usually are not. It forms a useful contrast to other purely qualitative thematic analysis approaches.

The essence of content analysis is to classify units of the data into a set of clearly defined categories. For example, a researcher may be interested in what kinds of things clients talk about in cognitive therapy for eating disorders. She could classify the content of recorded sessions into categories of, say, peer relationships, family relationships, body image, food, and so on. A content analysis would count the frequency of occurrence of each of these categories, possibly in different time segments of a therapy session. More than one rater could be used to establish how reliable the categories were.

The content categories could be predetermined, either from theory or from an existing coding system. An example of the latter is Gottschalk and Gleser's (1969) content analysis system for therapeutic interactions, which classifies speech into such categories as Anxiety, Hostility Outward, and Hostility Inward (see https://www.gb-software.com/develop.htm). Alternatively, the categories could be derived from an examination of the interviews themselves (usually a subset), and then applied systematically to all the interviews.

The strengths and weaknesses of this approach reflect those of quantitative versus qualitative research discussed earlier—principally, that the numbers enable easy comparison, but the quantitative data are limited in their meaning.

Framework. Framework is a fully qualitative approach, the most highly structured of the purely qualitative approaches in the thematic analysis family. It was developed by Ritchie and Spencer (Ritchie & Spencer, 1994; Ritchie et al., 2014), initially for research in the field of social policy. It featured prominently in an influential *British Medical Journal* article on analyzing qualitative data (Pope et al., 2000) and as result became popular in health psychology and medical investigations.

As in content analysis, the investigator develops a detailed coding framework, based on theory or on the interview topics covered. However, unlike content analysis, the analysis preserves the qualitative nature of the data—counting frequencies is not necessarily involved (although it can be). Charts, which cross-reference the occurrence of each code for each participant, are used to facilitate the analysis. However, the final step of transforming the initial codes into a manageable framework does require some inference from the researcher.

Grounded Theory. Grounded theory was one of the first systematic qualitative methods to be articulated. As its name suggests, its ultimate aim is not simply to describe and classify the data into categories but also to develop theory grounded in the data ("grounded" means solidly based on the data). It was developed in the 1960s by two sociologists, Barney Glaser and Anselm Strauss

(1967), who were dissatisfied with the predominantly quantitative direction of sociology at the time. Grounded theory has become a widely used method, in psychology as well as sociology (Henwood & Pidgeon, 1992, 2003; Rennie et al., 1988). The essence of the method is that the researcher identifies an initial set of categories or themes that stay fairly close to the data and then builds these categories into more abstract theoretical concepts, possibly culminating in an overarching theory.

Unfortunately, Glaser and Strauss subsequently disagreed about how to develop their approach, the core of the argument being about how prescriptive the method should be. (Willig, 2013). They later went their separate ways, so grounded theory is no longer a unitary method. Strauss coauthored a "how-to" book elaborating his more prescriptive approach (Corbin & Strauss, 2015), which has useful suggestions on carrying out qualitative research generally, not just within grounded theory.

Empirical Phenomenology. Empirical phenomenology was one of the earliest approaches to qualitative work within psychology. It was initially conceptualized by a small group of researchers based at Duquesne University in Pittsburgh (see Giorgi & Giorgi's, 2003, chapter in the first edition of this volume). They drew on the principles of European phenomenology to articulate an analytic method based on the intensive examination of individual experience. Studies using this approach are published in their house journals: the *Journal of Phenomenological Psychology* and the *Duquesne Studies of Phenomenological Psychology*.

Interpretative Phenomenological Analysis. Interpretative phenomenological analysis (see Smith & Fieldsend, Chapter 8, this volume) is a systematic method of conducting phenomenological analysis. It was developed within a health psychology context in the United Kingdom but has been more widely adopted. It stresses detailed examination of how individuals make sense of their personal experiences (the "phenomenological" aspect), while also acknowledging the researcher's role in making sense of the participants' own sense-making (the "interpretative" aspect). It tends to focus on small numbers of participants, sometimes single cases. Its developer, Jonathan A. Smith, has articulated the approach in various user-friendly publications (e.g., Smith et al., 1999, 2009), and its clarity makes it an appealing method for first-time qualitative researchers to try.

Generic Thematic Analysis. Finally, some approaches to thematic analysis, unlike those just described, do not have a "brand name"; they simply describe themselves as thematic analysis. Boyatzis (1998) is one influential early example. More recently, the work of Braun and Clarke (2006, 2013) has been highly cited. They set out a systematic, six-phase approach to conducting a thematic analysis. The clarity of their descriptions and their relative lack of theoretical baggage makes it another user-friendly approach suitable for the beginning researcher.

Family 2: Narrative Approaches

Human beings are storytelling animals; the essence of narrative approaches is that they take into account that storied nature. Approaches in the narrative family foreground the longitudinal aspect and are suited to addressing questions concerning the chronological nature of participants' accounts.

Narrative approaches address one criticism of the approaches in the thematic analysis family: that the resulting categories or themes can seem disconnected and static by not giving any sense of development over time. Narrative approaches attempt to rectify this problem and have time as an ever-present thread.

Narrative Analysis. Narrative psychology (see Bamberg, Chapter 3, this volume) and narrative analysis (see Murray, Chapter 6, this volume) attempt to describe and characterize the nature and structure of narratives. For example, narratives can be analyzed by genre (into romance, tragedy, comedy, etc.) or by their underlying structure (e.g., starting with a quest, then encountering obstacles or setbacks, then overcoming those obstacles).

One intriguing example is Humphrey's (2000) study of the narratives told by group members in Alcoholics Anonymous meetings. He classified these into five different story types, for example, the Drunk-a-Log and the Serial Story, describing the characteristics and function of each type.

Life History Research. Narrative analysis takes account of the chronology of people's lives, although sometimes in small, focused snapshots. Life history research takes this tendency to its logical conclusion and looks at people's whole lives. Such a perspective is surprisingly rare in psychology. Given that the way to understand people fully is to view their whole development in context, it is odd that so few research publications have looked at people's whole lives. Life history studies often involve intensive interviewing of individuals, over several occasions, to build a complete picture of the person's development from childhood to the present day (Cole & Knowles, 2001).

One moving example is Bogdan and Taylor's (1976) single-case study of "Ed Murphy," a man with severe intellectual disabilities who spent his life in state institutions. The researchers' synthesis of extensive interviews into the form of a first-person account showed that he possessed considerable degree of reflective self-awareness and helped give voice to a member of a stigmatized and often forgotten social group.

Family 3: Language-Based Approaches

The third family, language-based approaches, pays close attention to participants' speech. (For simplicity, we refer just to spoken language, but what we have to say applies equally to the analysis of written texts.)

Language-based approaches differ from phenomenological approaches in that they are less interested in participants' inner experiencing and more focused on the details of the language used and how speakers achieve their ends in a conversation.

Discourse Analysis. Discourse analysis (Potter, Chapter 7, this volume) attempts to identify the "discourse repertoires" that speakers use (i.e., the type of language they draw upon) and how speakers attempt to present a "subject position" (i.e., a certain standing for themselves in the eyes of their listeners). For instance, a would-be politician may try to position herself as a strong-willed authority figure, a technocratic expert, or as an ordinary "woman of the people."

Madill and Barkham (1997) used discourse analysis to examine the transcripts of a single case of psychodynamic therapy. They showed how the client, at various points in the therapy, took on a number of subject positions, which they labeled the "dutiful daughter," the "bad mother," and the "damaged child." They were then able to locate the client's discourse within its sociocultural context. For instance, the dutiful daughter subject position drew upon a set of discourses that emphasized women's subjectivity, which the researchers were able to place within its historical context, tracing it back to the emphasis on female domesticity in Victorian times.

Conversation Analysis. Conversation analysis was developed by the sociologists Harvey Sacks, Emmanuel Schegloff, and Gail Jefferson in the 1970s. It has been described as microsociology, that is, looking at social structure at its finest level of detail. It addresses the minutiae of talk at a micro level, examining some of the taken-for-granted aspects of how people interact, such as how speakers organize turn-taking in a conversation (Sacks et al., 1974).

For instance, McCabe et al. (2002) analyzed consultations between patients with psychosis and their psychiatrists, focusing on patients' attempts to engage their psychiatrists to talk about their (the patients') psychotic symptoms. The findings showed that although the patients attempted to talk actively about their experiences, their doctors tended to avoid engaging with them, for example, by ignoring them or asking a question, rather than responding directly.

Process Analysis. *Process analysis* is a wide-ranging term that covers a variety of approaches, both qualitative and quantitative. It is usually applied to the analysis of help-intended communication, such as counseling and therapy, peer support, mentoring, and so on. It aims to analyze the detailed features of the communication, often focusing on what is helpful and what is not.

For example, Balmforth and Elliott (2012) used a method called comprehensive process analysis to look at the antecedents and consequences of a single event in psychotherapy: the client's disclosure to the therapist of her childhood abuse. The analysis showed how the therapist facilitated the client's gaining insight into how the historical abuse was linked to her present problems of victimization.

Family 4: Ethnographic Approaches

Ethnographic approaches were the first systematic qualitative research method, articulated by anthropologists such as Franz Boas and Bronislaw Malinowski at the beginning of the 20th century (Emerson, 2001), although their roots go back to the ancient Greek travelers and historians, such as Herodotus.

In contrast to all of the approaches described earlier, which focus on the individual or the small group, ethnographic studies have a broader focus, encompassing a whole culture, or subculture, and its practices (Causey, Chapter 11, this volume). They typically involve researchers immersing themselves in the culture to be studied, using participant observation. Researchers take copious field notes, which are subsequently assembled into a (often book-length) report on the intricate features of that culture. It is therefore good for addressing research questions about a wider cultural or social system.

Ethnography.   Classic ethnographic studies involved sustained observation (*fieldwork*) of a cultural group, in a participant-observer role. The early anthropological studies often involved European or North American anthropologists spending months or years immersing themselves in the culture that they were studying. Margaret Mead's (1928/2017) *Coming of Age in Samoa* is a classic example of the genre, which has sparked considerable debate. Later studies have often been conducted in the researcher's own country of residence but focusing on a specific social group, often a marginalized one, within it. Whyte's (1943) *Street Corner Society*, which examined a youth gang in South Boston, is a well-known example of this genre.

As is evident from the preceding description, ethnography is extremely time-consuming and requires considerable expertise and commitment to carry out.

Focused Ethnography.   Focused ethnography (sometimes called rapid ethnography) is a stripped-down version of the full ethnographic approach. Rather than attempting to characterize a whole culture, it draws on ethnographic principles to focus on a smaller social system, such as a school or hospital ward, focusing on a more restricted research question (Simonds et al., 2012; Vindrola-Padros & Vindrola-Padros, 2017).

One example is a study of an intervention aimed at enhancing contact and decreasing stereotyping across generations on an inner-city housing project (Alcock et al., 2011). The intervention involved young and old people collaborating on a photovoice project (Wang & Burris, 1997) depicting their local environment. A focused ethnographic approach was used to evaluate its effectiveness.

Choosing an Approach

Having summarized the key features of each approach, we now look at how researchers can go about selecting the best one to use. Our pragmatic, pluralist position proposes that all approaches have their respective advantages and disadvantages and that it is the researcher's task to select the best method for answering their particular research question.

As we have said, this choice is a two-stage process. First, you decide which of the four families of methods best fits your question. This is the easier of the two decisions, as the four families are distinct in their aims and approaches (see Table 2.2 for a summary of the main research question that each family addresses).

Harder is the choice within each family of methods because, by definition, the approaches within a family tend to resemble each other, just like people within an actual family do. It is that choice that this section focuses on, using a running example.

Of course, factors other than pure pragmatism may play a role in the choice of approach. You may find yourself more drawn to a particular one because it fits in more with your personal cognitive style. Perhaps you find that you resonate with particular authors or find others harder to understand. Finally, external factors may play a role: A decisive factor may be the availability of a supervisor, or the presence of knowledgeable colleagues, who have expertise in a given approach.

Running Example

We illustrate the choice process using a running example of a specific research topic, based on our own research interests. The general topic is partner support (see, e.g., Harris et al., 2006; Pistrang et al., 2001). When people encounter life stresses or difficulties, they tend to turn for support first to their family and friends; those individuals who are in close relationships tend to turn to their partner (Barker et al., 1990). However, the process is complicated because attempting to help and support someone you are close to can raise some difficult dilemmas (Coyne et al., 1990). It is important to study the phenomenon of partner support to understand when and how it works and does not work; this knowledge can possibly be drawn upon in the design of psychological interventions.

Choosing a Thematic Analysis Approach

Within our running example, research questions concerning people's experiences of receiving and giving support to their partner would lend themselves to a thematic analysis approach. Suppose that the researcher is interested in how partners think and feel about giving support; for example, what are some of the dilemmas they experience when attempting to support their partner (Coyne et al., 1990)—let's say, someone who is depressed (cf. Harris et al., 2006)?

If the researcher wanted a general understanding of individuals' reports of the main difficulties in giving support, then a *generic thematic analysis* approach would be suitable. If they wanted a more structured approach, then the *framework* approach would be appropriate: it produces charts and tables and generates a map detailing which respondents endorsed which themes. If frequency counts of each theme was desired, then either the framework approach or *content analysis* would provide this, requiring a coding manual so that instances of themes could be counted. Other approaches can also produce frequency counts, although this is controversial because some qualitative researchers think that numerical data are contrary to the ethos of qualitative research.

If the research question concerned each individual's unique experiences and ways of making meaning, then a phenomenological approach, such as *interpretative phenomenological analysis*, would be preferable. Finally, *grounded theory* could be used if the researcher was aiming to produce an overarching theory of partner support, such as the central role of empathy (or the lack thereof) in supportive interactions.

Choosing a Narrative Approach

The central feature of narrative approaches is that they focus on the storied nature of the phenomenon. So, within our running example, *narrative analysis* would be good for addressing questions about how particular episodes of support played out—what was the precipitating problem, how did the partner initially respond, what happened next, and how was it finally resolved? Perhaps these accounts could be classified into a small number of prototypes: for example, the smooth resolution, the partner feeling criticized, coming up against a brick wall, and so on.

Life history approaches might be used to take a longer view, such as looking at how partners attempted to support each other over the course of their relationship. What do they remember of their early supportive interactions? How did these develop over time? Have they become more attuned to each other needs, or have they become more annoyed by their partner's perceived deficiencies?

Choosing a Language-Based Approach

Language-based approaches look at the fine details of interpersonal interactions—in our running example, actual interactions between partners would need to be recorded (rather than relying on self-report). *Conversation analysis* would be appropriate if the research question concerned micro-level aspects of an interaction, such as how partners give advice to one another. Advice can be couched in all sorts of linguistic forms—questions are a common one (e.g., "Why don't you try exercising more?")—and conversation analysis could address the antecedents and consequences of each form.

Discourse analysis could examine the different "subject positions" that each partner takes in the interaction (e.g., victim, expert, helpless child) and what linguistic resources they draw upon, much as in the Madill and Barkham (1997) therapy study described earlier.

Process analysis would look more broadly at the features of the interaction. If one partner is trying to support another, how does she go about it? Is she generally directive or nondirective? How does she gather background information, if at all?

Choosing an Ethnographic Approach

Finally, *ethnographic methods* shift the focus on to broader cultural issues. In terms of the running example, how does partner support fit into cultural norms, roles, and practices in the society in which it is taking place? What are the expectations for partners to provide help and support to each other in North American or British culture, and do they differ from, say, Chinese or Indian cultural expectations? Are there differences within each culture, for example according to ethnicity, religion, social class, or sexual orientation?

A *focused ethnography* might address some of the same questions, but within a single restricted cultural setting, such as a religious community, hospital clinic, or neighborhood.

CONCLUSION

This chapter has aimed to acquaint readers with the main approaches to qualitative research. Space restraints, and our not wanting to overload the reader, mean that we have just given a brief thumbnail sketch of each of the approaches. We hope that this has been sufficient to give you a taste of each of them and to whet your appetite for investigating more fully those that seem like a possibility for your particular line of research.

Subsequent chapters in this volume, and those in its previous edition (Camic et al., 2003), give full introductions to the approaches that we have covered. Furthermore, many other texts on qualitative research (e.g., Creswell, 2013; McLeod, 2011, Wertz et al., 2011; Willig, 2013, Willig & Stainton Rogers, 2017) are available to give a more expanded introduction.

One of the appealing aspects of qualitative research is that it is both an art and a science. It is a science in that it is systematic and has respect for the general principles of scientific investigation (e.g., locating the study in the context of previous literature, transparency of methods of data collection and analysis, grounding interpretations in the data, and not going beyond the data). It is an art in that it requires some inspiration and an ability to see patterns in the data and to synthesize a mass of observations into a compelling picture. It is also a profoundly human experience, and that, for many researchers, is the ultimate motivation: the privilege of being able to make contact with, and gain a deeper understanding of, one's fellow human beings.

REFERENCES

Ahern, K. J. (1999). Ten tips for reflexive bracketing. *Qualitative Health Research*, *9*(3), 407–411. https://doi.org/10.1177/104973239900900309

Alcock, A., Camic, P. M., Barker, C., Haridi, C., & Raven, R. (2011). Intergenerational practice in the community: A focused ethnographic evaluation. *Journal of Community & Applied Social Psychology*, *21*(5), 419–432. https://doi.org/10.1002/casp.1084

Balmforth, J., & Elliott, R. (2012). "I never talked about, ever": A comprehensive process analysis of a significant client disclosure event in therapy. *Counselling & Psychotherapy Research*, *12*(1), 2–12. https://doi.org/10.1080/14733145.2011.580353

Banyard, V. L., & Miller, K. E. (1998). The powerful potential of qualitative research for community psychology. *American Journal of Community Psychology, 26*(4), 485–505. https://doi.org/10.1023/A:1022136821013

Barker, C., & Pistrang, N. (2005). Quality criteria under methodological pluralism: Implications for conducting and evaluating research. *American Journal of Community Psychology, 35*(3–4), 201–212. https://doi.org/10.1007/s10464-005-3398-y

Barker, C., & Pistrang, N. (2012). Methodological pluralism: Implications for consumers and producers of research. In L. A. Jason & D. S. Glenwick (Eds.), *Methodological approaches to community-based research* (pp. 33–50). American Psychological Association. https://doi.org/10.1037/13492-003

Barker, C., Pistrang, N., & Elliott, R. (1994). *Research methods in clinical and counselling psychology*. John Wiley & Sons.

Barker, C., Pistrang, N., & Elliott, R. (2002). *Research methods in clinical psychology: An introduction for students and practitioners* (2nd ed.). John Wiley & Sons. https://doi.org/10.1002/0470013435

Barker, C., Pistrang, N., & Elliott, R. (2016). *Research methods in clinical psychology: An introduction for students and practitioners* (3rd ed.). John Wiley & Sons. https://doi.org/10.1002/9781119154082

Barker, C., Pistrang, N., Shapiro, D. A., & Shaw, I. (1990). Coping and help-seeking in the UK adult population. *The British Journal of Clinical Psychology, 29*(3), 271–285. https://doi.org/10.1111/j.2044-8260.1990.tb00885.x

Baruch, E., Pistrang, N., & Barker, C. (2018). "Between a rock and a hard place": Family members' experiences of supporting a relative with bipolar disorder. *Social Psychiatry and Psychiatric Epidemiology, 53*(10), 1123–1131. https://doi.org/10.1007/s00127-018-1560-8

Bogdan, R., & Taylor, S. (1976). The judged, not the judges. An insider's view of mental retardation. *American Psychologist, 31*(1), 47–52. https://doi.org/10.1037/0003-066X.31.1.47

Boyatzis, R. E. (1998). *Transforming qualitative information: Thematic analysis and code development*. Sage Publications.

Braun, V., & Clarke, V. (2006). Using thematic analysis in psychology. *Qualitative Research in Psychology, 3*(2), 77–101. https://doi.org/10.1191/1478088706qp063oa

Braun, V., & Clarke, V. (2013). *Successful qualitative research: A practical guide for beginners*. Sage Publications.

Camic, P. M., Rhodes, J. E., & Yardley, L. (Eds.). (2003). *Qualitative research in psychology: Expanding perspectives in methodology and design*. American Psychological Association. https://doi.org/10.1037/10595-000

Carlson, R. (1972). Understanding women: Implications for personality theory and research. *Journal of Social Issues, 28*(2), 17–32. https://doi.org/10.1111/j.1540-4560.1972.tb00015.x

Centers for Disease Control and Prevention. (2019). *Laveran and the discovery of the malaria parasite*. https://www.cdc.gov/malaria/about/history/laveran.html

Cole, A. L., & Knowles, J. G. (2001). *Lives in context: The art of life history research*. Altamira Press.

Corbin, J., & Strauss, A. (2015). *Basics of qualitative research: Techniques and procedures for developing grounded theory* (4th ed.). Sage Publications.

Coyne, J. C., Ellard, J. H., & Smith, D. A. (1990). Social support, interdependence, and the dilemmas of helping. In B. R. Sarason, I. G. Sarason, & G. R. Pierce (Eds.), *Wiley series on personality processes. Social support: An interactional view* (pp. 129–149). John Wiley & Sons.

Creswell, J. W. (2013). *Qualitative inquiry and research design: Choosing among five approaches* (3rd ed.). Sage Publications.

Douglas, H. (2009). *Science, policy, and the value-free ideal*. University of Pittsburgh Press. https://doi.org/10.2307/j.ctt6wrc78

Emerson, R. M. (2001). Introduction: the development of ethnographic field research. In R. M. Emerson (Ed.), *Contemporary field research: Perspectives and formulations* (2nd ed., pp. 1–26). Little, Brown & Co.

Finlay, L. (2003). The reflexive journey: mapping multiple routes. In L. Finlay & B. Gough (Eds.), *Reflexivity: A practical guide for researchers in health and social sciences* (pp. 3–20). Blackwell. https://doi.org/10.1002/9780470776094.ch1

Fischer, C. T. (2009). Bracketing in qualitative research: Conceptual and practical matters. *Psychotherapy Research, 19*(4–5), 583–590. https://doi.org/10.1080/10503300902798375

Fiske, D. W., & Shweder, R. A. (Eds.). (1986). *Metatheory in social science: Pluralisms and subjectivities.* University of Chicago Press.

Gearing, R. E. (2004). Bracketing in research: A typology. *Qualitative Health Research, 14*(10), 1429–1452. https://doi.org/10.1177/1049732304270394

Geertz, C. (1973). *The interpretation of cultures.* Basic Books.

Gergen, K. J. (1985). The social constructionist movement in modern psychology. *American Psychologist, 40*(3), 266–275. https://doi.org/10.1037/0003-066X.40.3.266

Ghosh, P. K. (Ed.). (1984). *Appropriate technology in third world development.* Greenwood Press.

Giorgi, A. P., & Giorgi, B. M. (2003). The descriptive phenomenological psychological method. In P. Camic, J. E. Rhodes, & L. Yardley (Eds.), *Qualitative research in psychology: Expanding perspectives in methodology and design* (pp. 243–273). American Psychological Association. https://doi.org/10.1037/10595-013

Glaser, B. G., & Strauss, A. L. (1967). *The discovery of grounded theory: Strategies for qualitative research.* Aldine.

Gottschalk, L. A., & Gleser, G. C. (1969). *The measurement of psychological states through the content analysis of verbal behavior.* University of California Press.

Harris, T. J. R., Pistrang, N., & Barker, C. (2006). Couples' experiences of the support process in depression: A phenomenological analysis. *Psychology and Psychotherapy, 79*(Pt. 1), 1–21. https://doi.org/10.1348/147608305X41218

Henwood, K. L., & Pidgeon, N. F. (1992). Qualitative research and psychological theorizing. *British Journal of Psychology, 83*(Pt. 1), 97–111. https://doi.org/10.1111/j.2044-8295.1992.tb02426.x

Henwood, K., & Pidgeon, N. (2003). *Grounded theory in psychological research.* In P. M. Camic, J. E. Rhodes, & L. Yardley (Eds.), *Qualitative research in psychology: Expanding perspectives in methodology and design* (pp. 131–155). American Psychological Association. https://doi.org/10.1037/10595-008

Hughes, C., & Cohen, R. L. (2010). Feminists really do count: The complexity of feminist methodologies. *International Journal of Social Research Methodology, 13*(3), 189–196. https://doi.org/10.1080/13645579.2010.482249

Humphreys, K. (2000). Community narratives and personal stories in Alcoholics Anonymous. *Journal of Community Psychology, 28*(5), 495–506. https://doi.org/10.1002/1520-6629(200009)28:5<495::AID-JCOP3>3.0.CO;2-W

Humphreys, K., & Piot, P. (2012). Scientific evidence alone is not sufficient basis for health policy. *BMJ (Clinical Research Ed.), 344,* e1316. https://doi.org/10.1136/bmj.e1316

Inazu, J. D. (2016). *Confident pluralism: Surviving and thriving through deep difference.* University of Chicago Press. https://doi.org/10.7208/chicago/9780226592572.001.0001

Joffe, H., & Yardley, L. (2003). Content and thematic analysis. In D. F. Marks & L. Yardley (Eds.), *Research methods for clinical and health psychology* (pp. 56–68). Sage Publications.

Krippendorff, K. (2013). *Content analysis: an introduction to its methodology* (3rd ed.). Sage Publications.

Levitt, H. M., Bamberg, M., Creswell, J. W., Frost, D. M., Josselson, R., & Suárez-Orozco, C. (2018). Journal article reporting standards for qualitative primary, qualitative meta-analytic, and mixed methods research in psychology: The APA Publications and

Communications Board task force report. *American Psychologist, 73*(1), 26–46. https://doi.org/10.1037/amp0000151

Madill, A., & Barkham, M. (1997). Discourse analysis of a theme in one successful case of psychodynamic-interpersonal psychotherapy. *Journal of Counseling Psychology, 44*(2), 232–244. https://doi.org/10.1037/0022-0167.44.2.232

McCabe, R., Heath, C., Burns, T., & Priebe, S. (2002). Engagement of patients with psychosis in the consultation: Conversation analytic study. *British Medical Journal, 325*(7373), 1148–1151. https://doi.org/10.1136/bmj.325.7373.1148

McLeod, J. (2011). *Qualitative research in counselling and psychotherapy* (2nd ed.). Sage Publications.

Mead, M. (2017). *Coming of age in Samoa a study of adolescence and sex in primitive societies.* Penguin Books. (Original work published 1928)

Oakley, A. (1999). Paradigm wars: Some thoughts on a personal and public trajectory. *International Journal of Social Research Methodology, 2*(3), 247–254. https://doi.org/10.1080/136455799295041

Peplau, L. A., & Conrad, E. (1989). Beyond nonsexist research: The perils of feminist methods in psychology. *Psychology of Women Quarterly, 13*(4), 379–400. https://doi.org/10.1111/j.1471-6402.1989.tb01009.x

Pinker, S. (2014). *The sense of style: The thinking person's guide to writing in the 21st century.* Viking Penguin.

Pistrang, N., & Barker, C. (2010). Scientific, practical and personal decisions in selecting qualitative methods. In M. Barkham, G. E. Hardy, & J. Mellor-Clark (Eds.), *Developing and delivering practice-based evidence: A guide for the psychological therapies* (pp. 65–89). Wiley-Blackwell. https://doi.org/10.1002/9780470687994.ch3

Pistrang, N., & Barker, C. (2012). Varieties of qualitative research: A pragmatic approach to selecting methods. In H. Cooper, P. M. Camic, D. L. Long, A. T. Panter, D. Rindskopf, & K. J. Sher (Eds.), *APA handbook of research methods in psychology: Vol. 2. Research designs: Quantitative, qualitative, neuropsychological, and biological* (pp. 5–18). American Psychological Association. https://doi.org/10.1037/13620-001

Pistrang, N., Picciotto, A., & Barker, C. (2001). The communication of empathy in couples during the transition to parenthood. *Journal of Community Psychology, 29*(6), 615–636. https://doi.org/10.1002/jcop.2000

Pope, C., Ziebland, S., & Mays, N. (2000). Qualitative research in health care. Analysing qualitative data. *British Medical Journal, 320*(7227), 114–116. https://doi.org/10.1136/bmj.320.7227.114

Potter, J., & Wetherell, M. (1987). *Discourse and social psychology.* Sage Publications.

Rennie, D. L., Phillips, J. R., & Quartaro, G. K. (1988). Grounded theory: A promising approach to conceptualization in psychology. *Canadian Psychology, 29*(2), 139–150. https://doi.org/10.1037/h0079765

Richardson, J. T. E. (Ed.). (1996). *Handbook of qualitative research methods for psychology and the social sciences.* British Psychological Society.

Ritchie, J., Lewis, J., Nicholls, C. M., & Ormston, R. (Eds.). (2014). *Qualitative research practice: A guide for social science students and researchers.* Sage Publications.

Ritchie, J., & Spencer, L. (1994). Qualitative data analysis for applied policy research. In A. Bryman & R. G. Burgess (Eds.), *Analyzing qualitative data* (pp. 173–194). Routledge.

Rosenberg, M. (1965). *Society and the adolescent self-image.* Princeton University Press. https://doi.org/10.1515/9781400876136

Sacks, H., Schegloff, E. A., & Jefferson, G. (1974). The simplest systematics for the organization of turn-taking in conversation. *Language, 50*(4), 696–735. https://doi.org/10.1353/lan.1974.0010

Simonds, L. M., Camic, P. M., & Causey, A. (2012). Using focused ethnography in psychological research. In H. Cooper, P. M. Camic, D. L. Long, A. T. Panter, D. Rindskopf, & K. J. Sher (Eds.), *APA handbook of research methods in psychology: Vol. 2. Research designs: Quantitative, qualitative, neuropsychological, and biological* (pp. 157–170). American Psychological Association. https://doi.org/10.1037/13620-010

Smith, J. A., Flowers, P., & Larkin, M. (2009). *Interpretative phenomenological analysis: Theory, method and research.* Sage Publications.

Smith, J. A., Jarman, M., & Osborn, M. (1999). Doing interpretative phenomenological analysis. In M. Murray & K. Chamberlain (Eds.), *Qualitative health psychology: Theories and methods* (pp. 218–240). Sage Publications. https://doi.org/10.4135/9781446217870.n14

Vindrola-Padros, C., & Vindrola-Padros, B. (2017). Quick and dirty? A systematic review of the use of rapid ethnographies in healthcare organisation and delivery. *BMJ Quality & Safety, 27*(4), 321–330. https://doi.org/10.1136/bmjqs-2017-007226

Wang, C., & Burris, M. A. (1997). Photovoice: Concept, methodology, and use for participatory needs assessment. *Health Education & Behavior, 24*(3), 369–387. https://doi.org/10.1177/109019819702400309

Wertz, F. J. (2014). Qualitative inquiry in the history of psychology. *Qualitative Psychology, 1*(1), 4. https://doi.org/10.1037/qup0000007

Wertz, F. J., Charmaz, K., McMullen, L. M., Josselson, R., Anderson, R., & McSpadden, E. (2011). *Five ways of doing qualitative analysis: phenomenological psychology, grounded theory, discourse analysis, narrative research, and intuitive inquiry.* Guilford Press.

Whyte, W. F. (1943). *Street corner society: The social structure of an Italian slum.* University of Chicago Press.

Willig, C. (2013). *Introducing qualitative research in psychology.* Open University Press.

Willig, C., & Stainton-Rogers, W. (Eds.). (2017). *The SAGE handbook of qualitative research in psychology* (2nd ed.). Sage Publications.

Winter, D. A. (2003). Repertory grid technique as a psychotherapy research measure. *Psychotherapy Research, 13*(1), 25–42.

Narrative in Qualitative Psychology

Approaches and Methodological Consequences

Michael Bamberg

Giving narrative and narrative analysis a prominent place within the overall frame of doing qualitative inquiry requires proceeding on two—if not three—tracks that do not necessarily run parallel: On one hand, we may want to determine with more clarity which aspects of our engagement with qualitative methodologies we value most—that is, why we approach our research question(s) qualitatively. Simultaneously, we may need to clarify: Why narrative? That is, which aspects of narrative inquiry do we deem particularly relevant in our overall qualitative approach, and which "definitions" of narrative do we embrace as productive in pursuit of more specific research questions? As a third potential track, we may need to specify the particular kind of narrative analysis—that is, how we define our unit(s) of analysis of what we tackle empirically—in concert with how we do it, so our analysis not only makes sense to others but can also be followed in pursuit of their own research questions. And although theoretically, and maybe also in principle, the sequence of steps (first, why and how qualitative; next, why and how narrative; and third, what kind of analytic procedures) should follow exactly this kind of top-down reasoning, it typically doesn't work that way. First, working through the options of qualitative approaches and picking one over the other is by no means simple or straightforward; the same holds for definitions of narrative and deciding which approach might be more attractive and productive. Second, and especially as beginners, we typically don't enter psychology research having taken Qualitative 101 as our startup course

https://doi.org/10.1037/0000252-003
Qualitative Research in Psychology: Expanding Perspectives in Methodology and Design, Second Edition, P. M. Camic (Editor)

and from there move on and survey the different approaches available. Rather, we enter working with narratives from somewhere in the middle, having seen or being attracted by others' work with narratives in how they approach particular research questions. Or we even enter after hearing and seeing actual narratives performed in real-life settings that we found intriguing and worth following up analytically, realizing only later that we bought into hidden assumptions with regard to narrative and qualitative frameworks that early on simply felt right and above suspicion.

Having successfully assisted undergraduate and graduate psychology students to engage in qualitative research for more than 25 years now, it still comes as a surprise how often the potential of narrative methodologies goes unrecognized. When facing analytic work with documents, interview data, or naturally occurring conversations that are full of storied accounts, students, particularly newcomers to qualitative inquiry, commonly rely on surfacing the data in terms of their content, and thereafter fall back on quantifying the thematic content across the data collected. This chapter is designed to help forge helpful pathways through the thickets of choices we have when engaging in narrative inquiry under the premise of qualitative inquiry as our overarching umbrella. As such, it attempts to bridge Chapters 1 (Camic), 2 (Barker & Pistrang), and 6 (Murray) of this volume. In addition, it shows connections with other qualitative methods, as discussed subsequently. I start with a brief consideration of two questions: First, what forms do qualitative (narrative) data take, and where do we find that data? Second, having made decisions with regard to what counts as valid (narrative) data to pursue our investigations, what are the implications with respect to what to do with those data—that is, how to analyze them? We work through these two questions in the first part of this chapter before turning, in the second part, to five methodological guideposts for qualitative inquiry that will serve as yardsticks to evaluate potential merits and drawbacks for narrative approaches. The chapter ends with a somewhat critical perspective on how we might be able to broaden future work by incorporating narrative research into a more critical and inclusive endeavor.

NARRATIVES AS QUALITATIVE DATA—UNITS OF ANALYSIS

Narratives and Stories—What Are They Made of?

Before discussing narratives as qualitative data and how to analyze them as qualitative data within the frame of psychological research, a brief excursion into what narratives are and what makes them potentially interesting may be necessary. I start by discussing four simple stories—all consisting of the same "events" (Figure 3.1).[1] However, what is different is their sequence as well as

---

[1]The term *event* is used here as expressed in the form of a proposition or clause; it typically depicts an actor and an action ("Lee went to the store") in contrast to a happening or a state ("Lee had no candy").

FIGURE 3.1. Four Simple Stories: The Same Event

Story A	Story B
1. Lee had no candy at home	1. Lee felt good
2. went to the store	2. went to the store
3. bought a package of candy	3. bought a package of candy
4. ate it all up	4. ate it all up
5. Lee felt good	5. Lee had no candy at home
Story C	Story D
2. Lee went to the store	2. Lee went to the store
1. after Lee had no candy at home	1. Lee was out of candy at home
5. Lee felt good	? Lee felt good
4. after having eaten up all the candy	? Lee ate up all the candy
3. that Lee had bought	? Lee bought a package of candy

their contribution to what can be called *story-hood* (prototypical or "well-formedness"). For Story A, we want to make the argument that all five propositions follow sequentially—that is, form a cohesive and an overall coherent whole. Story A starts with a state description of *lacking* a potentially desirable object and ends with a state description of *being satisfied*. *Not having (candy)* in this context is interpretable as posing a problem that is followed by three action clauses, depicting intentional actions to solve the problem; resulting in the final state description, the positive evaluation: problem solved. Story B still makes sense as a (kind of) story, although there is less overall coherence. For instance, "feeling good" doesn't necessarily result in "going to the store." And "not having" as a result of "having eaten it up" is no surprise and not particularly note- or tell-worthy. Thus, although still following a story format (starting and ending with state descriptions), Story B qualifies as less of a prototypical story construction (and somewhat [more] boring) compared with Story A.

Story C refers to the same sequence of events as Story A, despite the fact that the sequence of clauses seems scrambled. However, this is possible due to the way speakers of English can make use of tenses and aspectual markers to still signal the order of events in the story-world even if the order of clauses does not follow their canonical order. Nevertheless, the sequential arrangement of clauses in Story C may be chosen to contribute to the interpretation of a particular grounding—that is, making particular events as foregrounded—and as such may signal how a speaker positions these events with regard to one another. In contrast to Stories A through C, Story D is hard to make sense of. It contains a lot of ambiguity and would require a lot of inferences (i.e., harder interpretive efforts) to come to a somewhat cohesive and coherent interpretation. It is possible to interpret Lee's journey to the store as a consequence of being out of candy, but the rest of the clauses just don't follow—at least not easily. It should be clear that all stories (A–D) are fictional and that I chose deliberately to construct Lee as a third-person other rather than insinuating that the state descriptions of Lee's lack of candy and their (final) satisfaction might be interpretable as disclosures of a first-person's interiority.

Although the preceding stories are most likely not the kinds of data that analysts will have to deal with in their psychological research, relating them to the following four points will be relevant for the arguments to follow. First, narrative is a discourse mode that orders events in a temporal sequence, where characters and locations (places) are placed into this sequence of unfolding events, allowing the navigation of constancy and change. Second, not "everything" is expressed in language (or, if visual means of event presentation are picked, visual means). What this implies is that storytellers pick and choose events they deem relevant, but they also leave gaps: Most of it remains unsaid. For instance, what is not mentioned in Stories A and C is how long it took Lee to get to the store—10 minutes, 3 hours, a year; whether Lee got there on foot, by taxi, or by plane; what happened when Lee consumed the candy; how long it took to consume it; and so on. All of this information could have been unpacked and tied into the unfolding sequence as state or action descriptions, showing that it is up to speakers to decide which events they choose to tell in their story and that different speakers consequently may tell what they assumed to have happened quite differently; the same narrator may choose different events and tell their story at different occasions to different audiences differently. Third, the language chosen to construct characters in place and time, so that stories can come into existence, is not chosen without method or conscious decision; it is intentional. Further, the language used is not a transparent or direct window into narrator's minds, emotions, and identities. Finally, as the preceding examples demonstrate, there is a close interplay of form and content in the construction of stories, although this is in total disregard of a context in which these stories actually might have served a communicative and relational function.

Narratives as Stories in Context

Returning to narratives as qualitative data, it should be noted that both qualitative and quantitative data-gathering procedures take data "out of their context." Both look at certain aspects of the world as relevant for their research questions and set other aspects of the world aside as not relevant. The difference between them is that gathering qualitative data does not aim to turn them into numerical values and that aspects of the contexts of data collection are considered to be highly relevant (for an example and discussion about mixed methodologies, see Harding et al., Chapter 12, this volume). The reason for being open to context is simple: For once, having no hypothesis that allows researchers to strip a priori what is considered irrelevant for the hypothesis to be tested, the analysis of contextual factors becomes an important—if not a central—part of the investigation. Second, as a consequence, qualitative analysis typically works in depth—that is, from a set of data moving inside-out—to understand how context is constitutive to the data and to our understanding thereof. If this may still sound somewhat mystic, here is a simpler formulation of the same idea: Qualitative data come as situated data; they are situated in immediate and micro-local contexts, in communal and cultural contexts, and, last but not least, in historical contexts. Qualitative data only exist due to their contextual nature; therefore, these contexts are considered to be highly relevant to the phenomena we study and for our analytic work with them (for a discussion about situational analysis, see Wasburn et al., Chapter 9, this volume).

With regard to the general study of narratives and the use of narratives in psychological research, we follow up from the premise that narratives occur in contexts. The fact that researchers have tried to differentiate and distinguish between narrative and story; between storytelling and narrative practice; among life story, life history, and biography; between master and counter or alternative narratives; and between other dimensions of oral performance should not confuse us at the moment. In the following, I subsume all of them simply under the header of "narrative" because they all share three dimensions that lend themselves to be accessed analytically. Narratives—and here we follow Murray's directives in Chapter 6 of this volume—are considered first to be an interactive activity or discourse mode (in contrast to other discourse modes such as descriptions or argumentations). To qualify as narrative, they first need to meet particular structural constraints—that is, conveying a temporal contour that gives meaning to a sequence of events or happenings, typically performed in oral or visual modality. Now, with regard to analyzing or working with narratives, we are confronted by three options. We could analyze their form and structure, which has a history in linguistic and literary investigations, or we could analyze their content, which typically is the center of interest for research in the social and human sciences. As a third option, narrative research can also center on or around the circumstances in which narratives are put to use and attempt to analyze the functions they serve; that is, it can follow up on the question of why the construct of narrative form and the construal of narrative characters in time and space (content) were put to use in a particular context, including the potential uptake by the audience or viewer. To put this differently, the latter approach pursues the question: What is being accomplished by telling a particular narrative at a particular point in time and making a past event relevant to a particular audience? Of course, it is possible to draw on and connect these three analytic perspectives (form, content, and function) in our interpretive business of answering our particular research questions. We return to these options and their consequences in due course.

Shifting Narratives—Stories, Memories, Experiences

As foreshadowed in Chapter 2 by Barker and Pistrang and explicated in Chapter 6 by Murray, psychologists seem to be particularly interested in the middle part—that is, the contents of narratives, and here in the way narrators thematize themselves. Realizing around the mid-1960s that aging as a research field was gaining recognition as a social problem, which in turn opened up new funding resources for sociologists and psychologists, culminating in the emergence of the new field of lifespan psychology, researchers revived early explorations of life histories, life stories, and biographical approaches (cf. Thomas & Znaniecki, 1918–1920); this catapulted the biographical interview into the center as a new wave of qualitative research (for an overview, see Murphy et al., 2010). Although the type of interview technique originally was left relatively unstructured to open the floor for interviewees to structure their responses in their own (subjective) ways, the biographically centered interview soon became an added instrument to explore participants' experiences of a narrower scope, such as divorce (Riessman, 1990), particular types of illness or disease (Kleinman, 1988), or even more specific issues, such as the employability of former refugees in New Zealand (Greenbank, 2020). The central argument here for engaging in qualitative inquiry still is upheld—namely, that the quality of particular kinds of experiences could be better captured and understood when narrated in the context of individuals' life constructions—their childhood, upbringing, and experiential background up to the point of the interview. In addition, biographical approaches to lives and lived experience can be supplemented by autobiographic and autoethnographic writings, in which narrators write about themselves and critically take on culturally dominant discourses or master narratives within which they see themselves constrained and unfolding. Although these analytical approaches use the construct of narrative to explore the construct of life—or of particular aspects of life (types of experience, such as divorce, illness, etc.)—some psychologists have argued that it is actually memories that encapsulate experiences and surface in the form of narratives. In other words, the full life story as well as the biographically centered interview elicits memories that arguably reflect interviewees' experience and as such may lead researchers to their interviewees' identities and sense of self (cf. Smorti, 2011).

This is not the place to take on this line of argument or be critical, but it should be noted how the unit of analytic interrogation gradually began to change: first, narrowing the three analytic options (form, content, function) to converge mainly into an analysis of content; next, moving the analysis from narratives in large (which would include third- and second-person narratives) to center on first-person disclosures only (i.e., excluding stories about others); from there to life-story biographies (which automatically are taken to be stories or narratives); to becoming typically elicited in biographical interviews (where the interview became the unit of analysis); and from here to theme-centered interviews (e.g., divorce, where arguably the theme became what's being analyzed). Overall, simple stories or narratives as the original unit of inquiry mutated into constructs that were deemed to "sit" inside of participants' interiorities, and particular types of interviewing techniques were deemed in turn to be able to extract these aspects of interviewees' internal constructs. Another way of conceiving the ways narratives have analytically been appropriated in qualitative research is in terms of a change from narratives *told* to memories people *have*—which are taken to stand in as proxies for experiences that people *had*—which in turn are taken as proxies for the phenomena we are interested to explore and better understand, such as divorce, illness, or having been abducted by extraterrestrials. Noteworthy in this context are attempts to develop research interview procedures that strongly resemble psychoanalytic and deep interview techniques aiming to reveal unconscious meaning and intrapsychic processes by adopting an interviewer stance nearly identical to that of a therapist (cf. Kvale, 2003).

In the early days of collecting qualitative data in the form of personal documents (letters and autobiographies) and narrative interviews, the reporting of this kind of data largely refrained from deep analysis and interpretation and arguably tried to let the data "speak for themselves." For instance, the classic *The Polish Peasant* (Thomas & Znaniecki, 1918–1920) contained little commentary, let alone deeper interpretive analysis, of the rich ethnographic data that form the majority of the book. Reasons for not engaging with comments or anything that could reveal an interpreter's stance were to record aspects of social life and to document change, as well as to preserve voices that otherwise would be lost. In a second wave of working with biographies and life-story data, qualitative researchers began to condense and paraphrase the collected documents and data, trusting that their reports—at times copublished with their participants—were preserving the gist of their interviewees' experience and sense of who they were. However, a critique of these reports could demonstrate how interpretive categories smuggled into such attempts to condense and modify were not necessarily those of the interviewees but rather show traces of second-order categorial analysis. Subsequent debates of what kinds of categorization were appropriate stirred up discussions around issues of methodology and epistemological positions (discussed earlier in Chapter 2 under the headers of realism, phenomenology, and constructivism, and less so also positivism). It also should be noted that two other theoretical approaches began to take hold and gain prominence in work with narrative data: (a) psychodynamic and (b) discourse analytic theorizing. Psychodynamic approaches, and here particularly psychodynamic interpretative frames, view the interview as opening interviewees' narratives as a window into their unconscious sensemaking; discourse analysis (see Potter, Chapter 7, this volume) considers interviews a method to approach and analyze the interactive context in which narratives surface, including interview contexts.

GUIDELINES FOR QUALITATIVE RESEARCH USING NARRATIVES

Having been tasked by the American Psychological Association (APA) to establish guidelines and reporting standards for qualitative research (Levitt et al., 2018), we started out by developing criteria that differentiate among various qualitative research agenda. Because our guidelines were appearing in the new edition of the APA (2019) *Publication Manual* side by side with the guidelines for quantitative research and because psychological researchers are more likely to have some familiarity with the guidelines that had been developed and in place for decades for quantitative research only, the idea was to make the new guidelines relevant in terms of their new implications. I recently attempted to condense them into five general principles (Bamberg, 2020, p. 244, having been originally inspired by Marecek, 2003) that in principle could serve as guideposts for qualitative inquirers. Using them here in an elaborated form for this chapter, they form the backdrop against which to work up and compare several narrative approaches and their implications for doing analytic work:

1. allowing for inductive (non–hypothesis-testing) methodologies

2. allowing subjectivity and experience into research

3. interrogating the outsider perspective and allowing a blurred (although reflective) stance on the researcher–researchee divide

4. aiming for insights or findings that have "real-life implications," allowing for civic or social engagement of researchers

5. taking language seriously—that is, allowing intentional and cultural practices—as well as body and emotions (as more than mental [reflective] processes)

Inductive—and Generalizable

Investigations of narrative formed alongside narrative structure historically were typically not inductive or exploratory; originally, the development of categories to qualify instances of narratives very closely followed comparative-inferential procedures, having a lasting tradition in the discipline of narratology (literary history and literary theory). This is no longer the case. These days, academic work on structures and forms of narratives typically builds on more or less well-established canonical cases (such as the Stories A–D used earlier for the purpose of illustration) to demonstrate what nonlinear, disjointed narratives look like; how they are put to use; and how they are made sense of by readers, viewers, and audiences at large. Within literary analytic and critical traditions, this line of inquiry has led to the inductive development of widely accepted categorial distinctions—for instance, between literary genres (Frye, 1957) or folk and fairy tales (Propp, 1927).

As established earlier in the chapter and laid out in more detail in Chapter 6 of this volume, inductive procedures that work up categories of themes in single narratives (or narrative interviews) and establish content categories abducted from comparisons across narratives or interviews are more relevant for psychological work with narratives. According to Hammersley (1989), it is Blumer's (1979) critique of Thomas and Znaniecki's (1918–1920) relatively loose use of categorial distinctions and their interpretive theorizing that led to the development of grounded theory (see Griffiths, Chapter 10, this volume), which can be considered the first explicitly inductive and scientific approach to qualitative data. Collecting narrative data and sifting through these data to compare and contrast narratives to "find" commonalities (and differences) is an intrinsically inductive process, codified in what thematic and content analytic procedures are trying to accomplish. When it comes to the use of categories to code—and this holds for any form of data—we should be aware that we may be using these categories as hypotheses, looking into and testing whether these categories play out in quasi-numerical values that can further differentiate between qualitative data sets. Although there is nothing wrong in following these kinds of procedures, strictly speaking we enter the broad field of hypothesis testing. To summarize, qualitative interpretive work on the content of narratives or narrative interviews customarily does not try to import preconceived codes or categories. Rather, it approaches narratives (typically as texts) from which the interpretation of the interpreter emerges—bracketing and delaying interpretive categories as long as possible and beginning to reflect on categorial assumptions as soon as they are recognizably "kicking in." This kind of interpretive procedure follows the hermeneutic tradition of working with texts: The interpreter attempts to approach the meaning of texts by cycling through a number of methodical steps and typically reapplies these steps several times. Each cycle brings what has been learned in the previous cycle to the next cycle. However, a full and total understanding is never reached but only approached. And although the interpretive process always starts from a kind of preunderstanding and brings background assumptions into the interpretative engagement, bracketing—that is, setting these assumptions aside and delaying the use of interpretive categories—serves as a guidepost to what is recently discussed under the header of trustworthiness (cf. Levitt et al., 2018).

Analyses of narratives' functions—that is, entering the interpretive territory of an assessment of why narrators chose to share their story, or why a particular content was given a particular (story) format and why it was shared in the here-and-now of an ongoing interaction—is, for obvious reasons, the most bracketed interpretive commitment. In other words, the process of reaching an interpretation of how the participant's response, including their narrative form and content, contributed to answering our research question, will have to be the result of a slow inductive process in working with the data in which the interpretive framework (whether it be psychoanalytic or discourse analytic, hermeneutic or phenomenological) is laid open and documented in the analytic section of our report.

Allowing Subjectivity and Experience

Seeking to understand participants' experience and how they make sense of themselves and the world commonly falls into the domain of phenomenological approaches (see Smith & Fieldstone, Chapter 8, this volume), often relying on narratives or interviews (or both) as data for analytic work. Frequently, making the claim for narrative theorizing starts with the statement that stories in human interaction are universal and ubiquitous—implying that all we need to do is listen. True! So why must we be selective with regard to participants and engaging them in storytelling situations that we claim to be relevant to our research question? Why not just—seemingly simply— listen in on everyday and mundane conversations that just happen? Well, a number of narrative researchers, especially those following ethnographic, interactionist, and conversation-analytic orientations, claim to be doing exactly that. For them, storytelling events (narrative practices) are the empirical domain in which participants are subjects and express their subjectivity "naturally" by engaging in their daily business, although always constrained by sociocultural and institutional forces that limit—but also enable, as I have argued elsewhere (Bamberg & Wipff, 2020b)—communication and storytelling. The fact that they talk about past events in which they figured as actors or experiencer, or simply as bystanders, is not necessarily central to our analytic work with stories. Rather, any storytelling activity, including narratives about others or the sharing of well-established tales, is analyzable as narrative. We, as ethnographers or interaction analysts, *experience* our participants as subjects *in the experience* or recording or interacting with them; it is this "experience" that forms the unit of analysis. To clarify: First-person narratives—that is, instances of storytelling in which narrators thematize themselves—are special cases. However, their analysis follows the same procedures as third-person stories that thematize others (as with Lee's story earlier in the chapter). What is analyzed is the construction of characters in the there-and-then of the temporal contour of the story and how they are contextually made relevant for the here-and-now in the interaction.

Having spelled out this theoretical argument, this does not mean that interviews are ruled out as sites for the gathering of qualitative data or that they are "unnatural." Rather, it calls for the analysis of interviews as interactive settings, and as such, they form the units of analysis. The fact that interviewees may share stories about themselves and may reflect on their memories or experiences does not, per se, make these accounts more subjective or privilege them as experiential. Imagine, for instance, the stories we tell about the actions (and nonactions) of our students: those stories may be more colored by our subjectivity and experience—and more "telling" about ourselves—than stories we tell about ourselves. To sum up, there is more to narratives and qualitative work with narratives than the typical assertion that narratives preserve the experience of narrators and express their subjective ways of making sense, a claim that privileges the content of personal first-person narratives. Although not incorrect, this assertion confines the analysis of subjectivity and experience to the level of content of narratives, without interrogating why this particular content had been framed in the particular narrative form and been shared, at a particular moment, in the interview interaction.

Questioning or Interrogating the Outsider Perspective: The Roles of Reflection and Reflexivity

As exemplified in several narrative approaches presented by Murray (Chapter 6, this volume), qualitative data do not exist independently from a researcher's perspective. This may sound radically relativistic, as if narrative research generates its own data, but any research interest and subsequent question is formulated within a historical, societal, and communal setting and as such brings perspectives to the business of inquiry. Therefore, it is incorrect to attribute an inbuilt "research bias" to qualitative narrative research because this would presuppose the possibility of an "unbiased," bird's-eye perspective from which narratives can be approached and made sense of. However, as already touched on in the previous section, the bringing to bear of interpretive categories can be (and should be, as much as this is possible) bracketed; here we face a spectrum of options: Ethnomethodological, ethnographic narrative methodologies assume a different relationship to be optimal for the generation of interpretative categories that are supposed to surface in their work with the data collected. Even in participatory designs, research traditionally takes place in between the categories that are practiced by the members of a community and the researcher's perspective.[2] Empathy has also been proposed as an important precondition for qualitative inquiry in general but particularly for narrative inquiry, and here especially for the elicitation of quality data so that participants' subjectivities are able to "speak" and can become heard. This seems to be an interesting but also potentially complicated argument because it is widely accepted—in narratological circles (as *narrative empathy*, cf. Keen, 2007) as well as among communication researchers (as *emotion transportation*, cf. Green & Brock, 2002)—that narratives, especially of personal experience, rest on and proliferate an overall empathetic stance. This may complicate narrative analysis because it calls into question how the collection and analytic work with narratives from, for example, earthquake or tsunami survivors can be attended upholding the same standards as held for narratives from rapists or pedophiles.

To begin with, recognizing the multiple and complicated entwinement between researcher and participants raises questions about interpretive authority that go beyond discussions about *insider* and *outsider* or *emic* and *etic* perspectives. In response, this complexity enforces a deep and continuous reflection of the researcher's motives, cultural expectations, and subjectivities that are brought into the process of data collection as well as into the analytic process of working up these data into *generalizable interpretations*. The original plan and the values and intentions imported into the study will have to be explicitly acknowledged and closely monitored throughout. Furthermore, decisions to highlight certain interpretations and not others in the final reporting may

---

[2]See, however, attempts to break away from this form of navigation between insider and outsider perspectives by what runs under the header of "complete-member ethnography" (cf. Coffey, 2018) as well as claims by autoethnographers (cf. Bochner, 2014).

deserve equal attention in the form of critical reflection, moving reflection and reflexivity into a key role in the process of conducting narrative research (cf. Alvesson & Sköldberg, 2000; Jackson & Mazzei, 2012; Riessman, 2015; see also Barker & Pistrang, Chapter 2, this volume).

Aiming for Insights and Findings That Have "Real-Life Implications"

Teaching qualitative methods to undergraduate psychology students—60 per semester, over 2 decades—centering on doing ethnography and narrative analysis, the following question was asked repeatedly: What is it good for, and why do we need to learn this? And, interestingly, although only in recent years, some of our best students began to slight what they learned as just another way to interpret and make sense of psychology and maybe life and maybe even world but not contributing to making a difference—that is, change. My answer used to be that ethnography and narrative analysis are alternative methodologies and as such add to your repertoire of choices when we have to work up data; they serve as tools to enable you to ask your own research questions, collect your own data, and perform analyses along the lines learned. Plus, there is a certain transferability when working with other methods on different problems. I gathered my answer was operating with the premise that it was "the problem" researchers were investigating that would give them the opportunity to leave a mark on their surroundings, making a difference, and contribute to change. However, there may be more that we may be able to accomplish.

Up-front, there remains the premise that narrative inquiry with populations that are underserved would significantly help in shifting the spotlight toward issues of equity and social justice (cf. McKenzie-Mohr & Lafrance, 2017; Palacios et al., 2015). However, the integration of populations who have been on the fringe of qualitative research thus far may not be sufficient either. Therefore, and in conjunction with the imperative to move toward more diversity in work with vulnerable populations, I would like to orient readers toward a shift in analytic emphasis as well. Out of recent work with counternarratives, that is, narratives that are "intended to counter background assumptions that support another alternative narrative" (Bamberg & Wipff, 2020b, p. 80; cf. Stanley, 2007; Stanley & Haynes, 2019), the call has emerged to make use of positioning analytic procedures (see next section) that are able to microanalytically, in depth, explore how dominant master narratives can be interrogated and subverted in narrative practices.

Taking Language Seriously as Culturally Embodied and Intentional Practices

To "take language seriously" is undoubtedly a vague recommendation that requires some unpacking, starting with two common misconceptions of language: (a) language as distorting true feelings and intentions and (b) language as a transparent window into people's inner thoughts and determinations.

First, a common and precarious misconception in some quarters of qualitative theorizing claims that language—especially the actual wording and its performance—are surface and epiphenomena that stand in between people's true feelings and thoughts—that is, what they would have liked (intended) to express and what actually comes across and is understood by others. This misconception of language and communication as distorting people's "true" intentions then is likely to be used to disqualify analytic approaches that center on or around the actual language used by participants as "linguistic" or "discursive" analyses that do not get to the bottom of people's "true" determinations. A second and similar simplification starts from the opposite premise, holding language to be a transparent window into the phenomena under qualitative scrutiny. The transparency metaphor falls in line with our folk belief that we use language to read each others' minds, that is, with little effort to be able to figure out what they intend to communicate. Thus, so the argument continues, what qualitative analysis should focus on is what people mean, which is transparent from what they say—that is, does not require additional analysis. Although there is no doubt that debates over these issues will continue, setting up approaches that scrutinize language use will increasingly allow researchers to recognize the merits of microgenetic processes in the business of meaning production and of microanalytic approaches to work up these processes and lay them open for readers of our research.

Thus, the guideline of "taking language seriously" calls for a principal shift in the unit of analysis from formal and content aspects of story production to how form and content are tied together in the service of navigating and managing interpersonal relationships. Consequently, it is most prominently displayed in acts of story performance—that is, the minutiae of its telling, which have also been termed *narrative practices* (cf. Bamberg, 2020); and it is through these minutiae that storytellers position a sense of how they intend to be understood by others. Additionally, the way third- or first-person characters are positioned inside the story becomes a function of story performance (cf. Bamberg, 1997). Positioning analysis as a principled form of narrative analysis (Deppermann, 2013), building on Davies and Harré's (1990) original article, posits that storytellers engage in a continuous navigation process between having faith in and maintaining existing background assumptions (also called *master narratives*) on one hand and testing or rescripting—up to the possibility of challenging and openly countering—them on the other. Both aspects of story performance—being complicit and countering—are at work in narrative practices simultaneously and always in concert. An analysis of them can lay open how they are at work and result in micro-discursive practices that without question require analysts to go beyond the analysis of words, grammar, and semantics. Hitherto largely neglected aspects of bodily interactive performance features (e.g., paralinguistic qualities, such as intonation and pauses, and also visual elements, such as posture, gesture, gaze, and facial expressions) have become central to the analysis of how narrative practices are enacted. This turn to regarding and analyzing language as *culturally embodied* and *intentional practices* finds support in recent interrogations of the traditional affect–language divide, postulating that both language and affectivity unfold jointly and dynamically in situated relational settings (cf. Slaby et al., 2019; Wetherell, 2012), where they are rehearsed and polished in daily narrative storytelling practices from childhood on.

CONCLUSION

This chapter set up a larger background from where the roles of narrative and narrative research may be considered more central to qualitative inquiry than just being one method among others. First, it may have become apparent how narrative research cuts across the other three families of qualitative inquiry that Barker and Pistrang (Chapter 2, this volume) set apart from narrative approaches (i.e., thematic, language based, and ethnographic approaches); evidently, work with narratives is woven into each of them—often centrally— and cuts across them all. Second, one of the central feature of narratives, namely, their ability to configure the temporal dimension of human experience (past, present and future), confers a privileged status vis-à-vis other approaches for the analysis of stability, continuity, and change—one of the central aspects of human and organizational identity formation. Third, expanding the focus of narrative in qualitative research from what is represented in stories in terms of content to the relational function of the use of narratives in interpersonal relationships provides a powerful argument for devoting analytic endeavor to achieve a deeper understanding of users' relational context and experiences. Finally, as I have tried to argue here, incorporating aspects of bodily performed narrative practices as substantial facets into narrative analytic projects will help to develop more detailed analytic concepts for how dominant master narratives can be interrogated (cf. Bamberg & Wipff, 2020a) and subverted and through the stories research participants share—in everyday performances as well as in institutional practices such as research interviews, police interrogations, or doctor–patient and therapist–client interactions. As such, this chapter aimed to provide an additional link between the introductory and subsequent chapters and, in particular, to prepare readers for Chapter 6 of this volume (Murray), which provides an excellent diversification and exemplification of aspects I have raised here.

REFERENCES

Alvesson, M., & Sköldberg, K. (2000). *Reflexive methodology: New vistas for qualitative research*. Sage Publications.

American Psychological Association. (2019). *Publication manual of the American Psychological Association: The official guide to APA Style* (7th ed.).

Bamberg, M. (1997). Positioning between structure and performance. *Journal of Narrative and Life History*, 7(1–4), 335–342. https://doi.org/10.1075/jnlh.7.01int

Bamberg, M. (2020). Narrative analysis, an integrative approach—Small stories and narrative practices. In M. Järvinen & N. Mik-Meyer (Eds.), *Qualitative analysis—Eight traditions* (pp. 243–264). Sage Publications.

Bamberg, M., & Wipff, Z. (2020a). Counter narratives of crime and punishment. In M. Althoff, B. Dollinger, & H. Schmidt (Eds.), *Conflicting narratives of crime and punishment* (pp. 23–41). Palgrave MacMillan. https://doi.org/10.1007/978-3-030-47236-8_2

Bamberg, M., & Wipff, Z. (2020b). Re-considering counter narratives. In K. Lueg & M. Wolf Lundholt (Eds.), *The Routledge handbook of counter narratives* (pp. 71–84). Routledge. https://doi.org/10.4324/9780429279713-7

Blumer, H. (1979). *An appraisal of Thomas and Znaniecki's "The Polish peasant in Europe and America."* Transaction Books.

Bochner, A. (2014). *Coming to narrative: A personal history of paradigm change in the human sciences.* Left Coast Press.

Coffey, A. (2018). *Doing ethnography* (2nd ed.). Sage Publications.

Davies, B., & Harré, R. (1990). Positioning: The discursive production of selves. *Journal for the Theory of Social Behaviour, 20*(1), 43–63. https://doi.org/10.1111/j.1468-5914.1990.tb00174.x

Deppermann, A. (2013). Editorial: Positioning in narrative interaction. *Narrative Inquiry, 23*(1), 1–15. https://doi.org/10.1075/ni.23.1.01dep

Frye, N. (1957). *Anatomy of criticism: Four essays.* Princeton University Press. https://doi.org/10.1515/9781400866908

Green, M. C., & Brock, T. C. (2002). In the mind's eye: Transportation-imagery model of narrative persuasion. In M. C. Green, J. J. Strange, & T. C. Brock (Eds.), *Narrative impact: Social and cognitive foundations* (pp. 315–341). Lawrence Erlbaum Associates.

Greenbank, E. (2020). *Discursive navigation of employable identities in the narratives of former refugees.* Benjamins. https://doi.org/10.1075/sin.27

Hammersley, M. (1989). *The dilemma of qualitative method: Herbert Blumer and the Chicago tradition.* Routledge.

Jackson, A. Y., & Mazzei, L. A. (2012). *Thinking with theory in qualitative research: Viewing data across multiple perspectives.* Routledge.

Keen, S. (2007). *Empathy and the novel.* Oxford University Press. https://doi.org/10.1093/acprof:oso/9780195175769.001.0001

Kleinman, A. (1988). *The illness narratives: Suffering, healing, and the human condition.* Basic Books.

Kvale, S. (2003). The psychoanalytic interview as inspiration for qualitative research. In P. M. Camic, J. E. Rhodes, & L. Yardley (Eds.), *Qualitative research in psychology: Expanding perspectives in methodology and design* (pp. 275–297). American Psychological Association. https://doi.org/10.1037/10595-014

Levitt, H. M., Bamberg, M., Creswell, J. W., Frost, D. M., Josselson, R., & Suárez-Orozco, C. (2018). Journal article reporting standards for qualitative primary, qualitative meta-analytic, and mixed methods research in psychology: The APA Publications and Communications Board task force report. *American Psychologist, 73*(1), 26–46. https://doi.org/10.1037/amp0000151

Marecek, J. (2003). Dancing through minefields: Toward a qualitative stance in psychology. In P. M. Camic, J. E. Rhodes, & L. Yardley (Eds.), *Qualitative research in psychology* (pp. 49–69). American Psychological Association.

McKenzie-Mohr, S., & Lafrance, M. N. (2017). Narrative resistance in social work research and practice: Counter-storying in the pursuit of social justice. *Qualitative Social Work: Research and Practice, 16*(2), 189–205. https://doi.org/10.1177/1473325016657866

Murphy, J. W., Arxer, S. L., & Belgrave, L. L. (2010). The life course metaphor: Implications for biography and interpretive research. *Qualitative Sociology Review, 6*(1), 4–15. http://www.qualitativesociologyreview.org/ENG/archive_eng.php

Palacios, J. F., Salem, B., Schanche Hodge, F., Albarrán, C. R., Anaebere, A., & Hayes-Bautista, T. M. (2015). Storytelling: A qualitative tool to promote health among vulnerable populations. *Journal of Transcultural Nursing, 26*(4), 346–353. https://doi.org/10.1177/1043659614524253

Propp, V. (1927). *Morphology of the folktale* (L. Scott, Trans.; 2nd ed.). University of Texas Press.

Riessman, C. K. (1990). *Divorce talk: Women and men make sense of personal relationships.* Rutgers University Press.

Riessman, C. K. (2015). Entering a hall of mirrors: Reflexivity and narrative research. In A. De Fina & A. Georgakopoulou (Eds.), *The handbook of narrative research* (pp. 219–238). Wiley-Blackwell. https://doi.org/10.1002/9781118458204.ch11

Slaby, S., Mühlhoff, R., & Wüschner, P. (2019). Affective arrangements. *Emotion Review*, *11*(1), 3–12. https://doi.org/10.1177/1754073917722214

Smorti, A. (2011). Autobiographical memory and autobiographical narrative: What is the relationship? *Narrative Inquiry*, *21*(2), 303–310. https://doi.org/10.1075/ni.21.2.08smo

Stanley, C. A. (2007). When counter narratives meet master narratives in the journal editorial-review process. *Educational Researcher*, *36*(1), 14–24. https://doi.org/10.3102/0013189X06298008

Stanley, C., & Haynes, C. (2019). What have we learned from critical qualitative inquiry about race equity and social justice? An interview with pioneering scholar Yvonne Lincoln. *The Qualitative Report*, *24*(8), 1915–1929. https://nsuworks.nova.edu/tqr/vol24/iss8/7/

Thomas, W. I., & Znaniecki, F. (1918–1920). The Polish peasant in Europe and America (5 Vols.). University of Chicago Press.

Wetherell, M. (2012). *Affect and emotion: A new social science understanding.* Sage Publications. https://doi.org/10.4135/9781446250945

Information Power

Sample Content and Size in Qualitative Studies

Kirsti Malterud, Volkert Siersma, and Ann Dorrit Guassora

Assessment of the capacity of an empirical *sample* to answer the research question is vital at all stages of a research project: planning, execution, and dissemination. In certain areas, such as clinical trials, this is formalized as power calculations, while in other areas, such as qualitative research, this is often only loosely defined. In this chapter, we present a broad framework for appraisal of a sample of qualitative data in psychological and health sciences, comprising content as well as size. We define the concept of information power and suggest specific criteria for sample assessment as an alternative to naive use of saturation, the prevailing criterion for discontinuing data collection in qualitative studies.

AN APPROPRIATE SAMPLE OF QUALITATIVE DATA

Qualitative researchers within psychology and other disciplines need tools to evaluate sample content and size first while planning a study, then during the research process to appraise sample size continuously, and finally to ascertain whether the sample composition is adequate for analysis and final publication

Portions of this chapter were previously published in the journal article "Sample Size in Qualitative Interview Studies: Guided by Information Power," by K. Malterud, V. D. Siersma, and A. D. Guassora, 2016, *Qualitative Health Research, 26*(13), pp. 1753–1760. This material has been further developed and republished with the permission of the original publisher, SAGE Publications.

https://doi.org/10.1037/0000252-004
Qualitative Research in Psychology: Expanding Perspectives in Methodology and Design, Second Edition, P. M. Camic (Editor)

(Guest et al., 2006; Morse, 1995; Sandelowski, 1995). Moreover, readers of qualitative papers need to be able to ascertain whether the sample holds the capacity to answer the research question. In quantitative studies, *power calculations* determine what sample size (*N*) is necessary to demonstrate effects of a certain magnitude from an intervention. For qualitative interview studies, no similar formal standards for assessment of an appropriate sample exist.

Reviews indicate that qualitative researchers across disciplines demonstrate a low level of transparency regarding sample content and size and the underlying arguments for these (Carlsen & Glenton, 2011; Mason, 2010). Often the authors simply claim that saturation was achieved, inferring that addition of more participants did not add anything to the analysis, without specifying their understanding of how saturation has been assessed (Saunders et al., 2018). The *saturation* concept was originally coined by Glaser and Strauss (1967) as a specific element of *constant comparison* in grounded theory. Within the grounded theory framework, sample size is appraised as an element of the ongoing analysis where every new observation is compared with previous analysis to identify similarities and differences until no additional data can be found from which properties of the category can be developed. However, the saturation concept is recurrently claimed as standard in studies based on other analytic approaches, without explanation of how the concept should be understood in contexts beyond grounded theory and how it serves to justify the number of participants. Recently, the concept and its various applications has been more systematically examined (Nelson, 2017; Saunders et al., 2018).

A commonly stated principle for determining sample size in a qualitative cross-case study is that the sample should be sufficiently large and varied to elucidate the aims of the study (Kuzel, 1999; Marshall, 1996; Patton, 2015). However, this principle provides no guidance for planning. Experienced researchers seem to follow their own rules of thumb about the approximate numbers of units that were needed in previous comparable studies to arrive at a responsible analysis (Mason, 2010).

The authors of the present chapter have extensive experience from planning, conducting, publishing, and supervising qualitative as well as quantitative studies, and we share a concern for methodology across research methods and disciplines. We agree with Mason (2010) that as qualitative researchers, we should work to make our methods as robust and defensible as possible, aiming for intersubjectivity on decisions regarding design, sampling, and analysis (Malterud, 2001). We share the preconception that an assessment of sample composition is necessary for planning and that the adequacy of the sample must be continuously evaluated during the research process. Reviewing principles of sample size in qualitative cross case studies, we argue here that although sample size can be determined neither by formulae nor by perceived redundancy, certain principles may be proposed to guide sample composition, including size, in psychological research.

Sample composition should not rely on procedures from a specific qualitative method but rest on shared methodological principles for estimating an adequate number and type of units, events, or participants. For this purpose, we propose the concept *information power* (IP). The larger IP the sample holds, the lower the number of participants (*N*) is needed and vice versa. The aim of this chapter is to present and discuss a pragmatic model for the assessment of sample composition in qualitative studies, reflecting on how the IP needed for a specific study can be obtained.

THE CASE: AN INTERVIEW STUDY ON DIABETIC FOOT ULCER EXPERIENCES

The IP concept and the corresponding model were developed in a pragmatic focus group conversation between the authors, taking our shared experiences and a fictional case study as point of departure (Malterud et al., 2016). We situated the case as the first of three subprojects of a PhD study where the overall objective was to contribute to theories of motivation for self-care and to describe patients' practices for health professionals. The aim of the present subproject was to explore self-care among patients with diabetic foot ulcers by describing activities performed by patients to treat the ulcers and their motivation for doing so. The PhD student was a young psychologist who already had some experience with qualitative research from a previous project where descriptive cross-case analysis had been conducted. For the current project, a more interpretive and conceptual approach would be expected. Participants would be recruited among patients in a diabetes outpatient clinic who had recently been diagnosed with their first ulcer. Further sampling strategies and criteria would be informed by stepwise analysis, along with data collection by means of semistructured individual interviews.

How to plan and when to stop recruitment during this process would not be simple for the novice researcher. Our grant proposal, as is often the case for most research proposals, requested an advance estimate of the number of interviews to plan how many participants were needed to elucidate the aim of the study and to get an idea of how much time the data collection would require. The PhD supervisor had some ideas about the number of participants needed for this project from previous research she had conducted. The student, however, preferred to plan his study and make his decisions based on certain standards about which participants he would need to conduct a responsible analysis. In the following, we present the model we developed as a tool to appraise sample composition and its application in the case study. We discuss five items that in different ways determine the IP of the sample and the corresponding need for participants in relation to corresponding elements of the case.

ITEMS CONSTITUTING INFORMATION POWER

IP is related to the composition and the content potential of the sample. Reviewing alternative choices of design and method for the fictional interview study, we identified five items that have an impact on the IP of the sample: (a) study aim, (b) sample specificity, (c) use of established theory, (d) quality of dialogue, and (e) variation. In this section, we present these items and their dimensions separately and systematically. In practice, however, the items are related, have an impact on each other, and may offer mutual trade-offs.

1. Study Aim—Narrow or Broad?

IP, guiding an adequate sample, is related to the study aim. A broad study aim requires a larger sample than a narrow aim to offer sufficient IP because the phenomenon under study is more comprehensive. For example, a study aiming to explore how patients with their first diabetic foot ulcer are motivated to manage shift of bandages would need notably fewer participants than a study about how patients with foot ulcer generally manage self-care in everyday life.

In our case, the student had to choose between increasing the number of participants by recruiting a larger, purposive sample or narrowing the aim of the study to maintain appropriate IP. If, on the other hand, the aim of the study had concerned a very specific or rare experience, such as motivation for self-care among blind patients with diabetic foot ulcers, this would in itself have limited the number of eligible participants. An alternative emphasis of the study could have been to explore how individual resources can interfere with self-care of diabetic foot ulcers. If so, a study based on one or more interviews with one single participant might have provided access to exciting hypotheses from data with a strong IP concerning the aim. Defining the aim of the interview study, the researcher also would have offered some assurances regarding transferability of the findings. Hence, the IP of the sample will be critical to achieve the aim.

2. Sample Specificity—Dense or Sparse?

IP is also related to the specificity of experiences, knowledge, or properties among the participants included in the sample. To offer adequate IP, a less extensive sample is needed with participants holding characteristics that are highly exclusive for the study aim compared with a sample containing participants of sparse specificity. Specificity indicates participants who belong to the actual target group holding a capacity across participants to elucidate the actual study aim. In our case, high specificity means recruiting only patients with diabetic foot ulcers, capable to communicate about motivational issues. Alternatively, if the aim was to study challenges with self-care of foot ulcers, recruitment only of patients reporting self-care of their ulcers would give high specificity. If we did not constrain recruitment procedures to include only patients with foot ulcers, a much larger number of participants would be needed to cover those whose experiences we study. Still, a sample, established with specificity in mind, is not always feasible. The strategy of convenience sampling, accepting participants who are available, without trying to influence the configuration of the sample, implies the risk of limited specificity, thereby requiring more participants. Following such a recruitment strategy, we would probably have needed more interviews and participants to obtain a sufficient scope of reflections upon activities performed by patients to treat the ulcers and their underlying motivations, while acquiring much noise to be sorted out. On the other hand, we might have been fortunate, dropping into a group of unexpectedly specific participants. Hence, sample specificity cannot always be predetermined but can be supported by suitable recruitment.

3. Established Theory—Applied or Not?

Furthermore, IP, guiding adequate sample composition, is related to the level of theoretical background of the study. Relevant theory complements the analysis by adding interpretative capacity to the empirical data. A study supported by limited theoretical perspectives would usually require a larger sample to offer sufficient IP than a study where particular theories are applied in planning and analysis. This is perhaps why many grounded theory studies, departing with no guiding theoretical perspectives, include a large number of participants. Psychological theories about the authority that professionals exercise might, for example, have enhanced the IP of our cross-case study about self-care experiences with diabetic foot ulcers. New knowledge, even from a rather small sample, might be obtained by looking for patients' subjective construction of experiences of strategies to counter professional authority intended to make them perform specific self-care. Theory serves to synthesize existing knowledge as well as extending the sources of knowledge beyond the empirical interview data. On the contrary, another study, starting from scratch with no theoretical background, must establish its own foundation for grounding the conclusions. If so, a larger sample size would probably be needed to grant appropriate IP. Theoretical frameworks offer models and concepts that may explain relations between different aspects of the empirical data in a coherent way. Empirical studies with even very small numbers can make a difference if they address and elucidate something crucial to theory.

4. Quality of Researcher–Participant Dialogue—Strong or Weak?

IP is also related to the quality of the dialogue and "thickness of data" (Geertz, 2000) regarding interpretation. An interview study with strong and clear communication between researcher and participants requires fewer participants to offer sufficient IP than a study with ambiguous or unfocused dialogues. An interaction with tensions and conflicting views may reduce the confidence needed to talk about or understand intimate details. On the other hand, researchers who never challenge their participants may run the risk of developing data that, during analysis, only reproduce what is known beforehand, hence holding low IP. From a social constructivist perspective, empirical data in a qualitative study are coconstructed by complex and subjective interaction between researcher and participant, and a number of issues determine the communicative quality from which the IP is established. Analytic value of the empirical data depends on the skills of the interviewer and on the trust between researcher and participant. It is difficult to predict the quality of the dialogue or interpretation in advance. Correspondingly, rich and vivid observational and visual data may contribute substantially to interpretation and hence to IP.

In our study, the PhD student held more-than-average background knowledge about psychological aspects of diabetic foot ulcers. He had been a psychological consultant for the home nursing service in his area within this field the previous 2 years and previously established a special interest in motivational drivers for health behavior. The interviews were not his first encounter with the subject area, and he easily approached the participants' experiences of self-care practices. However, it took him some time to establish trust and understanding. It was therefore necessary for him to obtain additional interview training in advance, including undertaking practice interviews with other students. His supervisor, well read in diabetes complications and an experienced interviewer, had conducted six interviews in her previous project to establish a sample with adequate IP for an analysis that could contribute to existing knowledge.

5. Sample Variation—Homogenous or Diverse?

In a qualitative cross-case study aimed for exploration, description, and analysis of different aspects of a phenomenon, empirical data that are similar or mostly repetitious are not as valuable for in-depth analysis as are data with more variation of relevant aspects. IP is enhanced and supports substantial analysis when participants provide diverse aspects of equivalent and specific phenomena. Knowing that motivation for self-care is limited by patient resources, we could, for example, in the development phase of the study, aim for an especially varied sample of patients. These could be identified by discussions with the nurses at the diabetic clinic and include patients with successes as well as failures handling their ulcers across different age groups, genders, and types of diabetes. When the data content of the sample complies with the research question, different examples of related experiences or expressions add further depth as well as breadth and allow for more sustainable interpretation.

In our study, potential participants of various ages were recruited from a diabetes outpatient clinic with a broad uptake area, covering patients with foot ulcers from all age groups and having different comorbidities. Furthermore, the PhD student knew the staff of the clinic well from his previous collaborations as a psychological consultant. He assumed they would be cooperative and capable as recruitment agents, if only he was able to express the kind of variation he was pursuing. A limited but still strongly purposive sample with appropriate IP would be within reach, and he would avoid unnecessary duplication of experiences among the participants.

INFORMATION POWER IN QUALITATIVE CROSS-CASE STUDIES— THE MODEL

From the preceding reflections, we have conceptualized the five items constituting IP as well as the dimensions of each of them as a model intended as a tool to appraise sample size in qualitative cross-case studies (see Figure 4.1). The model can be used to reflect systematically on items determining the IP of the sample in the actual study.

According to the model, considerations about study aim, sample specificity, theoretical background, quality of dialogue, and variation should determine whether appropriate IP will be obtained with less or more participants included in the sample. A study will need the least number of participants when the study aim is narrow, if the combination of participants is highly specific for the study aim, if it is supported by established theory, if the interview dialogue is rich and relevant, and if the empirical data contain relevant diversity. A study will need a larger number of participants when the study aim is broad, if the combination of participants is less specific for the research

FIGURE 4.1. Information Power: Items and Dimensions

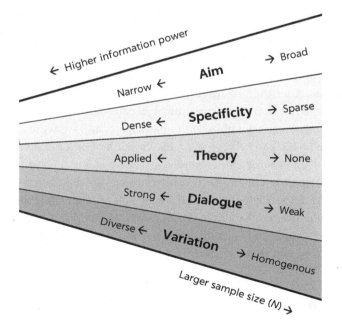

Note. From "Sample Size in Qualitative Interview Studies: Guided by Information Power," by K. Malterud, V. D. Siersma, and A. D. Guassora, 2016, *Qualitative Health Research*, *26*(13), p. 1756 (https://doi.org/10.1177/1049732315617444). Copyright 2016 by SAGE Publications. Adapted with permission.

question, if it is not theoretically informed, if the interview dialogue is weak, or if data are very repetitive. Please note that this framework guides the sampling but does not determine the sample size.

The dynamic interaction between the different items included in the model involves a trade-off between conditions that require more or fewer participants in a sample. For example, a researcher who express a narrow aim and achieves an excellent interview dialogue and a varied sample may be able to conduct a cross-case analysis even with a small sample. On the other hand, a researcher with limited theoretical or background knowledge may need a larger group of participants to reveal something new although the aim is well focused and the interview dialogues are good.

Our model is not intended as a checklist to calculate a specific number of participants but is meant as a recommendation of which items and dimensions of these to consider systematically about recruitment at different steps of the research process. An initial appraisal of the sample's composition—the number and type of participants needed—should consider whether the researcher is a novice. Researchers' interview skills and personal attributes affect their ability to establish a prolific dialogue, and additional interview skills training may be needed. Psychologists should be especially aware of important differences between clinical interviews and research interviews, taking care to establish the necessary competence for the latter. For new researchers, the addition of more participants may be necessary if the quality of the initial interviews does not generate relevant information. If the study is theoretically adequate, however, fewer participants may be needed. On the other hand, for a study in which recruitment leads to participants with limited variation regarding the phenomena under study, a larger sample size might be needed.

Appraisal of IP should be repeated along the process, supported by preliminary analysis. After the first three interviews, an initial review of the data is conducted, and relevant theory preliminarily considered (Malterud, 2016). In our case, some patients did not want to participate, and we were concerned it might not be possible to achieve as much variation of motivation for self-care as expected. Due to some extra interview training and extensive reading, the researcher managed to make good report and steer the dialogue well. The first interviews conducted appeared to be highly relevant for the research question, helping to narrow the aim of the study. Altogether, the IP developed was unexpectedly strong, and the anticipated number of participants needed could consequently be adjusted downward.

DISCUSSION

We have now substantiated why concepts beyond saturation are necessary for appraisal of sample content and size in qualitative studies. The IP concept and a model for sample assessment have been presented. We now discuss epistemological issues, comparing IP with existing concepts and frameworks, especially saturation.

The Logic of Particularities

Formal power calculations have been proposed as an alternative to what have been called informal, heuristic rules of thumb in qualitative studies for appraisal of sample size (DePaulo, 2000; Guest et al., 2006). The basic principle behind such attempts assumes a realist approach with a population where a set of information (e.g., self-care methods for management of diabetic foot ulcers) is available, each with different prevalence, and the aim is to identify as much of this information as possible with the least number of participants, selected at random. Although we do not repudiate the existence of settings where such assumptions might be adequate, most often they will be challenged in a qualitative study. The main argument against formal power calculations for qualitative studies is that there is no a priori hidden and complete set of data to be discovered. Furthermore, the objective of qualitative studies in psychology and health sciences is not to produce a complete listing of all possibilities and experiences available for a certain aim. Participants and study settings are selected purposively to provide the most hoped for salient information but will need to be elaborated by the researcher interacting with participants and supported by relevant theory (Kvale, 1996; Patton, 2015; Sandelowski, 1995).

A straitjacket of untenable, and maybe even misguiding, assumptions may harm the research process (Bacchetti, 2010). McWhinney (1989) urged medical researchers to focus more on particularities, not only universals, and Sandelowski (1996) argued that the single case is the basic unit of analysis in any qualitative study, independent of the amount of empirical data. Qualitative research in psychology, belonging to the interpretative paradigm, emphasizes the logic of exploration rather than the logic of justification, and other assumptions for sampling are usually more adequate than what can possibly be predicted or calculated (Kuhn, 1962; Malterud, 2001; Marshall, 1996; Sandelowski, 1996).

We have presented a pragmatic model for appraisal of sample content and size in qualitative cross-case studies. Our model offers a manageable strategy where we have explicated the principal assumptions for implementation so that the model can be contested for methodological elaboration. Next, we discuss this model and compare it with current leading standards regarding sample composition in qualitative studies.

The Model—Reflections and Challenges

Information power is the core concept of our model. We have argued that the IP of qualitative data is determined by *items* such as study aim, sample specificity, use of established theory, quality of dialogue, and variation. For each of these items, we have proposed *dimensions* along a continuum on which researchers are invited to position themselves and their study to assess an approximate number of participants or events needed for appropriate analysis. We argue that such an assessment should be revisited along the research process and not determined in advance. In this way, recruitment can be brought to an end when the sample holds sufficient IP. Still, the model may also offer support in the initial planning of a qualitative interview study.

The five items we have included in our model are neither mutually exclusive nor the only conceivable determinants of IP. Some of the criteria suggested by Nelson (2017) for conceptual depth, such as complexity and subtlety, for example, could also have been considered. A common denominator is that exploration of a comprehensive phenomenon, such as motivation for self-care, requires data with appropriate variation regarding some selected qualities. However, a pragmatic model intended for implementation calls for prioritization. We therefore decided to include a limited and feasible amount of vital compatible items whose dimensions with an impact for IP could be easily identified, appraised, and presented.

On a list of potential items to be included in the model, we have omitted the ease of recruitment issue, which actually raises a paradox. When recruitment is easy, the researcher is at liberty to select a relevant and purposive sample and thereby reduce the number of participants. On the other hand, if only a few among many potential participants volunteer, the specificity and variation of the sample may be jeopardized and thereby increase the number of participants needed. If so, IP may be enhanced by considering the reasons for the declines. Simple changes in procedure, such as interviewing at home instead of in the clinic, may remove these obstacles and contribute to a sample in which fewer participants are needed. The five items do not have universal impact, and their relative importance may therefore change from project to project and over the course of the research process.

To make the model simple and readily understood, we initially chose to develop it for the context of individual interview studies, where the question of sample size usually refers to the number of participants or events (Malterud et al., 2016). The issue of sample size may be more ambiguous when it comes to other qualitative research designs, such as focus group studies (number of groups, number of participant, or number of interviews?), observational studies (number of events to be recorded, number of people to be included, number of sites to visit?), or studies with data from written sources (pages of text, number of documents, number of organizations?). However, in this chapter we have extended the application to qualitative cross-case studies, independent of procedure for data collection or academic discipline.

Something Old, Something New, Something Borrowed, Something Blue

The IP concept and the items it comprises share some features with existing concepts and ideas within qualitative methodology. In our model, specificity covers issues usually discussed as matters of sampling (Patton, 2015). The role of aim in our model as regards sample size has also been discussed by Morse (2000), and it is likewise related to Patton's (2015) discussion of trade-offs between breadth and depth in a study. Nelson's (2017) criteria for conceptual depth include range, complexity, subtlety, resonance, and validity as an evaluative framework for sampling. Some of these criteria are related to items constituting IP (specificity, variation), while others deal with associated matters although within the grounded theory tradition. The final criterion—validity—is a major generic term holding different connotations, where external validity seems to be emphasized by Nelson, while internal validity is more accentuated with IP. Testing conceptual depth is finally presented as numeric scores on a scale, while IP is intended as a tool for overall reflection.

The dialogue item in our model shares some features with Spradley's (1979) notion of "good informants," which is discussed as an aspect of adequacy by sampling (Morse, 1991, 2000, 2015b). Our model differs, however, in that we emphasize the quality of the dialogue rather than the nature of the topic, even though these dimensions both cover the accessibility of the data. Dialogue in our model may be interpreted more figuratively, as the productive interaction between the researcher and data. Adequacy, as discussed by Morse, concerns the sufficiency and quality of data. Unlike the concept of adequacy, our model is not tied to development of theory or theoretical sampling, which are specific procedures of grounded theory.

The best qualitative analysis is conducted from empirical data containing abundant, heterogeneous accounts of new aspects of the phenomenon we intend to explore (Morse, 1991, 2015a; Patton, 2015). The sample should be neither too small nor too large (Kvale, 1996; Sandelowski, 1995). In our experience, reviewers often seem to be more concerned with samples being too small than being too large (possibly because of some misunderstood application of quantitative thinking on qualitative sample composition), instead of appraising the outcome of analysis from these particular empirical data. We therefore—as seen in Figure 4.1—find the left section of our model more useful than the right section because we particularly want to encourage samples that are not too large. We would warn against methodological ideologies or strategies unreflectedly leading to too large samples (Chamberlain, 2000). By initial and consecutive assessment of IP, the researcher may avoid wasting time and resources collecting unnecessary data. An even more important objection is that too large samples often provide information overload, thereby impeding overview and contaminating analysis by increasing the amount of information only marginally related to the aim. Our model indicates that abundant, heterogeneous accounts of new aspects can be obtained even with a sample of rather few participants, provided that the IP is appropriate.

"Information Power" Replacing "Saturation"?

Saturation is often mentioned as a criterion for sample size in qualitative studies (Morse, 1995). The concept was presented as an element of the *constant comparative method*, which is a central element of grounded theory, intended to generate theories from empirical data (Glaser & Strauss, 1967). Theoretical sampling based on preliminary theory developed in the study is required for saturation in a grounded theory analysis to finally arrive at saturation. Saturation occurs when the researcher no longer receives information that adds to the theory that has been developed.

These procedures are, however, not part of all qualitative studies. O'Reilly and Parker (2013) argued that adopting saturation as a generic quality marker is inappropriate, whereas Saunders et al. (2018) questioned its application across the spectrum of qualitative methods. Grounded theory has clear guidance about what constitutes theoretical saturation, but the meaning of saturation within other qualitative approaches is far from clear. Authors claiming saturation are not always transparent about how it has been achieved (Morse, 2015a), and several studies are simply not compatible with the saturation concept of GT. Reviews reveal that the concept is often poorly specified (Nelson, 2017; Saunders et al., 2018) and does not correspond with the original meaning of saturation from grounded theory (Carlsen & Glenton, 2011).

In a qualitative study, we do not head for a complete description of all aspects of the phenomenon we study. We will usually chase new insights that contribute substantially to or challenge current understandings. Furthermore, the epistemological anticipation of grounded theory that exhaustive sampling of a definite set of variations can be obtained and covered by saturation is not the theory of science at the heart of most qualitative research (Malterud, 2012). To be sure, Morse (2015a) rejected such an understanding of saturation, spelling out characteristics within categories as the domain to be saturated.

We consider Morse's accuracy (2015a) on this point as rather unusual among qualitative researchers, who more often refer to their perception of repetition—"heard it all"—as a criterion for saturation being accomplished. Research with social constructivist roots, where knowledge is considered as partial, intermediate, and dependent of the situated view of the researcher, does not support an idea that qualitative studies ideally should comprise a "total" amount of facts (Alvesson & Sköldberg, 2009; Haraway, 1991).

There are differences in how various approaches frame research questions, sample participants, and collect data to achieve richness and depth of analysis. DePaulo (2000) warned against the risk of missing something important when the sample of a qualitative study is inappropriate or too small. We agree with his point but not with his ambitions of covering the full range of the phenomenon in question. Finally, saturation is not as objective and indisputable as it might appear, at least from a peer reviewer's perspective. One researcher may regard the case as closed and get bored by further interviewing, while another colleague, perhaps with a less thorough knowledge of the field or with empirical data containing less variation, may assess further data as new information (Malterud, 2012; Morse, 1995).

IP is a concept that differs from saturation in several respects, and certain dimensions of IP may even oppose some of the saturation standards. With homogeneity among participants (e.g., with snowball sampling) or in the empirical data (e.g., due to low dialogical quality), saturation can be quickly, but inappropriately, declared. In such cases, appraisal of IP would entail a larger sample size. Our model is, however, not based on a very original methodological idea. We look upon IP as an aspect of internal validity, influencing the potential of the available empirical data to provide access to new knowledge by means of analysis and theoretical interpretations (Cohen & Crabtree, 2008; Kvale, 1996). In this regard, the content of the sample is often more important than size. Hence, IP of a sample is not very different from being sufficiently large and varied to elucidate the aims of the study but can be considered a specification of how to accomplish it (Kuzel, 1999; Marshall, 1996; Morse, 1995; Patton, 2015; Sandelowski, 1995).

Transferability of the Concept of Information Power

The applicability of the IP concept reaches beyond qualitative cross-case studies and is also relevant to single case studies and observational studies from any academic discipline. Although the concept of sample size may be ill defined in, for example, a single videotaped narrative on the psychological experiences of treatment and healing of a foot ulcer, the five items that comprise the model are reasonably well defined and can be used to get an indication for the assessment of IP for empirical qualitative data in general.

We suggest that the inherent, generic meaning of IP can also be applied to quantitative studies. The aim of a quantitative analysis, often the quantification of the effect of some exposure on an outcome, is usually easier achieved with fewer data when (a) the aim is narrow (a single, clear exposure is evaluated on a single specific outcome), (b) the sample is specific (a well-defined narrow target population to avoid effect modification), (c) the research question is backed up by theory (no data are to be used on plugging theoretical gaps), (d) the quality of the gathered data is high (no measurement error), and (e) variation is high (all interesting exposure groups and outcome modalities are well represented). Some of the applications of IP as illustrated in this chapter for qualitative cross-case studies (e.g., sequential appraisal of data in the execution phase and the danger of too many data) may well prove inspirational for the conduct of quantitative analysis.

CONCLUSIONS AND IMPLICATIONS FOR RESEARCH PRACTICE

Qualitative studies may benefit from sampling strategies where attention is shifted from the amount of input to the content of input, providing new knowledge from the analysis. IP indicates that the more information the sample holds that is relevant for the actual study, the lower the number of participants needed. An initial approximation of sample size is necessary for planning, but the adequacy of the final sample size must be evaluated continuously during the research process whenever possible. The results presented in the final publication will demonstrate whether the actual sample held appropriate IP to develop new knowledge, referring to the aim of the study at hand.

REFERENCES

Alvesson, M., & Sköldberg, K. (2009). *Reflexive methodology: New vistas for qualitative research* (2nd ed.). Sage Publications.

Bacchetti, P. (2010). Current sample size conventions: Flaws, harms, and alternatives. *BMC Medicine, 8*(1), 17. https://doi.org/10.1186/1741-7015-8-17

Carlsen, B., & Glenton, C. (2011). What about N? A methodological study of sample-size reporting in focus group studies. *BMC Medical Research Methodology, 11*(1), 26. https://doi.org/10.1186/1471-2288-11-26

Chamberlain, K. (2000). Methodolatry and qualitative health research. *Journal of Health Psychology, 5*(3), 285–296. https://doi.org/10.1177/135910530000500306

Cohen, D. J., & Crabtree, B. F. (2008). Evaluative criteria for qualitative research in health care: Controversies and recommendations. *Annals of Family Medicine, 6*(4), 331–339. https://doi.org/10.1370/afm.818

DePaulo, P. (2000, December). Sample size for qualitative research. *Quirk's Marketing Research Review, 14*(11), Article 20001202. https://www.quirks.com/articles/sample-size-for-qualitative-research

Geertz, C. (2000). *The interpretation of cultures: Selected essays*. Basic Books.

Glaser, B., & Strauss, A. (1967). *The discovery of grounded theory: Strategies for qualitative research*. Wiedenfeld and Nicholson.

Guest, G., Bunce, A., & Johnson, L. (2006). How many interviews are enough? An experiment with data saturation and variability. *Field Methods, 18*(1), 59–82. https://doi.org/10.1177/1525822X05279903

Haraway, D. (1991). Situated knowledges: The science question in feminism and the privilege of partial perspective. In D. Haraway (Ed.), *Simians, cyborgs, and women: The reinvention of nature* (pp. 183–201). Routledge.

Kuhn, T. S. (1962). *The structure of scientific revolutions*. University of Chicago Press.

Kuzel, A. (1999). Sampling in qualitative inquiry. In W. Miller & B. Crabtree (Eds.), *Doing qualitative research* (2nd ed., pp. 33–45). Sage Publications.

Kvale, S. (1996). *InterViews: An introduction to qualitative research interviewing*. Sage Publications.

Malterud, K. (2001). Qualitative research: Standards, challenges, and guidelines. *Lancet, 358*(9280), 483–488. https://doi.org/10.1016/S0140-6736(01)05627-6

Malterud, K. (2012). Systematic text condensation: A strategy for qualitative analysis. *Scandinavian Journal of Public Health, 40*(8), 795–805. https://doi.org/10.1177/1403494812465030

Malterud, K. (2016). Theory and interpretation in qualitative studies from general practice: Why and how? *Scandinavian Journal of Public Health, 44*(2), 120–129. https://doi.org/10.1177/1403494815621181

Malterud, K., Siersma, V. D., & Guassora, A. D. (2016). Sample size in qualitative interview studies: Guided by information power. *Qualitative Health Research, 26*(13), 1753–1760. https://doi.org/10.1177/1049732315617444

Marshall, M. N. (1996). Sampling for qualitative research. *Family Practice, 13*(6), 522–525. https://doi.org/10.1093/fampra/13.6.522

Mason, M. (2010). Sample size and saturation in PhD studies using qualitative interviews. *Forum Qualitative Social Research, 11*(3). Advance online publication. https://doi.org/10.17169/fqs-11.3.1428

McWhinney, I. R. (1989). "An acquaintance with particulars. . . ." *Family Medicine, 21*(4), 296–298.

Morse, J. M. (1991). Strategies for sampling. In J. M. Morse (Ed.), *Qualitative nursing research: A contemporary dialogue* (pp. 127–145). Sage Publications. https://doi.org/10.4135/9781483349015.n16

Morse, J. M. (1995). The significance of saturation. *Qualitative Health Research, 5*(2), 147–149. https://doi.org/10.1177/104973239500500201

Morse, J. M. (2000). Determining sample size. *Qualitative Health Research, 10*(1), 3–5. https://doi.org/10.1177/104973200129118183

Morse, J. M. (2015a). All data are not equal. *Qualitative Health Research, 25*(9), 1169–1170. https://doi.org/10.1177/1049732315597655

Morse, J. M. (2015b). "Data were saturated. . . ." *Qualitative Health Research, 25*(5), 587–588. https://doi.org/10.1177/1049732315576699

Nelson, J. (2017). Using conceptual depth criteria: Addressing the challenge of reaching saturation in qualitative research. *Qualitative Research, 17*(5), 554–570. https://doi.org/10.1177/1468794116679873

O'Reilly, M., & Parker, N. (2013). "Unsatisfactory Saturation": A critical exploration of the notion of saturated sample sizes in qualitative research. *Qualitative Research, 13*(2), 190–197. https://doi.org/10.1177/1468794112446106

Patton, M. Q. (2015). *Qualitative research and evaluation methods: Integrating theory and practice* (4th ed.). Sage Publications.

Sandelowski, M. (1995). Sample size in qualitative research. *Research in Nursing & Health, 18*(2), 179–183. https://doi.org/10.1002/nur.4770180211

Sandelowski, M. (1996). One is the liveliest number: The case orientation of qualitative research. *Research in Nursing & Health, 19*(6), 525–529. https://doi.org/10.1002/(SICI)1098-240X(199612)19:6<525::AID-NUR8>3.0.CO;2-Q

Saunders, B., Sim, J., Kingstone, T., Baker, S., Waterfield, J., Bartlam, B., Burroughs, H., & Jinks, C. (2018). Saturation in qualitative research: Exploring its conceptualization and operationalization. *Quality & Quantity: International Journal of Methodology, 52*(4), 1893–1907. https://doi.org/10.1007/s11135-017-0574-8

Spradley, J. (1979). *The ethnographic interview.* Holt, Rinehart, & Winston.

II

METHODOLOGIES FOR QUALITATIVE RESEARCHERS: HELPING TO UNDERSTAND THE WORLD AROUND US

5

Participation, Power, and Solidarities Behind Bars

A 25-Year Reflection on Critical Participatory Action Research on College in Prison

Michelle Fine, María Elena Torre, Kathy Boudin, and Cheryl Wilkins

In this chapter, we introduce the notion of *research collaboratories* in which critical inquiry-based collaboration flourishes; where critical participatory action research (CPAR) projects are conceived and implemented across universities and communities or movements to build theory, transform policy, support social change, and forge new solidarities. In these spaces, academics, policy makers, community members, students, and activists design research projects together; pool intentionally diverse standpoints; and integrate qualitative, quantitative, archival, and historic evidence to probe questions of (in)justice, enacting the principle—No Research About Us, Without Us! These projects rely on mixed methods, deeply rooted in the ethical and democratic production of knowledge, committed to a qualitative and participatory understanding of the evidence gathered, centering the perspective of those most impacted by social injustice.

Throughout the latter half of the 20th century, and across the globe, demands for research justice gained momentum, voiced by, for example, *campesinos* (country-people) and fishermen in South America, Maori communities in New Zealand, mining families in Appalachia, women demanding sexual and reproductive justice across the world, and people of color struggling for antiracist schools, among others. In the 1960s, people with physical disabilities active in the independent living movement rejected "experts'" call for special education, housing segregation, "normalization," and rehabilitation, insisting on a new paradigm framed by activists with disabilities. Denouncing research and policy driven by nondisabled "experts," fueled by diagnoses, pity, and

https://doi.org/10.1037/0000252-005
Qualitative Research in Psychology: Expanding Perspectives in Methodology and Design, Second Edition, P. M. Camic (Editor)

calls for medical intervention, they instead demanded radical inclusion. In the late 1980s, the same commitment to No Research on Us, Without Us could be heard as AIDS activists grew frustrated by the slow, detached pace of HIV/AIDS research controlled by the medical profession. Following the formation of the activist group ACT UP, some HIV+ community members refused to participate in medically managed clinical trials and organized grassroots, homegrown community-run trials.

A SHORT BIOGRAPHY OF COMMUNITY-BASED RESEARCH

Collaborations between universities and other research organizations, social scientists, organizers, advocates, and marginalized communities have a long, albeit sometimes hidden, history, even within the discipline of psychology (Fine, 2017; Fine & Ruglis, 2009). Indeed, since the late 1800s, social scientists have been centrally engaged in critical, community-based policy research, but many of these research stories have been exiled from the disciplinary canon.

In the late 1890s, in Philadelphia, the great scholar W. E. B. Du Bois, who had worked with William James at Harvard, was asked by Susan Wharton to investigate "the Negro problem." Understanding that the invitation focused on the Black community as the *cause* of the problem (rather than the effect of racialized state policies), Du Bois nevertheless took up the challenge and proceeded, with community members, to systematically map the housing, health, education, and financial conditions that showed up in the Black community and systematically revealed these conditions as an outcome of human-made history, structures, and policies of exclusion and discrimination. Du Bois produced scholarly documents, including the groundbreaking sociological text *The Philadelphia Negro* (1899) and also wrote policy documents and newspaper articles; published a novel, *The Quest of the Silver Fleece* (1911/2008); and produced an extravagant pageant, *The Star of Ethiopia*, to educate African Americans about their history and sociology.

Post–World War I, across the Atlantic, in Marienthal, Austria, when a worldwide economic depression meant that the looms in the textile factories stopped in 1930, Maria Jahoda and colleagues from the Institute of Psychology at the University of Vienna joined with community members to document the material and embodied consequences of massive unemployment on community life. They published popular and academic texts, including the brilliant text *Marienthal*; translated the research into materials for political organizers; and circulated the materials on a socialist radio program, after which Jahoda was briefly imprisoned under the regime of Kurt Schuschnigg, in 1936, for her underground work with the Social Democratic Party. Government officials accused her of using the research center as a front for secret maildrops by the party (Jahoda, Lazarsfeld, & Zeisel, 2001).

In 1946, Kurt Lewin called for a practice of "action research" aimed at changing communities and social institutions, involving spirals of self-reflective cycles of fact-finding, action, observation, evaluation, and then replanning and more fact-finding, action, and evaluation. Convinced that social science should play a role in informing social change, Lewin launched the Commission on Community Interrelations in partnership with the American Jewish Congress (Cherry & Borshuk, 1998) to develop research and methodologies in which community groups joined researchers as "fact-finders" to study "real-life" situations and produce knowledge that would effect social change. One such method, formalized through the leadership of Margot Wormser and Claire Seltiz, was the community self-survey. Called a "tool of modern democracy" by Gordon Allport (1954), community self-surveys brought together diverse teams of community members and researchers to engage in large-scale participatory research on discriminatory practices in housing, employment, education, and public services in their communities (see Torre & Fine, 2011).

In the Appalachian Mountains in the 1960s, Myles Horton, director of the Highlander Folk School/Research and Education Center in Tennessee, and sociologist Helen Lewis, director of Appalachian Research at Berea College, joined with White coal-mining housewives who were already collecting incidence records of fathers, husbands, and sons with black lung disease. They invited environmental scientists to meet with disabled miners, black lung physicians, leaders of the United Mine Workers, and musicians to document, in epidemiology and song, the embodied consequences of the coal-mining industry.

During this period scholars across the globe were challenging the "knowledge monopoly" (Fals Borda & Rahman, 1991) of university elites. Orlando Fals Borda (1985, 1995) had been working with rural communities in Colombia calling for the revolutionary potential of a "people's science" to weave popular education, community organizing, and social science. Coining the language of "participatory action research," he insisted on a praxis that was intended to build knowledge to transform social conditions.

In 1982, social psychologist and Jesuit priest Ignacio Martín-Baró returned to El Salvador from graduate School at the University of Chicago to initiate a series of "the people's" research projects at Universidad Centroamericana, where he was the director of the University Institute for Public Opinion. He argued that participatory research, of and by "the people," was essential to "challenge the official lies" of the dictatorship. In his short career, Martín-Baró seeded and launched a line of liberation psychology, rooted in a blend of liberatory theology and activist research "for the people" of El Salvador, including what he called the "people's survey" to offer a "social mirror" of lives in struggle and to contest the dominant stories being told by the government. He and five colleagues were murdered by a counterinsurgency unit of the Salvadoran government elite in November 1989. While he was committed to publishing only in Spanish for Latin American communities, in the 1990s, a set of Boston-based psychologists translated his brilliant and inspiring writings on critical participatory research, available in *Writings for a Liberation Psychology: Ignacio Martín-Baró* (1994).

During this same era, in the late 1980s, the Center for NuLeadership coalesced within the Greenhaven Think Tank, at Greenhaven Prison in New York State. A research team of men in the prison, led by Eddie Ellis, was dedicated to investigating and preventing the rising numbers of Black and Latino men consigned to the New York State prison system. Under the direction of Ellis, who was imprisoned for 23 years, and with the help of psychologist Kenneth Clark, the men of the center—all incarcerated "street penologists"—designed a study that systematically determined that 85% of the New York state prisoners were Black and Latino, and 75% of them originated in seven neighborhoods downstate. Members of the Blacks' Resurrection Study group and the Latino-based group Conciencia published the Seven Neighborhood study results into a Greenhaven Think Tank (1997) policy document, revealing the systematic links between seven "symbiotic neighborhoods"—Lower East Side, South Bronx, Harlem, Brownsville, Bed/Sty, East New York, and South Jamaica—and the then 62 state prisons. The policy document recommended a nontraditional vision: that these men, while in prison, should be trained in community development, mentorship, and adult education and, once paroled back to those communities, should be funded to help rebuild the community through internships, mentoring, and community programs. The men even detailed their vision for a prisoner-run model prison. Although Ellis has since passed away, the center survives in Brooklyn, rooted in the leadership of those most impacted by what they call the "criminal punishment" system.

CRITICAL PARTICIPATORY ACTION RESEARCH: EPISTEMIC ROOTS

CPAR stems from these radical demands for research justice and community participation, cultivated at the porous borders of universities and communities/movements. Unapologetically extending the borders of the academy, insisting on academic accountability and complicity, and centering the wisdom of those most impacted by injustice, CPAR embodies a distinct epistemology about whose knowledge matters and the dangerous limits of a "knowledge monopoly" tainted by an epistemology of privilege. With a range of methods, CPAR projects draw on quantitative, qualitative, ethnographic, archival, historic, folkloric, and visual methods to challenge dominant narratives, generate counternarratives, and democratize knowledge production (Collins, 1991).

We write as four CPAR researchers. We met in 1994 at the Bedford Hills Correctional Facility for Women, the maximum-security prison for women in New York State, where we collaborated on a participatory research team documenting the impact of college in prison on women prisoners, their children, the prison environment, and postrelease outcomes. We know, intimately, that sweet and fragile coalitions for research and action can be filled with good science, good friendship, laughter, and a vibrant sense of possibility and can be sustained in spaces carved within universities where academic–community/activist movement collaborations flourish. (see Torre, 2009; Torre & Ayala, 2009)

The Public Science Project (PSP) at the Graduate Center, City University of New York (CUNY; where María and Michelle work) and the Center for Justice at Columbia University (where Kathy and Cheryl work) grew as separate, if intertwined, sprouts rising from our rich collaboration at Bedford Hills. For the past 25 years through PSP at CUNY, María and Michelle have extended Kurt Lewin's ideas about action research and Ignacio Martín-Baró's commitment to liberation psychology, into a field we call CPAR (Torre et al., 2012; Fine & Torre, 2016). We have participated in CPAR projects nationally and internationally, in prisons and schools, and with social movements and community-based organizations. We offer weeklong summer institutes on CPAR, where scholars and activists engage with a range of multimethod, community-based research projects (see https://www.publicscienceproject.org).

In the same 25 years, Kathy and Cheryl also continued to work together, first inside Bedford and now at Columbia University, building community and opportunities with and for women in prison and after coming home. In prison, we joined other women in the effort to bring higher education back to prison, and reestablishing the college program at Bedford in the post–Pell grant era (described in more detail in the following section). Once home, Cheryl followed her commitment to higher education through becoming an academic counselor for College Initiative, supporting people who are pursuing college after prison, while Kathy extended her work in health care, creating the Coming Home program at St. Luke's Roosevelt Hospital for people returning from prison. Cheryl worked on the "Ban the Box" campaign on SUNY college admissions applications and restoring Pell grants to people inside prison, while Kathy worked with the long-termers in prison—those convicted of violent offenses with lengthy sentences and multiple parole denials—and helped create both the Long-Termers program and a movement to change parole policy and the underlying issues that keep people in prison with violent crimes almost forever. Kathy received her doctoral degree from Teachers College in 2009, focused on adolescents with incarcerated mothers; Cheryl earned her master's degree in urban affairs at Hunter College. We joined the faculty at Columbia in fall 2009 with the vision of infusing the issues surrounding ending mass incarceration into the entire university, with a multidisciplinary reach and always working with and centering the perspectives of the communities most impacted. Within 5 years, in partnership with Geraldine Downey, we helped create the Center for Justice.

In the remainder of this chapter, we reflect upon our original collaborative research project, Changing Minds, initiated in 1994 after federal policy eliminated prisoners' access to Pell grants for college.

CHANGING MINDS: A STUDY OF THE IMPACT OF COLLEGE IN PRISON

In 1994, President Bill Clinton signed the Violent Crime Control and Law Enforcement Act. With the sweep of a pen, much changed—including the withdrawal of Pell grants for persons in prison. Within a year, the 350 college-in-prison programs quietly operating throughout the United States dwindled to eight. The 15-year-old college program at Bedford was shuttered. The women who had lived with and participated in college inside initiated the idea for restoring it and conducting an evaluation of its impact.

A Policy Crisis: Collaborative Evaluation Rooted in the Wisdom of Those Most Impacted

As the Pell Grants were withdrawn and financial aid for college in prison was drying up, participating colleges began to withdraw support. The lights in the college classrooms were dimming at Bedford, and the energy in GED, Adult Basic Education, and English as a Second Language classes rapidly evaporated. After months of facing the loss of college, leaders among the women in prison approached the superintendent of Bedford to ask if she could imagine reestablishing a college program with private funding. The political "tough on crime" context made it unclear whether reinstituting college in the prison would even be acceptable to the governor of New York. Once permission was granted to explore the possibility, an Inmate College Bound Committee was formed. After meeting with the superintendent and other administrators, the next step was to invite community members from local universities, churches, and community groups to help strategize how we might resurrect college in the prison. Regina Peruggi, president of Marymount Manhattan College, offered to sponsor a BA program, assuming a more expansive consortium of universities would contribute one or two faculty per year. The university faculty, with women in the prison, developed a curricular plan for a sociology BA program to be offered at the prison to women who could pass the entrance examination for Marymount Manhattan College. With the approval of the superintendent, the inmate committee designed the governance of the program, authored a statement on the rights and responsibilities of students (e.g., requirement to tutor other students within the prison and/or upon release), established a minimal fee for enrollment, and built a warm, book-filled space for the program to operate in, humming with the sounds of students hungry to be educated, typing, chatting, taking notes, discovering writers, authoring their own pieces, engaging in "read arounds" (collective readings of original and published essays, poems, and stories) with prominent authors, cramming for midterms and finals, and reading until late into the evening. Within 6 months, college at Bedford was up and running.

The energy around the reestablishment of college was palpable, but so too was a sense of precarity. The program could be shut down at any moment; faculty could be denied entrance; the colleges' boards of trustees could decide to withdraw financial or political support; the correctional officers might resent the program and call on the significant power of their union to undermine the effort. The women in the prison recommended we commission an empirical evaluation of the impact of college in prison on the women prisoners, their children, the prison environment, and their postrelease outcomes. We decided that only a participatory design would work: Together we would design a systematic, multimethod participatory evaluation in collaboration with the Department of Corrections in Albany, the prison administration, the universities' administrators and faculty and with a set of women in prison as coresearchers.

Building a Research Collaborative

To our team, building such a collaborative meant holding space where diverse knowledges engage, rooted in the wisdom of those most impacted. To create our research team, we needed to facilitate a process that Torre (2009) called a *participatory contact zone* (2009), where insiders and outsiders could share what we know and do not know, so we could participate as equally as possible, learning from each others' distinct sources of expertise and experience. We offered a master's-level social science research methods course and spent months reading and discussing prison, college, feminist theory, capitalism, patriarchy, racism, mothering, politics, Whiteness, punishment, and transformation as well as methodology, sampling, crafting research questions, standpoint epistemology, feminist theory, critical justice studies, and critical race theory (see Fine et al., 2001). That is, we read together a range of critical theory texts rooted in questions of epistemology, gender, race, and class; challenging traditional conceptions of science, the prison–industrial complex, and social inquiry; and developing a collective set of questions we could pursue about if, how, why, and for whom college in prison mattered. This commitment to building a team of shared and distinctive knowledges is crucial to any CPAR project.

The course was designed to build a research-literate, dialogue-rich, highly diverse "participatory contact zone." Two PhD students, Rosemarie Roberts and Melissa Rivera, cotaught an advanced research methods course in the prison in which 15 students investigated personally meaningful questions about the impact of college, interviewing five women per question. Under a general "umbrella question" (What is the impact of college in prison?), the women fashioned their own unique questions: How does your involvement in college affect women's relationship with their children? Does college shift women's relationship to religion? How does college help women who have experienced domestic violence? Why do some women drop out? How do the correction officers feel about college? Within the semester, 75 "pilot" interviews were conducted. By the end of the course, seven of the women, by then trained as researchers, agreed to join the research team. For the next 4 years, every other week and then once a month, our research team gathered from 9 a.m. to 11 a.m. when the prison came to a halt for "count" and those of us not wearing green were escorted out.

Curating Intentional Diversity Within the Participatory Contact Zone

We were intentionally diverse: More than half of us were prisoners, the rest of us were free, but across our group we were also mothers and not mothers;

women who had suffered serious illness and those of us who had been spared, thus far; some who had experienced family violence as children and some who only witnessed or heard about it; women who engaged in activist community politics as adults and those who stayed away; women who grew up speaking Spanish and those of us who primarily spoke English; we were Black, Latina, Caribbean, White; a few lesbian, a few straight, and lots between. No one had a monopoly on expertise, but we built a research community that was delicately mindful of power dynamics, challenging taken-for-granted assumptions about who had capacity and expertise throughout.

Over time, we all came to realize how our different contributions would fundamentally shape the work. The women in prison held vital knowledge about the struggles that got them into prison; the structural and gendered abuse within the prison; the possibilities opened by college; the community built within the college; why reading, writing, and learning science mattered; and also the sustained class, race, and gender oppressions they had and would endure before, during, and after prison. Those of us from CUNY contributed methodological expertise, possible theoretical frameworks, and strong feminist and critical race understandings of the prison–industrial complex. Each of us raised critical questions about ethics, often reflecting aspects of our varying standpoints and communities we felt accountable to. We discussed confidentiality and anonymity of the interviews; where we might store the interviews at the prison and be able to guarantee privacy; the potential vulnerability of interviewed women who were critical of the prison or the college program; how to interview the children of women in prison without interfering with their precious time with their mothers in the prison and without interrupting their "real lives" back home; how or if to reference women's racial and ethnic identities or their crimes and sentences; who among the correction officers we might interview; how to describe public university involvement with the program given that the governor explicitly forbade public universities to be involved; whether we should write in "many voices" to narrate and explore the diversity of our research team or in a single voice to influence policy; and whether to focus on "traditional" indicators of success including recidivism and tax savings when really we were interested in transformation and liberation.

Together we pooled our wisdoms and aspired toward *strong objectivity* (Harding, 1994), in which differently positioned people intentionally and delicately work across distinct standpoints to generate robust evidence to complicate simple dominant narratives.

Working Through Differences as Resources and Power Dynamics

Across the 4 years of the project, our intimacies grew. We witnessed parole denials, canceled family visits, sons picked up by the police, cells unjustly searched by correctional officers, the beautiful intergenerational relationships among the women in prison, and why college—even in hell—mattered so much. Across our years of collaboration, some project participants were released; some developed cancer or kidney disease; a few were punishingly placed in solidarity confinement; and one member was "drafted" to prison at the Canadian border for no apparent reason other than what we felt was an abuse of state power.

All this to say that in CPAR projects, relationships develop, knowledge production democratizes, and deficit assumptions dissolve. The labels that psychologists and policy makers often blithely apply, describing people as "at risk" or "criminal," explode and are banished. As researchers, we committed to a design principle Michelle Fine and Lois Weis have called *critical bifocality*, always connecting "lives" to history, political structure, and desire (Weis & Fine, 2012). We worked through power dynamics and difficulties around who would write, how not to either demonize or romanticize the women in prison (or the women in the academy), how to code collaboratively (when there was no place to secure interviews and preserve confidentiality). We took seriously Foucault's invitation "to criticize the working of institutions which appear to be both neutral and independent; to criticize them in such a manner that the political violence . . . will be unmasked" ("Human Nature," 1971). We set out to document structural violence and radical possibilities.

Across 4 years of working together, we unmasked the "political violence" Foucault described; chronicled the luscious joy of education among women, even behind bars; and worked through tricky power dynamics that will always emerge in university–community collaborations (see Fine et al., 2003). Beautiful and spontaneous alliances developed among us, draping across CUNY and Bedford lines, dulling but never erasing the oppressive green uniforms that severely differentiated us as free or not. Some left after a meeting to weep on the train ride home; others were strip searched before returning to their cells.

Understanding the Political and Affective Context Around College in Prison

Our collective task was to document the impact of college within the prison, but the women inside Bedford Hills Correctional Facility understood the far reaches of college beyond the classrooms; the messy context in which the college program was situated; and the profound impact on children, on women who returned home, on correctional officers and college campus faculty, and on administrators. They explained how college spilled onto "the yard" where reading groups on Alice Walker and Michel Foucault convened; how college reduced disciplinary incidents and transformed the climate in the Children's Center, the "anger management" classes, "trailer visits" with loved ones, the summer camp for the children of the women, and evening discussions across cells. Our design grew more complex, enriched by the wide spectrum of expertise shaping the work. We tracked broadly the intellectual, relational, emotional, and political transformations of and by the women who participated in college and others around them; their writings, letters and poetry; their relationships with children, nieces, and nephews; their desires to give back to society, emergent leadership within the prison, and vibrant engagements in justice movements upon release; and their (unexpected!) delight in paying taxes, indicating a complicated recognition of "citizenship."

A Collaborative Approach to Design and Methods

Together we designed a multimethod project to address four key questions (see Table 5.1). We wanted to answer "how many" questions (e.g., how many women return to prison after college? How many disciplinary incidents occurred before and after college was introduced? How much money would be saved if college were available?) but also "why" and "how" questions (e.g., why do college graduates not return to prison at equivalent rates? How do their children think about higher education? How do the correction officers view the program?). We pondered together how to recruit a representative sample including leaders of the College Bound program, students, nonstudents, and dropouts; and officers who liked the program and those who were critical. We drafted slightly distinct interview questions for students, dropouts, graduates and women no longer in prison, children of students, correction officers, faculty, and university presidents. We sent a collective Research Request to the director of research at the Department of Corrections for 36-month recidivism data on matched samples of women who had and had not attended college, controlling for incoming criminal justice history and level of education.

All interviews and focus groups were conducted by pairs of researchers, one from the "inside" of the prison and one from the "outside," with the exception of interviews with corrections officers and with college students after release from prison, which were conducted by María. Each step was a deliberative and deep conversation swirling around a small table in the College Bound office, as we sometimes smuggled in cookies and fresh strawberries, over cross-tabs and transcripts, tears and laughter, across 4 years (Fine et al., 2001).

Organizing and Presenting the Findings

Our theoretical framework, methods, and findings are available in full at https://www.publicscienceproject.org. We spent a lot of time talking about who we wanted to reach with our findings—that is, who was our audience? We wanted the report to speak to women (and men) in and out of prison, their families and children, legislators, educators, religious leaders, advocates, and general members of society. To address all of these folks, we grouped the data simply into three "buckets" of impact: on the women and their children, on the prison environment, and on society. In summary, our research demonstrated:

- *College in prison transforms the lives of students and their children and promotes lasting transitions out of prison.* Interviews with the children of women in

TABLE 5.1. Changing Minds: Research Design

Research questions	Method	Sample	Outcomes
1. What are the costs of providing or withholding college from inmates?	1. Reincarceration analysis	$n = 274$ women in college	• Costs of imprisonment
	2. Cost–benefit analysis	$n = 2,031$ women not in college	• Costs of college education
			• Costs of reincarceration
2. What is the impact of college-in-prison on the safety and management of the prison environment?	3. Surveys of faculty	$n = 33$	• Changes in prison disciplinary environment
			• Prison climate
	4. Interviews with corrections officers and administrators	$n = 6$	• Correction officers' views of and experiences with college in prison
			• Attitudes of women not in the college program about college
			• Faculty views of college program
3. What are the personal and social effects of college in prison on students and their children?	5. One-one-one interviews conducted by inmate-researchers	$n = 65$	• Academic persistence and achievement
			• Personal transformation
	6. Focus groups with inmates, children, university presidents, and faculty	Focus groups: $n = 43$ (inmates) $n = 20$ (faculty) $n = 9$ (children) $n = 7$ (presidents)	• Expression of responsibility for crime and for future decision
			• Reflection on choices made in the past and decisions to be made in the future
			• Civic engagement and participation in prison and outside
4. What is the impact of the college experience on the transition home from prison?	7. In-depth interviews with former inmates	$n = 20$	• Reincarceration rates
			• Economic well-being
			• Health
	8. Student narratives	$n = 18$	• Civic participation
	9. Reincarceration analysis of former inmates who attended college while in prison	$n = 274$ college students $n = 2,031$ women not in college	• Persistence in pursuing higher education post-release
			• Relations with family and friends

Note. Adapted from *Changing Minds: The Impact of College in a Maximum-Security Prison* (p. 12), by M. Fine, M. E., Torre, K. Boudin, I. Bowen, J. Clark, D. Hylton, M. M. Martinez, R. Roberts, P. Smart, and D. Upegui, 2001, Prison Policy Initiative (https://www.prisonpolicy.org/scans/changing_minds.pdf).

prison, and interviews with more than 20 released women who had attended college in prison revealed the extent to which higher education afforded women the opportunity to craft new identities, develop new networks, take responsibility for the past and cultivate a commitment to "give back," and embody a sense of responsibility to repair the world.

- *College in prison significantly reduces reincarceration rates.* In our collaboration with the New York State Department of Correctional Services, we commissioned a study that tracked 274 women who attended college while in prison and compared them with 2,031 women who did not attend college while in prison, controlling for crime and incoming education level. Women who attended college while in prison were significantly less likely to be reincarcerated (7.7%) than those who did not attend college while in prison (29.9%).

- *College in prison enhances the sense of safety in the prison.* Interviews with prison administrators, corrections officers, women in prison, and college faculty revealed that the presence of a college program permeates the culture of the prison environment so that prisoners and officers report feeling safer, with fewer disciplinary incidents committed, especially by women in the college program.

Brainstorming Dissemination: Who Do We Want to Influence?

Given the "good news" emanating from the statistical data; confirmed by the interviews with women, correction officers, university faculty, and the children; and given our policy goals to reestablish both Pell grants (federal) and TAP (Tuition Assistance Program) grants (in New York State) for women and men in prison, we (those of us not in prison at the time) met with members of the Black, Puerto Rican, Latino, and Asian Legislative Caucus in New York State to solicit their advice on converting research to policy and advocacy. Then Chairman Jeffrion Aubry told us, "We can only support this report if you can demonstrate statistically that access to higher education yields tax savings, reduction in crime, and no risk to public safety." And so we did. Michael Jacobson, a prominent criminologist, volunteered to conduct a cost–benefit analysis of college-in-education for a hypothetical group of 100 women, estimating annual costs of additional incarceration to be $30,000 and annual cost for college in prison to be $2,500. Jacobson determined that providing access to college in prison is far more cost-effective than reincarceration, foster care, health complications, and diminished employability.

Eager to move these extremely positive findings to audiences beyond the pro–college-in-prison advocates, we then held confidential meetings with members of Governor Pataki's staff, legislators, conservative prison reformers, and victims' rights advocates, including Janice Grieshaber, the executive director of the Jenna Foundation for Non-Violence, a mother of a murder victim and powerful advocate of long sentences for men and women convicted of violent crimes. Michelle asked if Ms. Grieshaber would consider a quote for the back of the report. Within a few weeks, we received a generous endorsement:

> Educating the incarcerated is not an exercise in futility, nor is it a gift to the undeserving. It is a gift to ourselves and to our children, a gift of both compassion and peace of mind. It is a practical and necessary safeguard to insure that those who have found themselves without the proper resources to succeed have these needs met before they are released. We are not turning the other cheek to those who have hurt us. We are taking their hands and filling them with learning so that they can't strike us again. (endorsement on back cover of *Changing Minds*, Fine et al., 2001)

As a group, we deliberated and ultimately decided to create multiple products, written in distinct "voices"—policy, scholarship, organizing, and popular culture. On the official report, we determine that authorship would be alphabetical but Michelle's name would be listed first, to increase the perceived legitimacy and university grounding of the research. We sent copies of the final report to every governor in the country and all the state legislators in New York State, streaming quotes alongside statistics, cost–benefit analyses and photographs, opening with a letter of gratitude from a college graduate sent upstate to Albion Prison. We produced 1,000 evidence-based advocacy brochures in English and Spanish, flooding community-based organizations, advocacy groups, and local libraries, and also postcards with quotes from the research: "Get tough on crime, educate men and women in prison!" "Since my mother has been enrolled in college, all she wants to talk about is school, and reading and homework!" "As a corrections officer, I don't like the college program much—since I can barely afford college for myself or my kids—but I know they are reading at night, not getting in fights and won't be coming back."

The full research team has coauthored multiple chapters and articles in widely recognized methods texts, academic journals (including the first edition of *Qualitative Research in Psychology*), corrections journals, and local newspapers, and as coresearchers are newly released from prison, our "we" expands as we speak in person across the state and country.

Assessing the Impact on Policy and the Academic Research

We can assess the impact of this project in terms of (a) changes in public policy and (b) the range of projects developed as participatory, prisoner-led research.

Policy. Did the research change policy? Yes and no. Today, Pell grants remain inaccessible to most people in prison. Nevertheless, there is a massive national movement to restore Pell grants in prison and open higher education access postprison, as well as some shifts in state-level and even federal legislation, led by formerly incarcerated advocates. As state legislatures review their budgets in contexts of austerity and realize anew the financial burden of funding jails and prisons, politicians are increasingly calling us, downloading the report, and asking us to consult. A national coalition led by formerly incarcerated advocates and foundations has mobilized to restore Pell Grants and support public–private initiatives for college in prison, bolstered in part by our findings.

Research. Much more obviously, there has been a dramatic turn toward participatory designs for projects conducted on, with, and by people in prison and formerly incarcerated researchers—an expectation that research on criminal justice will be grounded in the wisdom of formerly incarcerated researchers, affected families, and communities. Since the release of the *Changing Minds* report, a series of CPAR projects in, after, and about prisons has been launched, all rooted in the perspective of those most affected: a research-based video designed by and for the children of women and men in prison (Echoes of Incarceration, 2009); a participatory study of the "gifts" formerly incarcerated students bring to college (Halkovic et al., 2013); a multimethod analysis of the recidivism rates and biographies of "long-termers"—in this case, men and women with sentences longer than 10 years—and their lives after prison, challenging the logic and perverse consequences of very long sentences (Marquez-Lewis et al., 2013); and a community-inspired study of aggressive and discriminatory policing in the Bronx borough of New York City (Stoudt et al., 2015). Cheryl and Kathy were recently awarded a significant grant to establish the Collective Leadership Institute to support the organizing and movement-building of women who were incarcerated or directly impacted by mass incarceration; to produce an oral history, film, and longitudinal research study documenting and elevating the growth and role of women's leadership in bringing higher education back to Bedford; and to create a model of university–community collaboration in documenting the role of women's leadership in challenging mass incarceration.

All of these projects reflect our signature CPAR elements: the research is deeply rooted in community; designed by collectives of academics and community members; centers on the perspectives of those most impacted; integrates evidence from history, statistics, and narratives; and results in publishing and disseminating "products" that are scholarly, policy-oriented, and accessible to the local community. We have produced executive summaries of our research for legislators and amicus briefs for courts; distributed T-shirts with key qualitative quotes from our research on police violence, including children's T-shirts that read "Why do I always fit the description?" and "It's not a crime to be who I am." We have presented findings at community gatherings by and for those impacted by mass incarceration, collectively published scholarly papers on college in prison as a form of Affirmative Action, and helped to produce—led by children of people who have been incarcerated—films by and for children impacted by it. Our audiences are first and foremost the communities to whom we are accountable, and also policy makers, academics and college students, organizers, and the general public.

REFLECTIONS ON THE CHANGING MINDS STUDY AND RESEARCH JUSTICE

In a world fraught with widening inequities and spiking White nationalisms; heightened state violence against communities of color; and a ruthless state apparatus targeted to disproportionately contain, hurt, and exile Black and

Brown people, we find that authoritarian and racist stories about "criminals" amplify, racism swells, and universities are increasingly viewed as irrelevant and elitist colonial outposts. At this deeply precarious moment, we need an insurgent movement of "by and for" university–community collaborations, vibrant and brimming with "differences" and dissent, that focus on critical policy work locally in communities, across state lines, and transnationally. The academy has a long-overdue obligation to nurture a generation of critical scientists, diverse by gender, sexuality, race, ethnicity, immigration status, socioeconomic class, and including those who have been incarcerated or those who are committed to participatory work with communities under siege; to open doors to community members and movements; to challenge dangerous epistemologies of academic ignorance and privilege, often rooted in White supremacy; and to recognize the wisdom brewing in communities that have struggled due to systematic inequality over generations.

CONCLUSION

In 1994, we forged an alliance of research and imagination between CUNY and the women inside Bedford Hills Correctional Facility. From that collaboration, a spirit and dedication to research justice has survived, permeating policy and practice, research, and organizing. Over the past 25 years, these relationships, research projects, and policy challenges have only strengthened because of deep participation and the leadership of formerly incarcerated women. Critical participatory inquiry can and must be a tool in progressive policy reform, community organizing, popular education, theory building, and movements for social justice. *Changing Minds* remains an open-access document and a strong multimethod example of how universities can humbly work in solidarity with communities, through a critical participatory framework, in the fight for a more just tomorrow.

REFERENCES

Allport, G. W. (1954). *The nature of prejudice*. Addison-Wesley.

Cherry, F., & Borshuk, C. (1998). Social action research and the Commission on Community Interrelations. *Journal of Social Issues, 54*(1), 119–142.

Collins, P. H. (1991). *Black feminist thought: Knowledge, consciousness, and the politics of empowerment*. Routledge.

Du Bois, W. E. B. (1899). *The Philadelphia Negro: A social study*. Ginn.

Du Bois, W. E. B. (2008). *The quest of the silver fleece*. Dover Publishers. (Original work published 1911)

Echoes of Incarceration [Documentary initiative]. (2009). https://www.echoesofincarceration.org

Fals Borda, O. (Ed.). (1985). *The challenge of social change*. Sage Publications.

Fals Borda, O. (1995, April 8). *Research for social justice: Some North–South convergences* [Plenary address]. Southern Sociological Society Meeting, Atlanta, GA. http://comm-org.wisc.edu/si/falsborda.htm

Fals Borda, O., & Rahman, M. A. (1991). *Action and knowledge: Breaking the monopoly with participatory action-research*. The Apex Press. https://doi.org/10.3362/9781780444239

Fine, M. (2017). *Just research in contentious times: Widening the methodological imagination.* Teachers College Press.

Fine, M., & Ruglis, J. (2009). Circuits and consequences of dispossession: The racialized realignment of the public sphere for U.S. youth. *Transforming Anthropology, 17*(1), 20–33. https://doi.org/10.1111/j.1548-7466.2009.01037.x

Fine, M., & Torre, M. E. (2016). The Public Science Project at the City University of New York. In R. Tandon, B. Hall, W. Lepore, & W. Singh (Eds.), *Knowledge and engagement: Building capacity for the next generation of community-based researchers* (pp. 186–196). PRIA.

Fine, M., Torre, M. E., Boudin, K., Bowen, I., Clark, J., Hylton, D., Martinez, M. M., Roberts, R., Smart, P., & Upegui, D. (2001). *Changing minds: The impact of college in a maximum-security prison.* https://www.prisonpolicy.org/scans/changing_minds.pdf

Fine, M., Torre, M. E., Boudin, K., Bowen, I., Clark, J., Hylton, D., & Martinez, M. M., Smart, P., Rivera, M., Roberts, R., & Upegui, D. (2003). Participatory action research: Within and beyond bars. In P. Camic, J. E. Rhodes, & L. Yardley (Eds.), *Qualitative research in psychology: Expanding perspectives in methodology and design* (pp. 173–198). American Psychological Association.

Greenhaven Think Tank. (1997). *The non-traditional approach to criminal and social justice.* Center for NuLeadership, Resurrection Study Group.

Halkovic, A., Fine, M., Bae, J., Greene, A., Gary, C., Riggs, R., Evans, D., Campbell, L. Taylor, M., Tejawi, A., & Tebout, R. (2013). *The gifts they bring: Welcoming "first generation" college students into higher education after prison.* Public Science Project and the Prisoner Re-Entry Institute at John Jay College, CUNY.

Harding, S. (1994). Rethinking standpoint epistemology: What is "strong objectivity"? In L. Alcoff & E. Potter (Eds.), *Feminist epistemologies* (pp. 49–82). Routledge.

Human nature: Justice versus power. Noam Chomsky debates Michel Foucault. (1971). https://chomsky.info/1971xxxx/

Jahoda, M., Lazarsfeld, P., & Zeisel, H. (2001). *Marienthal: The sociography of an unemployed community.* Transaction Publications.

Marquez-Lewis, C., Fine, M., Boudin, K., Waters, W., DeVeaux, M., Vargas, F., Wilkins, C., Martinez, M., Pass, M., & White, S. (2013). How much punishment is enough? Designing participatory research on parole policies for persons convicted of violent crimes. *Journal of Social Issues, 69*(4), 771–796. https://doi.org/10.1111/josi.12041

Martín-Baró, I. (1994). *Writings for a liberation psychology.* Harvard University Press.

Stoudt, B. G., Torre, M. E., Bartley, P., Bracy, F., Caldwell, H., Downs, A., Greene, C., Haldipur, J., Hassan, P., Manoff, E., Sheppard, N., & Yates, J. (2015). "We come from a place of knowing": Experiences, challenges, advantages and possibilities of participating in Morris Justice Project. In C. Durose & L. Richardson (Eds.), *Re-thinking public policy making: Why co-production matters.* Policy Press.

Torre, M. E. (2009). Participatory action research and critical race theory: Fueling spaces for nos-otras to research. *The Urban Review, 41*(1), 106–120. https://doi.org/10.1007/s11256-008-0097-7

Torre, M. E., & Ayala, J. (2009). Envisioning participatory action research Entremundos. *Feminism & Psychology, 19*(3), 387–393. https://doi.org/10.1177/0959353509105630

Torre, M. E., & Fine, M. (2011). A wrinkle in time: Tracing a legacy of public science through community self-surveys and participatory action research. *Journal of Social Issues, 67*(1), 106–121. https://doi.org/10.1111/j.1540-4560.2010.01686.x

Torre, M. E., Fine, M. E., Stoudt, B. G., & Fox, M. (2012). Critical participatory action research as public science. In H. Cooper, P. M. Camic, D. L. Long, A. T. Panter, D. Rindskopf, & K. J. Sher (Eds.), *APA handbook of research methods in psychology: Vol. 2. Research designs: Quantitative, qualitative, neuropsychological, and biological* (pp. 171–184). American Psychological Association. https://doi.org/10.1037/13620-011

Weis, L., & Fine, M. (2012, Summer). Critical bifocality and circuits of privilege. *Harvard Educational Review, 82*(2), 173–201. https://doi.org/10.17763/haer.82.2.v1jx34n441532242

Some Ways of Doing Narrative Research

Michael Murray

The central core of qualitative research is exploring how people make sense of their everyday worlds and how to contribute to processes of personal and social transformation (Murray, 2019). Narrative inserts itself into this task based on the argument that people make sense of their worlds in narrative form. We exist in a stream of time, and narrative is a way of bringing order to this constant change by linking past events with the present and the future. However, although narrators are actively involved in constructing these narratives, they are doing so within a particular social context and drawing on broader cultural narratives. The challenge for the narrative researcher is not only to explore the character of particular narratives but also how they are shaped in certain contexts and how they shape our identities. This chapter considers the many sources of narrative accounts and how these can be explored further.

NARRATIVE DATA

There are a variety of sources of narrative data. The most common potential sources are considered in this section.

Interviews

Forms of Interview

The primary source of narrative data for research has been the interview, which can take many forms ranging from the biographical or life-course interview to

https://doi.org/10.1037/0000252-006
Qualitative Research in Psychology: Expanding Perspectives in Methodology and Design, Second Edition, P. M. Camic (Editor)

the topic or focused interview. The former is concerned with eliciting a detailed largely unstructured account of a person's life, while the latter invites the interviewee to provide detail about a certain experience. However, the focus of the interview is to draw out the temporal nature of the phenomenon, how it evolved over time from the past through the present and can extend into the future.

In the life-course interview, the researcher outlines at the outset the purpose of the interview and then guides the participant through the account. For example, in a biographical interview the interviewer could start as follows: "I would like you to tell me the story of your life beginning as far back as you wish and recounting as much detail in your life up until the present." During the account, the interviewer can intersperse the account with such comments as "What happened next?" or "Can you recall anything else?" The main emphasis is on how the participant connects past events together with current experience and possible futures.

The researcher can use an interview guide such as the Life Story Protocol developed by Dan McAdams (1995). This guide starts by inviting the participant to tell the story of their life. The participant is encouraged to focus on key experiences and to structure their account almost in the form of chapters about their past, present, and future. Rosenthal (2004) provided a detailed guide to conducting a biographical interview which begins in a very open-ended format:

> Please tell me/us your family story and your personal life story; I/we am/are very interested in your whole life. Anything that occurs to you. You have as much time as you like. We/I won't ask you any questions for now. We/I will just make some notes on the things that we would like to ask you more about later, if we haven't got enough time today, perhaps in a second interview. (p. 51)

Rosenthal found that this open-ended format often led to an extensive response from research participants, frequently lasting several hours.

Within the psychoanalytic tradition, Hollway and Jefferson (2012) have promoted the use of the free association narrative interview technique, an open-ended interview approach designed to encourage the participant to talk extensively about an issue. The researcher subsequently identifies any inconsistencies or confusions in the account, which can be discussed in a subsequent interview.

Frequently, the researcher is interested not in whole life stories but in particular experiences, although these can be situated within a biographical interview. In this case, the interview is designed to encourage participants to tell stories about particular experiences or turning points in their lives. Flick (2002) has promoted the *episodic* interview. In this format, the aim is to develop narrative accounts about particular experiences (episodes) combined with reflections on causes and consequences.

Although most research is conducted with individual participants, narrative research can also be conducted in group settings. An example of this is the study by Lohuis et al. (2016), which was designed to explore how health care teams make sense of their effectiveness through telling their team story.

In this study, five teams of health employees participated in a narrative focus group in which they were guided by McAdams's (1995) life-story protocol adopted for a group. At the outset, the moderator asked the question "Imagine you are going to write a book about your team, what would the index of the book look like?" (McAdams, 1995, p. 412). The responses to this question formed the starting point to encourage the team members to reflect on how their team worked. Subsequently one of the authors spent time with each of the teams building up an understanding of how they worked.

Collecting Narrative Accounts

One of the particular strengths of the narrative interview is that it gives the research participant more control in shaping the discussion agenda. In the standard interview, researchers bring a series of questions or theories they would like to explore. In the narrative interview, the researcher adopts a more open approach. For example, the narrative interview can start with the open request, such as "Tell me about yourself" or "Tell me about your job," and follow up with a few related questions. The successful narrative interviewer develops a relationship with the research participant. The interviewee needs to feel that their story is deeply valued. They may be initially suspicious at the openness of the narrative approach and need to be reassured.

In collecting narrative accounts, the researcher needs to be aware that the very interview process itself may encourage a certain structure for those accounts. In particular, it may encourage a certain narrative coherence. As Hollway (1989) argued, "Participants usually strive for coherence in the narratives they produce (for research as for other purposes). This is one effect on subjectivity of the dominant Western assumption of the unitary rational subject" (p. 43).

Squire (2013), in her study of personal accounts of people with HIV, questioned the constraints placed on an individual in a narrative life-course interview. She felt that there is a tendency to create a false "seamlessness, homogeneity" (p. 199). In addition, narrative accounts emphasize the central role of the narrator to the neglect of others in their life story.

One way to challenge this tendency to coherence is to encourage the telling of a series of stories rather than a single life story. Such an approach combines the episodic with the traditional narrative life-course interview. Another strategy is to dispense with the single interview but to conduct a series of interviews or to engage in a process of extended conversations over time. This is the strategy adopted by Squire (2007) in her study of the experience of living with HIV/AIDS in South Africa. Realizing the weaknesses of a single interview, Squire developed a more extended discursive process through which she attempted to get to know the participants. This was a form of participatory research in which she attempted to actively involve the participants in the project.

Another alternative to the sit-down interview is the walk-along interview in which the researcher engages in a more free-flowing conversation with the participant about their lives or particular experiences while the research participant is going about everyday tasks. This method is part of the ethnographic tradition, which requires the researcher to spend considerable time with the research participant getting to know their lives and collecting data in a more extensive and informal manner (Kusenbach, 2003). It is through engaging in such unstructured conversations that the stories about everyday lives can be exchanged and a more sophisticated understanding of human experience developed. The researcher also gets to grasp the context within which the narrator lives and within which the narrative is developed.

Role of the Interviewer

The narrator is not simply telling their story in a vacuum but telling it to someone. The narrative is a coconstruction in which the interviewer plays a role in shaping the narrative either deliberately or through who they represent in the eyes of the narrator. It is for this reason that the researcher needs to reflect on who they are and how they contribute to the shaping of the narrative account. Squire (2013), in discussing the role of the researcher in shaping the interview, admitted that this reflexive caution can be an ongoing challenge: "I could be almost endlessly reflexive about this research. To ignore the power relations of interviews may implicitly reproduce them" (p. 59).

Despite this concern, Squire found that many of the participants in her research declared that they were telling their own story. Indeed, not only within the relative privacy of interviews but also in more public spheres, many people are happy to disclose extended personal details.

Although interviews are a primary source of narrative data, they can be supplemented with information that can help locate the experiences described. This is illustrated in the study by Toolis and Hammack (2015) of the narratives of homeless youth that combined life-story interviews with ethnographic fieldwork. Before conducting the interviews, Toolis had spent a year employed in a drop-in center for homeless youth. This provided her with the opportunity to observe the users of the center (the guests) and to become familiar with staff and the organization. She then conducted detailed interviews with a sample of the guests using the Life Story Protocol developed by McAdams (1993, 1995). The analysis of the narrative accounts was informed by their understanding of the organizational setting coupled with a reflection on the interview process.

Documents

Both published and unpublished documents are an important means of accessing narrative accounts. Although not written for research, they potentially provide a rich source for the narrative researcher.

Diaries

Diaries have historically been used by many individuals to record their reflections on events. There are various forms of the diary from the personal and intimate journal that the author may be reluctant to share to the more formal appointment diary, which is simply a listing of events. Recently there has been the development of research diaries designed to collect contemporaneous descriptions of particular experiences. Research diaries can vary in format from simple pencil-and-paper exercises to telephone interviews, to electronic formats. Some research diaries follow a structured format, whereas others are unstructured and simply request that the participants regularly record their experiences over a certain period.

The use of research diaries can be supplemented with follow-up interviews providing the research participants with the opportunity to reflect on certain incidents they reported and to place them within a larger narrative frame. An example of this approach was the study by Kenten (2010) of the experiences of lesbians and gay men. In this study, a sample of participants were initially interviewed about their experience of being gay. After the interview, they were invited to keep a diary record of when they became aware of their sexuality in their everyday lives. The content of the diaries was transcribed and loosely analyzed, providing a guide to subsequent interviews that focused on the experience of keeping a diary and the participants' reflections on the various experiences described. The diary and the matched interviews were then analyzed in tandem.

The diaries can also be used to promote reflection by the participants in the research project. For example, in her study of women's views of breast self-examination, Kearney (2006) organized group discussions on the topic. These discussions were supplemented with diary entries about breast self-examination, which the women were encouraged to record between the discussions. These diary entries could then be discussed at the subsequent meetings.

Autobiographies

Traditionally these have been written by major political or military figures, celebrities, and artists. However, this is changing with the proliferation of published accounts by the ordinary person. Frequently, these have centered on the experience of some traumatic event or series of events. Thus, there are published accounts of living through various social conflicts, such as war (e.g., Orwell, 2000), but also of more personal trauma, such as abuse, the onset of serious illness, or the death of a loved one (e.g., Didion, 2006).

Contemporary autobiographies often center on traumatic personal events such as sexual assault or serious illness. Murray (2009), in his analysis of a selection of published accounts of breast cancer, noted how at the beginning of the accounts, the women often emphasized how normal their lives had been. The women were just ordinary people; they were blameless. They had lived healthy lives until suddenly they were diagnosed with cancer. The middle of the story concerned their dealings with the health system and the treatment they had received for the disease. At the end, they looked back on the experience with relief but also with a certain amount of gratitude around the lessons that they had learned about life but apprehension about the future.

An increasingly popular phenomenon is online narrative accounts by people who have experienced some traumatic episode in their lives. There are a large number of websites devoted to such stories that provide a new source of narrative data for research (e.g., https://www.cancercenter.com/patient-stories). Overberg et al. (2006) conducted an analysis of cancer stories in Dutch on the Internet and found that most had provided a structure to aid the reader, and some offered the opportunity for readers to post their reactions to a particular story. Another example is the work of Pederson (2013), who explored the content of stories posted on the internet by unemployed youth. He conducted a narrative thematic analysis of a sample of these internet stories and classified them as presenting five identity types that worked to engage in different ways with the master narrative of the American Dream of upward social mobility against adversity.

A final example is that of various types of political memoir. The most common form is that by the political leader. A less recognized genre is the *testimonio* and the autobiographical account of the community activist. The *testimonio* is the account of the social activist written at the time of the action to publicize and to draw attention to some injustice. An example is the account written by Domitila De Chungara (1978), which detailed her work organizing women in Bolivian mining communities. The accounts of the community activist mix the political memoir with the *testimonio* and tell a story of social injustice which the narrator has struggled to challenge at a local level (Murray, 2021). These political memoirs were written not just to record certain events but to convince others of the value of the author's actions and beliefs. An important factor in reviewing these memoirs is the extent to which they were written by the author alone or with the help of someone else.

Archives

There is a wealth of narrative and related material contained in archives that have been compiled by a range of organizations. These archives contain extensive accounts—written, oral, and visual—by individuals who have participated in certain events. Some of these archives may be more accessible and organized than others.

An example is the archive of Peter Cheeseman, who established a theatre in the English midlands in the 1950s. This archive contains transcripts of narrative accounts of particular events that were collected in fieldwork interviews. It was from these transcripts that play scripts were developed. In a subsequent research project exploring changing representations of aging, material from some of these archival interview transcripts was supplemented with contemporary interviews with actors, theatre makers, and audience members. Together this information was used to develop a new narrative drama about the process of growing old (Bernard et al., 2015).

With the growth of the internet, the digital storage of narrative accounts collected from a variety of sources has become commonplace. For example, Anderson (2019) detailed the Belfast prison memory archive (http://prisonsmemoryarchive.com). This resource contains 175 filmed "walk-and-talk" recordings of those who had some connection with prisons during the

"Troubles" in Northern Ireland (1970–1990). The archive participants include prisoners, prison staff, relatives, and others. Access to these archives can open up debates about their subsequent interpretations and usage. Certain narrative records may have been stored to record and to promote action against various social injustices, but these may be interpreted contrary to their original intention.

Some archives contain not only written narrative accounts, but also videoed accounts sometimes supplemented with other material. The Fortunoff Video Archive for Holocaust Testimonies, which was established in 1982, now contains more than 4,400 videotaped narrative accounts by individual survivors, witnesses, and liberators of the Holocaust. Some of this material has been made available on the internet (https://web.library.yale.edu/testimonies). These testimonies range in length from half an hour to 40 hours. Extracts from the interview transcripts have been published, and more detailed analyses have been produced.

The Global Feminisms Project is an online repository of the oral histories of women who have devoted their lives to promoting social change. The interviews followed a similar format. They were "semi-structured oral histories prompting women to speak about their familial background, career and academic experiences, and engagement with activism and movements" (Dutt & Grabe, 2014, p. 111). The website provides the interview transcripts and videos of the interviews (https://sites.lsa.umich.edu/globalfeminisms/). It also contains a basic thematic analysis of some of the interview transcripts. Researchers have begun to explore in more detail the character of these narrative accounts.

Letters

An early example of the use of letters in social research is the study conducted by Thomas and Znaniecki (1918–1920), which explored the experience of emigration to the United States by Polish peasants. The work contained multiple sources of data including more than 700 to-and-fro letters from immigrants and family members. Stanley (2010) provided a detailed commentary of the original analysis of these letters. She also led an extensive project developing an "epistolary dataset" of the 4,600 letters by the socialist feminist Olive Schreiner (1855–1920; https://www.oliveschreiner.org/), which has been used to explore the rise of socialist feminism (e.g., Stanley et al., 2012).

The work by Thomas and Znaniecki provoked substantial debate in the 1940s among social scientists about the use of letters and similar materials in social science research. One of the commissioned reports was by Gordon Allport, who later published his own collection of *Letters From Jenny* (Allport, 1946/1965), which was a selection from more than 300 letters written to him over a period of time by the mother of a former college friend. In the letters, "Jenny" details her frustration at what she perceives to be the misbehaviors of her son. Allport supplemented his account of these letters with a detailed analysis of the personality of the mother.

Letters normally record details of recent events. Sools et al. (2015) reversed this process by exploring letters from the future. In this study, participants were encouraged to write letters about potential events in the future. These narrative accounts were then explored to consider how they were structured and considered intentions and hopes about the future and the pathway from the present.

Visual and Other Sources

With the growth of qualitative research, narrative researchers have begun to explore other potential sources of narrative data. Some new approaches are considered in this section.

Videos and Images

While the initial turn to narrative placed emphasis on verbal and written sources of data, there is increasing interest in a wider range of sources. One such source is the visual medium, which can range from the use of video through photographs to graphic novels. Because these are often in the public domain, the task of the researcher is to identify particular media that connect with the focus of the research. Hoecker (2014) considered the organization of visual narratives produced by national truth commissions in Peru and Guatemala. They considered how different media, including photographs and illustrations, were used to convey different perspectives.

Another example is the Waterford Memories project, which has placed on its website (https://www.waterfordmemories.com) videotaped narrative accounts of women who had been confined to one of the Magdalene laundries that was established in Ireland by various religious orders in the early 20th century as custodial institutions for young, unmarried women who had given birth. The videotaped narrative accounts by women who had been confined in these institutions and details of other related educational projects illustrate the combination of narrative and action research. Together, the public display of these narrative accounts becomes part of a process of advocacy and social change by challenging the Irish state's historic complicity with the religious orders in confining these women (O'Mahoney, 2018).

Exhibitions and Events

The broader rapprochement between social science and the arts has also enabled narrative researchers to explore the potential of other artforms, such as performance and drama. Langellier (1999) detailed the qualities of performance that add to the individual oral narrative. These include the voice and body of the narrator and that the performance is a conversation with the listening audiences both present and absent.

Washington and Moxley (2008) described an extensive participatory project of women's experiences of homelessness. Part of this project involved extended conversations with a sample of eight women, which produced lengthy narrative transcripts for each woman supplemented with photographs they had taken. The women mounted an exhibition that included photographs and other material that conveyed their experience of homelessness. The women were the curators of the exhibition and took turns discussing the contents with visitors. In this way, the research turned into a participatory action research project, which, through the portrayal of the women's experiences, contributed to stimulating "public awareness, arousing public indignation, and fostering collaborative action" (p. 155).

A final example is the work of Global Dialogues (https://www.globaldialogues.org), a nonprofit organization that aims to use creative methods to involve young people in a range of activities designed to enhance global public health. These activities include a competition for young people across sub-Sahara Africa to write a script for a potential film about HIV/AIDS. More than 150,000 young people participated in this study between 1997 and 2014. Global Dialogues organized local juries to pick the best scripts submitted. At least 39 films have been developed from these scripts, and an archive of more than 75,000 narratives was created (Winskell, 2020). This massive narrative data source has begun to be explored to develop an understanding of how different groups of young Africans make sense of HIV/AIDS. By developing films from the scripts, the whole study constitutes a form of action research by exploring with the young people their views of HIV/AIDS as conveyed in the film scripts.

NARRATIVE ANALYSIS

A major challenge faced by the narrative researcher is the multiple forms of analysis. There is no single standard method but rather a variety of approaches nested in different epistemological assumptions. Riessman (2008) distinguished between the thematic, the structural, and the performative–dialogical approaches. This framework tends to underplay the broader sociocultural context within which narrative is constructed. Mishler (1995) suggested consideration of narrative content, context, and syntax. This approach tends to lose sight of the agency of the narrator.

A third approach that attempts to connect both agent and context in narrative analysis considers the intrapersonal, interpersonal, positional, and societal processes within narrative telling (Murray, 2000). Each of these processes is not distinct but overlaps such that we can begin to explore connections across the processes or levels of analysis. Here we consider each of these four analytic levels illustrated with a range of examples. Considering the levels of analysis allows us to integrate the personal with the social and to consider narrative as performance within a particular setting. Langellier (1999) described this process vividly:

> From a pragmatic perspective, personal narrative performance is radically contextualized: first in the voice and body of the narrator; second, and as significantly, in conversation with empirically present listeners; and third in dialogue with absent or ghostly audiences (Minister, 1999). (p. 127)

Although the focus is largely on researcher-led analysis, group-based and participatory forms of analysis are also considered. The analysis begins with a transcript of each narrative account, which can be accompanied by a short summary and a visual representation.

Intrapersonal Level of Analysis

This approach focuses on the narrative account as being the personal construction of the narrator. This level of analysis begins with exploration of the structure and content of the narrative account. The researcher begins by reading the whole interview and familiarizing themselves with the various issues raised. The basic structure of a standard narrative is the beginning, middle, and end. However, how these phases are connected differ, as does the emphasis placed on the role of the central character (e.g., victim, hero) and the overall tone of the narrative. The structure of different accounts can be contrasted.

Suggestions on how to explore the narrative structure can draw on various linguistic and literary theorists. The approach developed by Labov and Waletsky (1967) distinguished among six narrative elements:

- *Abstract:* summary of the narrative account
- *Orientation:* the orientation in terms of time and place
- *Complicating action:* details of the action and turning points and overall plot
- *Evaluation:* the overall tone of the narrative
- *Resolution:* the outcome of the narrative
- *Coda:* the endpiece and reflection on the narrative

These elements can be condensed into three core elements of orientation, complicating action and evaluation. Adopting this approach provides a starting point for more detailed analysis of the content of the narrative account. However, often narrative accounts are not so easily categorized. They may be open-ended, without a clear conclusion. Awareness of this unfinished structure can contribute to the analysis.

Other structural approaches attempt to provide an assessment of the plot underlying the narrative account. In his analysis of Western literature, Frye (1957) argued that there were four archetypal forms: *comedy, romance, tragedy*, and *satire*. More contemporary critics have extended this classification scheme. For example, Plummer (1994) described the basic plots of the modernist tale as being (a) taking a journey, (b) engaging in a contest, (c) enduring suffering, (d) pursuing consummation, and (e) establishing a home. He suggested that the common elements in these stories are (a) suffering which gives tension to the stories, (b) a crisis or turning point or epiphany, and (c) a transformation.

Gergen and Gergen (1986) proposed three broad temporal narrative structures: *progressive,* where progress toward a goal is enhanced; *stability*, where no change occurs; and *regressive*, where progress is impeded. They suggested that their threefold structure was similar to the romance, comedy, and tragedy genres described by Frye. An example of the use of this structural approach was the study by Murray (2007) of fish harvesters' narrative accounts of injuries they had incurred. Their accounts were read and reread before being classified as opportunity, challenge or phenomenon, and destruction, which was similar to Gergen and Gergen's (1986) threefold categorization. These three narrative orientations were also similar to the temporal orientations in Crossley's (1999) study of the narrative accounts of people with a positive diagnosis of HIV/AIDS, which she in turn linked with broader cultural narratives. She classified the three orientations as "living with a philosophy of the present," associated with a general cultural story of conversion and growth; a "living in the future" narrative orientation, associated with a normalizing cultural narrative; and a "living in the empty present" orientation, associated with a cultural story of loss.

The content of the narrative account can be explored through a form of thematic analysis (Braun & Clarke, 2006) to identify the key issues raised in the narrative. Here the challenge is not to break the narrative account down into its component parts but rather to grasp the coherence of the narrative. This requires a reading and rereading of the narrative account to identify, either inductively or deductively, the key themes. Inductively, the analyst reads across the whole narrative and identifies recurrent issues, whereas deductively, the analyst approaches the narrative with certain theoretical constructs in mind, which is used to engage with the transcript. Abduction is the combination of these approaches. For example, in the analysis of narrative accounts of the fish harvesters (Murray, 2007), a recurrent theme developed inductively was strength and fortitude, which was deductively connected with theorizing around Western notions of maleness.

In a study of the experience of being a refugee, Pavlish (2007) conducted interviews with a sample of 30 refugee men and women. The interview transcripts were then subjected to inductive thematic analysis which produced four main themes for the women (Leaving the good life behind, Worrying about their daughters, Feeling ambivalent about marriage, and Lacking hope) and three themes for the men's narrative accounts (Leaving the good life behind, Having no peace in the heart, and Fearing the future). These themes provided a way of organizing how the refugees made sense of the experience of being a refugee through the stories they told. The analyst reads and rereads the accounts searching for evidence for particular themes and noting how they are developed in different settings and presented in different ways.

In conducting this form of narrative thematic analysis, the researcher might conduct some coding to help them identify specific units within the narrative account. This is a process of breaking down the narrative account before rebuilding it in a more concentrated form. In the inductive form of coding, this process proceeds atheoretically in a bottom-up approach. In the deductive form, the researcher is informed by some theoretical approach that guides their coding. For example, in their study of the narrative accounts of women activists, Dutt and Grabe (2014) were informed by theories of social identity, marginalization, and *conscientization* (consciousness raising). They noted that they were also informed by their own political viewpoints. This attention to the subjectivity

of the researcher emphasizes the double hermeneutic involved in constructing an account of the narrative accounts whereby the researcher is developing
their interpretation of the narrative.

Further, some researchers might use thematic analysis to focus their attention on certain aspects of personal narrative accounts. For example, Savaş and
Stewart (2019) used Braun and Clarke's (2006) guide to thematic analysis to
code a selection of narrative accounts by women activists from the Global
Feminisms Project archive. They were interested in what factors contributed
to the women following an activist life pathway. They began by reading for
familiarization before proceeding to coding and then the development of
themes. Their analysis was a mixture of induction and deduction. They identified inductively five broad coding categories: initial activism, experience of
injustice, metanarrative (of personal narrative in broader context), family
atmosphere, and reflection. They then interpreted these codes within three
themes that they developed deductively: activism as normal, activism as
identity, and activism as action.

Researchers focusing at the personal level can also begin to explore the role
of unconscious processes in the development of narrative accounts. This is the
psychosocial approach developed by Hollway and Jefferson (2012). They argued
that anxiety is inherent in the human condition and that threats to the self,
engender feelings of anxiety. In response to such threats, various psychic
defences are mobilized at the conscious and unconscious levels. In narrating
experiences that could provoke anxiety, the narrator will use various techniques
to reduce the anxiety, (e.g., not discussing the issue or minimizing its importance). In their discussion of psychoanalytic approaches to narrative, Saville
Young and Frosh (2016) stressed the importance of this form of narrative analysis
that draws attention to unintended (or unconsciously intended) messages being
expressed. For this reason, they argued that at we should attend to the "breaks,
pauses and other 'breaches' in smooth sense-making" (p. 2), which reveal
underlying emotional aspects.

This attention to silence in the narrative accounts is particularly important
in understanding trauma narratives. Narrative accounts are not something
people can automatically provide when they are invited to do so. Rather
researchers have indicated that in the face of trauma, individuals are often
at a loss for words. An example of this is a study of the narrative accounts
of refugees. The current period in our history is one of mass migration as
millions of people flee from situations of war and oppression. This has promoted
a turn to research designed to both understand the experience of migration
and also to contribute to enhancing the lives of those who migrate. One such
study is that by Puvimanasinghe et al. (2014), which aimed to further our
understanding of the experiences of African refugees to Australia. This study
focused on the individual life stories of a sample of refugees. These interviews
adopted an unstructured life story approach in which the participants were
invited to tell the story of their lives. One important aspect of the analysis of
the narrative accounts was the concern not just with what the participants
said but also their silences. It is not just the absolute silences but also the

avoidance of certain issues such that, although the narrator may talk about many issues the researcher is also interested in, those topics are ignored.

Interpersonal Level of Analysis

A problem with the intrapersonal approach is the tendency to focus on the structure and content of the narrative to the neglect of the interpersonal context within which it is constructed. The narrator is telling the story to someone and is trying to create a certain impression. The story is a type of discursive performance. Narration is an active process that takes place within an interpersonal and societal context. It is a cocreation that not only conveys the experience but affirms the identity of the narrator. As such, the analyst is concerned with discursive coconstruction of the narrative account not just with what the narrator says but the discursive exchange with the other, real or imagined.

The discursive narrative analyst considers the process of storytelling rather than the intrinsic structure of the narrative. In analyzing the narrative, the aim is not just to consider the structure but the way the story is told in a certain social context and what it says about the identity of the narrator. The researcher considers what both the narrator and the researcher say. Blix et al. (2015) used Bamberg's (1997) threefold positioning approach to explore the narrative construction of the accounts of the lives of two Sami women in Norway. Bamberg proposed three levels in his analysis:

1. Positioning within the story: How is the narrator and others positioned in the story?

2. Positioning with the interaction: How does the narrator position themself with respect to the researcher and audience?

3. Positioning within the broader sociocultural context: How does the narrator position themself with the broader master narrative?

At the first level, the women told a story of a changing Sami life within which they were positioned as being the chosen ones. They felt that they were chosen by someone to live a certain life. This positioning was by an educator or a parent. At the second level, the concern was with the interaction between the researcher and the narrators. The researcher was an educated Norwegian who was interested in the life stories of Sami women. The narrators refer to their own lack of education and their limited knowledge of Norwegian. With a different researcher, their narrative account may have been different. At the third level, the concern is with the wider sociocultural narrative of Sami assimilation and the dependent position of the Sami. This analysis explores the exchanges in the interview how the narrative account is constructed in the immediate and broader social context.

The psychoanalytic approach is also concerned with the interpersonal context within which the narrative is constructed. With the psychoanalytic focus on subjectivity, this concern is explored in terms of intersubjectivity and the role of transference and countertransference (Saville Young & Frosh, 2016).

The researcher explores how these unconscious processes could influence how the narrative is constructed in the interaction.

Positional Level of Analysis

This level of analysis is an extension of the interpersonal level but considers more the power differential between the participants in the exchange. Thus, we can begin to consider the difference between a conversation between two participants of equal status and another where there is a particular power relationship between them. This relationship can be a reflection of gender, class, ethnicity, age, and professional status. In each of these interactions, the character of the narrative is somewhat changed.

This form of analysis considers the power relationship (real or imagined) between the narrator and the audience. It can also consider the positions adopted by the narrator and the subject of the narrative account. In the study by Blix et al. (2015), the Sami women were constructing their narrative account to an educated Norwegian researcher; thus, their narrative account emphasized deficiencies rather than strengths. Another example is the study by Sargeant et al. (2017) of the experience of simulated patients (SPs) who are often used in the training of medical students. This study drew on Harré and van Langenhove's (1991) positioning theory, which argues that people position themselves within particular individual and institutional frames of reference. In this study, a sample of SPs were interviewed about their experience of being a patient. Across all accounts, the SPs positioned the students as future doctors and themselves as patients. Making sense of these positions, the SPs drew on broader social representations of the two roles and of the perceived power differential between doctors and patients.

It is the power differential that is the key issue in the positional analysis. For example, the narrator may avoid discussion of certain topics lest they attract criticism from the perceived superior interviewer. This is the reason for the interest in more causal, free-flowing conversation that aims to reduce this power differential.

Societal Level of Analysis

The final level of analysis is concerned with how the personal narrative is constructed in a particular sociocultural context. This level of analysis can consider the character of the dominant or master cultural narrative and how the personal narrative engages with it. Dominant cultural narratives can be defined as "overlearned stories communicated through mass media or other large, social and cultural institutions and social networks" (Rappaport, 2000, p. 3). They are also materialized through everyday social practices and institutions. In exploring personal narratives at this level, the researcher is analyzing them with reference to these cultural narratives.

However, in any society there may be conflicting cultural narratives. Hammack (2011) explored the conflicting narratives of Palestinian and Israeli youth. In his study, he conducted narrative interviews with a sample of these youth and interpreted the transcripts with reference to conflicting national master narratives. The narratives of the Israeli youth were of a redemptive form emphasizing historic persecution and the need for oppression of the Palestinians. Conversely, the narratives of the Palestinian youth emphasized themes of loss and dispossession and the legitimacy of resistance. The narrative identities of both sets of youth were intertwined in conflicting cultural national narratives.

In their study of contested national identity among German youth, Moffitt et al. (2018) conducted interviews with White and Turkish German young adults. They conducted an analysis of the interview transcripts informed by the idea that there are three dominant narratives of German identity: muted national pride, integration, and Germanness as being ethnically based. Their analysis also adopted a discursive approach exploring the interaction between and researcher and the young adults. They identified sections of the interview that discussed issues of identity. This highlighted how the young Germans negotiated in their discussions how they engaged with the dominant narratives. For example, when asked if their self-definition of being German was sufficient, one participant replied: "I'm used to it, so it doesn't bother me. But sometimes I think it would be much simpler, simply, if I could just say one sentence" (Moffitt et al., 2018, p. 885).

Pederson (2013) used a discursive approach to develop five narrative themes in his analysis of Internet stories of unemployed youth. In those narratives labeled "victim," the narrators positioned themselves as people who had been wronged by the company or the whole economic system. They had done nothing wrong. In those narratives labeled "redeemed identity," the narrator presented the self as someone who had suffered through losing their job but was overcoming it and finding new opportunities. In those narratives labeled "hopeless," the narrator expressed the view that the job loss was a threat to their whole identity. The bitter narratives ranged from self-blame to regret. The final narratives presented an identity of "entitlement" and "astonishment" at losing their job. Overall, Pederson argued that these five narrative identities reflect different ways of engaging with the master narrative of the American Dream that people will achieve success through hard work and determination.

Another example of the connection with societal analysis is the study of frontier narratives conducted by Judith Kleinfeld (2012). This study took place over a 10-year period and combined participant observation and open-ended interviews with 75 people who had moved to live in Alaska. The interviews were transcribed and "analyzed for central themes and images." Kleinfeld explored the transcripts for evidence of engagement with America's frontier romance master narrative. She defined the master romance as "a ritualized story that moves through many imaginative forms—history, literature, art, advertising, film and television" (p. vii). This frontier romance moves through three stages: "the hero leaves the security of home, the hero goes out into the wilderness, the hero forges a better self and forges a better world" (p. viii). In exploring the transcripts, Kleinfeld was surprised to find that her participants, in detailing their life stories, often introduced the influence of iconic stories such as Jack London's *Call of the Wild* or television shows such as those about Davy Crockett. They were constructing a narrative identity drawing on these iconic stories.

Again, there is the importance of the relationship between the researcher and the narrator. Kleinfeld (2012) distinguished between the public stories initially told to the interviewer, which emphasized strength and fortitude, and the private stories, which introduced the trials and difficulties the participants had experienced and were disclosed as they got to know the researcher. Kleinfeld developed three types of personal story told to her by the women participants: the redemption story—how personal suffering was transformed into goodness; the quest for a dream man story, and the story of two individuals together in the wilderness. Each of these personal stories drew on the archetypal romance frontier story.

Caddick et al. (2015) examined the ways a group of male combat veterans talked about masculinity and how, with posttraumatic stress disorder (PTSD), they performed masculinities in the context of a surfing group and what effects this had on their health and well-being. Participant observations and life history interviews were conducted with a group of combat veterans who belonged to a surfing charity for veterans experiencing PTSD. Their analysis explored the ways in which the veterans enacted masculinities in accordance with the values that were cultivated during military service. These masculine performances in the surfing group had important effects both on and for the veterans' well-being. Significantly, the study highlighted how masculine performances could be seen alternately as a danger and as a resource for health and well-being in relation to PTSD.

In exploring the connection between the intrapersonal and the societal, narrative researchers can also explore the development of counternarratives (i.e., narrative accounts that directly conflict with and challenge the dominant sociocultural narrative). For example, Squire (2012) was interested in how the HIV/AIDS patients that she interviewed developed counternarratives to the dominant medical narrative. The narrators were working to challenge the dominant narrative through the story they told. The sharing of these counter narratives can be a means of collective resistance. Squire (2012) suggested in her study of people with HIV/AIDs that their narratives act as an agent for social change through two key processes: similarization and familiarization. *Similarization* is the process by which in their narrative accounts the individual defines himself as similar to others—thus as a person who is having similar experiences can through helping others like himself participate in a larger process of social change. *Familiarization* is the process by which the individual familiarizes their experience by making connections with family and friends and so "rhetorically opposing stigmatisation and building community" (Squire, 2012, p. 62).

The psychoanalytic approach is also concerned with the sociocultural context within which the narrative is constructed. This approach is concerned with how the narrator is positioned within or engages within dominant psychoanalytic narratives. This approach is particularly influential in literary analysis. For example, Cokal (2005) explored how certain psychoanalytic themes inform F. Scott Fitzgerald's 1934 novel *Tender Is the Night*. She argued that Freud provides Fitzgerald with "a plot template that explains character motivation and, on an even deeper level, creates a thematic architecture of loss and destruction that holds up the novel as a whole" (p. 76). In Moscovici's (1961/2008) classic work on social representations of psychoanalysis, he argued that it is not just in literary texts but throughout Western culture that psychoanalytic concepts have become widespread. Thus, in developing narrative accounts of everyday experiences, we can draw on such concepts as the unconscious, the id, and the ego.

Participatory Analysis

In the same way as research participants can work collectively in developing a narrative account of certain experiences, they can also be involved in the analysis. The sharing of stories in a group setting is different from the traditional interview not least because of the impact of the storytelling on members of the group. Awareness of this impact can change the character of the research from collecting narrative accounts to promoting group solidarity. An example of this is the work of Lechner and Renault (2018), who were interested in the migration experiences of refugees. Working with such a traumatized group brought to the fore the ethical issues around the research and its impact on the participants. The researchers saw their research not simply as a means of taking from the participants but as enhancing their strengths. Thus, they designed the project to be a form of action research.

The study by Lykes et al. (1999) illustrated the process of combining narrative analysis with participatory action research. In this study, Lykes worked with a group of Indigenous Mayan women to explore their experiences of violence. The researchers used photography and oral history to develop an account of their experiences. Then they collectively analyzed the corpus of material—"clustering ideas, identifying similarities and differences between and across photos, contrasting holistic analyses of the photographs, as well as exploring processes and/or events that preceded the event" (pp. 218–219). The women moved from describing their own experiences to identifying the similarities in their experiences and the underlying causes of the violence and ways of combatting it.

CONCLUSION

In collecting narrative accounts, the researcher is involved from the outset in selecting and shaping those accounts. Further, in interpreting the accounts, the researcher is creating a new narrative that can potentially empower or undermine the narrator. It is for this reason that researchers must reflect on the personal and theoretical assumptions that guide their research. The ethics of the research needs to be considered at all stages. Mishler (1986) noted that "through their narratives people may be moved beyond the text to the possibilities of action" (p. 117). The researcher plays and an important role in shaping this action potential for personal and social change. W. B. Yeats (1938–1939/2016) worried about the impact of his writing on Irish revolutionaries: "Did that play of mine send out | Certain men the English shot? | Did words of mine put too great a strain | On that woman's reeling brain?" In a less dramatic fashion, the narrative researcher must reflect on the impact of their work on both the narrator and the broader audience. They need to consider how narratives can contribute to personal and social change and how they can participate in these processes of change (Haaken, 2010; Selbin, 2010; Squire, 2021).

REFERENCES

Allport, G. W. (1965). *Letters from Jenny*. Harcourt, Brace. (Original work published 1946)

Anderson, M. E. (2019). Community-based transitional justice via the creation and consumption of digitized storytelling archives: A case study of Belfast's prison memory archive. *The International Journal of Transitional Justice, 13*(1), 30–49. https://doi.org/10.1093/ijtj/ijy030

Bamberg, M. (1997). Positioning between structure and performance. *Journal of Narrative and Life History, 7*(1–4), 335–342. https://doi.org/10.1075/jnlh.7.42pos

Bernard, M., Rickett, M., Amigoni, D., Munro, L., Murray, M., & Rezzano, J. (2015). Ages and stages: The place of theatre in the lives of older people. *Ageing and Society, 35*(6), 1119–1145. https://doi.org/10.1017/S0144686X14000038

Blix, B. H., Hamran, T., & Normann, H. K. (2015). Roads not taken: A narrative positioning analysis of older adults' stories about missed opportunities. *Journal of Aging Studies, 35*, 169–177. https://doi.org/10.1016/j.jaging.2015.08.009

Braun, V., & Clarke, V. (2006). Using thematic analysis in psychology. *Qualitative Research in Psychology, 3*(2), 77–101. https://doi.org/10.1191/1478088706qp063oa

Caddick, N., Smith, B., & Phoenix, C. (2015). Male combat veterans' narratives of PTSD, masculinity, and health. *Sociology of Health & Illness, 37*(1), 97–111. https://doi.org/10.1111/1467-9566.12183

Cokal, S. (2005). Caught in the wrong story: Psychoanalysis and narrative structure in *Tender Is the Night*. *Texas Studies in Literature and Language, 47*(1), 75–100.

Crossley, M. L. (1999). Making sense of HIV infection: Discourse and adaptation to life with HIV positive diagnosis. *Health, 3*(1), 95–119. https://doi.org/10.1177/136345939900300104

De Chungara, D. B. (with Viezzer, M.). (1978). *Let me speak. Testimony of Domitila: A woman of the Bolivian mines*. Monthly Review Press.

Didion, J. (2006). *The year of magical thinking*. Harper.

Dutt, A., & Grabe, S. (2014). Lifetime activism, marginality, and psychology: Narratives of lifelong feminist activists committed to social change. *Qualitative Psychology, 2*(2), 107–122. https://doi.org/10.1037/qup0000010

Flick, U. (2002). *An introduction to qualitative research*. Sage Publications.

Frye, N. (1957). *Anatomy of criticism*. Princeton University Press. https://doi.org/10.1515/9781400866908

Gergen, K., & Gergen, M. (1986). Narrative form and the construction of psychological science. In T. R. Sarbin (Ed.), *Narrative psychology: The storied nature of human conduct* (pp. 22–44). Praeger.

Haaken, J. (2010). *Hard knocks. Domestic violence and the psychology of storytelling*. Routledge.

Hammack, P. L. (2011). *Narrative and the politics of identity. The cultural psychology of Israeli and Palestinian youth*. Oxford University Press.

Harré, R., & van Langenhove, L. (1991). Varieties of positioning. *Journal for the Theory of Social Behaviour, 21*(4), 393–407. https://doi.org/10.1111/j.1468-5914.1991.tb00203.x

Hoecker, R. (2014). Visual narrative and trauma recovery. *Narrative Inquiry, 24*(2), 259–280. https://doi.org/10.1075/ni.24.2.05hoe

Hollway, W. (1989). *Subjectivity and method in psychology: Gender, meaning and science.* Sage Publications.

Hollway, W., & Jefferson, T. (2012). *Doing qualitative research differently. A psychosocial approach* (2nd ed.). Sage Publications.

Kearney, A. J. (2006). Increasing our understanding of breast self-examination: Women talk about cancer, the health care system, and being women. *Qualitative Health Research, 16*(6), 802–820. https://doi.org/10.1177/1049732306287537

Kenten, C. (2010). Narrating oneself: Reflections on the use of solicited diaries. *Forum Qualitative Sozialforschung/Forum: Qualitative Social Research, 11*(2), 6. https://doi.org/10.17169/fqs-11.2.1314

Kleinfeld, J. (2012). *The frontier romance: Environment, culture, and Alaska identity.* University of Alaska Press.

Kusenbach, M. (2003). Street phenomenology: The go-along as ethnographic research tool. *Ethnography, 4*(3), 455–485. https://doi.org/10.1177/146613810343007

Labov, W., & Waletsky, J. (1967). Narrative analysis: Oral versions of personal experience. In J. Helm (Ed.), *Essays on the verbal and visual arts* (pp. 12–44). American Ethnological Society/University of Washington Press.

Langellier, K. M. (1999). Personal narratives, performance and performativity: Two or three things I know for sure. *Text and Performance Quarterly, 19*(2), 125–144. https://doi.org/10.1080/10462939909366255

Lechner, E., & Renault, L. (2018). Migration experiences and narrative identities: Viewing alterity from biographical research. *Critical Hermeneutics, 2*, 1–25.

Lohuis, A. M., Sools, A., van Vuuren, M., & Bohlmeijer, E. T. (2016). Narrative reflection as a means to explore team effectiveness. *Small Group Research, 47*(4), 406–437.

Lykes, M. B., Matco, A. C., Anay, J. C., Caba, A. L., Ruiz, U., & Williams, J. W. (1999). Telling stories—Rethreading lives: Community education, women's development and social change among the Maya Ixil. *International Journal of Leadership in Education, 2*(3), 207–227. https://doi.org/10.1080/136031299293039

McAdams, D. P. (1993). *The stories we live by: Personal myths and the making of the self.* Guilford Press.

McAdams, D. P. (1995). *The life story interview.* Northwestern University.

Mishler, E. G. (1986). *Research interviewing: Context and narrative.* Harvard University Press.

Mishler, E. G. (1995). Models of narrative analysis: A typology. *Journal of Narrative and Life History, 5*(2), 87–123. https://doi.org/10.1075/jnlh.5.2.01mod

Moffitt, U., Juang, L. P., & Syed, M. (2018). Being both German and Other: Narratives of contested national identity among white and Turkish German young adults. *British Journal of Social Psychology, 57*(4), 878–896. https://doi.org/10.1111/bjso.12268

Moscovici, S. (1961/2008). *Psychoanalysis: Its image and its public.* Polity Press.

Murray, M. (2000). Levels of narrative analysis in health psychology. *Journal of Health Psychology, 5*(3), 337–347. https://doi.org/10.1177/135910530000500305

Murray, M. (2007). "It's in the blood and you're not going to change it": Fish harvesters' narrative accounts of injuries and disability. *Work, 28*(2), 165–174.

Murray, M. (2009). Telling stories and making sense of cancer. *International Journal of Narrative Practice, 1*, 25–36.

Murray, M. (2019). Some thoughts on qualitative research in psychology in Europe. *Qualitative Research in Psychology, 16*(3), 508–512.

Murray, M. (2021). Hidden from view: Some written accounts of community activism. In C. Squire (Ed.), *Stories changing lives.* Oxford University Press. https://doi.org/10.1093/oso/9780190864750.003.0005

O'Mahoney, J. (2018). Advocacy and the Magdalene laundries: Towards a psychology of social change. *Qualitative Research in Psychology, 15*(4), 456–471. https://doi.org/10.1080/14780887.2017.1416803

Orwell, G. (2000). *Homage to Catalonia.* Penguin.

Overberg, R., Toussaint, P., & Zwetsloot-Schonk, B. (2006). Illness stories on the Internet: Features of websites disclosing breast cancer patients' illness stories in the Dutch language. *Patient Education and Counseling, 61*(3), 435–442. https://doi.org/10.1016/j.pec.2005.05.010

Pavlish, C. (2007). Narrative inquiry into life experiences of refugee women and men. *International Nursing Review, 54*(1), 28–34. https://doi.org/10.1111/j.1466-7657.2007.00510.x

Pederson, J. R. (2013). Disruptions of individual and cultural identities. How online stories of job loss and unemployment shift the American Dream. *Narrative Inquiry, 23*(2), 302–322. https://doi.org/10.1075/ni.23.2.05ped

Plummer, K. (1994). *Telling sexual stories: Power, change and social worlds.* Routledge.

Puvimanasinghe, T., Denson, L. A., Augoustinos, M., & Somasundaram, D. (2014). Narrative and silence: How former refugees talk about loss and past trauma. *Journal of Refugee Studies, 28*(1), 69–92. https://doi.org/10.1093/jrs/feu019

Rappaport, J. (2000). Community narratives: Tales of terror and joy. *American Journal of Community Psychology, 28*(1), 1–24. https://doi.org/10.1023/A:1005161528817

Riessman, C. K. (2008). *Narrative methods for the human sciences.* Sage Publications.

Rosenthal, G. (2004). Biographical research. In C. Seale, G. Gobo, J. F. Gubrium, & D. Silverman (Eds.), *Qualitative research practice* (pp. 48–64). Sage Publications. https://doi.org/10.4135/9781848608191.d7

Sargeant, S., McLean, M., Green, P., & Johnson, P. (2017). Applying positioning theory to examine interactions between simulated patients and medical students: A narrative analysis. *Advances in Health Sciences Education: Theory and Practice, 22*(1), 187–196. https://doi.org/10.1007/s10459-016-9691-8

Savaş, Ö., & Stewart, A. J. (2019). Alternative pathways to activism: Intersections of social and personal paths in the narratives of women's rights activists. *Qualitative Psychology, 6*(1), 27–46. https://doi.org/10.1037/qup0000117

Saville Young, L., & Frosh, S. (2016). Psychoanalysis in narrative research. In K. Stamenova & R. D. Hinshelwood (Eds.), *Methods of research in the unconscious: Applying psychoanalytic ideas to social sciences* (pp. 199–210). Karnac Books.

Selbin, E. (2010). *Revolution, rebellion, resistance: The power of story.* Zed Books.

Sools, A. M., Tromp, T., & Mooren, J. H. (2015). Mapping letters from the future: Exploring narrative processes of imagining the future. *Journal of Health Psychology, 20*(3), 350–364. https://doi.org/10.1177/1359105314566607

Squire, C. (2007). *HIV in South Africa: Talking about the big thing.* Routledge. https://doi.org/10.4324/9780203946503

Squire, C. (2012). Narratives, connections and social change. *Narrative Inquiry, 22*(1), 50–68. https://doi.org/10.1075/ni.22.1.04squ

Squire, C. (2013). *Living with HIV and ARVs: Three-letter lives.* Palgrave.

Squire, C. (Ed.). (2021). *Stories changing lives.* Oxford University Press.

Stanley, L. (2010). To the letter: Thomas and Znaniecki's *The Polish Peasant* and writing a life, sociologically. *Life Writing, 7*(2), 139–151. https://doi.org/10.1080/14484520903445271

Stanley, L., Salter, A., & Dampier, H. (2012). The epistolary pact, letterness and the Schreiner epistolarium. *a/b: Auto/Biography Studies, 27*(2), 263–293.

Thomas, W. I., & Znaniecki, F. (1918–1920). The Polish peasant in Europe and America (5 Vols.). University of Chicago Press.

Toolis, E. E., & Hammack, P. L. (2015). The lived experience of homeless youth: A narrative approach. *Qualitative Psychology, 2*(1), 50–68. https://doi.org/10.1037/qup0000019

Washington, O. G. M., & Moxley, D. P. (2008). Telling my story: From narrative to exhibit in illuminating the lived experience of homelessness among older African American women. *Journal of Health Psychology, 13*(2), 154–165. https://doi.org/10.1177/1359105307086702

Winskell, K. (2020). Social representations theory and young Africans' creative narratives about HIV/AIDS, 1997–2014. *Journal for the Theory of Social Behaviour, 50*, 1–14. https://journals.plos.org/plosone/article?id=10.1371/journal.pone.0227878

Yeats, W. B. (2016). The man and the echo. In *Collected poems*. Macmillan. (Original work published 1938–1939)

7

Discursive Psychology

Capturing the Psychological World as It Unfolds

Jonathan Potter

The following transcript is from a family mealtime. Anna has not been eating; her sister Katherine has (note that names have been changed throughout).

Discursive psychologists work with material of this kind. The psychological world here is unfolding naturally, not staged by the researcher. It is captured on digital video (allowing us, for example, to see the spitting on Line 9) and transcribed in a way that captures delay, overlap, intonation, and volume (Hepburn & Bolden, 2017). This is the stuff of real life. It records how the interaction unfolds for the participants—it is not a functional MRI recording of Mum's or Anna's brain, nor has the family been interviewed about what is going on. However, their actions, and their psychological implications, are intelligible to one another. The building of interaction for intelligibility makes interaction, and language learning, possible. For example, Mum's "you need to eat your <u>di</u>nner please" on Line 1 is recognizable to all parties, and most relevantly to Anna, as an action directing her to eat (Craven & Potter, 2010). The strangled, half-sobbing sound that Anna produces is recognizably resisting this direction.

Portions of this chapter were previously published in the chapter "Discourse Analysis and Discursive Psychology" by J. Potter, in H. Cooper, P. M. Camic, D. L. Long, A. T. Panter, D. Rindskopf, and K. J. Sher (Eds.), *APA Handbook of Research Methods in Psychology: Vol. 2. Research Designs: Quantitative, Qualitative, Neuropsychological, and Biological* (pp. 119–138), 2012, American Psychological Association (https://doi.org/ 10.1037/13620-008). Copyright 2012 by the American Psychological Association.

https://doi.org/10.1037/0000252-007
Qualitative Research in Psychology: Expanding Perspectives in Methodology and Design, Second Edition, P. M. Camic (Editor)

FIGURE 7.1. Mum Gazes at Anna

Note. Low-resolution images are used deliberately in this chapter to preserve the
anonymity of research participants.

```
01 Mum:      Anna: you need to eat your dinner plea:se,
02           (0.4)   [
03 Anna:     #↓Mm:::[uhmuh ((protest plus sob))
04 Mum:             [((Gaze to Anna until end of line 17))
05           (0.4)
06 Anna:     °°↑uh
07           (.)
08 Mum:      >↑Come on↑<
09 Anna:     ((spitting/dribbling to line 16))/(1.3)
10 Mum:      ↑What you doing.
11               (2.0)
12 Mum:      [((does double-take, continued gaze to A))]
13           [                (1.7)                     ]
14 Mum:      ↑What'you ↑↑dhoing.
15           (1.9)
16 Mum:      NO:.=That's naughty.
```

These materials allow us to consider how the interaction unfolds, and each bit of the interaction is relevant to what came before and what came after. After Mum's direction for Anna to eat, she not only doesn't eat but, but after Mum's urging on Line 8, she starts to spit or dribble. There is something fascinating about this. Food is being ejected just where Mum most pressed the need for eating. It is not just ejecting food, but it is recognizable (by us as analysts, and by Mum as participant) as defiance. After a directive is issued, a relevant next item is compliance; doing the opposite is defiance.

After the onset of the defiant spitting or dribbling, Mum does something striking. Although she is gazing straight at Anna (see Figure 7.1) and can see very clearly what is going on, she issues an interrogative: "↑**What you doing.**", repeated on Line 14 with pumped up intonation (↑**What'you ↑↑dhoing**.) when Anna continues to spit. Although she is using the syntax of a question, Mum is not in pursuit of information. The interrogative form nevertheless treats Anna as able to answer the question. It works to draw attention to Anna's delinquency, treats her as a conscious agent of her own wrongdoing, and puts her in the position of either reporting that delinquency or defying the requirement to answer. Mum stretches the wait after these interrogatives (Lines 13 and 15) where the moral flaws in Anna's behavior are, as it were, dangling for all to see, before providing the stressed injunction followed by the moral categorization: "NO:.=That's naughty." Mum's contributions can be seen in a profound way as "shaming interrogatives" (Potter & Hepburn, 2020).

In these concrete materials that can be readily studied, some of the big issues of social relations are played out. We see the sociological truism that power and resistance go together. We have a way into questions of socialization that have been at the heart of developmental psychology (Hepburn, 2019), and we have a way at looking at how issues of emotion and embodiment play out in natural interaction (Edwards & Potter, 2020; Hepburn & Potter, 2012; Potter & Hepburn, 2020). These are basic themes of discursive psychology.

Discursive psychology begins with psychological matters as they arise for people as they live their lives. It studies how psychological issues and objects are constructed, understood, and displayed as people interact in both everyday and institutional situations. The preceding example is from a mundane mealtime, but discursive psychological work has looked at a range of institutional settings as well as situations where interaction is digitally mediated (Meredith & Potter, 2013). It focuses on questions such as the following:

- How do medical personnel manage issues of empathy in end-of-life hospice care conversations (Ford et al., 2019)?

- What roles do "first impressions" play in naturalistic settings (Humă, 2015)?

- How does a successful female politician manage multiple dilemmas when attending to gender and misogyny in her own situation (Sorrentino & Augoustinos, 2016)?

Questions of this kind involve a focus on matters that are "psychological" for people as they act and interact in particular settings—in families, in workplaces, on public political platforms, and so on.

The nature and scope of "psychology" are understood very differently in discourse analytic work compared with other approaches such as social cognition. Instead of starting with inner mental or cognitive processes, with behavioral regularities, or with neural events that are happening below and behind interaction, it starts with the public displays, constructions, and orientations of participants. The history of psychology has tended to work with a picture of an individual perceiving the world and its features directly. However, in actual settings, people are overwhelmingly working with versions of events, actions, and relationships that are built in talk and texts. People read news accounts and tweets that formulate a candidate supreme court judge inflamed by unjustified accusations or displaying the unstable fury of an abuser; couples' counseling sessions are filled with vivid descriptions of episodes from relational history. And these descriptions are themselves built to perform actions.

The social world immerses people in talk and texts that can be studied for their psychological implications. That discourse is the primary arena for human action, understanding, and intersubjectivity (Schegloff, 1992). We communicate with one another, express our desires and fears, and come to understand others' feelings and concerns primarily though talking. It is important to recognize that discursive psychology is not a psychology *of* language; it is psychology working *through* language (Edwards, 1997; Stokoe, 2018).

Contemporary discursive psychology is a program that overwhelmingly works with naturalistic materials: audio and video records of people interacting with one another within their everyday and institutional settings (Potter & Shaw, 2018). One conclusion of this work is that social life is organized with an extraordinary degree of granularity and orderliness; to understand it properly involves following its real-time unfolding as people respond to one another's talk and display, moment by moment, a subtle, practical understanding of one another. In real life, psychology is in motion; that is how it is experienced. Discursive psychology is an approach that attempts to capture that motion. As analysts, we have the advantage of being able to freeze time and rerun the sequences, holding them up to the light for inspection and bringing to bear the now-considerable body of research findings to help unlock their operation.

Discursive psychology is an approach to psychological life rather than a method that can be used to answer questions developed with different assumptions. Philosophically, it can be linked to Ludwig Wittgenstein's view of psychology dispersed across multiple language games and his attack on the idea of each individual having a private language of thought. Discursive psychology's basic methodological and analytic principles follow from its meta-theoretical, theoretical, and conceptual arguments, although these are further supported through the empirical fruitfulness in particular studies (Tileagă & Stokoe, 2015).

This chapter briefly reviews the development of discursive psychology, outlines some of its basic features, and overviews its core methodological stages and procedures; it ends with a discussion of prospects and debates.

DEVELOPMENT OF DISCURSIVE PSYCHOLOGY

Discourse analysis is a broad interdisciplinary field that has evolved in different forms and with different assumptions within linguistics, sociology, cultural studies, and psychology. The coverage here highlights three main strands of work.

Strand 1: Interviews and Repertoires

From the mid-1980s onward, the focus of discourse analytic work in psychology was on identifying the different "interpretative repertoires" that are used to build social action (Potter & Wetherell, 1987). An interpretative repertoire is a cluster of terms, categories, and idioms that are closely conceptually organized. Repertoires are typically assembled around a metaphor or vivid image. In most cases, interpretative repertoires are identified by analyzing a set of open-ended interviews in which participants address a set of different themes.

The repertoire notion is derived from Nigel Gilbert and Michael Mulkay's (1984) pioneering study of the different repertoires that scientists use to construct their social world when they are writing research papers and arguing with one another. It was further developed by Margaret Wetherell and Jonathan Potter (1992) in a major study of the way Pākehā (White) New Zealanders constructed versions of social conflict and social organizations to legitimate particular versions of relations between groups. Much of the interest was in ideological questions of how the organization of accounts, and the resources used in those accounts, could be used to help understand the reproduction of broad patterns of inequality and privilege. Put simply, how did White Europeans undermine Maori land claims and other historically grounded grievances without appearing self-interested or racist?

This strand of work was closely allied to, and influenced by, Michael Billig's (1996) rhetorical psychology and incorporated the central notion of ideological dilemmas (Billig et al., 1988), which itself builds on the notion of interpretative repertoires from Potter and Wetherell (1987). For example, Billig (2002) found in talk about the British royal family a web of arguments and assumptions that work to sustain the familiar social hierarchies and avoid questioning privilege.

This work was based largely on the analysis of open-ended interviews, or group discussions, that provided the ideal environment for generating the kinds of ideological themes or interpretative repertoires that were a key topic of study. Note that the interviews were conceptualized as an arena for generating ideological talk rather than a pathway to participants' beliefs or feelings. This kind of analysis has been a continuing theme in discourse research, particularly on topics such as gender, race, and nationalism (for a recent example on immigrant cultural identity in family therapy, see Sametband & Strong, 2018).

Strand 2: Discursive Psychology and Constructionism

From the early 1990s, the main focus of discursive psychology work moved away from the analysis of open-ended interviews to studies of records of naturalistic interaction such as conversations, legal argument, newspaper reports, parliamentary debates, and news interviews. Its focus was on the role that descriptions of the world and of psychological states play in the formation of particular actions, such as blamings, and the management of accountability.

The earlier style of work was developed under the title *discourse analysis*; an explicit *discursive psychology* was refined out of this (Edwards & Potter, 1992). Discursive psychology developed with a distinctive approach to constructionism focused on texts and talk (Potter, 1996; Potter & Hepburn, 2008). This work continues to critically engage with mainstream cognitive psychology, respecifying notions such as memory, scripts, emotion, attribution, and perception in terms of interactional practices (Edwards, 1997; Hepburn, 2004; Stokoe & Hepburn, 2005). For overviews of these two strands of work, see Augoustinos and Tileagă (2012), Hepburn (2003, Chapter 7), Humă et al. (2020), and McKinlay and McVittie (2008).

Strand 3: Discursive Psychology and Sequential Analysis

From around the middle of the 1990s, these two strands of discursive psychology work started to be joined by a third. The specific characteristics of this strand reflect a continuing and deeper engagement with conversation analysis (Sidnell & Stivers, 2012). Indeed, at times these two fields blur together. This engagement with conversation analysis is reflected in distinct characteristics:

1. working with a corpus of conversational materials;
2. intensive use of audio or video recording and transcript;
3. use of existing discursive and conversation analytic studies to leverage claims;
4. attention to psychological phenomena in both everyday and institutional settings; and
5. analysis of word choice is supported by systematic attention to prosody, delivery, and embodied action.

Sally Wiggins (2016) offered a book length overview of studies in this strand of discursive psychology. This strand of work sustained the interest in the way facts are built as factual and the way conduct is made accountable. However, it increasingly exploits the sophisticated understanding of sequence, position, and turn design provided by conversation analysis. Indeed, there has been a convergence of issues in both conversation analysis and discursive psychology because both are concerned with mundane epistemics and the management of intersubjectivity (Bolden et al., 2019; Heritage, 2012). Hepburn and Potter (2021) presented an overview of the essentials for conducting conversation analysis.

This strand of work also provides an approach to social categories and how they are conversationally and sequentially occasioned in, for example, race and gender talk (Durrheim et al., 2015; Stokoe, 2012). There is continued analytic and theoretical discussion of the place of cognitivism in analysis (e.g., te Molder & Potter, 2005) and work on interaction in psychological methods (Gibson, 2019). Discursive psychology and conversation analysis have converged to study the ways psychological matters play out in practices taking place in institutional settings such as psychotherapy (Peräkylä, 2012), counseling (Kiyimba & O'Reilly, 2016), mediation (Sikveland & Stokoe, 2016), environments supporting atypical populations (Antaki & Wilkinson, 2012), and others. Much of the change in discursive psychology in the past decade has involved broadening and deepening; this combines with increasing engagement with conversation analysis which is itself fast evolving.

GENERAL THEORETICAL ORIENTATION OF DISCURSIVE PSYCHOLOGY

Discursive research treats discourse as having four key characteristics.

1. Discourse Is Action Oriented

Discourse is the primary medium for action. Actions may be relatively discrete objects associated with speech act verbs—an admonishment, say, or a compliment. Yet they can also be complex and embedded within institutional practices without a clear speech act verb, such as when questions are used to indirectly deliver advice in "person-centered" counseling (Butler et al., 2010). There is no lay term for this practice; even the semitechnical description "client-centered" is only a global catchall for a range of discrete practices. As work in the second strand of discursive psychology has shown, actions are often performed indirectly via descriptions, sometimes thereby avoiding the "on-the-record" accountability of speech act constructions. Crucially, discursive psychological work differs from mainstream psychology of language because of its focus on how actions are formed, and responded to, rather than treating language as a pathway to putative mental objects. This also distinguishes it from a range of humanistic and qualitative approaches such as interpretative phenomenological analysis (e.g., Smith & Fieldsend, Chapter 8, this volume).

2. Discourse Is Situated

Discursive psychology treats action as situated in three senses. First, action is situated *sequentially*. That is, actions are situated within the specifics of unfolding conversation. They are located in time, orienting what has just happened and building an environment for what happens next. The massive significance of this context has been shown repeatedly in conversation analysis. For example, when an invitation is issued, this sets up an ordered array of possible next actions, of which accepting or turning down are most relevant. It is not possible simply to ignore the invitation without this itself being, potentially, interpretable as the specific and consequential action of ignoring the invitation. Moreover, when the recipient accepts or rejects an invitation, the recipient is locally displaying an understanding that an invitation is precisely what has been issued, so the turn by turn unfolding of talk provides an ongoing check on understanding (Schegloff, 1992). Explicating the intricate order of interaction has been the central project of conversation analysis (Schegloff, 2007).

Second, action is situated *institutionally*. Institutions often require special identities that are pervasively relevant—patient, hostage negotiator, therapist—such that actions will be understood in relation to those identities. And they often involve collections of local interactional goals that all parties orient to (Heritage & Clayman, 2010). These institutional goals are often themselves refined from broader everyday practices (compare Edwards, 2008, on "intention" in police interrogation with Potter & Hepburn, 2003, on "concern" in helpline calls). The specific analytic relevance here is how psychological matters are introduced, constructed, and made relevant to the setting's business (Edwards & Potter, 2001).

Third, action is situated is *rhetorically*. Billig (1996) emphasized the pervasive relevance of rhetorical relations, even where there is an absence of explicit argument (as Myers (2004) showed in an analysis of "opinion" discourse). Discourse research highlights, for example, the way descriptions are built to counter actual or potential alternatives (Potter, 1996). A major theme in discursive psychology is the way epistemic issues are managed using a wide range of conversational and rhetorical resources (Potter, 2020; Potter & Hepburn, 2008). This theme cuts through, and is deeply relevant to, the conventional psychological topics of memory, attribution, attitudes, and persuasion.

3. Discourse Is Both Constructed and Constructive

Discourse is *constructed* out of a range of resources—grammatical structures, words, categories, rhetorical commonplaces, repertoires, conversational practices, and so on, all of which are precisely assembled in real time with relevant prosody, timing, and so on. These resources, their use, and their conditions of assembly can become topics of discursive study.

Discourse is *constructive* in the sense that it is used to build versions of psychological worlds, of social organizations, action, and of histories and broader structures. Such versions are an integral part of action. Some discursive research focuses on the way constructions are built and stabilized and how they are made neutral, objective, and independent of the speaker. People are skilled builders of descriptions; they have spent a lifetime learning this art. Discursive analysis aims to reveal the complex and delicate work that goes into this seemingly effortless building. There are complex issues yet to be fully explicated at the boundary of discursive constructive work and conversation analysis focused on epistemics (Heritage, 2012; Potter, 2020).

4. Discourse Is Produced as Psychological

Discursive psychologists focused on the way psychological matters play out in interaction. People can construct their own and other's dispositions, assessments, and descriptions as subjective (psychological) or objective. For example, an assessment of a minority group can be couched in the language of attitudes (I am generally positive about Polynesian Islanders) or build as an objective feature of this social group using a range of descriptive procedures (Potter & Wetherell, 1988).

Edwards (2007) distinguished "subject-side" from "object-side" descriptions and highlighted the way producing discourse in either of these ways can be a central element in a range of practices. A person can be described as having a legitimate complaint about something in the world (an "object-side description") or as whining (a "subject-side description" that highlights things wrong with the speaker rather than the world; Edwards, 2005). Object-side and subject-side assessments may be combined to form different kinds of actions (Potter et al., 2020). One of the features of the normative organization of interaction is that it provides a baseline calibration for marking out a speaker's psychological investment in any claim, action, or outcome.

SIX STAGES IN THE EXECUTION OF DISCURSIVE RESEARCH

The discussion of the different stages in the execution of discursive research is illustrated by examples from a program of research focused on psychological issues and interaction in family mealtimes.

Let me start with the broadest of considerations. We chose to focus on family mealtimes as they provided materials rich in issues to do with interaction, psychology, and asymmetry. This is a site where parties are often trying to manage one another's behavior. Food and eating are often an area of family conflict. There are a wide range of descriptions, assessments, and emotional displays, particularly in families with younger children. There is a more pragmatic reason for focusing on this topic, as well: Traditional mealtimes when a small group sit around a single table are ideal for capturing continuous interaction between a set of parties on video. There are also broader applied interests in parenting, socialization, diet, and eating disorders of different kinds. One subsample included families in which one child has a serious enduring health condition, opening up new and possibly applied topics.

For simplicity, I will break the research process into six stages: access and consent; data collection; transcription and data management; developing research questions; corpus building and preliminary analysis; and developing and validating analysis. In practice, these stages are somewhat overlapping—transcription, data management, and question development tend to iterate through all stages of the research process.

Stage 1: Obtaining Access and Consent

One of the features that makes discursive psychology different from most other psychological methods is its primary focus on audio or video records of interaction that takes place in natural settings. This makes the process of gaining access and consent, developing appropriate ethics scripts, and working closely with participants in a way that sustains and merits a strong degree of trust an integral part of the research process. Gaining access and consent can be a challenge—particularly in sensitive institutional settings. Nevertheless, experience shows that with the right approach and a proportionate commitment of time and effort trust can be developed and consent can be obtained for working in the most sensitive of sites. In the past 20 years, discursive research has focused, for example, on neonatal intensive care, family therapy, police interrogation, neighbor mediation, physiotherapy for stroke patients, hostage negotiation, and social work assessments of abusive parents, as well as everyday conversations between families and friends.

Ethics procedures depend on local institutional review board protocols and are sensitive to different institutional requirements. Digital records allow for a range of anonymization, even when using video materials. Audio programs such as Adobe Audition allow easy editing out or obscuring of proper names and other identifying details. A wide range of video programs include effects that can disguise the identity of individuals while allowing the research team, or conference audience, to see physical layouts of interaction and features, such as bodily orientation or even eye gaze. Discourse researchers have become more sophisticated about the informed element of informed consent, and particularly at tailoring information to groups and individuals with different linguistic skills. In institutional settings, discourse researchers work closely with the relevant professionals to mitigate possible risks of compromising anonymity or putting sensitive information into the public domain, while collecting materials that are, as far as possible, uninfluenced by the processes of collection. Discourse workers sometimes use secure, password-protected storage for the most sensitive materials.

The mealtimes study recruited families with the help of undergraduate and PhD student researchers. At this stage, the aim was not to be representative of different demographics or ethnic groups. Indeed, by starting with families that had regular shared meals at a table, the sample was probably tilted toward middle-class professional people. They were shown research illustrations to indicate the kind of work that we were conducting. We used a standard ethics protocol with the parents and developed a specific, simplified version for younger children. This made clear that audio and video recordings would be played in one-on-one and research group meetings. It also made clear that short, anonymized extracts would appear in research publications. Participants could tick a further option that gave permission for the researchers to show short video clips in conferences or embedded in training materials. We emphasized that we were not trying to collect material that the participants considered private; we suggested that they delete any recording that they wanted to remain private. In practice, this did not appear to be an issue.

Ironically, across the range of different discursive psychological studies, it is often the professionals rather than clients or laypeople that are most guarded. They sometimes worry that their professional practice will be found wanting, perhaps because the materials they were trained with used unrealistic idealizations of what interaction should look like. David Silverman (1997) referred to this as the "problem of the Divine Orthodoxy": Practitioners feel they are not living up to idealized, normative standards completely removed from actual practice and wish that failure not be exposed. Hepburn and Potter (2003) covered issues in obtaining access to professional settings in detail.

Stage 2: Data Collection

The main aim in discursive research is to develop an archive of high-quality records of interaction in the setting under study. There are no hard-and-fast rules for the size of such a collection. Even small amounts of material can be a basis for useful research, but the more material there is, and the more appropriate the sampling, the more questions will become analytically tractable and the more confident we can be in research conclusions. Some considerations are paramount here.

First, the quality of recording has an exponential knock-on effect on transcription and analysis. Time and resources devoted to getting high-quality recordings will pay off handsomely when it comes to transcribing the recordings and working with them in data sessions. Hours are wasted relistening to a key piece of talk submerged in a loud recording hum or attempting to work out whether a child has taken a mouthful of food or just put the fork near her mouth. Modern recording technology is compact and combines high sound and image quality with high-volume storage.

Second, if embodied activities are available to participants, they can be relevant for what they are doing. That means that it will be important to have video records of face-to-face interaction (or non–face-to-face interaction that is technologically mediated with a visual modality). Ideally, more than one camera can help with issues of eye gaze and facial expressions, but there is a compromise in simplicity and intrusion.

Third, once the whole process has been put into place, actually making recordings is almost always simpler and easier than analyzing and transcribing them. This means that researchers should err on the side of collecting more data rather than less. Digital recordings can be stored cheaply, and they provide an important resource for future research.

Fourth, it is common for participants record their own data. This minimizes the reactivity arising from extended researcher involvement and allows the participants to be in control of ethical issues. This means that simplicity is a key consideration. We gave families a single small recorder with high-capacity storage and asked them to record 15 or so mealtimes. Sometimes a meal was recorded with only some of the participants in shot—but with plenty of redundancy, we were able to focus on the best-quality recordings.

In terms of sample size, we started with around 15 meals from each of five families. Then we added in smaller collections of meals from three families with a child with health issues, led by Laura Jenkins (2012). This allowed a focus on pain expressions in family settings. A further collection was set up under the direction of Alex Kent (2011) that returned to three families for annual recordings. At this stage, we were not sure what we were looking for; we wanted a sample that would help us with the generation of research questions and would have enough interaction to be able to build collections of specific phenomena. For example, we had no difficulty assembling large collections of directives or sufficient numbers of threats to build a study.

Stage 3: Data Management and Transcription

As research projects evolve, effective data management is vital. Much of this is focused on systems of folders that collect recordings, different levels of transcript, and analytic notes. Such a system can facilitate data sharing (discourse research is often collaborative) and can assist full backup of data and analysis. We used cloud storage to facilitate data sharing and analytic sharing. Encryption and secure storage may be required depending on the agreements with participants and the sensitivity of the materials.

Data management of this kind is a prelude for data reduction. This involves the systematic building of a particular corpus that is of a size that is small enough to be easily worked with but large enough to be able to make appropriate generalizations.

In our case, each family was assigned a pseudonym and given a root folder. Within this, we had a subfolder with all the ethics agreements scanned and some potentially relevant ethnographic background (ages, occupations, ethnicity, and so on). Each meal had its own subfolder with the raw video within it clearly labeled (e.g., Crouch meal 07), and it also included transcript with different levels of detail.

Discourse research works with both the original audio or video recordings and the transcript. Unlike some other approaches, transcripts and recording are used together and are both essential to the research.

It is common to use two forms of transcript. A basic "first pass" transcript is often generated by a transcription service. This has just the words rendered as effectively as the service can hear them. This kind of transcript has two uses:

1. It allows the researcher to quickly go through a stretch of interaction and get an overall feel for what is there. This can be a particularly important shortcut where there are many hours of recordings.

2. It is searchable, allowing a sift through an entire set of materials (quickly when using an indexing program) for the kinds of phenomena that can be identified through the appearance of individual lexical items or transcriber descriptions.

The second form of transcription is an attempt to capture on the page features of the delivery of talk relevant to participants. The standard system used in discursive psychology and conversation analysis was developed by Gail Jefferson. The best full overview is by Hepburn and Bolden (2017). It was designed to be easy to learn and simple to generate using standard word processing software. It encodes features such as overlaps and pauses, volume and emphasis, features of prosody such as rising and falling intonation, and features of the speed of delivery. These are captured because they are the features of talk that are attended to by participants and consequential for interaction.

Jeffersonian transcript is extremely labor-intensive. The ratio of record time to transcription time can be 1:20 or more, with key factors being the quality of the recording, the complexity of the interaction, and whether there are nonvocal elements that need to be represented. It also takes time to learn to do good-quality transcription. It is necessary both to understand the roles of the different symbols and to learn to apply them consistently. This is facilitated by listening to the audio that goes with a high-quality transcript; a good, open-access web resource with examples is found online (http://rucal.rutgers.edu/transcription/).

Because of the time investment in producing quality transcript, there are rarely sufficient resources for completely transcribing a full set of recordings. Various criteria can be used to decide what to transcribe and in what order. After getting a first-pass transcript of most of the meals, we chose a small number (because they seemed typical or simply seemed interesting or intriguing for one reason or another) and produced high-quality Jeffersonian transcript for some sequences to facilitate question generation.

Stage 4: Developing Research Questions

It has been common in psychological research to stress the importance of formulating a clear research question before starting the research. And there are often good reasons for such a rule, particularly when using experimental designs, questionnaires, or open-ended interviews. However, with discursive research, much of the discipline comes from working closely with a set of naturalistic materials—records of people living their lives in a particular setting. And many of the questions formulated for more traditional research have a causal form—what is the effect of X on Y—which is rarely appropriate for discourse work. Rather than posing a causal question, the focus is often on attempting to explicate the workings of a social practice, perhaps with the ultimate aim of making broader sense of the setting as a whole (reporting abuse to a helpline, crisis negotiation with a potential suicide). And this often means that questions are continually refined over the course of a program of work and a study within that program.

One of the benefits of working with naturalistic materials is that they produce their own challenges that lead to novel questions. Collecting high-quality recordings of natural interaction helps the research open up to new ideas; they often feature actions or occurrences that are unexpected or not easily understood with the repertoire of explanatory concepts available in contemporary psychology. This can provide an exciting starting point for analytic work. A common practice in the discursive community is to use different levels of engagement with the materials to generate questions. A key part of this is often data sessions with analytically minded colleagues. There is no set model for such sessions. One approach is to take a short, relatively self-contained sequence; play the video repeatedly; and then spend a few minutes where each participant writes notes on one feature of the sequence. These observations are then shared, they are compared with the video, unnoticed features may be highlighted, and this may be a basis for question generation or even developing a specific hypothesis about a phenomenon or a practice to be pursued in further materials.

It is customary in psychology to develop questions and hypotheses from existing theory and research traditions. The research instruments are built around these questions, with the consequence that progress is often restricted to a familiar terrain. It is hard to overestimate how novel it is for psychologists who have spent their careers designing experiments based around a small number of variables or analyzing interview responses on restricted topics to be opened up to the world in motion in all its richness.

As we engaged with the collection of family meals, we were intrigued by the sheer amount of time that parents spent trying to get their children to eat—to finish food or eat putatively more healthy food. This encouraged us to take as an early theme requests and directives, and how they are recognized, how they are built, and how they are resisted. And we started to look at the orderly progression from mere noticings (you have some beans left), to requests (would you eat your beans), to directives (eat those beans—now). And what happens next in this progression? We were intrigued by the occurrence of threats (if you don't eat those beans, there will be no dessert) and different kinds of admonishments (what did I say, that's naughty). Alongside these things are the use of food descriptions and assessments. These topics cut across, and provide new perspectives on, more standard psychological topics such as the nature of socialization, the operation of social influence and behavior modification, the role of emotion, the nature of bodily conduct.

Stage 5: Analysis

In some forms of psychological research, data analysis is a relatively brief element, conducted in an afternoon with the support of statistical software such as SPSS. In discursive psychology, in contrast, the analytic stage of work is often the most time-consuming and the most crucial. The same materials may be subject to different analyses that identify different practices or highlight different themes. A high-quality data set is an enormously rich and generative resource.

Discursive psychological analysis often uses a systematic trawl through the materials to build a corpus of examples. This early trawl is typically inclusive rather than exclusive with the aim of including central examples and borderline cases. It is expected that such a corpus will be refined. When analytic understanding has been improved it is likely that some of the cases will be dropped from the corpus and new cases will be seen as appropriately part of the corpus.

The process of analysis will involve increasingly precise attempts to specify what is going on—how some practice or practices are unfolding. This stage is akin to hypothesis testing because the researcher often has a number of initial ideas that cannot survive a careful exploration of cases that account for the specific details of what is there.

Something that struck us as interesting and deserving of study early on was the appearance of threats. The interest was partly in how threats are built and responded to and partly in what they can tell us about how social influence operates as a practical issue for participants. Take the following from Hepburn and Potter (2011).

Crouch 06 6:40 (Crouch is the family pseudonym, 06 the meal number and 6:40 the time)

```
01  Mum:    [An]na?
02          (1.6)
03  Anna:   U↑hhuh ((more of a sob than a response))
04          (0.6)
05  Mum:    If you don' eat your dinner:,  (0.4)
06          there'll be no pudding.
07          [             (1.2)              ]
08  Anna:   [((spits mouthful onto her plate))]
09  Mum:    That's horrible.
```

Some observations about this fragment: First, it does not come out of nowhere; it is positioned after a period of Anna not eating and what interaction analysts would describe as a cline of increasingly intensified attempts at parental behavioral modification. Note Mum's use of "Anna?" with what can be heard as warning intonation on Line 1, perhaps implying that something bad will happen if she does not head it off by eating. Second, note the way Mum manipulates contingencies she has control of in Lines 5 and 6 using the "if–then" construction. The (expected in this family) reward of pudding will be removed if Anna does not eat. This is the threat (in other examples from the corpus, instead of withholding rewards, the contingency might be banishment to the bottom step or the bedroom).

Third, note that a threat is an intensified attempt at influence (beyond noticing, requesting or directing), but as such, it sets up the potential for intensified resistance. Issuing a threat sets up *defiance* as a potential next action. When Anna spits out her food in Line 8, it is not just spitting, it is a highly visible rejection of the strong push for compliance embodied in the threat. Precisely because there is so much interactional pressure on generating the particular outcome, not going along with the pressure can be rendered a "strong" thing to do.

There is a strong analytic temptation to view material such as this from the parents' perspective and to see socialization as a one-way process that has adults acting on children. One of the magical features of working with naturalistic materials such as these is that we have the actions, orientations, and perspectives of both parent and child. We can supplement analysis of the way threats are formed in parents' talk with analysis of how they are variously complied with, defied, ignored, or managed in other ways. In the following extract from the same family, Mum and Anna are having a meal together (see Figure 7.2).

Here Anna announces that she is finished and gradually pushes her chair back from the table (Lines 6–7). All the while, she looks sideways in a way that disattends to possible expressions of disapproval from Mum—a frown, say. In this household leaving the table is subject to a range of rules, including ask first. Mum responds by saying Anna's name with a stretch and prosody that might be described as "warning intonation"; this suggests displeasure and

FIGURE 7.2. Anna Drinks, Watched by Mum

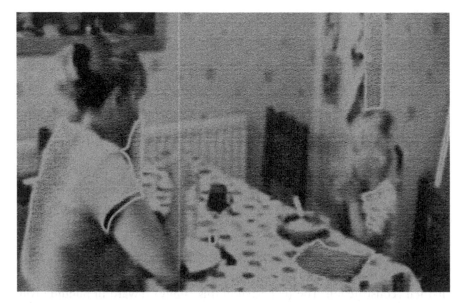

Note. Low-resolution images are used deliberately in this chapter to preserve the anonymity of research participants.

<u>Crouch 08 9:15</u>

```
01 Anna:    Now (all funnish:.)((with mouth full))
02          (0.5)
03 Mum:     Mm:.
04          (0.7)
05 Mum:     Finish your mouthful.
06          [                  (8.1)              ]
07 Anna:    [((Gradually pushes back from table))]
08 Mum:     Anna::,!
09          (1.1)
10 Mum:     If y'want some pudding you sit still
11          on your chai:r don't you.
12          (2.6)
13 Anna:    [((leans forward to get drink, gulps noisily))]
14          [                  (9.6)                        ]
15 Anna:    .hh Ha:ve [you: finsd mu::m, ]
16 Anna:              [((cup over mouth))]
17 Mum:     Nearly:
```

maybe more to come, although not immediately. At this point Anna stops pushing back and looks directly at Mum. She has not left the table, but neither has she pulled back in.

Here Mum issues a somewhat softened threat: "If y'want some pudding you sit still on your chai:r don't you." It has the conditional structure of a threat, but the tag question format produces it as something that Anna already knows, and therefore as a reminder. In socialization terms, it builds Anna as someone who already knows this social rule. The tag question takes the form of a yes–no polar question. But Anna does not produce an answer, nor does she display compliance by returning her chair to the table. Neither does she continue to push back, which here, after a warning and threat, would show defiance. Instead, she reaches forward to take her drink while closely watching Mum, who closely watches Anna. This close mutual inspection is no doubt attentive to cues from each about what they will do next—each needs to calibrate their actions relevantly to the other. Anna has, by taking the drink, produced herself as still (somewhat) at the table (see Figure 7.2) while actually having moved her chair quite far back. In a sense, this is compliance as Anna has not fully gotten down off the chair, but it is *softened* compliance (compliance with a flavor of defiance). This is an alternative, then, to full compliance and full defiance.

More generally, Mum is manipulating the contingencies that she is in control of to encourage Anna's eating, but while this sets up an environment for Anna's next action, it does not cause that action, just as Mum's threat to withhold the dessert it oriented to her eating but (plainly) does not cause her to eat. The challenge for the discursive psychologist is to capture and unpack the action, interaction, and its organization in a way that does justice to the specifics of the interaction and the unfolding situated understandings of the participants. This involves careful and specific focus on the way the parties are building actions, how these are coordinated, and the various lexical, prosodic, and embodied elements that contribute to that building.

Stage 6: Validation

In practice, there is not a clearcut distinction between analysis and validation. Building a successful analysis that works and is attentive to all the details of the materials that are being studied is already a major part of validating the findings. Nevertheless, there are some considerations that are worth highlighting:

1. *Participants' orientations.* One of the enormous virtues of working with open ended, naturally occurring materials is that they provide a major resource in validating findings that is absent in most other psychological methods. That resource is the turn-by-turn nature of interaction. Any turn of talk is oriented to what came before, and it sets up an environment for what comes next. At its simplest, when someone provides an acceptance it provides evidence that what came before was an invitation. If an analyst claims that, say, some conversational move is an indirect invitation we would want to see evidence that the recipient is orientating (even indirectly) to its nature as an invitation.

2. *Deviant cases.* Apparently deviant cases are often analytically and theoretically informative. They can show whether a generalization is robust or breaks down. For example, studies of media interviews show that interviewees rarely treat interviewers as accountable for views expressed in their questions (Heritage & Clayman, 2010). There are occasional deviant cases, however, where a news interviewer is treated as responsible for some view. However, rather than showing that this pattern is not normative, they show precisely its normative organization.

3. *Coherence.* The accumulation of findings from different studies allows new studies to be assessed for their coherence with what comes before. For example, work on the organization of food assessments in mealtime conversations (Wiggins, 2002, 2019) builds on and provides further confirmation of earlier work on assessments and compliments (Pomerantz, 1984). Looked at the other way around, a study that clashed with some of the basic findings in discourse work would be treated with more caution—although if its findings seemed more robust, it would be more consequential.

4. *Readers' evaluation.* One of the most fundamental features of discursive psychology compared with other psychological perspectives is that its claims are accountable to the detail of the empirical materials and that the empirical materials are presented in a form that allows readers, as far as possible, to make their own checks and judgments. Discourse articles typically present a range of extracts from the transcript alongside the interpretations that have been made of them. This form of validation contrasts with much traditional experimental and content analytic work, where it is rare for anything close

to "raw data" to be included or for more than one or two illustrative codings to be provided (and then often in an appendix). Sacks's (1992) ideal was to put the reader as far as possible into the same position as the researcher with respect to the materials. Such an ideal is unrealizable in practice, but discourse work is closer than many analytic approaches in psychology.

CONCLUSION: PROSPECTS FOR DISCURSIVE PSYCHOLOGY

For much of the past 100 years, psychology has developed as a hypothetico-deductive science that has conceptualized the world in terms of the effects and interactions of variables on one another that can best be assessed using experiments analyzed using multivariate statistics. This methodological apparatus has been combined with a cognitivist or neuroscientific form of explanation where the causes of human action are seen to lie within individuals. In some ways, this has been a hugely impressive and successful enterprise. Yet this has had a number of unintended consequences that restrict its approach to human action.

First, the search for general relationships that underlie behavior has the consequence of moving research away from the specifics of human action. Action is typically modeled, restricted, or reported and transformed into the kind of counts that are amenable to multivariate analysis. On the extremely rare occasion that records of actual interaction in natural settings are used, it is quickly transformed into counts (using, say, content analysis—see Potter & Shaw, 2018).

Second, this search for general relationships combined with the need for simple controlled designs means that little attention has been paid to the nature and organization of the rich local and institutional settings in which human conduct invariably takes place.

Third, the hypothetico-deductive approach has led researchers away from careful descriptive studies in favor of studies that start with some kind of relationship or model to be tested. This combines with the legacy of the competence performance distinction that has become a central part of modern cognitivism and treats "performance data" as enormously messy and something to be bypassed by focusing, via hypothetical models, directly on competence.

In contrast to this, discursive psychology starts with the concrete particulars of human action recorded in specific settings with minimal researcher interference. In many ways it is a classically empiricist enterprise. Its analytic approach is focused on the way practices are built in real time and how their organization and intelligibility is dependent on the normative organization of talk. Psychological matters come into discursive psychological study through their emergence as issues that are relevant for participants. Instead of attempting to capture underlying competence, it is focused on how psychological matters are public and intelligible.

Thus, the study of threats (a) started with materials collected as parts of actions that the participants would do irrespective of their researched status, (b) first involved a descriptive project that started to explicate the form through which threats are built, (c) focused on threats in terms of broader action sequence, and (d) explicated the different ways in which threats could be responded to (with compliance, defiance, or sometimes softened compliance). The key focus is on threats as an object for the participants and how they are built to do the business of behavior change, and how they succeed and fail in achieving this outcome.

The program of discursive psychology offers an alternative approach that respecifies core psychological notions such as cognition, perception, embodiment, and emotion and offers an alternative analytic approach that places the situated understandings of the participants at the core of the research. Its focus on people's practices makes it distinct from both mainstream experimental psychology and from a range of alternative qualitative methods (narrative psychology, interpretative phenomenological analysis, ethnography) that typically use open-ended interviews as their main technique of data generation.

REFERENCES

Antaki, C., & Wilkinson, R. (2012). Conversation analysis and the study of atypical populations. In T. Stivers & J. Sidnell (Eds.), *The handbook of conversation analysis* (pp. 533–550). Blackwell. https://doi.org/10.1002/9781118325001.ch26

Augoustinos, M., & Tileagă, C. (2012). Twenty five years of discursive psychology. *British Journal of Social Psychology*, *51*(3), 405–412. https://doi.org/10.1111/j.2044-8309.2012.02096.x

Billig, M. (1996). *Arguing and thinking: A rhetorical approach to social psychology* (2nd ed.). Cambridge University Press.

Billig, M. (2002). *Talking of the royal family*. Routledge. https://doi.org/10.4324/9780203414910

Billig, M., Condor, S., Edwards, D., Gane, M., Middleton, D. J., & Radley, A. R. (1988). *Ideological dilemmas: A social psychology of everyday thinking*. SAGE Publications.

Bolden, G. B., Hepburn, A., & Potter, J. (2019). Subversive completions: Turn-taking resources for commandeering the recipient's action in progress. *Research on Language and Social Interaction*, *52*(2), 144–158. https://doi.org/10.1080/08351813.2019.1608096

Butler, C. W., Potter, J., Danby, S., Emmison, M., & Hepburn, A. (2010). Advice-implicative interrogatives: Building "client-centered" support in a children's helpline. *Social Psychology Quarterly*, *73*(3), 265–287. https://doi.org/10.1177/0190272510379838

Craven, A., & Potter, J. (2010). Directives: Entitlement and contingency in action. *Discourse Studies*, *12*(4), 419–442. https://doi.org/10.1177/1461445610370126

Durrheim, K., Greener, R., & Whitehead, K. A. (2015). Race trouble: Attending to race and racism in online interaction. *British Journal of Social Psychology*, *54*(1), 84–99. https://doi.org/10.1111/bjso.12070

Edwards, D. (1997). *Discourse and cognition*. SAGE Publications.

Edwards, D. (2005). Moaning, whining and laughing: The subjective side of complaints. *Discourse Studies*, *7*(1), 5–29. https://doi.org/10.1177/1461445605048765

Edwards, D. (2007). Managing subjectivity in talk. In A. Hepburn & S. Wiggins (Eds.), *Discursive research in practice: New approaches to psychology and interaction* (pp. 31–49). Cambridge University Press. https://doi.org/10.1017/CBO9780511611216.002

Edwards, D. (2008). Intentionality and *mens rea* in police interrogations: The production of actions as crimes. *Intercultural Pragmatics, 5*(2), 177–199. https://doi.org/10.1515/IP.2008.010

Edwards, D., & Potter, J. (1992). *Discursive psychology*. SAGE Publications.

Edwards, D., & Potter, J. (2001). Discursive psychology. In A. W. McHoul & M. Rapley (Eds.), *How to analyse talk in institutional settings: A casebook of methods* (pp. 12–24). Continuum International.

Edwards, D., & Potter, J. (2020). A word is worth a thousand pictures: Language, interaction, and embodiment. In S. Wiggins & K. Osvaldsson Cromdal (Eds.), *Discursive psychology and embodiment: Beyond subject–object binaries* (pp. 277–303). Palgrave. https://doi.org/10.1007/978-3-030-53709-8

Ford, J., Hepburn, A., & Parry, R. (2019). What do displays of empathy do in palliative care consultations? *Discourse Studies, 21*(1), 22–37. https://doi.org/10.1177/1461445618814030

Gibson, S. (2019). Obedience without orders: Expanding social psychology's conception of "obedience." *British Journal of Social Psychology, 58*(1), 241–259. https://doi.org/10.1111/bjso.12272

Gilbert, G. N., & Mulkay, M. (1984). *Opening Pandora's box: A sociological analysis of scientists' discourse*. Cambridge University Press.

Hepburn, A. (2003). *An introduction to critical social psychology*. SAGE Publications. https://doi.org/10.4135/9781446218884

Hepburn, A. (2004). Crying: Notes on description, transcription, and interaction. *Research on Language and Social Interaction, 37*(3), 251–290. https://doi.org/10.1207/s15327973rlsi3703_1

Hepburn, A. (2019). The preference for self-direction as a resource for parents' socialisation practices. *Qualitative Research in Psychology, 17*, 1–19. https://doi.org/10.1080/14780887.2019.1664679

Hepburn, A., & Bolden, G. B. (2017). *Transcribing for social research*. SAGE Publications. https://doi.org/10.4135/9781473920460

Hepburn, A., & Potter, J. (2003). Discourse analytic practice. In C. Seale, D. Silverman, J. Gubrium, & G. Gobo (Eds.), *Qualitative research practice* (pp. 180–196). Sage Publications.

Hepburn, A., & Potter, J. (2011). Threats: Power, family mealtimes, and social influence. *British Journal of Social Psychology, 50*(Pt. 1), 99–120. https://doi.org/10.1348/014466610X500791

Hepburn, A., & Potter, J. (2012). Crying and crying responses. In A. Peräkylä & M.-L. Sorjonen (Eds.), *Emotion in interaction* (pp. 195–211). Oxford University Press. https://doi.org/10.1093/acprof:oso/9780199730735.001.0001

Hepburn, A., & Potter, J. (2021). *Essentials of conversation analysis*. American Psychological Association.

Heritage, J. (2012). Epistemics in action: Action formation and territories of knowledge. *Research on Language and Social Interaction, 45*(1), 1–29. https://doi.org/10.1080/08351813.2012.646684

Heritage, J. C., & Clayman, S. (2010). *Conversation analysis and institutional interaction*. Cambridge University Press.

Humă, B. (2015). Enhancing the authenticity of assessments through grounding in first impressions. *British Journal of Social Psychology, 54*(3), 405–424. https://doi.org/10.1111/bjso.12089

Humă, B., Alexander, M., Stokoe, E., & Tileagă, C. (2020). Special issue on discursive psychology. *Qualitative Research in Psychology, 17*(3), 313–335. https://doi.org/10.1080/14780887.2020.1729910

Jenkins, L. (2012). *Children's expressions of pain and bodily sensations in family mealtimes* [Unpublished doctoral thesis]. Loughborough University.

Kent, A. (2011). *Directing dinnertime: Practices and resources used by parents and children to deliver and respond to directive actions* [Unpublished doctoral thesis]. Loughborough University.

Kiyimba, N., & O'Reilly, M. (2016). The value of using discourse and conversation analysis as evidence to inform practice in counselling and therapeutic interactions. In M. O'Reilly & J. N. Lester (Eds.), *The Palgrave handbook of adult mental health* (pp. 520–539). Palgrave Macmillan. https://doi.org/10.1057/9781137496850_27

McKinlay, A., & McVittie, C. (2008). *Social psychology and discourse*. John Wiley & Sons. https://doi.org/10.1002/9781444303094

Meredith, J., & Potter, J. (2013). Conversation analysis and electronic interactions: Methodological, analytic and technical consideration. In H. L. Lim & F. Sudweeks (Eds.), *Innovative methods and technologies for electronic discourse analysis* (pp. 370–393). IGI Global. https://doi.org/10.4018/978-1-4666-4426-7.ch017

Myers, G. (2004). *Matters of opinion: Talking about public ideas*. Cambridge University Press. https://doi.org/10.1017/CBO9780511486708

Peräkylä, A. (2012). Conversation analysis in psychotherapy. In T. Stivers & J. Sidnell (Eds.), *The handbook in conversation analysis* (pp. 551–574). Blackwell. https://doi.org/10.1002/9781118325001.ch27

Pomerantz, A. M. (1984). Agreeing and disagreeing with assessments: Some features of preferred/dispreferred turn shapes. In J. M. Atkinson & J. Heritage (Eds.), *Structures of social action: Studies in conversation analysis* (pp. 57–101). Cambridge University Press.

Potter, J. (1996). *Representing reality: Discourse, rhetoric and social construction*. SAGE Publications. https://doi.org/10.4135/9781446222119

Potter, J. (2012). Discourse Analysis and discursive psychology. In H. Cooper, P. M. Camic, D. L. Long, A. T. Panter, D. Rindskopf, and K. J. Sher (Eds.), *APA handbook of research methods in psychology: Vol. 2. Research designs: Quantitative, qualitative, neuro-psychological, and biological* (pp. 119–138). American Psychological Association. https://doi.org/10.1037/13620-008

Potter, J. (2020). Discursive psychology: A non-cognitivist approach to practices of knowing. In K. Krippendorf & N. Halabi (Eds.), *Discourses in action: What language enables us to do* (pp. 71–85). Routledge. https://doi.org/10.4324/9780429356032-4

Potter, J., & Hepburn, A. (2003). I'm a bit concerned—Early actions and psychological constructions in a child protection helpline. *Research on Language and Social Interaction*, *36*(3), 197–240. https://doi.org/10.1207/S15327973RLSI3603_01

Potter, J., & Hepburn, A. (2008). Discursive constructionism. In J. A. Holstein & J. F. Gubrium (Eds.), *Handbook of constructionist research* (pp. 275–293). Guilford Press.

Potter, J., & Hepburn, A. (2020). Shaming interrogatives: Admonishments, the social psychology of emotion, and discursive practices of behaviour modification in family mealtimes. *British Journal of Social Psychology*, *59*(2), 347–364. https://doi.org/10.1111/bjso.12346

Potter, J., Hepburn, A., & Edwards, D. (2020). Rethinking attitudes and social psychology—Issues of function, order, and combination in subject-side and object-side assessments in natural settings. *Qualitative Research in Psychology*, *17*(3), 336–356. https://doi.org/10.1080/14780887.2020.1725952

Potter, J., & Shaw, A. (2018). The virtues of naturalistic data. In U. Flick (Ed.), *The SAGE handbook of qualitative data collection* (pp. 182–199). SAGE Publications. https://doi.org/10.4135/9781526416070.n12

Potter, J., & Wetherell, M. (1987). *Discourse and social psychology: Beyond attitudes and behaviour*. SAGE Publications.

Potter, J., & Wetherell, M. (1988). Accomplishing attitudes: Fact and evaluation in racist discourse. *Text*, *8*(1–2), 51–68. https://doi.org/10.1515/text.1.1988.8.1-2.51

Sacks, H. (1992). *Lectures on conversation* (Vols. I & II, G. Jefferson, Ed.). Basil Blackwell.

Sametband, I., & Strong, T. (2018). Immigrant family members negotiating preferred cultural identities in family therapy conversations: A discursive analysis. *Journal of Family Therapy, 40*(2), 201–223. https://doi.org/10.1111/1467-6427.12164

Schegloff, E. A. (1992). Repair after next turn: The last structurally provided defense of intersubjectivity in conversation. *American Journal of Sociology, 97*(5), 1295–1345. https://doi.org/10.1086/229903

Schegloff, E. A. (2007). *Sequence organization in interaction: Vol. 1. A primer in conversation analysis*. Cambridge University Press. https://doi.org/10.1017/CBO9780511791208

Sidnell, J., & Stivers, T. (Eds.). (2012). *The handbook of conversation analysis*. Wiley-Blackwell. https://doi.org/10.1002/9781118325001

Sikveland, R., & Stokoe, E. (2016). Dealing with resistance in initial intake and inquiry calls to mediation: The power of "Willing." *Conflict Resolution Quarterly, 33*(3), 235–254. https://doi.org/10.1002/crq.21157

Silverman, D. (1997). *Discourses of counselling: HIV counselling as social interaction*. SAGE Publications.

Sorrentino, J., & Augoustinos, M. (2016). "I don't view myself as a woman politician, I view myself as a politician who's a woman": The discursive management of gender identity in political leadership. *British Journal of Social Psychology, 55*(3), 385–406. https://doi.org/10.1111/bjso.12138

Stokoe, E. (2012). Moving forward with membership categorization analysis: Methods for systematic analysis. *Discourse Studies, 14*(3), 277–303. https://doi.org/10.1177/1461445612441534

Stokoe, E. (2018). *Talk: The science of conversation*. Robinson.

Stokoe, E., & Hepburn, A. (2005). "You can hear a lot through the walls": Noise formulations in neighbour complaints. *Discourse & Society, 16*(5), 647–673. https://doi.org/10.1177/0957926505054940

te Molder, H., & Potter, J. (Eds.). (2005). *Conversation and cognition*. Cambridge University Press. https://doi.org/10.1017/CBO9780511489990

Tileagă, C., & Stokoe, E. (Eds.). (2015). *Discursive psychology: Classic and contemporary issues*. Routledge. https://doi.org/10.4324/9781315863054

Wetherell, M., & Potter, J. (1992). *Mapping the language of racism: Discourse and the legitimation of exploitation*. Harvester/Wheatsheaf and Columbia University Press.

Wiggins, S. (2002). Talking with your mouth full: Gustatory mmms and the embodiment of pleasure. *Research on Language and Social Interaction, 35*(3), 311–336. https://doi.org/10.1207/S15327973RLSI3503_3

Wiggins, S. (2016). *Discursive psychology: Theory, method and applications*. Sage Publications. https://doi.org/10.4135/9781473983335

Wiggins, S. (2019). Moments of pleasure: A preliminary classification of gustatory mmms and the enactment of enjoyment during infant mealtimes. *Frontiers in Psychology, 10*, 1404. https://doi.org/10.3389/fpsyg.2019.01404

8

Interpretative Phenomenological Analysis

Jonathan A. Smith and Megumi Fieldsend

Interpretative phenomenological analysis (IPA; Smith et al., 2009) is a well-established qualitative approach developed to investigate individuals' lived experiences. It is concerned with the particular experiences that individuals have and their meaning making that occurs in relation to those experiences. This approach enables researchers to conduct microlevel explorations of meanings that tap into the wholeness of experiences a person encounters. In trying to understand lived experience, IPA is collaborative because it explores experiential meanings through the interpretative work between the researcher and the participant rather than being a theory-driven examination.

In this chapter, we first outline the theoretical underpinnings of IPA, then offer a description of the general principles of the IPA research process. We then present an example of IPA analysis with data taken from a PhD research project conducted by the second author (Fieldsend, 2019) under the supervision of the first author (Smith) on the lived experience of involuntary childlessness. Finally, we point to methodological developments currently happening in the IPA world. Our aim with this chapter, then, is to offer readers an understanding of what IPA is and how it works, and we do this by outlining the key steps in the research process.

THEORETICAL UNDERPINNINGS OF IPA

IPA is phenomenological in its focus on lived experience, and through interpretative work, it attempts to explore and understand individuals' personal experiences. Phenomenology is often referred to as a "philosophical movement"

https://doi.org/10.1037/0000252-008
Qualitative Research in Psychology: Expanding Perspectives in Methodology and Design,
Second Edition, P. M. Camic (Editor)

(Moran, 2000, p. 287), with philosophers debating the study of "human experience and the way in which things are perceived as they appear to consciousness" (Langdridge, 2007, p. 10). There are many phenomenological thinkers examining different ways of understanding lived experience. Among them, Husserl, Heidegger, Merleau-Ponty, and Sartre are particularly influential theorists.

Husserl was the first to write programmatically of the phenomenological perspective. He emphasized that a personal experience needs to be examined in the way that it manifests itself to us, so that we can find the essence of a given phenomenon (experience). In doing so, he expressed the necessity for us to "go back to the things themselves" (Husserl, 1900/2001, p. 168). He also introduced a method that involves the process of phenomenological reduction, bracketing all judgments, preconceptions, and assumptions. This, Husserl believed, would offer a way of seeing and describing "the experiential content of consciousness" (Smith et al., 2009, p. 12) and also set out scientific and phenomenological foundations (Ashworth, 2008).

Heidegger (1923/1999), who was Husserl's student, acknowledged the latter's phenomenological concept of going back to the *things themselves*; however, he was notably recognized for his divergence from Husserl's viewpoint, focusing more on ontological perspectives, or the "doctrine of being" (p. 1). Heidegger used the term *Dasein* to refer to human beings, emphasizing that Dasein is always "being-*there*-involved-in" (p. 5, emphasis in original) the world. Heidegger pointed out that our experiences have relatedness with others, things, and environments but also represent engagement "in time, standing at the present moment, but aware both of past and future" (Warnock, 1970, p. 50). Heidegger here added the aspect of temporality in phenomenological investigation. He also argued that to understand human beings living in such complex modalities, "hermeneutical explication" (Heidegger, 1923/1999, p. 25) or interpretative endeavor is needed, and this is a way of making hidden experiential meanings visible.

While IPA acknowledges Husserl's major contribution to the establishment of phenomenological principles, it also takes account of Heidegger's hermeneutic recasting of phenomenology (Larkin et al., 2006). This contrasts it with what is described as descriptive phenomenology, the leading proponent of which is Giorgi. Giorgi's project is to construct an empirical phenomenological method that stays as true as possible to the principles of Husserl. Therefore, descriptive phenomenological research works toward the investigation of "what is the essential structure" of "x" (Lopez & Willis, 2004, p. 731) by searching for "the most invariant meaning for a context" (Giorgi, 1997, p. 244).

IPA, in contrast, sees empirical phenomenological research as involving interpretation, emphasizing that "without the phenomenology, there would be nothing to interpret; without the hermeneutics, the phenomenon would not be seen" (Smith et al., 2009, p. 37). This refers also to the practical focus of IPA: Researchers engage actively in interpreting participants, who are attempting to interpret their own experiences. Hence, a double hermeneutic is involved (Smith et al., 2009). Interpretative explication in IPA is, therefore, a vital part of the explorative processes toward understanding a personal lived experience.

IPA also draws on the embodied and existential conceptions of Merleau-Ponty and Sartre. Merleau-Ponty (1945/1962) stated, "The world is not what

I think, but what I live through" and "the world is what we perceive" (p. xviii). Merleau-Ponty here emphasized perception. Perception is referred to as the manifestation each individual finds in their own meaningful world (Matthews, 2006) and is "an experience of my body-in-the world" (Merleau-Ponty, 1945/1962, p. 164). Merleau-Ponty focused on embodied features of our existence, offering another dimension of lived experience: *lived body*. (Lewis & Staehler, 2010). The concept of lived body is importantly associated with one's *felt sense* of human experience. His phenomenological stance on the-person-in-context and embodied-self in the world contribute a holistic dimension to understanding human existence.

Sartre is another key figure who brought existential ontology into phenomenological psychology (Lewis & Staehler, 2010). In his view, "man[kind] will only attain existence when he [or she] is what he [or she] purposes to be" (Sartre, 1946/1948, p. 28), meaning to refer to the importance of *becoming* rather than *being*. The process of becoming involves one's responsibility to an act where many possibilities and relatedness to others exist. Sartre stressed how individuals making sense of their experiences are influenced by personal as well as social relationships. Moran (2000) explained:

> Sartre's most interesting discussions concern the manner by which we come to consciousness of ourselves in the light of how others see us. Not only do we give ourselves projects, we also have ourselves as we are viewed by others, our being-for-others (etre-pour-autrui). This is a "third-person" perspective on ourselves. (p. 388)

Sartre's existential philosophy adds the necessity of understanding human experience in relation to the existence of others because our experiences are "contingent upon the presence and absence of our relationships to other people" (Smith et al., 2009, p. 20).

The final distinctive feature of IPA is idiography. An idiographic approach, in contrast to a nomothetic one, concerns the particular—or a researcher's commitment to a detailed analysis of each case in its own right—and it is a crucial feature of IPA (Smith et al., 1995). IPA tries to understand lived experience as unique to each individual and "not subordinated to a general theoretical position" (Smith et al., 1995, p. 62). The hermeneutic and idiographic principles of IPA can provide ways to explore the personal world as far as is possible and also experience-close understandings of a topic under investigation. In practice, an IPA study usually presents an analysis of more than one participant's experience. A key part of the skill in IPA is constructing the narrative account to enable the reader to appreciate both the patterning of similarity among participants and, at the same time, the particular way in which that patterning is manifest for different individuals. Thus, the aim is to produce an analysis that speaks to both convergence and distinctiveness in participants' experience.

PUTTING IPA INTO PRACTICE

In this section, we take readers through the stages involved in conducting an IPA study. See Smith et al. (2009) for a more detailed guide.

Formulating a Research Question

Essentially, researchers using IPA have interests in exploring and understanding processes where individuals are trying to make sense of things of significance that happen to them in their lives. IPA is, therefore, useful when a research question concerns the personal experiential meanings a particular topic (event or thing) has for a particular person in a particular context. Phenomenological thinking also plays a part in ways of developing research questions. These aim to be broad and open. To illustrate this, following are research questions informing some actual IPA studies:

- What is the first experience of depression like (Smith & Rhodes, 2015)?
- How do athletes experience social support after retirement from elite sport (Brown et al., 2018)?
- What is it like for cancer patients to be involved in an improvisational music therapy program (Pothoulaki et al., 2012)?
- What is it like for Japanese mothers to live with multiple children who have intellectual disabilities (Kimura & Yamazaki, 2013)?
- How do engineering students in the United States experience the transition to becoming engineers (Huff et al., 2018)?

Purposive Homogenous Sampling

To investigate detailed accounts of individuals who share a particular context that is significant to those people, IPA principally uses homogeneous and purposive sampling. The aim is to look in detail at the meaning of experience for individuals in this particular group, and, by keeping the group relatively homogenous, analysis is able to concentrate on that meaning making at the individual level. IPA values the richness of qualitative insights over quantitative significance, and therefore, the number of participants in IPA research tends to be small. To maintain homogeneity, inclusion and exclusion criteria are usually set for a study. A typical sample size for a doctoral dissertation is now eight to 10. This is a large enough number to give a rich, patterned analysis of convergence and divergence within the sample but also small enough to be manageable within the time constraints. However, it is important not to reify a certain number. There is a wide range of factors to be taken into account when considering sample size, for example, complexity of design, richness of data, and number of studies being conducted. Doing IPA well is time-intensive, and the aim is to do a good analysis of a reasonably small sample rather than a superficial analysis of a large number of people. By sampling within a homogeneous group, one is able to focus on the micro-psychological features of people in that group as opposed to broader demographic variables. Thus, for example, in examining the experience of starting a new job, one might decide to have the following inclusion criteria:

- female
- age 25–35
- educated to bachelor's degree level
- working in the retail sector

When conducting the analysis, it is likely one will find similarities and differences between participants. Because the sample is relatively homogeneous, one is more able to focus on psychological characteristics or individual features connected with the differences rather than the demographic variables that have been kept constant. Of course, in reality, one needs to be pragmatic, and there will be many contextual factors that affect who one ultimately includes in the study.

Collecting Data

Semistructured interviews are the most common method for generating detailed experiential data for IPA studies (Smith et al., 2009; Smith & Osborn, 2008). Semistructured interviews allow a researcher to be flexible in exploring areas that matter to the participant without being fixed to a particular order or overly controlled by prepared questions (Smith, 1995). Unlike structured interviews, this further allows the researcher to engage in those elements the participant is trying to make sense of and provides rich data of what the participant is "expert on" (Smith, 1995, p. 12). This is consistent with the phenomenological underpinnings of IPA. The aim of the questioning is to enable the participant to reveal their account of their experience as far as possible in its own terms. The interview schedule can be developed as a guide for semistructured interviews. At the beginning of an interview, it is important to establish rapport with the participant for them to feel comfortable as they engage in the interview. Maintaining sensitivity to and curiosity about the participant's responses is vital in gaining rich experiential data. Each interview is, in general, audio-recorded and transcribed verbatim.

Analysis[1]

IPA offers a systematic analytical procedure that can rigorously investigate both within a case and across cases. The first stage of the analysis starts with reading and rereading the first transcript to familiarize oneself with the world of the participant. This provides the researcher with an entry point to capture what seems to be of importance to the participant. This is followed by the initial note-taking stage. Here, the researcher comments on, for example, concerns, ideas, and impressions through a line-by-line reading. There are no set rules to this, but the notes the researcher makes usually draw on descriptive, linguistic, and conceptual levels of importance. Initial notes are then converted into "a concise and pithy statement of what was important in

---

[1] This chapter introduces some improvements to the terminology used in IPA arising from discussion between Jonathan and two other senior figures in IPA, Paul Flowers and Michael Larkin, while preparing the second edition of the IPA book (Smith et al., 2021). What used to be called *emergent themes* are now called *experiential statements*. This is a better term for this stage of analysis. Then, a collection of *experiential statements* is clustered to form a personal *experiential theme*. How this works is explained in detail in this chapter.

the various comments attached to a piece of transcript" (Smith et al., 2009, p. 92), transforming it into an experiential statement. Experiential statements, therefore, speak of the elements of the participant's experience together with the researcher's psychological and conceptual interpretations of them, but based on the participant's words. The next stage involves looking for connections across experiential statements and clustering those that gravitate toward each other. Clusters of experiential statements become personal experiential themes and are compiled in a table for the first case with subthemes where appropriate and evidenced with a short extract taken from the original transcript. This process is then repeated for each case in turn, only after which the following stage is to examine patterns across cases.

Writing Up

Writing up is a process whereby the researcher presents a full account of the results of the analytic process for the reader. Personal experiential themes are explicated and evidenced with quotes from participants followed by close interpretative readings of those quotes. It is also in writing up that new insights often emerge, and therefore, analysis continues into writing up in IPA. A good IPA paper offers a close interpretative analysis of participants accounts, and so it invites readers to engage in the world of other people and to feel "what it is like" to experience the phenomenon under investigation.

Ethical Issues

It is important that empirical researchers in the human and social sciences conduct their research ethically. IPA researchers need to think about the ethical implications of the particular features of their research practice. One of the avowed aims of IPA is to present clear and detailed accounts of individual lived experience. This is a worthy aim, but one must be extremely careful while attempting to implement this aim that one respects as far as is possible the confidentiality of the participants whose accounts are being presented. Participants names should be changed to pseudonyms and transcripts should be checked carefully so that extracts presented do not reveal other identifying information.

A second aspect of good practice is particularly salient in the typical semistructured interviews that IPA researchers conduct. The less structured form of this interview process means that, however carefully the interview has been planned, the participant may become distressed in talking about some aspect of their experience. It is good ethical practice for the research team to prepare for this possibility when constructing the schedule, discussing the interview technique, and considering appropriate ways to respond should the participant get upset. The responses should be proportionate to the degree of distress the participant is displaying. For example, usually it is sufficient to stop and let the participant take a moment, pull back slightly and move the conversation to a different area, or ask if the participant would like to take a short break. Only in the very unusual event that the distress was greater or more prolonged would one need to invoke a higher level of intervention. If you are a student, then what is appropriate in such circumstances should be discussed in advance with an adviser or supervisor.

A Worked Example: Searching for Meaning in Involuntary Childlessness in Midlife

This section describes the application of IPA to a research project on involuntary childlessness, which was conducted by the second author (Fieldsend) under the supervision of the first author (Smith).

Background and Research Question

Having children and creating a family is a major transition in adult development, bringing new meanings to life. For involuntarily childless people, however, living a life without the children they hoped for can impact their experience in a range of ways. Although the majority of studies in relation to involuntary childlessness have tended to focus on infertility and fertility treatments from medical or clinical viewpoints, little is known about the personal experiences of involuntary childlessness of people living beyond the phase of trying for a baby and the psychological impact that the absence of children has on them in everyday life (Fieldsend, 2018).

Given the lack of knowledge available in the extant literature on human reproduction and psychosocial adult development in relation to involuntary childlessness, this exploratory research set out to investigate the following research question: "What is it like for women in midlife living with involuntary childlessness?"

The Participants

In keeping with IPA's commitment to purposive homogeneous sampling, this study invoked the following inclusion criteria:

- women aged between 45 and 55;
- in long-term heterosexual relationships;
- no adopted children, stepchildren, or children of a partner from a previous relationship; and
- no longer trying to have a child.

Initially, 12 women were recruited via three leading childless support networks in the United Kingdom. However, of the 12, one was found to not meet the criteria and so was excluded from the study.

Data Collection

Data were collected via semistructured interviews. Rather than following a typical chronological sequence of past, present, and future, we employed an interview schedule (see Exhibit 8.1) that started with questions on the present, then looked at the future, and only then asked about the past. It was felt that it would be easier for participants to talk about their past after building a good rapport and establishing trust with the interviewer because talking about past experiences requires a lot of thought and reflection.

EXHIBIT 8.1

Interview Schedule

I. Life at the moment

  1. Could you tell me a bit about yourself?
     Prompts: job, family, hobbies, interests

  2. What sort of things do you usually do on weekends or when you have free time?
     Prompts: How do you spend your free time?
     Do you go out often on weekends? If so, with whom?

  3. What things make you feel good about yourself?
     Prompts: In what sort of situation do you find yourself feeling fulfilled?

II. Goals and meaning of life

  4. How do you feel about being your age (e.g., 50)?
     Prompts: What is the best thing about being (e.g., 50)?
     How about the worst thing about being (e.g., 50)?
     Mentally, physically, emotionally, spiritually?

  5. Do you think of yourself as having goals that you are working toward? If so, could you tell me about them?
     Prompts: Do you see yourself working toward something?

  6. When you think about your future, say in five years' time, what do you hope to be doing?

  7. Could you tell me who the important people are in your life?
     Prompts: Could you tell me why? In what ways?
     Personally? Socially? Family?

III. The past

  8. Could you tell me about the best thing that has ever happened in your life?
     Prompts: Personally? Socially?

  9. Could you tell me about the biggest change that has ever happened in your life?
     Prompts: Personally? Socially? Could you tell me about the biggest decision you've ever made?

  10. Do you see yourself as being the same person as you were when you were 25?
      Prompts: In what ways are you similar or different?

If there has been no reference to children, then I will bring it in here:

  11. You said that you wanted to have children. How do you feel about it now?

  12. Is there anything else that you feel we haven't covered that you would like to tell me?

Note. This interview schedule first appeared in Megumi Fieldsend's unpublished PhD thesis (Fieldsend, 2019) and was later reproduced in "'Either Stay Grieving, or Deal With It': The Psychological Impact of Involuntary Childlessness for Women Living in Midlife," by M. Fieldsend and J. A. Smith, 2020, *Human Reproduction, 35*(4), (supplementary material). Copyright 2020 by Oxford University Press. Reprinted with permission.

All participants spontaneously raised the topic of children and started to talk about their experiences, typically in conjunction with other everyday situations (e.g., going out with friends with or without children or doing things that are enjoyable). The participants completed the interviews, all of which lasted between 52 and 95 minutes, and all were audio-recorded and then transcribed verbatim.

Analysis: Renee's Case

We now introduce one of the participants, Renee (pseudonyms are used to protect confidentiality throughout this chapter) and take readers through the key analytical stages of her case. Renee responded to a recruitment advertisement posted on a webpage for an involuntary childless support group and volunteered to take part in this research. She is 54 years old and has been married to Ron for more than 27 years. The interview took place at her house and lasted for just over an hour. The verbatim transcript of her interview was used for the analysis.

Exploratory Noting. The transcript was read several times and, during the line-by-line reading, words and phrases that seemed interesting, stood out, appeared unusual, or were enigmatic were underlined. At the same time, any ideas and impressions that came to mind were noted in the left margin of the transcript. This was developed as forms of descriptive comments that pointed to things that mattered to Renee. The reading of the transcript in this way also drew attention to the language used. Linguistic elements, such as metaphors, pronouns, tenses, repetitions, words associated with time, positive–negative words, and long pauses between words, were all noted. The linguistic lens helped in linking the different meanings associated with Renee's statements.

Some exploratory notes operate at a more conceptual level where the analytical focus shifts toward a more abstract form of "sense-making" about what Renee was experiencing. Through this, new questions arose investigating the overarching meaning associated with her experience. However, the emphasis was always placed on the importance of the interpretation being grounded in what she actually said.

A short example taken from Renee's transcript is presented in Exhibit 8.2. Early in the interview, Renee had talked about tai-chi and yoga as being positive things in her life.

In the example given here, the researcher was interested in exploring Renee's meaning making in relation to her tai-chi experience. It shows the process of initial note taking, from writing thoughts freely as they come to mind, to shifting the focus on Renee's words, and then to developing the conceptual level of notation. For example, words such as *self-discovery* and *very very* were noted because these signified the embodied content of her tai-chi experience; and her use of *certainly* was noted because this explicitly connected tai-chi to her experience of being involuntarily childless.

The analytical process develops into more psychologically focused interpretations at conceptual levels, in this case, focusing on such features as distress, coping, and inwardness as shown in Exhibit 8.2. Renee's comment "Certainly after" was, together with the researcher's sense of concern, noted and conceptualized as an indication of the depth of her emotional suffering. In addition, when connections at this point in the transcript were noticed along with what was said in other sections, a link was marked with an arrow showing the page and line number.

Turning Exploratory Notes Into Experiential Statements. This stage continued the interactive and dynamic process of the researcher trying to make sense of Renee's world while Renee was trying to make sense of her own experience.

EXHIBIT 8.2

Exploratory Noting for Renee

Exploratory notes	
Loss of desire in her life.	Int: um . . . may I ask why you started doing this . . . [Renee: Why we traveled?] or doing this tai-chi . . . ?
Self-discovery was needed to find the meaning of her life.	Renee: Oh, the . . . the tai-chi . . . yeah . . . erm . . . I was finding it difficult to think . . . what I wanted in my life. Erm . . . and . . . really looking for more meaning . . . I think . . . and as part of that . . . I don't know if you call it a journey? It it . . . was something I wanted to do . . . to find out more about myself.
Doing tai-chi is a way to stop "all the thoughts" and give Renee some "comfort." → p. 3. 36 focus "here and now" How distressful "all the thoughts" are? Tai-chi is a coping strategy that provides self-compassion.	Erm . . . so "self-discovery" I suppose. And also sometimes I found it to be a comfort, because it stopped all the thoughts. So, in that respect, it was very good. Erm . . . so . . . I . . . read a lot of sort of self-help books, and erm . . . I like a lot of the books that sort of come from a Buddhist perspective . . . to
Tai-chi is "Very very helpful"; here the use of "very very" emphasizes her need to have help? The focus turns inward, toward herself. "Certainly" confirms the impact of not being able to have children has in her life. I wonder how much she is suffering emotionally?? — the depth of emotional suffering	do with mindfulness and focusing on . . . erm . . . sort of self-compassion those sorts of things. And I've found that very, very helpful. Certainly after . . . we found out we couldn't have children. Because that was quite hard. Erm so . . . yeah . . . it, it definitely has been something that has . . . has made me . . . erm . . . I don't know just . . . cope better with life, I think. And I enjoy it . . . [laughs] . . .

Through this process, each experiential statement was developed to capture not only Renee's account but also the researcher's interpretation of it. Thus, the IPA researcher is engaged in the double hermeneutic referred to earlier.

Developing experiential statements required concentration and time and was challenging. However, the analysis progressed by considering how a potential reader would perceive the dynamics or subtleties that were embedded within the experiential statements. Each of these was noted in the right margin of the transcript (see Exhibit 8.3).

Clustering Experiential Statements Into Personal Experiential Themes. In the case of Renee, 115 experiential statements were identified. Each was written on a separate piece of paper, and all these pieces of paper were placed on a large surface and examined for patterns. They were then grouped to enrich the understanding of the psychological impact and the meaning of childlessness for Renee. Similarity and difference, as well as contextual (temporal and relational) and positive and negative dimensions were considered as this helped to identify patterns across statements. Although some clustered fairly easily to form a new group, others did not appear to go anywhere and so were put aside at this stage. It was also useful to go back to the original transcript to recheck whether Renee's accounts were reflected in this patterning. As the analysis progressed, constant engagement in the hermeneutic circle continued.

Through these processes, the original 115 experiential statements were condensed and clustered into 12 groups. Further analysis was then conducted to look for connections across those 12 groups. This resulted in the emergence of four higher order clusters, which were named and became the personal experiential themes. Each personal experiential theme had shared properties within its theme group (subthemes). At the final stage of the case analysis, a table was created to represent the emergence of the personal experiential themes. This was made up of subthemes, illustrative extracts, and page and line numbers referring to the relevant places in the original transcript (see Exhibit 8.4).

Although a single person's experiences can be written up as a case study, IPA usually involves the analysis of a number of cases. This was true for the current research project, and so the analysis continued cross case. One characteristic that emerged among the 11 participants was differences in marital status: Participants included five married women, three single cohabiting women, and three divorced women living with a partner or remarried. To investigate this relational dimension on the experiences of childlessness, each of these three groups was analyzed separately.

The first cross-case analysis was conducted on the group of five married women. First, an analysis was conducted on each case in the way described earlier. Next, the five tables of personal experiential themes and subthemes, including Renee's, were established. To help illustrate this stage, an additional example from this group for Clare (54) is presented here as Exhibit 8.5.

The next process involved examining patterns across the five cases and constructing a table of group experiential themes that illustrates the shared accounts of the participants at the group level. This follows IPA's idiographic commitment. First, one does a thorough analysis of the personal experience of

EXHIBIT 8.3

Developing Experiential Statements for Renee

Exploratory notes		Experiential statements
	Int: um . . . may I ask why you started doing this . . . [Renee: Why we traveled?] or doing this tai-chi . . . ?	
Loss of desire in her life.	Renee: Oh, the . . . the tai-chi . . . yeah . . . erm . . . I was finding it difficult to think . . . what I wanted in	
Self-discovery was needed to find the meaning of her life.	my life. Erm . . . and . . . really looking for more meaning . . . I think . . . and as part of that . . . I don't know if you call it a journey? It, it . . . was something I wanted to do . . . to find out more about myself.	A journey of "self-discovery" as searching for purpose and meaning in life
Doing tai-chi is a way to stop "all the thoughts" and give Renee some "comfort." → p. 3. 36 focus "here and now" How distressful "all the thoughts" are?	Erm . . . so "self-discovery" I suppose. And also sometimes I found it to be a comfort, because it stopped all the thoughts. So, in that respect, it was very good. Erm . . . so . . . I . . . read a lot of sort of self-help books, and erm . . . I like a lot of the books	Focusing on the self now inhibits overloading thinking
Tai-chi is a coping strategy that provides self-compassion.	that sort of come from a Buddhist perspective . . . to do with mindfulness and focusing on . . . erm . . . sort	
Tai-chi is "Very very helpful"; here the use of "very very" emphasizes her need to have help? The focus turns inward, toward herself. "Certainly" confirms the impact of not being able to have children has in her life. I wonder how much she is suffering emotionally?? — the depth of emotional suffering	of self-compassion those sorts of things. And I've found that very, very helpful. Certainly after . . . we found out we couldn't have children. Because that was quite hard. Erm so . . . yeah . . . it, it definitely has been something that has . . . has made me . . . erm . . . I don't know just . . . cope better with life, I think. And I enjoy it . . . [laughs]	Self-compassion as coping

EXHIBIT 8.4

Personal Experiential Themes and Subthemes for Renee

Personal experiential themes
Subthemes
Illustrative extracts (page.lines)

1. Feeling the deficit
Children as people go through a life stage [realization of the loss]
now things like my nephews and nieces . . . I think at each stage, you . . . realize what you haven't got (7.28–32)

Childlessness leading to emotional insecurity
[Anxiety? Depression?]
because I had wanted them [ ] there's always regrets and the negatives that come in (10.41–44)

Endless search for positives on childlessness
who do you know who's found a life . . . "now they are having a great life." I want that. [ ] absolutely nothing (21.30–34)

2. Being isolated
Common everyday conversation triggers a sense of exclusion
I can't talk about these things that all these other women have got in common (8.32–33)

Childlessness remains taboo.
people are becoming more aware, but it's still almost a taboo subject (21.48–49)

Shrinking circle rather than expanding
it's difficult to make new friends . . . as I say more acutely, as we're losing people . . . shrinkage rather than expansion (11.15–19)

3. Working to change
Self-compassion as coping
sort of self-compassion . . . I've found that very, very helpful. Certainly after . . . we found out we couldn't have children. [ ] cope better with life (3.21–27)

Restoring self in creativity
this sort of real thing I want to do things, make things, create things (5.14–15)

Reframing self-belief as reconstructing life structure
you have to kind of reframe everything, you have to kind of start again and you have to come to terms with that (14.37–39)

4. Finding connections
Finding positives in doing something for others
I could see myself doing something like . . . voluntary work . . . spend time . . . with my nephews and nieces (12.24–27)

Bonding emerges through experience-close relation
who obviously have been more perhaps down the same route as myself . . . are people I can talk to about it (9.14–16)

Self-disclosure as a way of helping other childless people
by taking part in this [ ] that will be helpful for other people (21.5–6)

EXHIBIT 8.5

Personal Experiential Themes and Subthemes for Clare

Personal experiential themes
  Subthemes
    Illustrative extracts (page.lines)

1. **Battling through depression and grieving**
   The enormous impact of childlessness resulted in depression
     The fact that I couldn't have children [ ] went to this deep, deep depression
     (6.17–22)

   Unable to have children as a punishment
     I went through so many different emotions, but one of the emotions was, it's a
     punishment . . . I'd be a bad mother (3.11–15)

   Long-term effects of angst aligned with a grief journey
     I was 34 [ ] I wanted children. [ ] it's been a . . . a huge . . . grief journey [ ] probably
     from 34 to 44, it was 10 years of . . . angst (9.33–45)

2. **Being stuck**
   Avoiding friends with small children, leading to isolation
     I distanced myself from people who'd [pause] were having babies or got young
     children, and I lost quite a few friends (2.48–3.1)

   Children as informants for life
     With children you can see your life's progress, can't you? (18.28–29)

   Finding self as an outsider
     I still . . . feel a little bit . . . out of it. If you're with a group of mums and they're
     talking baby talk or children talk, it's quite difficult . . . to join in the conversation.
     [ ] you do get excluded. (3.41–46)

3. **Trying to move on**
   Looking for fulfillment in everyday life
     I probably am still on that journey [ ] something to do with your time that gives
     you fulfillment (17.32–39)

   Trying to choose to move on
     I'd like to emphasize the choice [ ] either stay grieving or . . . [ ] get on with it and
     find something else (9.5–14)

   Gaining emotional support through self-disclosure
     It's important to have at least one person you can talk to. If you can't talk . . . if it's
     all bottled up inside, it's horrendous, horrendous. (10.38–40)

4. **Evolving self**
   Conceptual shift ascribed to being a mother as "a" role in life
     there is actually more to life than being a mum [ ]. Even 5 years ago, I never thought
     I'd say that (5.33–39)

   Looking for similarities rather than differences
     don't keep saying you're different. . . . Looking for similarities [ ] I'm just like these
     people you know (19.23–32)

   Making contributions to society
     we do contribute in many, many ways. We don't take a lot from the society.
     We give a lot. [ ] I'm on my high horse now. (20.44–48)

each participant in their own terms. Only after that is complete does one then look for patterns of convergence and divergence across cases. Here, each of the five tables that were previously produced was printed on a separate sheet of paper and then placed on a large work surface. This allowed the researcher to look at the broad pattern of personal experiential themes across all five cases. Renee's and Clare's tables demonstrate some of their shared accounts. For example, both of their first personal experiential themes, "Feeling the deficit" and "Battling through depression and grieving," speak of their internal struggles. Similarly, their respective second personal experiential themes, "Being isolated" and "Being stuck," feature their relational problems. However, the focus here was to look for commonalities across all the five cases, and therefore, the analysis continued. As a result, it revealed four shared higher order features: intrapersonal problems, interpersonal problems, intrapersonal solutions, and interpersonal solutions. The personal experiential themes for each participant were resequenced to reflect this patterning, then the tables for each participant were drawn upon for the material fitting each new master theme. Hence, a table of group experiential themes for this group of five married women was developed (for a summary, see Table 8.1).

The same process was repeated for the remaining two groups, and two more master tables were developed, one for the three single cohabiting women, the other for the three divorced women living with a partner or remarried.

All three master tables were further examined by looking for convergences and divergences across the themes identified. At that point, similarities across the three groups were evidenced. However, no strong feature differentiating the groups was in evidence, suggesting that marital differences had little effect on the experiences of childlessness among the women in this study. Drawing on the findings, the analysis continued to develop higher order levels of themes that represented all 11 participants. Since the three master tables constructed previously were grounded in each participant's account, the analysis was conducted using the same tables with a shift in focus searching for connections across all the themes presented. At the end of the analytical process, a main

TABLE 8.1. Summary of the Main Table for Five Married, Involuntarily Childless Women: Group Experiential Themes and Subthemes

Group Experiential Theme	Subthemes
1. Being deprived—the loss	Emotional impact of the loss
2. Diverging from a normative world	Being isolated
	Being excluded
	Feeling different: compared with norms
3. Relational reconnections	Forming new connections
	Power of disclosure
	Making contributions
4. Dealing with inner turmoil	Reappraising self-belief
	Ways of coping
	Restoring self-worth in life

TABLE 8.2. Summary of the Main Table for 11 Women: Higher-Level Group Experiential Themes and Subthemes

Group Experiential Theme	Subthemes
1. Intrapersonal consequences of loss	Going through disenfranchised grief
	Uncertainty: layers of worries and fears
	Losing life purpose
2. Encountering relational losses	Unshared normative social values
	Being detached
	Losing affinity
3. Confronting internal pain	Evaluating internal conflicts
	Finding ways to move on
	Self-exploration: searching for fulfillment
4. Recontructing the self through relational reconnections	Building new connections
	Power of disclosure
	Connecting the self and the world

table for 11 women was developed with four higher level group experiential themes and subthemes (see Table 8.2 for a summary).

Writing Up. We now give a brief example of writing up by presenting one short section from the results. This presents part of the subtheme "Being detached" from the higher level Theme 2, "Encountering relational losses" (see Exhibit 8.6).

In the extract in Exhibit 8.6, Renee's quote speaks of the experiential significance of isolation caused by the absence of children. The interpretative narrative here unfolds the meaning of the loss of not having had children for Renee over her use of the word "shrinkage." Clare's and Kelly's quotes also point to their sense of isolation but, in their cases, through the boundaries they made. The meaning exposed in those quotes directs us also to feel their emotional pain. The final quote from Maggie describes role isolation caused by the unshared, everyday social roles of parenthood and refers to a possibly perceived sense of abnormality in a family-oriented social world.

This short passage has revealed the shared experience of isolation for those four participants; however, the idiographic importance of each woman's account remains. All 11 participants talked about their sense of relational loss at various levels, showing the actuality of the interpersonal relational struggles happening in their everyday lives.

METHODOLOGICAL DEVELOPMENTS IN IPA

Since IPA was first introduced in the early 1990s (Smith, 1991, 1994), its idiographic experiential approach has given researchers a better way of exploring and understanding insights into personal lived experiences. There is now a large corpus of research using IPA to address a wide range of experiential questions. It is also the case that recent years have witnessed a number of interesting methodological developments in the use of IPA.

EXHIBIT 8.6

Brief Example From Final Writing Up

Being detached

All participants have shown their concerns about relational connections in society. More than half of the participants explicitly described their detached feelings from others in everyday life. There appear to be three different, but interrelated, features: isolation, exclusion, and separation.

Isolation

The term *isolation* here refers to participants' feelings about a lack of or losing contact with people who have got children. There are difficulties in "widen[ing]" one's social world, as Renee describes:

> it's difficult to make new friends to to . . . widen your circle, and I think that's something that I feel . . . as I say more acutely, as we're losing people . . . that that . . . that it's this idea [little laugh] of shrinkage rather than expansion (11.15–19)

There is a deep sense of loss of connection that makes Renee feel isolated. She "acutely" feels a disconnection from society. But sadness and fear also seem to play a part in her felt sense of "shrinkage." Sadness embedded within the loss of having her own children appears possibly as a metaphor here for the physical image of the loss— shrinking rather than growing a pregnant bump. And because she does not want to experience another loss, a sense of fear appears around "this idea" of "losing people."

Engaging in society means interacting with people in various situations. Because children are everywhere, being with others in itself often evokes isolation. Clare and Kelly both have made boundaries between themselves and people with children:

> I distanced myself from people who'd . . . were having babies or got young children, and I lost quite a few friends. (Clare. 2.48–3.1)

> I think because I still find it hard to be around people with children, um . . . so I think it . . . brings up, sort of too much sadness . . . so it's nice . . . I kind of feel . . . I've, I've deliberately avoided my friends with children. (Kelly. 3.23–24)

As both extracts illustrate, children trigger "too much sadness" (Kelly). The participants' avoidance is a way of protecting themselves from emotional pain. At the same time, this behavior disables social connections and contacts and therefore leads to isolation.

Isolation for Maggie appears differently. For her, it results from role differences:

> when ordinary friends've got children erm . . . it's nice to find . . . it's hard to find . . . let me go back there . . . when you don't have children it's hard to find new friends, because parents find friends at the school gate. (3.36–40)

Children initiate social bonds. Maggie is isolated from social roles that "ordinary friends" of hers find—in this case, their friends "at the school gate." Because Maggie's friends are "parents," they connect with each other through parental roles in common everyday life. Maggie is in midlife role isolation and so finds it difficult to connect with her friends who are parents. It is interesting to note that her sense of childlessness is perceived as not "ordinary." Having a sense of abnormality regarding childlessness may also limit social connectedness.

Multimodal Designs

One development noticed in recent IPA studies is the application of multimodal designs, which here means incorporating visual methods, such as drawings, as a part of data collections in IPA studies (Kirkham et al., 2015; Nizza et al., 2018; Shinebourne & Smith, 2011). Boden et al. (2019) argued that "drawing taps into multiple sensory registers" helps researchers gain "hard-to-reach aspects" of participants' lived experiences (pp. 218–219).

One example of a multimodal study is that by Kirkham et al. (2015). In this study, patients attending a pain management clinic were asked to draw a picture of their pain, and they were provided with colored pencils and paper to do so. In the subsequent interview, the researcher asked participants questions about their drawings. The analysis of the data focused on examining participants' accounts of their visual representations of their pain. The report included the drawings to help readers follow the unfolding account. This is an approach with great potential for further development.

Multiperspectival Designs

In multiperspectival studies, accounts are collected from participants who can offer different points of view on the phenomenon. So, for example, in a study on the experience of the transition from primary to secondary school, interviews might be conducted with young people making the transition and their parents and teachers.

A study by Larkin and Griffiths (2004) looked at two distinctive groups of people, one recreational drug users and the other bungee jumpers, who were connected by the underlying feature of "rewards" and "risks." This is an example of multiperspectival designs where the aim of the study is to explore the question "How do persons evaluate and understand the relationship between risk and pleasure?" (p. 217). Larkin et al. (2019) offered a valuable discussion of multiperspectival designs in IPA.

The development of new types of design in IPA studies shows its growing maturity and illustrates its potential for extending the ways in which personal experience is examined. The important thing about these developments is that they are within an integrated IPA framework. Thus, visual images are not being added on as a separate extra. The image being produced is of the experience under investigation; the image is then usually used as a stimulus for the participant to talk about that experience. Similarly, in a multiperspectival study, care is taken to make sure the multiple perspectives are of the same or a related phenomenon and that the multiple perspectives will therefore help illuminate the analysis of the experience of the participants included. We look forward to further methodological developments in these type of IPA designs. Finally, a caveat. It is indeed encouraging to see such methodological innovation. However, these more complex designs are suitable for some research questions, less so for others. We still expect, in the future, to see the carrying out of excellent IPA studies that involve only in-depth interviews with a small number of participants. IPA affords a broad palette, and there is room on it for a wide range of research designs.

CONCLUSION

In this chapter, we have outlined the theoretical and practical foundations of IPA and specified the stages taken for an IPA research project—in this example, involuntary childlessness. Through phenomenologically oriented qualitative analysis with an idiographic commitment as its focus, IPA enables researchers to explore and give voice to the experience of the participants at deeper levels, and the methodological development of IPA also has shown its expansive and creative applications. We hope this chapter has given readers an understanding of the underpinnings of IPA and of what it is like to do an IPA research project, together with useful resources for conducting good IPA research. If you wish to read in more detail on IPA, we recommend you look at Smith et al. (2009, 2021) or Smith and Nizza (in press).

REFERENCES

Ashworth, P. (2008). Conceptual foundations of qualitative psychology. In J. A. Smith (Ed.), *Qualitative psychology: A practical guide to research methods* (2nd ed., pp. 4–25). Sage Publications.

Boden, Z., Larkin, M., & Iyer, M. (2019). Picturing ourselves in the world: Drawings, interpretative phenomenological analysis and the relational mapping interview. *Qualitative Research in Psychology, 16*(2), 218–236. https://doi.org/10.1080/14780887.2018.1540679

Brown, C. J., Webb, T. L., Robinson, M. A., & Cotgreave, R. (2018). Athletes' experiences of social support during their transition out of elite sport: An interpretative phenomenological analysis. *Psychology of Sport and Exercise, 36*, 71–80. https://doi.org/10.1016/j.psychsport.2018.01.003

Fieldsend, M. (2018). What is it like being involuntarily childless? Searching for ways of understanding from a psychological perspective. In N. Sappleton (Ed.), *Voluntary and involuntary childlessness: The joys of otherhood?* (pp. 49–70). Emerald. https://doi.org/10.1108/978-1-78754-361-420181003

Fieldsend, M. (2019). *Facing and dealing with the challenge of involuntary childlessness: An interpretative phenomenological analysis* [Unpublished doctoral dissertation]. Birkbeck College, University of London.

Fieldsend, M., & Smith, J. A. (2020). "Either stay grieving, or deal with it": The psychological impact of involuntary childlessness for women living in midlife. *Human Reproduction, 35*(4), 876–885. https://doi.org/10.1093/humrep/deaa033

Giorgi, A. (1997). The theory, practice, and evaluation of the phenomenological method as a qualitative research procedure. *Journal of Phenomenological Psychology, 28*(2), 235–260. https://doi.org/10.1163/156916297X00103

Heidegger, M. (1999). *Ontology: The hermeneutics of facticity* (J. van Buren, Trans.). Indiana University Press. (Original lecture 1923)

Huff, J. L., Smith, J. A., Jesiek, B. K., Zoltowski, C. B., & Oakes, W. C. (2018). Identity in engineering adulthood: An interpretative phenomenological analysis of early-career engineers in the United States as they transition to the workplace. *Emerging Adulthood, 7*(6), 451–467. https://doi.org/10.1177/2167696818780444

Husserl, E. (2001). *Logical investigations* (J. N. Findlay, Trans.). Routledge. (Original work published 1900)

Kimura, M., & Yamazaki, Y. (2013). The lived experience of mothers of multiple children with intellectual disabilities. *Qualitative Health Research, 23*(10), 1307–1319. https://doi.org/10.1177/1049732313504828

Kirkham, J. A., Smith, J. A., & Havsteen-Franklin, D. (2015). Painting pain: An interpretative phenomenological analysis of representations of living with chronic pain. *Health Psychology, 34*(4), 398–406. https://doi.org/10.1037/hea0000139

Langdridge, D. (2007). *Phenomenological psychology: Theory, research and method.* Pearson.

Larkin, M., & Griffiths, M. D. (2004). Dangerous sports and recreational drug-use: Rationalizing and contextualizing risk. *Journal of Community & Applied Social Psychology, 14*(4), 215–232. https://doi.org/10.1002/casp.770

Larkin, M., Shaw, R., & Flowers, P. (2019). Multiperspectival designs and processes in interpretative phenomenological analysis research. *Qualitative Research in Psychology*, *16*(2), 182–198. https://doi.org/10.1080/14780887.2018.1540655

Larkin, M., Watts, S., & Clifton, E. (2006). Giving voice and making sense in interpretative phenomenological analysis. *Qualitative Research in Psychology*, *3*(2), 102–120. https://doi.org/10.1191/1478088706qp062oa

Lewis, M., & Staehler, T. (2010). *Phenomenology: An introduction*. Continuum International.

Lopez, K. A., & Willis, D. G. (2004). Descriptive versus interpretive phenomenology: Their contributions to nursing knowledge. *Qualitative Health Research*, *14*(5), 726–735. https://doi.org/10.1177/1049732304263638

Matthews, E. (2006). *Merleau-Ponty: A guide for the perplexed*. Continuum.

Merleau-Ponty, M. (1962). *Phenomenology of perception* (C. Smith, Trans.). Routledge. (Original work published 1945)

Moran, D. (2000). *Introduction to phenomenology*. Routledge.

Nizza, I. E., Smith, J. A., & Kirkham, J. A. (2018). "Put the illness in a box": A longitudinal interpretative phenomenological analysis of changes in a sufferer's pictorial representations of pain following participation in a pain management programme. *British Journal of Pain*, *12*(3), 163–170. https://doi.org/10.1177/2049463717738804

Pothoulaki, M., MacDonald, R., & Flowers, P. (2012). An interpretative phenomenological analysis of an improvisational music therapy program for cancer patients. *Journal of Music Therapy*, *49*(1), 45–67. https://doi.org/10.1093/jmt/49.1.45

Sartre, J. P. (1948). *Existentialism and humanism* (P. Mairet, Trans.). Methuen. (Original work published 1946)

Shinebourne, P., & Smith, J. A. (2011). "It is just habitual": An interpretative phenomenological analysis of the experience of long-term recovery from addiction. *International Journal of Mental Health and Addiction*, *9*(3), 282–295. https://doi.org/10.1007/s11469-010-9286-1

Smith, J. A. (1991). Conceiving selves: A case study of changing identities during the transition to motherhood. *Journal of Language and Social Psychology*, *10*(4), 225–243. https://doi.org/10.1177/0261927X91104001

Smith, J. A. (1994). Reconstructing selves: An analysis of discrepancies between women's contemporaneous and retrospective accounts of the transition to motherhood. *British Journal of Psychology*, *85*(Pt. 3), 371–392. https://doi.org/10.1111/j.2044-8295.1994.tb02530.x

Smith, J. A. (1995). Semi-structured interviewing and qualitative analysis. In J. A. Smith, R. Harré, & L. Van Langenhove (Eds.), *Rethinking methods in psychology* (pp. 9–26). Sage Publications. https://doi.org/10.4135/9781446221792.n2

Smith, J. A., Flowers, P., & Larkin, M. (2009). *Interpretative phenomenological analysis: Theory, method and research*. Sage Publications.

Smith, J. A., Flowers, P., & Larkin, M. (2021). *Interpretative phenomenological analysis: Theory, method and research* (2nd ed.). Sage Publications.

Smith, J. A., Harré, R., & Van Langenhove, L. (1995). Idiography and the case-study. In J. A. Smith, R. Harré, & L. Van Langenhove (Eds.), *Rethinking psychology* (pp. 59–69). Sage Publications.

Smith, J. A., & Nizza, I. E. (in press). *Essentials of interpretative phenomenological analysis*. American Psychological Association.

Smith, J. A., & Osborn, M. (2008). Interpretative phenomenological analysis. In J. A. Smith (Ed.), *Qualitative psychology: A practical guide to research methods* (2nd ed., pp. 53–80). Sage Publications.

Smith, J. A., & Rhodes, J. E. (2015). Being depleted and being shaken: An interpretative phenomenological analysis of the experiential features of a first episode of depression. *Psychology and Psychotherapy: Theory, Research and Practice*, *88*(2), 197–209. https://doi.org/10.1111/papt.12034

Warnock, M. (1970). *Existentialism*. Oxford University Press.

Situational Analysis

Mapping Relationalities in Psychology

Rachel Washburn, Adele Clarke, and Carrie Friese

Situational analysis (SA) is a qualitative research method that enables textured, "thick analyses" (Fosket, 2015) of social life through analytic mapping strategies. Developed by Adele Clarke (2003, 2005, 2009, 2019), SA extends and regrounds grounded theory around what is now called the *interpretive turn*. This umbrella concept refers to shifts in understandings of social life that spread across the social sciences and humanities in the latter part of the 20th century. Provoked by the theoretical interventions of postmodern and poststructural thinkers, the interpretive turn coalesced around a rejection of core positivist assumptions about truth and knowledge production in favor of relational, ecological, and situated understandings of meaning and inquiry. A major pioneer in the social sciences, Clifford Geertz (1973, Chapter 1), asserted that the fundamental contrast was between positivism as an "experimental science in search of laws" and an "interpretive science in search of meaning" (p. 5). Rabinow and Sullivan (1979/1987) further noted that the interpretive turn was based on "the realization that all human inquiry is necessarily engaged in understanding the human world from within a specific situation. This situation is always and at once historical, moral, and political" (pp. 20–21).

On the basis of these theoretical and methodological developments, Clarke (2003, 2005) developed SA as a new approach to qualitative analysis deriving from both Straussian grounded theory (Strauss, 1987; Strauss & Corbin, 1990, 1998) and constructivist grounded theory (GT) (Charmaz, 2000, 2006, 2007,

https://doi.org/10.1037/0000252-009
Qualitative Research in Psychology: Expanding Perspectives in Methodology and Design, Second Edition, P. M. Camic (Editor)

2008, 2014) approaches and sharing most of their epistemological roots.[1] Like GT, SA has been widely taken up transnationally and across many disciplines and professions, including psychology. Thus, we note several exemplary SA works from psychology in this chapter.

To accomplish its new goals, SA has a different conceptual infrastructure or guiding metaphor from the action-centered "basic social process" focus central to GT. In SA, basic social processes of action are replaced by a focus on "the situation" as the key unit of analysis. This enables analysts to more fully elaborate the dense complexities of a particular situation broadly conceived. In doing SA, the researcher uses cartographic approaches to analysis, making four kinds of maps to frame and analyze the situation of inquiry:

1. *Situational maps* specify all the major elements found in the situation, human and nonhuman.

2. *Relational maps* then analyze relations among all the major elements specified in the situational map.

3. *Social worlds/arenas maps* diagram all the collective actors (social worlds, organizations, institutions) and their arenas of commitment and action in the situation.

4. *Positional maps* detail positions taken and not taken in all the major debates in the discourses found in the situation.

All four maps are intended as analytic exercises, fresh and distinctive ways into empirical social science data that attend to its complexities, relationalities, and ecologies. Mapping is followed by memoing to capture analysis and to provoke and plan further lines of inquiry. For researchers in psychology, SA provides a powerful method for analyzing the important ways in which individuals' experiences are shaped by and coconstituted through a constellation of elements ranging from other people to discourses and policies, to technologies and organizations.

---

[1]As many readers may know, there are various approaches to GT today, including Glaserian, Straussian, dimensional, constructivist, and situational. Although there are shared commitments across these approaches, there are also areas of importance difference, especially in epistemological groundings and specific processes used in analysis. Anselm Strauss was trained as a Chicago School sociologist and mentored by Herbert Blumer, one of the originators of symbolic interactionism. Straussian GT reflects Strauss's deep commitments to interactionism and his worldview as a social constructionist qualitative researcher. See Morse and colleagues (2021) for detailed differences. Charmaz (2000; see also 2014, pp. 13–14) initially distinguished between *constructivist* and *constructionist approaches*, asserting that constructionists did not necessarily reflexively view their own work as constructed interpretations, while constructivists did. Today, she sees many constructionists taking a considerably more reflexive stance in their work. Thus, the in-practice differences have narrowed. With Charmaz, we view most everything as constructed and interpreted, an assumption integral to our version of interactionism (see also Blumer, 1969). On constructionism, Holstein and Gubrium (2007) offered chapters on constructionism across the disciplines. Charmaz (2000, 2006, 2014) focuses on constructivist GT.

In this chapter, we provide an overview of SA, including some key methodological and theoretical groundings, followed by a description of the four mapping strategies. For each mapping strategy, we provide an example of how the maps have been productively used by researchers in psychology. We conclude with reflections on the distinctive strengths and contributions of SA, especially for critical projects in psychology that seek to grasp the complexities and diversities of various situations of inquiry.

THE UNIQUE CONTRIBUTION OF SITUATIONAL ANALYSIS

Developed as a methodological extension of Straussian and constructivist GT by Clarke, SA has been expanded by Clarke and colleagues (2015, 2018; Clarke & Friese, 2007). In addition to its roots in Straussian GT, SA draws heavily from feminist theory; interactionist theory; Foucault and other poststructuralist theorists; cultural and postcolonial studies; and science, technology, and medicine studies.

For readers unfamiliar with GT, it is a method of qualitative inquiry developed by Barney Glaser and Anselm Strauss (Glaser & Strauss, 1967; see also Griffiths, Chapter 10, this volume). It offers an intensely empirical approach to the study of social life through distinctive systematic approaches to data analysis. Since its inception, GT has been elaborated and extended in several directions, including SA. The very term *grounded theory* means data-grounded theorizing, and SA sustains this tradition.

Although some grounded theorists, notably Strauss and Charmaz, generated more contemporary constructivist framings of GT (see especially Strauss, 1987; see also Charmaz, 2000, 2007, 2008, 2014), for Clarke (2005), some problematic positivist recalcitrancies remained. In pushing GT more fully around the interpretive turn, SA addresses these. In particular, it addresses the following key methodological issues: First, methods are needed that intentionally elucidate the complexities of situations as the grounds of social life. That is, a method must aim at capturing complexities rather than simplifying, must elucidate uneven processes of change as well as stabilities, and must untangle agents and positions sufficiently to make contradictions, ambivalences, and even irrelevances clear. Second, a method is needed that encourages analysts to elucidate marginalized perspectives and subjugated knowledges of social life that may even be illegitimate to some. We need to lucidly communicate what it means to dwell heterogeneously all over this planet in complicated and often highly unstable situations.[2]

Third, methods are needed that go beyond "the knowing subject" as the featured knower and decision maker to also address and analyze salient

---

[2]Some threads of interactionism moved toward interpretive cultural studies in ways Clarke sought to extend through SA (e.g., Denzin, 1989, 2001). See also Denzin and Lincoln (1994, 2018).

discourses within the situation of inquiry. We are all, like it or not, constantly awash in seas of discourses constitutive of life itself. SA therefore follows Foucault's poststructural "footsteps" (Prior, 1997) into historical, narrative-textual, and visual discourses to integrate the decentering of "the knowing subject" more deeply into empirical research.

Further, fresh methodological attention needs to be paid to objects in situations: cultural objects, technologies, media—all the nonhuman, animate, and inanimate things that also constitute the situations we study (see, e.g., Mead, 1934/1962; see also Foucault, 1972; Latour, 1987; McCarthy, 1984). Some are products of human action (and we can study the production processes); others are construed as "natural" (and we can study how they have been constructed as such). In the contemporary moment, studying action is far from enough.

Clarke (2005) also argued that we need methodologies that take individual and collective difference(s) into account in social life to generate more just and equitable social policies from education and welfare reform to health coverage, from caregiving to social security in old age or disability. Such visionary aspects of pragmatist philosophy are again vital after the interpretive turn for good reason: Because they are sorely needed (see, e.g., Denzin & Lincoln, 1994, 2018; Rabinow, 2011; Rorty, 1982). But they also need to be grounded through empirical research to effect more equitable policies through the explicit acknowledgment and incorporation of the complexities of situatedness and difference(s) rather than their erasure through subtly coerced assimilations or hopes for transcendence through shared education or beliefs.

In keeping with these aims, SA provides an alternative conceptual infrastructure from the GT focus on human action and social processes. In SA, this is replaced with a focus on the situation as a whole from diverse angles of vision. Using the cartographic strategies described later in this chapter, analysts map the key elements of all kinds in situations, social worlds/arenas, and positions within discourses. Through mapping and memoing, analysts move toward provocative yet provisional analytics and theorizing as an ongoing process rather than developing a substantive theory.

Methodologically, SA retains GT's strong systematic approach to analysis, which is accomplished through meticulous mapping rather than coding of data. Like GT, SA also relies on abductive as well as inductive analytic strategies, theoretical sampling, theoretical saturation, and assiduous memoing. Finally, like constructivist GT, SA also does not believe the researcher should be a *tabula rasa*—a blank slate—in terms of prior knowledge of theory and substantive research areas. Well-developed proposals and rigorous research are built on critically combining prior knowledge and scholarly preparation with informed analytic openness.

DEFINING THE SITUATION IN SITUATIONAL ANALYSIS

Important to the development of SA was that historically, qualitative inquiry has tended to ignore the situatedness of phenomena studied (Denzin, 1970, 1989; Haraway, 1991, Chapter 9), concentrating instead on action and interaction (in GT), selves (in autoethnography and social psychology), a specific culture (in anthropologically oriented ethnography), and so on. Inspired by the concept of "situation" as taken up by W. I. Thomas, Dorothy S. Thomas, John Dewey, Karl Mannheim, C. Wright Mills, Norman Denzin, Donna Haraway, and Brian Massumi, SA emphasizes the situatedness of phenomena as a needed corrective.

The notion of the situation in SA also engages and extends Strauss's emphasis on structural conditions in GT analyses. Although action is a major focus of traditional GT, Strauss's pragmatist interactionist sociology was based most of all in understanding action as a situated activity. For Strauss, the conditional matrix, an analytic device he developed with Julie Corbin, was a *situating device*—a means of enabling researchers to envision the specific empirical contexts or conditions under which the action is occurring.[3] Strauss and Corbin's (1990, 1998) conditional matrices were intended to push grounded theorists to consider how various facets of the context or broader situation "condition" or shape the action. Such facets might include an important upcoming election or a new technology that will change practices in a specialty.

Although the conditional matrices valuably pioneered new territory, Clarke found them inadequately empirical. Therefore, in SA, "the situation as a whole" is the key unit of analysis instead of the action focus of GT. Figure 9.1, The Situational Matrix, details the analytic foci of SA.

As depicted in Figure 9.1, in SA, the conditions *of* the situation are *in* the situation. There is no such thing as "context." The conditional elements of the situation need to be specified in analyzing the situation itself as they are constitutive of it, not merely framing it, contextualizing it, contributing to it, or shaping it. They are it. Regardless of whether some might construe them as local or global, internal or external, close in or far away or whatever, the fundamental question is, How do these elements appear—make themselves felt as consequential—*inside* the empirical situation under examination? SA features analyses of the complexities and relationalities of these conditional elements inside the situation and their ecologies.

Significant here, the varied elements in a situation are not bounded and autonomous but porous and "coconstitutive" of each other. The elements help make each other up through their shared presence and relations in the situation. SA was developed to aid in understanding precisely what coconstitutes and helps to shape what else in a given situation—analyzing the relationalities involved and their ecologies.

To clarify, in SA, a situation is not merely a moment in time, a narrow spatial or temporal unit or a brief encounter or event (or rarely so). Instead, it usually involves a somewhat enduring arrangement of relations among many different kinds of elements across a number of events over time. Most significant, each situation has its own ecology. These ecological relations are analyzed by doing the four kinds of maps, discussed next.

---

[3]See Strauss (1987, 1991, 1993, 1995; Strauss & Corbin, 1990, 1998; see also Corbin & Strauss, 1990). Strauss would likely have been familiar with Dewey's (1938) concept of "the matrix of inquiry" (p. 60) in his *Logic: The Theory of Inquiry.*

FIGURE 9.1. Situational Matrix

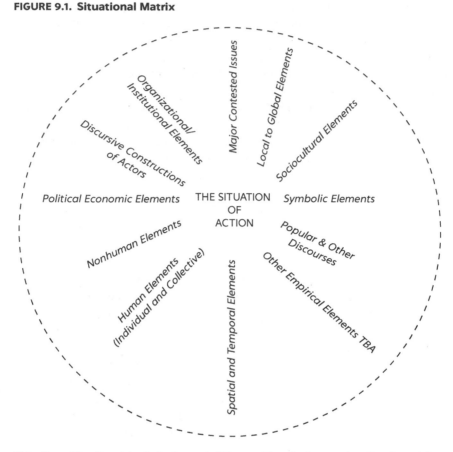

Note. From *Situational Analysis: Grounded Theory After the Postmodern Turn* (p. 73), by A. E. Clarke, 2005, Sage Publications (https://doi.org/10.4135/9781412985833). Copyright 2005 by Sage Publications. Reprinted with permission.

MAPPING SITUATIONS IN SITUATIONAL ANALYSIS

In doing an SA, the situation of inquiry is empirically constructed by the analyst through making four very different kinds of maps and following through with analytic work and memos of various kinds to document and detail the analysis-in-progress:

1. *Situational maps* lay out the major elements—human, nonhuman, discursive, and other empirical elements found in the research situation of inquiry.

2. *Relational maps*, made using situational maps, map and analyze the relations among the different elements in the situation.

3. *Social worlds/arenas maps* lay out the collective actors and the arena(s) of commitment and discourse within which they are engaged in ongoing negotiations—organizational or institutional interpretations of the situation.

4. *Positional maps* lay out the major positions taken, and not taken, in the data vis-à-vis particular axes of difference, concern, and controversy around issues in the situation of inquiry.

Data for an SA research project can be produced through in-depth interviews, ethnographic observations, or both, as is usual in GT. However, SA also strongly urges focusing on or also including extant discourse materials found in the situation under study as data—narrative, visual, and historical materials. These may include all kinds of documents, websites, imagery, material cultural objects, technological apparatuses, scientific or other specialized literatures, and social media, among others. In SA, whatever discursive materials exist in the situation of inquiry are viewed as constitutive of that situation—integral parts of it—and therefore worthy of analysis.

Next, we describe each kind of map in detail. (For more guidance in doing SA research, see Chapters 4–9 in Clarke et al., 2018.) For templates for making each of the four kinds of maps, see the Sage Companion Website at https://study.sagepub.com/clarke2e/student-resources/templates.

Situational Maps

The initial maps done in SA—situational maps—lay out the major human, non-human, discursive, historical, symbolic, cultural, political, and other elements in the research situation of concern and provoke analysis of relations among them. These maps capture the messy complexities of the situation in their dense relations and permutations. They intentionally work against the usual simplifications so characteristic of scientific work (Star, 1983) in particularly post-structural and interpretive ways (see Figure 9.2).

The messy situational map also works as an excellent "holding device," a place to "put"—easily write down—all the possible elements (deleting any that do not empirically pan out) and to add new elements as they emerge through fresh data gathering. Once an element is empirically confirmed through data, if it is seemingly important analytically, the researcher can follow through with further theoretical sampling (see Charmaz, 2014, Chapter 8).

Situational maps are also excellent research design tools. Even a very preliminary situational map helps in planning an SA research project, especially because researchers typically have to discuss many facets of the design in dissertation proposals and research grants long before any actual research has been done! Having some idea of the important elements to be researched in the situation under study enables writing stronger and clearer proposals.

Figure 9.3 is the Abstract Ordered Situational Map. Here you can see the basic categories more clearly. These categories derive in part from Clarke's work and from Strauss's (1993) "general orders" (p. 252) within his negotiated or processual ordering framework: spatial, temporal, technological, work, sentimental, moral, aesthetic, and so on. In terms of laying out the major elements in situations, these categories are fairly generic—common across research situations.

FIGURE 9.2. Abstract Messy Situational Map

Note. From *Situational Analysis: Grounded Theory After the Interpretive Turn* (p. 66), by A. E. Clarke, C. Friese, and R. Washburn, 2018, Sage Publications. Copyright 2018 by Sage Publications. Reprinted with permission.

It is important to note that there is no absolute need to include all of these categories in any given analysis. What appears in your situational map is based on your situation of inquiry—your project. Both messy and ordered situational maps are done and redone across the career of the research project along with analytic memos.

An exemplar of SA research in psychology that includes messy or ordered situational maps is Khaw (2012), discussed in the following section.

Mapping Relationality

Once you have an empirically based messy situational map, you can begin doing the second kind of map, the relational map—and the next phase of analytic work and memoing in SA. Here relations among the various elements in the situation are the analytic focus.

Taking each element in turn, the researcher thinks about it in relation to all the other elements on the map. In Figure 9.4, as an example, the element focused on is Organization #1. The memo on this map would specify the nature of the key relationships of Organization #1 by describing the nature of each line—each relation between two (or more) elements. This mapping is done systematically, one element at a time. Such relational analyses are the major work done with the situational map. It parallels the word by word, line

FIGURE 9.3. Ordered Situational Map

INDIVIDUAL HUMAN ELEMENTS/ACTORS e.g., key individuals and significant (unorganized) people in the situation, including the researcher	**NONHUMAN ELEMENTS/ACTANTS** e.g., technologies; material infrastructures; specialized information and/or knowledges; material "things"
COLLECTIVE HUMAN ELEMENTS/ACTORS e.g., particular groups; specific organizations	**IMPLICATED/SILENT ACTORS/ACTANTS** as found in the situation
DISCURSIVE CONSTRUCTIONS OF INDIVIDUAL AND/OR COLLECTIVE HUMAN ACTORS as found in the situation	**DISCURSIVE CONSTRUCTIONS OF NONHUMAN ACTANTS** as found in the situation
POLITICAL/ECONOMIC ELEMENTS e.g., the state; particular industry/ies; local/regional/global orders; political parties; NGOs; politicized issues	**SOCIOCULTURAL /SYMBOLIC ELEMENTS** e.g., religion; race; sexuality; gender; ethnicity; nationality; logos; icons; other visual and/or aural symbols
TEMPORAL ELEMENTS e.g., historical, seasonal, crisis, and/or trajectory aspects	**SPATIAL ELEMENTS** e.g., spaces in the situation; geographical aspects; local, regional, national, global spatial issues
MAJOR ISSUES/DEBATES (USUALLY CONTESTED) as found in the situation; and see positional map	**RELATED DISCOURSES (HISTORICAL, NARRATIVE AND/OR VISUAL)** e.g., normative expectations of actors, actants, and/or other specified elements; moral/ethical elements; mass media and other popular cultural discourses; situation-specific discourse
OTHER KINDS OF ELEMENTS as found in the situation	

Note. From *Situational Analysis: Grounded Theory After the Interpretive Turn* (p. 131), by A. E. Clarke, C. Friese, and R. Washburn, 2018, Sage Publications. Copyright 2018 by Sage Publications. Reprinted with permission.

by line coding procedures in GT, similarly relying on being highly systematic in carefully analyzing the empirical data to generate a rich analysis.

Relational maps portray the major and minor relationships or "relationalities" in the situation. Focusing on the most interesting relations and theoretically sampling them—gathering more data about them—ultimately helps the analyst decide which stories—which relations—to pursue as the heart of the project.

Both the situational and relational maps are usually working maps for the researcher(s). Thus, neither usually appears as the focus of a chapter or publication. Exceptions to this are often included to demonstrate the wide range of elements found in a particular situation—its inherent complexities—or to situate a particular element worthy of extended focus.

Excellent examples of situational and relational maps in psychology can be found in Khaw's (2012) research with mothers who experienced intimate partner abuse. Situating her work within the stages of change and boundary ambiguity literatures, Khaw was especially interested in understanding how

FIGURE 9.4. Abstract Relational Map

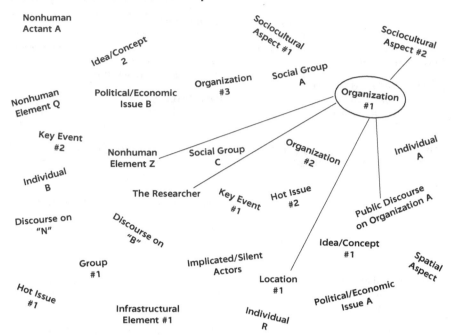

Note. From *Situational Analysis: Grounded Theory After the Interpretive Turn* (p. 139), by A. E. Clarke, C. Friese, and R. Washburn, 2018, Sage Publications. Copyright 2018 by Sage Publications. Reprinted with permission.

changing family boundaries can reshape the process of leaving an abusive partner. Khaw's engagement with key concepts from these literatures and her careful analysis of her interview data are reflected in her messy and relational maps. In these maps, she included a range of elements, including processes of change, stage of change, readiness to leave, physical absence or presence, and being a mother. As she described, her messy maps were not static but rather evolved throughout the research process and became more dense over time. In a relational map, she explored relationships between a number of elements, including how victim-blaming discourse is related to a fear of leaving and how the type of violence experienced is related to setting boundaries and fears of abusers. For Khaw, "situational maps became a visual reminder of the plethora of individual, relational, and societal factors that play a role in abused mothers' experiences in the process of leaving and in their attempts to end the abuse" (p. 146). Other researchers in psychology have found similar strengths in SA (described subsequently).

Social Worlds/Arenas Maps

Social worlds are groupings of varying sizes that are distinctively collective (e.g., a recreation group, an occupation, a theoretical tradition, or even a discipline or an organization), each of which has "a life of its own." They can be quite small or even vast. Participants in social worlds generate shared perspectives that form the basis for both individual and collective identities. These perspectives also undergird the commitments of that social world to collective action in the arenas in which it is involved. A social world has shared commitments to certain activities, and participants share resources of many kinds toward actions to achieve their goals.

Arenas of concern are constituted of multiple social worlds all committed to particular issues and prepared to act in some way in that arena. They may also have other commitments in other arenas. In arenas, "various issues are debated, negotiated, fought out, forced and manipulated by representatives" of the participating worlds and subworlds (Strauss, 1978, p. 124).[4] Social worlds typically actively participate in arenas in which their agendas are pursued. For example, a scientific discipline would be active in arenas where funding for their research is allocated, where knowledge relevant to their discipline is generated, where policy based on their research is decided, and so on. The empirical questions here are: Which worlds care about what issues, and what do they want to do about them?

Usually social worlds/arenas maps are initially done once you have gathered some data about your project—once you are beginning to get a handle on what might be going on more broadly. In doing a social worlds/arenas map, one tries to make collective sense out of the situation (see Figure 9.5).

The main goal of social worlds/arenas analysis is to delineate the collective organizational and institutional actors active in that situation. The overall goals are to make the broader situation of your project clear and legible to others and to provoke your own analysis. A clear understanding of what worlds are involved, why, and how so, can be important in terms of analysis of power relations and possibilities for change. Such issues are too often ignored in qualitative inquiry.

In Figure 9.5, the abstract social worlds/arenas map, the dotted lines indicate the usually quite porous boundaries of both social worlds and arenas. The porous nature of these boundaries and their plasticity are vital to SA, as it is through them that changes of many kinds enter—and leave—the situation of inquiry. This porousness gives social worlds/arenas analysis its flexibility, its plastic capacities to take change and different perspectives into account, its fluid poststructural analytic edge.

Many articles and dissertation and book chapters are based on social worlds/arenas maps (e.g., Alonso-Yanez et al., 2016). Helpful exemplars in psychology can be found in Strong and colleagues' (2012, 2017, 2018) research. In a series of articles, they used SA to analyze how medicalizing discourses are shaping counselor education in Canada. One of their social worlds/arenas maps (Strong et al., 2018, p. 169) detailed psychological, psychiatric, counseling psychology,

---

[4]On social worlds/arenas theory in SA, see Clarke et al. (2018, Chapter 3). For initial work, see Clarke (1991). For Strauss's final statement on his theory, see Strauss (1993, pp. 209–260).

FIGURE 9.5. Abstract Social Worlds/Arenas Map

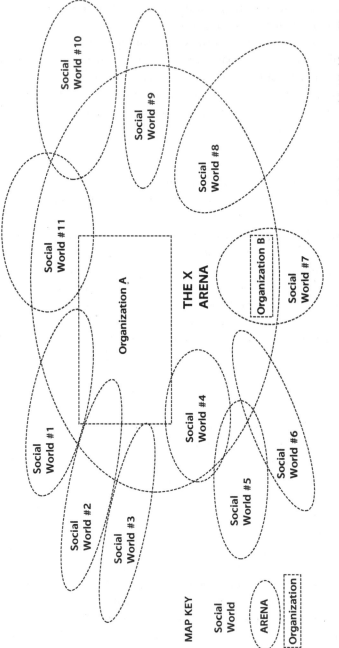

and counseling education arenas and related social worlds, helping to reveal key tensions students had to confront during their education.

Most recently, Murdy et al. (2020) productively used SA in counseling to explore and address clients' "situated concerns." Using a case example involving a client's gambling problems, Murdy and colleagues (2020) developed a social worlds/arenas map to examine the constellation of collective actors "who have something at stake in, and mutually influence" (p. 3) their clients' gambling practices. Their social worlds/arenas map includes major arenas such as the gambling industry, the political and economic arena, the medical and mental health and addictions arena, the personal and community arena, and the counseling and psychotherapy arena. Within these overlapping arenas are a variety of collective actors, including research bodies, government bodies, addiction specialists, counseling professionals, and advocacy groups. Importantly, for Murdy and colleagues (2020), SA mapping helped shift the focus from viewing their client's "gambling concern as an individually created and sustained problem, to recognizing his relational situatedness within a larger network of social actors" (p. 3).

Positional Maps

A particularly innovative aspect of SA is its integration of discourse analysis with GT (Clarke, 2003, 2005).[5] Positional maps are integral to—at the very core of—making SA a fully poststructural approach to qualitative inquiry. Positional maps are the analytic tools applied distinctively to the discursive materials in the situation, gathered through fieldwork, participant observation, interviewing, and the collection of documents, websites, and any and all other such discourse data found in the situation of inquiry.

Positional maps analyze the discourses in the situation of inquiry broadly conceived. They do very different kinds of analytic work from the situational and social worlds/arenas maps. The core goal of positional maps is to lay out the major positions taken on issues in the situation—topics of focus, concern, and often but not always contestation and controversy. Positional maps focus on issues, positions on issues, absences of positions where they might be expected (sites of discursive silence), and differences in discourses central to the situation under study.

Perhaps the most important and radical aspect of positional maps in SA is that positions are not correlated or associated with persons or groups or institutions. Instead, we seek to move with Foucault (1973, p. xiv) beyond "the knowing subject" here. Positions on positional maps are positions taken in discourses. Individuals and groups of all sorts may and commonly do hold

---

[5]As a doctoral student, Clarke asked Strauss whether one could use GT to analyze historical documents (one genre of discourse material). He said yes, and she then used it in several discourse analysis projects (e.g., Clarke & Montini, 1993), including her dissertation (Clarke, 1998), which integrated analyses of scientific literatures and primary archival materials as discourses with interview and observational data.

multiple and often contradictory positions on the same issue. Positional maps seek to represent this heterogeneity of positions in all its richness, not to link the positions to particular actors and thereby simplify them. This is a distinctively poststructural move, intentionally designed to reveal complexities.

Figure 9.6 offers an Abstract Positional Map that portrays positions on a particular issue in the larger situation of concern. There are two main axes, 1 and 2, and an infinite number of positions along them is possible. Six positions are shown on this map: A, B, C, D, E, and F. Positional maps also reveal possible positions for which you have not found any data. If, after searching further, this remains true, you have identified a site of silence. One of the powerful things positional maps do is to "help such silences speak," allowing

FIGURE 9.6. Abstract Positional Map

Note. From *Situational Analysis: Grounded Theory After the Interpretive Turn* (p. 167), by A. E. Clarke, C. Friese, and R. Washburn, 2018, Sage Publications. Copyright 2018 by Sage Publications. Reprinted with permission.

you to name them and explore reasons for the silence. Typically, a number of positional maps will be done for an SA project, each focusing on the positions found in relation to different axes of inquiry.

Positional maps center on complexities, differences, and controversies which are themselves heterogeneous. Thus, positional maps offer improved means of representing debates and positionality interpretively (see Clarke et al., 2018, Chapter 7). Because of this, many SA publications center on positional maps; see, for example, Friese's (2010) analysis of classification conundrums related to practices of cloning endangered species in zoos. Other examples include Fisher (2014) on posttraumatic stress disorder and the military, Gagnon and colleagues (2010/2015) on the deployment of fear in a public health sexually transmitted disease campaign, and Washburn (2015) on the politics sharing of biomonitoring test results with testing participants in the absence of accurate knowledge of the actual consequences of exposure to those chemicals found in their bodies.

In psychology, positional maps have been productively used by scholars conducting research on a variety of topics, including counselor education (Strong et al., 2017, 2018), intimate partners and sexual violence (Salazar & Öhman, 2015), media campaigns on queer youth suicide (Grzanka & Mann, 2014), the disclosure of eating disorders (Williams et al., 2018), and "situated forms of stuckness" in counseling (Murdy et al., 2020). For example, in their work on how masculinity, violence, and responsibility are negotiated by young Nicaraguan men, Salazar and Öhman (2015) constructed a positional map to frame the array of positions taken on men's responsibility for intimate partner violence, vis-à-vis a continuum of maintaining masculine hegemony and control. They found that the Nicaraguan men's discourses studied ranged from challenging gender inequality, intimate violence, and sexual abuse to strongly supporting the patriarchal gender order. In sum, the discourse supporting gender equality and men's full responsibility for intimate violence and sexual abuse is struggling to achieve recognition and legitimacy in this setting.

Another productive example comes from Murdy et al. (2020), who developed a positional map to explore discursive positions on the locus of responsibility for gambling practices and the source and location of the problem. On one axis, they plotted positions on the responsibility continuum, ranging from personal to collective. On the other, they plotted positions on the source and location of the problem continuum, ranging from internal-personal to external-societal. For Murdy and colleagues, positional maps helped in both identifying debates regarding sources and solutions to problems their clients might face as well as the ways in which these debates position clients in untenable ways, caught between competing messages about causes and cures.

In sum, each kind of map in SA does distinctive kinds of work in delineating and analyzing the situation under study and its different forms of complexity and relationality. Situational and relational maps detail the elements and their dense relations in the situation. Social worlds/arenas maps center on the relational ecologies of collective, organizational, and institutional entities, rarely pursued. Positional maps offer in-depth analyses of debates and contested issues in the discourses in the situation, including positions not taken or silenced.

Together, the four SA maps center on elucidating the key elements, relations, discourses, structures, and conditions of possibility that characterize the situation of inquiry. Thus, SA can deeply situate research projects individually, collectively, organizationally, institutionally, temporally, geographically, materially, discursively, culturally, symbolically, visually, and historically.

Together, the maps and memos about them constitute the overall SA research analysis—a relational ecology of the situation. They provide what Park (1952) called "the big picture" or "the big news" or what Star (1995) called "the ecology of knowledge" of the situation under study.[6] The maps portray the assemblage of elements and the ecology of relations among them, major collective actors and fundamental issues and debates in the broad situation studied.

Together these maps answer the following questions: Where in the world and when is this project going on? What and who are involved in this situation? What is going on in this situation? What is at stake in the situation for the different entities involved? What "conditions of possibility" for change are offered in this situation? What conditions render which changes essentially impossible? What and who are rendered invisible or marginalized—implicated actors?[7] By whom (who has what kinds of power in the situation)? Why and how do these conditions matter? To whom?

SA studies can stand on their own, independently, as the method is fully grounded and empirically ambitious. Alternatively, in a larger study such as a dissertation or book project, the researcher(s) might want to combine SA with constructivist GT (Charmaz, 2014) with which it is wholly compatible (see, e.g., Friese, 2013). Combining the study of action, situations, and discourses is analytically potent. In addition, researchers may use the maps to design *situated interventions* based on their research—policy-related actions to implement changes in counseling, psychology, education, clinical nursing or medicine, and so on. Although not discussed here, SA can also be used in the analysis of narrative, visual, and historical discourse materials per se (see Clarke et al., 2018, Chapters 10–13).

CONCLUSION

SA offers four kinds of maps as fresh analytic devices for analyzing social phenomena. Rooted in poststructural assumptions about truth, SA works to push GT analyses around the interpretive turn. By shifting the analytic gaze from human action to the situation, SA helps analysts attend to discourses

---

[6]Both Star (1995) and Clarke (1998) were deeply influenced by Rosenberg's (1979) concept of ecologies of knowledge.

[7]Implicated actors in a situation are actors defined solely by others in that situation for those others' own purposes. They cannot and do not represent themselves in any way. One example would be women users of contraception as defined by the makers of contraceptives (Clarke, 1998). By analyzing the constructions of implicated actors, the researcher can analyze the power dynamics in the situation (see Clarke et al., 2018, pp. 76–77).

(narrative, visual, and historical) and a wide array of nonhuman elements of various kinds, including technologies, policies, and guidelines. For researchers in the field of psychology, SA has been especially valued for its capacity to help analysts move beyond the knowing subject to analyses of the situations in which practitioners, people suffering from mental illnesses, therapeutic guidelines, diagnostic criteria, and the process of becoming a therapist exist and coconstitute one another.

A notable strength of SA is that it can be done not only with interview and ethnographic observational data generated as part of the project, but also with documents of all kinds and the full range of extant narrative, visual, and historical discourse materials found in the situation. Most organizations are self-documenting, and public, media, website, and other institutional discourses are growing in importance due to wide and fast electronic access. SA's capacities for analyzing such discourses are excellent, making the method especially useful for multisite research, which is increasingly common. Here several kinds of data are collected. Using SA, the data can be analyzed separately, comparing the outcomes, or all together to generate an overall analysis.

The outcomes of situational mapping should be "thick analysis" (Fosket, 2015, p. 196), paralleling Geertz's (1973, Chapter 1) "thick description." Thick analysis explicitly takes into account the full array of elements in the situation— human, nonhuman, discursive. Rather than simplify, the "thick analyses" of SA embrace relationalities and complexities. Inspired by C. Wright Mills's (1959) "sociological imagination," SA seeks to provoke the "analytic imagination" (James, 2012) in ways that can be particularly useful in psychology and social psychology. SA is embedded in and develops from pragmatist interactionism, and we draw upon pragmatists John Dewey (1939) and Herbert Blumer (1969), who are also key figures in social psychology. Pragmatism and interactionism combined with critical social theorizing inform the insistence in SA that the situation be the unit of analysis. Through analyzing the situation, SA is one of many qualitative research techniques appropriate in psychology.

REFERENCES

Alonso-Yanez, G., Thumlert, K., & de Castell, S. (2016). Re-mapping integrative conservation: (Dis)coordinate participation in a biosphere reserve in Mexico. *Conservation & Society, 14*(2), 134–145. https://doi.org/10.4103/0972-4923.186335

Blumer, H. (1969). *Symbolic interactionism: Perspective and method.* Prentice-Hall.

Charmaz, K. (2000). Grounded theory: Objectivist and constructivist methods. In N. Denzin & Y. Lincoln (Eds.), *Handbook of qualitative research* (2nd ed., pp. 509–536). Sage Publications.

Charmaz, K. (2006). *Constructing grounded theory: A practical guide through qualitative analysis.* Sage Publications.

Charmaz, K. (2007). Constructionism and grounded theory. In J. A. Holstein & J. F. Gubrium (Eds.), *Handbook of constructionist research* (pp. 397–412). Guilford Press.

Charmaz, K. (2008). The legacy of Anselm Strauss in constructivist grounded theory. *Studies in Symbolic Interaction, 32,* 127–142. https://doi.org/10.1016/S0163-2396(08)32010-9

Charmaz, K. (2014). *Constructing grounded theory: A practical guide through qualitative analysis* (2nd ed.). Sage Publications.

Clarke, A. E. (1991). Social worlds theory as organizational theory. In D. Maines (Ed.), *Social organization and social process: Essays in honor of Anselm Strauss* (pp. 17–42). Aldine de Gruyter.

Clarke, A. E. (1998). *Disciplining reproduction: Modernity, American life sciences and the "problem of sex."* University of California Press.

Clarke, A. E. (2003). Situational analyses: Grounded theory mapping after the post-modern turn. *Symbolic Interaction, 26*(4), 553–576. https://doi.org/10.1525/si.2003.26.4.553

Clarke, A. E. (2005). *Situational analysis: Grounded theory after the postmodern turn.* Sage Publications. https://doi.org/10.4135/9781412985833

Clarke, A. E. (2009). From grounded theory to situational analysis: What's new? Why? How? In J. Morse, Nerager Stern, P., Corbin, J., Bowers, B., Clarke, A. E., & Charmaz, K. (Eds.), *Developing grounded theory: The second generation* (pp. 194–235). Routledge.

Clarke, A. E. (2019). Situational analysis: A critical interactionist method. In M. H. Jacobsen (Ed.), *Critical and cultural interactionism* (pp. 189–209). Routledge. https://doi.org/10.4324/9781315141640-11

Clarke, A. E., & Friese, C. (2007). Situational analysis: Going beyond traditional grounded theory. In A. Bryant & K. Charmaz (Eds.), *Handbook of grounded theory* (pp. 362–397). Sage. https://doi.org/10.4135/9781848607941.n17

Clarke, A. E., Friese, C., & Washburn, R. (Eds.). (2015). *Situational analysis in practice: Mapping research with grounded theory.* Routledge.

Clarke, A. E., Friese, C., & Washburn, R. S. (2018). *Situational analysis: Grounded theory after the interpretive turn.* Sage Publications.

Clarke, A. E., & Montini, T. (1993). The many faces of RU486: Tales of situated knowl-edges and technological contestations. *Science, Technology & Human Values, 18*(1), 42–78. https://doi.org/10.1177/016224399301800104

Corbin, J., & Strauss, A. (1990). Grounded theory research: Procedures, canons, and eval-uative criteria. *Qualitative Sociology, 13*(1), 3–21. https://doi.org/10.1007/BF00988593

Denzin, N. (1970). *The research act: A theoretical introduction to sociological methods.* Aldine Transaction.

Denzin, N. (1989). *Interpretive interactionism.* Sage Publications.

Denzin, N. (2001). *Interpretive interactionism* (2nd ed.). Sage Publications.

Denzin, N. K., & Lincoln, Y. S. (Eds.). (1994). *Handbook of qualitative research.* Sage Publications.

Denzin, N. K., & Lincoln, Y. S. (Eds.). (2018). *Handbook of qualitative research* (5th ed.). Sage Publications.

Dewey, J. (1938). *Logic: The theory of inquiry.* Henry Holt.

Dewey, J. (1939). Experience, knowledge and value: A rejoinder. In J. A. Boydston (Ed.), *The later works of John Dewey (1925–1953): 1939–1941/essays, reviews, and miscellany* (Vol. 14; pp. 517–608). Southern Illinois University Press.

Fisher, M. P. (2014). PTSD in the U.S. military, and the politics of prevalence. *Social Science & Medicine, 115,* 1–9. https://doi.org/10.1016/j.socscimed.2014.05.051

Fosket, J. R. (2015). Situating knowledge. In A. E. Clarke, C. Friese, & R. Washburn. (Eds.), *Situational analysis in practice: Mapping research with grounded theory* (pp. 195–233). Routledge. (Original work published 2014)

Foucault, M. (1972). *The archeology of knowledge and the discourse on language.* Harper.

Foucault, M. (1973). *The order of things [discourses]: An archeology of the human sciences.* Vintage/Random House.

Friese, C. (2010). Classification conundrums: Categorizing chimeras and enacting species preservation. *Theory and Society, 39*(2), 145–172. https://doi.org/10.1007/s11186-009-9103-7

Friese, C. (2013). *Cloning wild life: Zoos, captivity and the future of endangered animals.* New York University Press. https://doi.org/10.18574/nyu/9780814729083.001.0001

Gagnon, M., Jacob, J.-D., & Holmes, D. (2015). Governing through (in)security: A critical analysis of a fear-based public health campaign. In A. E. Clarke, C. Friese, & R. Washburn (Eds.), *Situational analysis in practice: Mapping research with grounded theory* (pp. 270–284). Routledge. (Original work published 2010)

Geertz, C. (1973). *The interpretation of cultures: Selected essays*. Basic Books.

Glaser, B. G., & Strauss, A. L. (1967). *Discovery of grounded theory: Strategies for qualitative research*. Aldine.

Grzanka, P., & Mann, E. S. (2014). Queer youth suicide and the psychopolitics of "it gets better." *Sexualities*, *17*(4), 369–393. https://doi.org/10.1177/1363460713516785

Haraway, D. (1991). *Simians, cyborgs, and women: The reinvention of nature*. Routledge.

Holstein, J. A., & Gubrium, J. F. (Eds.). (2007). *Handbook of constructionist research*. Guilford Press.

James, A. (2012). Seeking the analytic imagination: Reflections on the process of interpreting qualitative data. *Qualitative Research*, *13*(5), 562–577. https://doi.org/10.1177%2F1468794112446108

Khaw, L. (2012). Mapping the process: An exemplar of using situational analysis in a grounded theory study. *Journal of Family Theory & Review*, *4*(2), 138–147. https://doi.org/10.1111/j.1756-2589.2012.00126.x

Latour, B. (1987). *Science in action: How to follow scientists and engineers through society*. Harvard University Press.

McCarthy, D. (1984). Towards a sociology of the physical world: George Herbert Mead on physical objects. In N. Denzin (Ed.), *Studies in symbolic interaction* (Vol. 5, pp. 105–121). Emerald Insight.

Mead, G. H. (1962). *Mind, self, and society from the standpoint of a social behaviorist* (Works of George Herbert Mead, Vol. 1). University of Chicago Press. (Original work published 1934)

Mills, C. W. (1959). *The sociological imagination*. Oxford University Press.

Morse, J., Stern, P. N., Corbin, J., Bowers, B., Charmaz, K., Clarke, A. E., & Porr, C. (2021). *Developing grounded theory: The second generation revisited* (2nd ed.). Routledge Press.

Murdy, T., Vegter, V., & Strong, T. (2020). Situational analysis mapping for transformative thinking, conceptualization and dialogues in counseling practice. *Counseling and Psychotherapy Research*. Advance online publication. https://doi.org/10.1002/capr.12351

Park, R. E. (1952). *Human communities*. Free Press.

Prior, L. (1997). Following in Foucault's footsteps: Text and context in qualitative research. In D. Silverman (Ed.), *Qualitative research: Theory, method, practice* (pp. 63–79). Sage Publications.

Rabinow, P. (2011). Dewey and Foucault: What's the problem? *Foucault Studies*, *11*(11), 11–19. https://doi.org/10.22439/fs.v0i11.3202

Rabinow, P., & Sullivan, W. M. (Eds.). (1987). The interpretive turn: A second look. In P. Rabinow & W. M. Sullivan (Eds.), *Interpretive social science: A second look*. University of California Press. (Original work published 1979)

Rorty, R. (1982). *Consequences of pragmatism: Essays, 1972–1980*. University of Minnesota Press.

Rosenberg, C. E. (1979). Toward an ecology of knowledge: On discipline, contexts and history. In A. Oleson & J. Voss (Eds.), *The organization of knowledge in modern America* (pp. 440–455). Johns Hopkins University Press.

Salazar, M., & Öhman, A. (2015). Negotiating masculinity, violence, and responsibility: A situational analysis of young Nicaraguan men's discourses on intimate partner and sexual violence. *Journal of Aggression, Maltreatment & Trauma*, *24*(2), 131–149. https://doi.org/10.1080/10926771.2015.1002652

Star, S. L. (1983). Simplification in scientific work: An example from neuroscience research. *Social Studies of Science*, *13*(2), 208–226. https://doi.org/10.1177/030631283013002002

Star, S. L. (Ed.). (1995). *Ecologies of knowledge: New directions in the sociology of science and technology.* State University of New York Press.

Strauss, A. L. (1978). A social worlds perspective. In N. Denzin (Ed.), *Studies in symbolic interaction* (pp. 119–128). JAI Press.

Strauss, A. L. (1987). *Qualitative analysis for social scientists.* Cambridge University Press. https://doi.org/10.1017/CBO9780511557842

Strauss, A. L. (1991). *Sociological awareness: Collective images and symbolic representation.* Transaction.

Strauss, A. L. (1993). *Continual permutations of action.* Aldine de Gruyter.

Strauss, A. L. (1995). Notes on the nature and development of general theories. *Qualitative Inquiry, 1*(1), 7–18. https://doi.org/10.1177/107780049500100102

Strauss, A. L., & Corbin, J. (1990). *The basics of qualitative analysis: Grounded theory procedures and techniques.* Sage Publications.

Strauss, A. L., & Corbin, J. (1998). *The basics of qualitative analysis: Grounded theory procedures and techniques* (2nd ed.). Sage Publications.

Strong, T., Chondros, K., & Vegter, V. (2018). Medicalizing tensions in counselor education? *European Journal of Psychotherapy & Counselling, 20*(2), 220–243. https://doi.org/10.1080/13642537.2018.1459765

Strong, T., Gaete, J., Sametband, I. N., French, J., & Eeson, J. (2012). Counsellors respond to the *DSM-IV-TR. Canadian Journal of Counselling and Psychotherapy, 46*(2), 85–106. https://cjc-rcc.ucalgary.ca/article/view/59273

Strong, T., Vegter, V., Chondros, K., & Job, C. (2017). Medicalizing developments in counsellor education? Counselling and counselling psychology students' views. *Canadian Journal of Counselling and Psychotherapy/Revue Canadienne de Counseling et de Psychothérapie, 51*(2). https://cjc-rcc.ucalgary.ca/article/view/61098

Washburn, R. (2015). Rethinking the disclosure debates: A situational analysis of the multiple meanings of human biomonitoring data. *Critical Public Health, 23*(4), 452–465. https://doi.org/10.1080/09581596.2012.752071 [Reprinted with reflection in A. E. Clarke, C. Friese, & R. Washburn (Eds.). (2015). *Situational analysis in practice: Mapping research with grounded theory* (pp. 241–269). Routledge.]

Williams, E. P., Russell-Mayhew, S., & Ireland, A. (2018). Disclosing an eating disorder: A situational analysis of online accounts. *Qualitative Report, 23*(4), 914–931. https://nsuworks.nova.edu/tqr/vol23/iss4/14

10

What Lies Beneath?

Eliciting Grounded Theory Through the Analysis of Video-Recorded Verbal and Nonverbal Interactions

Colin Griffiths

The anthropologist Clifford Geertz (2017) noted that in seeking to develop a thick description of a social phenomenon one starts from a "state of general bewilderment as to what the devil is going on" (p. 333) and proceeds from that indeterminate state to a more settled understanding on the basis that bewilderment disappears when the conceptual structures that inform subjects' acts are discovered. *Thick description* is an ethnographic term that may be contrasted with thin description; both approaches seek to describe people's behavior; however, thick description also describes the situations that surround individuals' behavior so that a total description of the context of any behavior may be available. This chapter aims to explain how thick descriptions of very focused research contexts may be obtained and how such descriptions may enable comprehension of areas of human research that for many have been off limits in the past due to the inaccessibility of the settings and the participants. It also tries to elucidate a method through which explanatory theory may be discovered that relieves some of the bewilderment that confronts researchers and students of human behaviors in trying to comprehend those who do not talk and therefore cannot be interviewed. This approach is particularly useful in understanding those who inhabit a confused reality, such as people with end-stage dementia and those with severe and profound intellectual disabilities. However, it may be that the methods outlined in the chapter also facilitate a deeper comprehension of all human behavior for reasons that will become clear as the chapter progresses.

https://doi.org/10.1037/0000252-010
Qualitative Research in Psychology: Expanding Perspectives in Methodology and Design, Second Edition, P. M. Camic (Editor)

The goal of this chapter, therefore, is to present a method of qualitative inquiry that enables an understanding of how individuals behave by not only delving into their verbal texts but also by considering visual as well as aural forms of data. Video by its nature presents a far deeper and potentially more complex insight into the communications, behaviors, and affective drives of an individual than audio alone because it potentially offers extraordinarily detailed observations of how a person is behaving. However, video has to be managed to allow this detail to emerge in a comprehensible way. This chapter explores how that may be achieved, and the key is to consider video as narrative.

Comprehension of narratives that explore what people do and potentially what they feel about what they do, therefore, is what the chapter seeks to accomplish. A key underlying assumption is philosopher and psychologist John Dewey's view that a person's experiences offer a window into the understanding of that person (Ollerenshaw & Creswell, 2002). If the experiences that underpin a person's behaviors and if the interaction between what the person is experiencing and his or her behaviors can be described using video in sufficient detail and with an inherent fluency, then a narrative picture may be derived from the video. This narrative must then be presented in a way that can potentially reveal the patterns inherent to and the meaning of those behaviors and experiences.

Dana Jack (1991) made the point that "the first person voice is the self that speaks from personal experience and observation . . . [it is] the authentic self" (p. 94), and it is this self that this chapter explores. Furthermore, it is often the authentic self of the disadvantaged, the disabled, and the marginalized that may be discovered by the methods that are considered here. Specifically, the chapter aims to uncover the nonverbal, the nonsymbolic and the apparently insignificant behaviors that all of us continually display but which in a predominantly verbal society are rarely considered important. So the narratives that this chapter considers are the nonverbal narratives that are often characterized by behaviors that are seen as fleeting, small, and unimportant. The development of a method that enables the construction of such narratives is the first aim of the chapter. The second and equally important aim is to find out what lies beneath the surface of the narratives to ascertain the theory that may underpin them.

Grounded theory is the approach used to achieve this goal. In considering grounded theory, a choice has to be made between competing analytic approaches. That choice is made on the basis of the utility of the analytic approach; the difficulty in carrying out the analysis; and, overidingly, the capability of the analytic method to achieve the goal of developing a theory that closely fits the data, explains it, and details the main concern of the participants in the data and how that concern is resolved. Grounded theory was developed by Barney Glaser and Anselm Strauss as a way of addressing the perceived mismatch between the empirical world and theories that explain it. In *The Discovery of Grounded Theory*, Glaser and Strauss, (1967) offered a method of eliciting theory from primarily qualitative data that is applicable to and explains the behaviors inherent in that data—specifically, by identifying the patterns of peoples' behaviors in the data. Over the years, three essential variations of the method have emerged: Barney Glaser's classic grounded theory, Strauss and Corbin's more structured approach, and Kathy Charmaz's constructivist approach. The difference between each approach is based on how one views the purity of the original (classic) approach. Classic grounded theory, Glaser and Strauss's original concept as developed in subsequent years by Glaser, relies heavily on a strict adherence to the constant comparative method and a sense that, if carried out consistently and with a genuine understanding of the process, the validity of the theory is beyond question simply because the theory will so closely fit the data on which it is based. By contrast, Strauss and Corbin's approach is more structured. It uses a process called *axial coding*, which formally explores multiple dimensions of the categories within the emerging theory in a structured manner (Strauss & Corbin, 1998). A third approach, advocated primarily by Kathy Charmaz (2006), is a constructivist approach, which suggests that the researcher is implicitly part of the research process, and as such, data and the resulting theory are inevitably coconstructed by the researcher and the research participants. All three approaches have their merits; however, this chapter adopts the classic grounded theory (Glaser, 1992, 1998) approach because, although it can take a little time to fully ingest, once understood, it is a simple and clear process that leads to the development of theory that closely reflects the data on which it is based.

This chapter now examines some of the possibilities of video and how it may be obtained, followed by an outline of the construction of narrative based on video. The derivation of theory from a cohesive narrative follows, and the chapter concludes with a case study of how this can be done.

OBTAINING VIDEO

At the outset the researcher has to make various decisions regarding how the video data are to be collected. First, the setting obviously determines much of what can be done and how it can be done. Is a static setting to be used for filming? Will it be one room or multiple locations? Will mobile filming be required, that is, will the location where the filming is taking place be moving (e.g., a car, a bus), or equally, will the researcher be moving around with a mobile handheld camera?

Second, a choice has to be made regarding the type of camera to be used, it's specifications, capabilities, size, cost, and maneuverability. Third, should the camera be fixed on a tripod, thereby leaving the researcher free to move around the setting; or if the target of the video is moving, does the handheld approach work better? The use of two cameras should also be considered because this enables a simultaneously recorded close-up view of the action, along with a second view that can picture a wider view of the context in which the interaction is playing out. Alternatively, a nonobtrusive 360-degree-type camera might be more appropriate for some situations where simultaneous interactions are important to capture (Camic et al., 2018, p. 6). The scope of this chapter does not extend to the technical aspects of which camera to use. There are many possibilities commercially available, and expert advice should be sought before purchasing equipment. It is important to note that technological improvements in equipment and software happen rapidly, so it would be wise to seek up-to-date advice regarding the most appropriate cameras and analytic equipment for the task in hand.

The researcher has to choose how visible he or she will be in the recording setting. Four possible stances can be taken, and these vary according to the degree of intrusion that the researcher is prepared to make into the recording setting. This classification is taken from Speziale and Carpenter (2007). The researcher can be a *complete observer*, taking no part in the action, or an *observer as participant*, participating only tangentially in the action. A more involved stance is *participant as observer*; this suggests that the researcher is then intentionally part of the action. Finally, the researcher could adopt the stance of *complete participant*, becoming a fully acknowledged actor in the proceedings. Obviously the requirements of the research itself, along with the sensitivities of the people in the research, setting will largely determine the choice; however, the potentially disruptive impact of the researcher should be factored into the decision that is made. The implications of the stranger's presence in a setting may be disruptive. All in all, the Hawthorne effect, as it is known, implies that a researcher's presence affects the observed action (Polit & Hungler, 1999); however, it has been suggested that this effect wears off over time (Mulhall, 2003), and research approaches can be developed to facilitate a gentle insertion of the researcher and the camera into the setting over time that lessens the intrusive effect on the action.

THE CAPABILITIES OF VIDEO

Video has major advantages compared with participant or nonparticipant observation in which the data are recorded using field notes. In considering the utility of video in examining the interactions of parents and infants, Beebe (2006) suggested that slowing the action down permits behaviors that were previously invisible to become apparent: "a videotape played in slowed time, or frame-by-frame, acts like a social microscope revealing subtleties and subliminal details of interactions which are too rapid and complex to grasp with the naked eye in ongoing time" (p. 151).

So, what processes does video reveal? According to Bezemer et al. (2017), video permits the viewing of aspects of clinical work that are too "small scale and ephemeral to be noticed in real time" (p. 584). This fine-grained analysis allows for the observation of teamwork and of "manners of talking, acting and reasoning that participants themselves are often unaware of" (p. 584). Video often appears to reveal what is going on beneath the surface of the interaction process and indeed beneath the surface of the individual's consciousness in some cases. It enables the detection of "habits, routines, and practices that are unnoticed by the participants involved, these are the tacit aspects of communication," according to Majlesi et al. (2018, p. 71).

But these behavioral processes must be revealed by specific behaviors, and these are detailed by various researchers. The variety of behaviors that video reveals can be classified as vocalizations such as crying, laughter, moaning, loud breathing, and, of course, silence. Eye expressions, such as the direction of eye gaze, the focus of attention, and joint attention, as well as eye behaviors, such as winking and blinking, are also observable. Facial expressions, such as smiling, mouth movements, lip movements, and frowning, can be identified. Body activities, including stretching, head turning, changing posture, and stillness, are all evident in video. Lastly, gestures such as arm movements, gross and subtle head movements, hand expressions, scratching, rubbing, and of course pointing and symbolic gestures are all identifiable through video (Griffiths, 2011). It is interesting to note that video offers a very detailed view of what is to be seen and can also capture those behaviors that are potentially observable or to be expected in a situation but are in fact not present.

Ultimately, the argument for using video in qualitative research is that it appears to allow individuals who cannot speak and interact in a conventional manner to "speak" through the observation of how they communicate using their bodies. By way of further illustration, Campbell and Ward (2018), who carried out research on the experiences of people with dementia in a hair salon, noted that "video has the ability to capture elements that are not easily seen or described such as responses to smells, temperatures or to the sensory feel of something" (p. 98). They further contended that the use of film enables those with dementia who rarely communicate verbally to make sounds and exhibit behaviors that reflect the internal processes going on within them. They poignantly described a woman who oscillated between periods of anxiety and calm as she progressed through the experience of having her hair washed and dried. In short, Campbell and Ward suggested that the some of the thoughts of people with advanced dementia whom they were observing were made apparent through the use of video by close observation of their behaviors.

Having decided how to film and collect the video data and what data to collect, the next step is to process the data. This is best done by uploading the video files to a PC or laptop for analysis. Technical advice is best sought before embarking on this process; however, a proprietary video-editing program will probably be used to hold, observe, and manipulate the video films. This is the precursor to the initial analysis of the data and its presentation in narrative form.

FROM VIDEO INTO NARRATIVE

The research design will dictate what the narrative framework that is used to analyze the data that has been collected in the video looks like. The general principles that underpin the design of such a bespoke analytic framework are explained in this section. A strong narrative framework should be able to include and name all the differing elements, such as the setting in which the action is taking place and the main activities that are proceeding in parallel with the target behaviors of interest, which may influence these behaviors.

Furthermore, it should be structured in a way that facilitates the unearthing of the relationships between the behaviors and between the actions in the setting so that the potential causes and effects are clearly evident. This process was lucidly described by Haslbeck (2014), who examined the impact of music therapy on two premature infants when she noted that she wished to identify the "patterns of interaction, coherence and possible causal relationships between . . . the child, therapist and environment within the music therapy process" (p. 11). The actual narrative itself depends on the target behaviors that are being observed, but in general, the aim of the researcher is, as noted previously, to develop a thick description of the events that have been filmed. That means describing the interaction, behaviors of interest, or events that are being targeted as well as the surrounding events. Specifically, the events that are antecedent to the behavior take place at the same time, and subsequent behaviors in detail and in sequence. Clearly, every observer will approach such a task with a degree of subjectivity; however, this may be obviated if the description is sufficiently detailed; furthermore, the use of two observers, each producing parallel accounts, may be helpful when the events being observed are potentially ambivalent or unclear.

Several steps are required to work up a manageable structure into which the data from a video can be inputted (see Figure 10.1). The implication is that the researcher must enumerate the different types of target behaviors that are of interest, identify the other factors that will affect the action that has been observed in the video, and identify the number of participants in the action. The analytic framework will be structured so that it contains boxes (compartments) for each type of data that is being sought. In general, these are probably best aligned horizontally. The vertical axis will then contain the temporal breakdown of the data so that a sequential narrative unfolds as the reader progresses downward through the figure's table. The timing structure will differ depending on the exact behaviors and the different external events that are being targeted in the research. The analytic framework will be designed to

FIGURE 10.1. Video Transcription Record

Name_____ Date_____ Recording numbers (start–finish)_____

	Participant	JM	Participant	MD	
Recording no. (time)	Nonverbal	Verbal	Nonverbal	Verbal	Comments

make explicit the sequence of events that are observed. One event or behavior is likely to be named and described on each horizontal line. Thus, the length of time that each horizontal line encompasses depends very much on the degree of temporal detail required by the research. In many ways, the decision as to how long a line within the analytic framework lasts for determines the degree of detail and the degree of temporal magnification of the action that is being sought. For example, one line could represent one second of action; this would allow for a reasonable view of most interactions. However, for some research that may be too detailed and not required, whereas for other types of research that are examining microbehaviors, each line may represent one frame of the action (1/24th of a second). An example of a typical analytic framework is illustrated in Figure 10.1.

MICROANALYSIS OF VIDEO DATA

As noted in the previous section, the types of target behaviors that are sought will be predominantly nonverbal behaviors, such as an individual's eye movements, gaze, head orientation, and facial expressions. Whole body movements and body posture are also potential target behaviors, as are limb movements and gestures. If available and relevant to the research, speech, vocalizations, and symbolic gestures can be recorded. One of the key abilities of this approach to data collection is that video potentially records everything that is going on and in such detail that microbehaviors are readily observed; therefore, the researcher must choose which behaviors to target. The researcher must also decide which additional elements should be noted, for example, what events are happening in the surrounding setting that are of interest, such as the ways people respond to peripheral stimuli and the ways that people subsequently reorient (de Barbaro et al., 2011). The key factor in this decision is what relationships are being investigated, that is, what links are being sought between potential events in the environment and specific behaviors—for example, the interrelationship of physical action between two people. Figure 10.2 (part 3.24) illustrates this where the action of one participant influences the action of the other. Another key aspect that this type of research approach can reveal is the minute microinteraction between two or more individuals' behaviors. A well-designed, tightly sectioned framework should allow for the minute interplay of nonverbal behaviors that occur in dyadic communication but are not normally evident.

The degree to which minute observations may be made is illustrated by de Barbaro et al. (2011), who, while observing infant interaction in a naturalistic setting, recorded infants' small saccades (rapid eye movements) and fine-grained measures of gaze distribution, then measured looking-time behaviors. Harrison (2005) commented on the utility of such an approach in determining patterns of interaction between family members; this capability to analyze cause, effect, and the complicated web and nuance of causality and impact is one of the determining strengths of the microanalytic approach.

FIGURE 10.2. Transcription Sample 1 (JM)

Name John Moore Date 22 April Tape numbers (start–finish) 3.20–3.40 Event—Walk 1. JM is being prompted to walk across the classroom from one staff to another.

Recording No.	Participant Nonverbal		JM Verbal	Participant Nonverbal	KM. Verbal	Comments	My interpretation	Staff's interpretation
3.20	Eye gaze	looks down at floor		Is in front of JM about 10 feet away but not in view		M standing behind holding JM by the [r] hand and [l] arm *Now you just go down another.*	JM is determined	
	Facial expression	Set jaw						
	Head movement							
	Arm movement							
	Leg movement							
	Other	JM standing in front of M. [l] arm held by M, wriggles in her hold.	Oooh					
3.21	Eye gaze	looking down				M withdraws [r] hand behind JM *Little bit*		
	Facial expression	grin						
	Head movement							
	Arm movement	[r] arm rises and comes across to M's hand						
	Leg movement							

	Other	Wriggles in M's arms	Ooh					
3.22	Eye gaze	Looks at his [I] hand				M *Call him*		JM is trying to get in front of M
	Facial expression							
	Head movement							
	Arm movement	[r] hand goes around to catch M's [I] which is holding his own [I]						
	Leg movement							
	Other							
3.23	Eye gaze	Down at hands		JM		M looking forward, releases his [I] hand and pulls her [I] hand back *Now*	JM anticipating a routine that he knows and likes well	JM is saying *I'll be there in a minute.*
	Facial expression	grinning						
	Head movement							
	Arm movement	Withdraws [I] hand from M's hold, his 2 hands come together						
	Leg movement							
	Other		Oooh					

(continues)

FIGURE 10.2. Transcription Sample 1 (JM) (Continued)

3.24	Eye gaze	Looking forward but down		M withdraws her hands completely and watches him set off *Off you go, JM*	
	Facial expression				
	Head movement				
	Arm movement	Hands unclasp arms stretch out			
	Leg movement	Moves forward			
	Other				
3.25	Eye gaze		Arms extended to catch JM	JM	M hand out
	Facial expression	Intent on looking at KM			
	Head movement				
	Arm movement	[r] arm extended wide and [l] also extended			M as if to support JM should he stumble
	Leg movement				
	Other	Walks rapidly forward			

				That's it	—	
3.26	Eye gaze	Looking at KM			—	
	Facial expression					
	Head movement					
	Arm movement	Extended				
	Leg movement					
	Other	Lurches slightly to [I] as he progresses toward KM	*Ooooh*			
3.27	Eye gaze	Looking directly at KM			Leaning forward, arms extended toward the oncoming JM, looking at him; retreats back as he catches her hands and slows down	
	Facial expression	Fond expression		M *Oh very good JM*		JM delighted to be about to meet KM
	Head movement	Turns [I] to look at camera as he passes				
	Arm movement					
	Leg movement					
	Other	Moves to catch KM's hands				

Note. Verbal statements are italicized.

Ultimately, the impact of a microanalysis of this type was summed up by Margaret Mead, who in 1963, while using multiple sequential photographs in her anthropological work, commented on "large numbers of pictures of interactional events to record minimal changes or differences which may be crucial to an analysis of events on a micro cultural level, but which would not be precisely observed without the use of the camera" (Collier, 1967, p. 75). However, the value of using camera and video is only realized if the structure for handling the data is well designed in terms of its orientation and precision, which in turn presents the data in a narrative form which is amenable to analysis.

THE DEVELOPMENT OF THEORY

The analytic framework in which the video data are presented constitutes the narrative data. The narrative data from the video equate to the interview transcript with which most qualitative research is concerned. So, the problem that presents itself is how to unearth the inherent structure (theory) that may underpin the narrative as presented in the analytic framework.

The approach to theory development recommended by this author (Griffiths & Smith, 2016) for video analysis is classic grounded theory as proposed by Glaser and Strauss (1967) and subsequently refined by Glaser. Classic grounded theory, in its initial iterations, was not conceived as being concerned with video data. Glaser (1998) repeatedly made the point that person-to-person interviews should not be (audio) recorded. Furthermore, this goes against the grain of classic grounded theory which suggests that data collection should be tightly targeted. Glaser goes on to suggest that excess data obtained from audio and video recording makes delimiting (focusing on what is precisely relevant for the emergence of the theory) very difficult. Subsequently the development of research methods that use video to study nonspeaking participants, as well as advances in video technology, have opened up new fields of research, thus requiring rethinking of Glaser's earlier assumptions. For example, Nilsson (2012) was using grounded theory to research people with profound cognitive difficulties. In her personal correspondence with Glaser in the early 2000s, he modified this stricture to enable the collection of data from an otherwise unreachable cohort.

Theories are abstract conceptualizations that aim to explain relationships between observed phenomena (Craig, 1980). They also enable prediction and explanation of behavior, and they should be applicable to practical, everyday situations (Glaser & Strauss, 1967). Theories therefore by their nature are approximations to the truth. To ensure that a theory is as close an approximation to the truth (what is inherent in the data) as possible, Glaser suggests that the constant comparative method be used to analyze the data, and that approach is explained subsequently in the section titled Coding the Data.

At the outset of the research, the researcher should adopt the approach of "not knowing" in order to have as blank a mental sheet as possible onto which the theory will be written. This implies that the researcher is comfortable with, or at least accepting of, uncertainty. An initial acceptance that ambiguity, confusion, and uncertainty are to be expected and indeed welcomed implies that the researcher adopt a fundamental state of mind, that of "trusting to emergence" (Glaser, 1998). Allowing the inherent patterns of social organization to emerge from the data through the constant comparative method of data analysis is fundamental to the data analysis process, and it is where it diverges most clearly from the other, aforementioned approaches to grounded theory. In many ways, the key to this data analysis approach is that the researcher can tolerate uncertainty and is willing to let the patterns that are inherent in the data speak.

Classic grounded theory aims to develop a theory that has logical consistency; is clear, parsimonious, states no more than is needed to make clear the inherent patterns; has density and scope; is integrated; fits the data; and works to explain what is going on in the data (Glaser, 1998). So, having determined one's approach to the data and having made the video recordings and transcribed the data, the next step is to code it.

VIDEO DATA ANALYSIS

The data analysis process initially pulls apart the narrative to identify patterns that are inherent but not obvious within it. Identification of these patterns enables the structure that lies beneath the surface of the data to emerge— namely, the theory that explains the main concerns of the participants in the narrative. The first step in the process is to code the data.

Coding the Data

At the outset, the researcher is confronted by an analytic framework that contains the narrative data. The procedure is to examine each aspect of the narrative line-by-line to identify significant single words, phrases, sentences, and sometimes paragraphs. The researcher must pay attention to the sequencing of the action, to the relationships between the verbal and nonverbal behaviors of all of the participants, and to the interplay between the behaviors and any external events that are evident in the data (see Figure 10.2 for an example of this). Thus, by looking closely at the details of the data, it becomes possible to name (code) discrete events, behavioral sequences, phenomena, and processes that are inherent in the data; this is the basic level of analysis, and it determines the fundamental building blocks of the theory.

The constant comparative method works by naming one incident as a code, then naming a second incident as code and comparing the two. They may be the same code, in which case the two incidents are combined under the same code name. If different they are named differently, and a third incident is examined and named. It may be related to one of the previous two codes, in which case it is subsumed under that name, or it may be different and be given a new name. This process continues as the researcher codes their way through the data. The key to the process is that as each new piece of coded data (incident) is compared with the previously coded data; the researcher asks if this new incident can be included in the previously named code because it is denotes a similar concept, or should a new code be named? For a fuller description of the coding process, see Griffiths (2011, p. 104).

As the process proceeds, codes can be grouped together under categories. Categories are formed of codes that appear to have something in common. It may take some time before the commonalities inherent in the codes are evident. However, after a while, it will become clear that some codes can be grouped under a category name because they share one or more properties. Subsequently, other codes will be grouped under a different name (because they refer to different concepts than those in the first category), and ultimately most codes are likely to end up in a category. The constant comparative process applies not only to the naming of codes but also to the naming of categories. An initial category name will be provisional as new codes are named. As the database grows, new codes may be added to the category; if its name is robust—if it effectively conceptualizes the codes that it contains, it will not need to be changed; however, it may be that the new codes alter the conceptual nature of the category, and consequently its name will change. It may also be that the addition of new codes changes the nature of the category to such an extent that some codes allocated to it are removed and allocated to different category. The point is that codes and categories are initially provisional and that only as the data analysis process continues do they become more fixed. As the process continues, the categories themselves will be clustered into higher order categories or themes. Eventually one category will emerge that is related to all or most of the other categories; this is the core category, and it will explain the main concerns of the participants in the research—that is, it provides the inherent, latent structure of the theory (Glaser, 1998), and it will in all probability give its name to the theory and answer the research question. It should be noted that the researcher's perspective necessarily guides the application of the coding and categorization process; however, classic grounded theory reduces—and Glaser would contend, eliminates—this subjective element because the constant comparative method implies that continually returning to the data to find out if the named code or category reflects what is there implies that the theoretical framework that emerges will possess an inherent validity that is derived from its fit with the data (see the section on rigor, later in the chapter). Glaser (1998) termed this "letting the data speak" and noted that "the goal [of grounded theory] is not to tell people what to find or to force but what to do to allow the emergence of what is going on" (p. 41).

Writing Memos

Coding data by its nature fractures the narrative. The narrative story is broken up into small pieces, allocated to boxes that contain it, and eventually arranged in a vertical structure that offers a view of what the bones of the narrative consist of. These are named substantive codes and categories because they represent the data in the substantive area—that is, they are derived from the topic being researched. When represented visually, they are the vertical lines of the theory. However, a theory by its nature requires the substantive components to be woven together or linked up so that the relationships between the different aspects of the substantive area become clear. Glaser (1998) termed these "theoretical codes" and noted that they "conceptualize how the substantive codes will relate to each other as interrelated, multivariate hypotheses in accounting for resolving the main concern of the participants" (p. 163). Thus, the theoretical codes weave together the fractured data into a whole; they provide the horizontal lines of the theory so that ultimately the theory can be construed as a grid with vertical lines (the substantive codes and categories) and horizontal lines namely the theoretical codes. Theoretical codes are generated by the writing of memos.

The role of memos is concisely summed up as intended to assist the researcher to "clarify creative leaps made when linking, merging or splitting categories and (also) to record emerging theoretical reflections" (Burck, 2005, p. 245). Memos can be said to assist in the description and analysis of the relationships that potentially exist between the codes and categories that have been identified from the data as the coding process and the analysis proceeds (Glaser, 1978). Glaser and Strauss (1967) carefully considered how the process of constantly comparing the emergent codes and categories impacts the researcher's thinking; they suggested that it soon induces the researcher, here termed the "analyst," to think about the theoretical links that might work to explain what is happening in the data: "The analyst starts thinking in terms of the full range of types or continua of the category, its dimensions, the conditions under which it is pronounced or minimized, its major consequences, its relations to other categories, its other properties" (p. 106).

What happens is that "after coding for a category perhaps three or four times, the analyst will find conflicts in the emphasis (way) he is thinking" (Glaser & Strauss, 1967, p. 107) about the category and its relationship to the code and will be musing over theoretical notions and ideas that the coding process is forcing them to consider (i.e., should the data be coded into this category or another, and what is the rationale for doing either? How should the next incident that is similar be coded?). This is the time to write a memo taking into consideration the researcher's thoughts about the different options they could take in regard to how they code incidents and what the consequences of these might be. Furthermore, the incident in the data may also be coded for other categories, and the rationale for consigning the incident to any other specific category should also be considered. In other words, the researcher should go back and forth over the data as each piece of data is coded, with the aim of allowing this roving process to stimulate ideas about the relationship of each code to each other and to the inherent categories that are emerging with the aim of then writing memos that will explore the possible relationships between the codes and the categories that are emerging. Two examples of memos are taken from the case study detailed later in the chapter are found in Exhibit 10.1. Analytic Memo 53 asks a question of the data, and memo 55 determines an

---

EXHIBIT 10.1

Examples of Analytic Memos

Analytic Memo 53
Two categories are similar:

> Gaze response to definite stimulus and reaction to being handled . . . should they be merged or are they telling different things?

Analytic Memo 55
The relationship between the categories:

> Ignoring, disinterest, and bored is framed by the connect of not engaging with the activity; however, each category represents a decreasing level of active disengagement.

---

emergent (theoretical) taxonomy of disinterest. Both these memos imply returning to the data to ascertain the answer to the issues they pose; this is a fairly typical role that memos may play in determining the eventual structure of the theory.

To sum up, the actual process of coding induces the researcher to think about what is happening, and these thoughts are then written down as memos. It may be that the researcher ends up with a large memo bank of tens or even hundreds of memos. When the researcher comes to examine these, some memos will prove to be interesting but useless from a theoretical viewpoint, but others may suggest theoretical links across the codes—and more especially the categories. The researcher then experiments by inserting the idea generated by the memo into the emerging theoretical structure to see if it fits; the question to be asked is whether the ideas expressed in the emergent theory fit the data. If so, the researcher may write a memo considering the implications of this. At this point, the theory is starting to emerge, the researcher may decide that some aspects of the theory require additional explanation, and so may return to the field to collect additional data and make further observations (often described as theoretical sampling) in specific areas. Alternatively, the researcher may understand that no further useful data is to be found, and data saturation or theoretical sufficiency has been achieved.

Rigor and Elegance of the Theory

Two additional matters should be addressed in considering the data analysis process and the production of (emergence of) a theory. The first relates to the rigor of the analysis and the theory. Conventional criteria for assessing qualitative research center on trustworthiness (does the work reflect the human experience in the data?), dependability (consistency of the analysis), credibility (does the work reflect the perceptions of the participants?), transferability (are results generalizable?), and confirmability (can the data be traced to its source?;

Holloway & Wheeler, 2002). Grounded theory eschews these measures for the criteria of relevance and instead asks the following questions: Is the theory applicable to those who were researched? Does the theory address the main concern of the participants? Does the theory work to explain the participants' behavior? Is the theory modifiable? And above all, does it *fit* (a key term) the substantive area? (Glaser, 1998). Achieving these criteria requires a thorough application of the constant comparative process. One further point that Glaser emphasized is that if there is a perception that the theory omits something or is manifestly wrong, then the researcher should refer to the data to ascertain whether this is the case. Glaser's injunction that the data are always right applies here.

The second issue is the question of the final shape of the theory. Glaser and Strauss (1967) made the point that as the theory develops delimiting occurs. That means that as noted previously, the theory changes very little as theoretical saturation is reached. Final modifications tend to be concerned with clarifying the logic of the theoretical structure and removing those aspects of the theory that are not relevant, thus reducing the theory to its essentials. The final theory aims to be elegant in addressing the main concern of the participants and in presenting an open and easily accessible face suggesting that this theory will tell something about how the world works.

CASE STUDY: ATTUNING, A THEORY OF INTERACTION OF PEOPLE WITH SEVERE AND PROFOUND MULTIPLE DISABILITY AND THEIR CARERS

The lives of people with severe, profound, and multiple intellectual disabilities are difficult to know. This is for various reasons but primarily because they have severely impaired cognitive and adaptive abilities. Numerically they may be considered to have an IQ below 35 (Hanzen et al., 2017). However, an influential school of thought suggests that reductionist approaches to the measurement of intelligence do not fully measure the abilities of people with such pervasive disabilities and that, as a result, existing standardized tests cannot meaningfully assess their capabilities (Nakken & Vlaskamp, 2007). Most will, however, have concomitant sensory disabilities, such that 81% of people with profound intellectual disability also have a visual disability, 31% an auditory problem (Zijlstra & Vlaskamp, 2005), up to 50% have epilepsy, and many have motor impairments. The result is that people in this group live largely apart, frequently in high-support residential units. They need assistance with washing, eating, dressing, and all self-help skills, and some form of support will be a lifelong requirement. In terms of communication, most people with severe and all those with profound intellectual disability will have greatly impaired cognitive processes such that they have little or no expressive or receptive language. People with severe intellectual disability may have some vocabulary and a limited comprehension of symbolic language, but those with profound intellectual disability will likely be nonverbal, will not communicate using symbolic language, and as a result have a "limited ability to use a formal linguistic code in any modality" (Grove et al., 1999, p. 190).

The aim of the study was to answer the following question: How do people with severe and profound intellectual and multiple disability interact with those with whom they come into contact? (Griffiths & Smith, 2016). The basic assumption behind the research was that communication is dyadic (i.e., that it takes at least two people and that communication emanates from a behavior that has an inherent meaning that can be interpreted). At its most effective, communication ensures that "mutual understanding rests on attaining a shared understanding of the interpretation to be ascribed to signals" (Griffiths & Smith, 2016, p. 125). To achieve this aim, research was carried out in a school for children and adolescents with severe and profound intellectual disability in Ireland. Purposeful sampling was used to select three dyads. Each dyad consisted of one child or adolescent with a profound intellectual disability and one staff member. However, only the data from two of the dyads were subsequently analyzed. Ethical permission was obtained from the service that administered the school in question and from the university that supervised the research. Consent was obtained from the nondisabled staff members and proxy consent from the parents or grandparents of those with intellectual disability.

One dyad consisted of an older teenager who was a semiambulant man with a profound intellectual disability and his key worker, who was his dedicated childcare worker (a brief section of this participant's transcript is included in Figure 10.2). The second dyad consisted of a man in his mid-20s who had a borderline severe–profound intellectual disability, was paraplegic and therefore used a wheelchair, and his key worker, who was a nurse (for full details, see Griffiths, 2011, and Griffiths & Smith, 2016). Each dyad was filmed for 1 hour while engaging in various school-based activities, such as one-to-one games, group games, group stories, painting sessions, motor activity sessions, and one mealtime. The interaction necessarily involved filming other staff and occasionally students as they participated in the activity sessions. Each particular session was chosen because it was thought likely that meaningful interaction would take place during it. Filming was carried out using an observer as participant stance. This meant that the researcher participated very little in the action but would not refuse to engage when interaction was prompted by students in the group. To prepare for the filming, I (the researcher) spent some time in the preceding weeks with the students and staff letting them know what would happen, getting to know them, and enabling them to get to know me.

The video camera was discreetly located on a tripod in whichever classroom was being used for the relevant activity. The video was made using a JVC GR-D240 digital video camera. The action was recorded and subsequently uploaded to a laptop computer. Ulead Video studio 7 (Corel Corporation, Ottawa, Ontario, Canada), a video-editing package, was used to handle and edit the video. This software enabled the film to be run backward and forward at normal, slow, or fast speeds; most importantly, it enabled the video to be run on a frame-by-frame basis (24 frames per second), which facilitated a very detailed analysis of the observed action and was especially useful in analyzing the detailed sequence of events where cause and effect occurred in microseconds.

Twenty-five minutes of data were purposefully chosen for transcription because they represented the most interaction-intensive sessions; this was split into 12 and 13 minutes between the two dyads. The initial data transcription process aimed to develop a highly detailed narrative that would encompass nearly every viewable aspect of the interaction in a selected session Figure 10.2 gives a representation of how a small part of the findings looked when transcribed into a fine, detailed narrative; please note that all names and abbreviations of names are pseudonyms. Please also note that JM is the person with a profound intellectual disability, KM his key worker, and M another staff member who works in the school. Data timings are in minutes and seconds. It should be emphasized that the fine detail of the interaction process was the focus of both the filming process and the subsequent distillation of the video into narrative. (For full details of the research method, see Griffiths, 2011, pp. 61–115.) In this vignette, JM, who has an unsteady gait, is engaged in one of his activities—namely, walking practice.

The study was analyzed using the grounded theory approach detailed earlier, and it revealed that the staff and students with severe/profound intellectual disability communicated by attuning to each other. The mechanics of this process were found to be regular and essentially procedural. Seven categories of data were identified, and attuning was found to be the core category, that is, the category that integrated the others and was the main concern of the participants. The categories were as follows: the *Setting*, that is, the physical environment in which the action took place; *Being*, which can be thought of as representing the person's state of mind; *Stimulus*, which is where one communication partner tried to induce an action from another; *Action*, which was defined as "an observable process of behavioral change in an individual which is demonstrated by movement, gesture, facial expression, vocalization or other behaviour" (Griffiths & Smith, 2017, p. 111); *Attention*, which was an indicator that a shared point of reference, or the actions of another partner in the dyad were being watched by the first communication partner; and *Engagement*, which was defined as "a category that describes the point in the interpersonal process where the attention of two or more people is focused on each other or one person is focused on an object or an event" (Griffiths & Smith, 2017, p. 112). *Attuning* was then seen as the process that integrated the other categories.

Multiple hypotheses were generated by the theory; however, the primary theoretical statement was that in communication between people with severe and profound intellectual disability and their nondisabled communication partners,

> the setting influences the state of mind of the person in it (his or her sense of being). A person's state of mind influences what stimuli the person offers to another, who may attend to the stimulus or not. Attending to the stimulus is influenced by the setting in which the interaction takes place and the state of mind of the person attending to the stimulus. If the other attends to the stimulus, he or she may act or may become engaged with the first person. (Griffiths & Smith, 2016, p. 130)

This is determined by the attuning process. Attuning is therefore described as a "process whereby communication partners move symmetrically or asymmetrically towards or away from each cognitively and emotionally" (Griffiths & Smith, 2016, p. 130).

CONCLUSION

The case study presented in this chapter offers one example of how a visual grounded theory approach to data collection and analysis can work. It was concerned with opening up understanding of one poorly understood group of people who are largely marginalized in society. In the view of this researcher, one of the great advantages of this approach to inquiry is that it opens up and gives a voice to those who cannot speak, those who have difficulty communicating, and those who are very impaired psychologically, such as those with severe intellectual disability. However, it is also relevant to the understanding of those in the later stages of dementia (Clare et al., 2020). I also suspect that application of this approach in examining the ordinary lives of those who are not disabled and not in any way "different" may reveal much that was previously unnoticed. To return to the suggestion of Bezemer et al. (2017), a fine-grained analysis of video allows for the observation of "manners of talking, acting and reasoning that participants themselves are often unaware of" (p. 584), implying that there is much ordinary interaction conducted in everybody's daily life that can be discovered by the application of these methods.

Two cautions must be mentioned, however. The first relates to the ethical issues underpinning the study of those who cannot fully consent to participate, for which there are two aspects to consider. Confidentiality, which in the case study described in the preceding section was secured through the use of initialled pseudonyms and by ensuring that no identifying information was present in the text. Second, consent is important for all research participants but especially so for those from vulnerable populations, as in this case study. For those participants who could give fully informed written consent, it was obtained from each participant directly. Consent for those who could not give fully informed written consent (i.e., those with severe or profound intellectual disability) was given by a close relative or guardian of the participant. However, for each participant's autonomy to be fully assured, the principles of process consent were applied. Process consent is person-centered, derives from the situation, and takes the welfare of the participant as paramount (Dewing, 2007). Thus, consent to participate should be based on a gradual introduction to the research, should be ongoing and should be judged "on how the person responds and what feelings they express" (Dewing, 2008, p. 63). This approach was applied in the case study.

The second caution is a methodological one—namely, that the analysis (particularly the transcription of the data from video into narrative format) of the 25 minutes of data in the case study described in this chapter took a long time. In general, it took more than 5 hours to transcribe 1 minute of video into narrative. There are only a few other examples of this type of data analysis. One of these is Schoenfeld's (1992) work. He made a video of one student who was playing an educational video game; his intention was to "understand virtually all the actions (of the student) taken in a problem session and the mental states that lay behind them" (p. 182). Schoenfeld reported that the 7 hours of video he made took 18 months to analyze. He noted that in the context of thick description of an event these descriptions were "thicker than most" (p. 209). The researcher must be cognizant of the length of time and the intensity of the work required by this approach to inquiry, but the prize it offers of revealing behaviors, actions, and interactions that participants themselves, health and social care professionals, family members, and others are not aware of surely makes it worth the effort.

REFERENCES

Beebe, B. (2006). Co-constructing mother-infant distress in face-to-face interactions: Contributions of microanalysis. *International Journal of Infant Observation and Its Applications, 9*(2), 151–164.

Bezemer, J., Cope, A., Korkiakangas, T., Kress, G., Murtagh, G., Weldon, S. M., & Kneebone, R. (2017). Microanalysis of video from the operating room: An underused approach to patient safety research. *BMJ Quality & Safety, 26*(7), 583–587. https://doi.org/10.1136/bmjqs-2016-005816

Burck, C. (2005). Comparing qualitative research methodologies for systemic research: The use of grounded theory, discourse analysis and narrative analysis. *Journal of Family Therapy, 27*(3), 237–262. https://doi.org/10.1111/j.1467-6427.2005.00314.x

Camic, P. M., Crutch, S. J., Murphy, C., Firth, N. C., Harding, E., Harrison, C. R., Howard, S., Strohmaier, S., Van Leewen, J., West, J., Windle, G., Wray, S., & Zeilig, H. (2018). Conceptualising artistic creativity in the dementias: Interdisciplinary approaches to research and practice. *Frontiers in Psychology, 9*, Article 1842. https://doi.org/10.3389/fpsyg.2018.01842

Campbell, S., & Ward, R. (2018). Video and observation data as a method to document practice and performances of gender in the dementia care hair salon. In J. Keady, L.-C. Hyden, A. Johnson, & C. Swarbrick (Eds.), *Social research methods in dementia studies* (pp. 96–118). Routledge.

Charmaz, C. (2006). *Constructing grounded theory*. Sage Publications.

Clare, A., Camic, P. M., Crutch, S. J., West, J., Harding, E., & Brotherhood, E. (2020). Using music to develop a multisensory communicative environment for people with late stage dementia. *The Gerontologist, 60*(6), 1115–1125. https://doi.org/10.1093/geront/gnz169

Collier, J. (1967). *Visual anthropology: Photography as a research method*. Holt, Rhinehart and Winston.

Craig, S. L. (1980). Theory development and its relevance for nursing. *Journal of Advanced Nursing, 5*(4), 349–355. https://doi.org/10.1111/j.1365-2648.1980.tb00975.x

de Barbaro, K., Chiba, A., & Deák, G. O. (2011). Micro-analysis of infant looking in a naturalistic social setting: Insights from biologically based models of attention. *Developmental Science, 14*(5), 1150–1160. https://doi.org/10.1111/j.1467-7687.2011.01066.x

Dewing, J. (2007). Participatory research: A method for process consent with persons who have dementia. *Dementia (London), 6*(1), 11–25. https://doi.org/10.1177/1471301207075625

Dewing, J. (2008). Process consent and research with older persons living with dementia. *Research Ethics Review, 4*(2), 59–64. https://doi.org/10.1177/174701610800400205

Geertz, C. (2017). Thick description: Towards an interpretive theory of culture. In P. Erickson & L. D. Murphy (Eds.), *Reading for a history of anthropological theory* (5th ed., pp. 136–160). University of Toronto Press.

Glaser, B. (1978). *Theoretical sensitivity*. Sociology Press.

Glaser, B. (1992). *Basics of grounded theory analysis*. Sociology Press.

Glaser, B. (1998). *Doing grounded theory: Issues and discussion*. Sociology Press.

Glaser, B., & Strauss, A. (1967). *The discovery of grounded theory: Strategies for qualitative research*. Aldine De Gruyter.

Griffiths, C. (2011). *Attuning: A theory of interaction of people with severe and multiple intellectual and multiple disability and their carers* [Unpublished doctoral dissertation]. Trinity College. http://www.tara.tcd.ie/handle/2262/77028

Griffiths, C., & Smith, M. (2016). Attuning: A communication process between people with severe and profound intellectual disability and their interaction partners. *Journal of Applied Research in Intellectual Disabilities, 29*(2), 124–138. https://doi.org/10.1111/jar.12162

Griffiths, C., & Smith, M. (2017). You and me: The structural basis for the interaction of people with severe and profound intellectual disability and others. *Journal of Intellectual Disabilities, 21*(2), 103–117. https://doi.org/10.1177/1744629516644380

Grove, N., Bunning, K., Porter, J., & Morgan, M. (1999). See what I mean: Interpreting the meaning of communications by people with severe and profound intellectual disabilities. *Journal of Applied Research in Intellectual Disabilities, 12*(3), 190–203. https://doi.org/10.1111/j.1468-3148.1999.tb00076.x

Hanzen, G., van Nispen, R. M., van der Putten, A. A., & Waninge, A. (2017). Participation of adults with visual and severe or profound intellectual disabilities: Definition and operationalization. *Research in Developmental Disabilities, 61*, 95–107. https://doi.org/10.1016/j.ridd.2016.12.017

Harrison, A. M. (2005). Herding the animals into the barn: A parent consultation model. *The Psychoanalytic Study of the Child, 60*(1), 128–153. https://doi.org/10.1080/00797308.2005.11800749

Haslbeck, F. B. (2014). Creative music therapy with premature infants: An analysis of video footage. *Nordic Journal of Music Therapy, 23*(1), 5–35. https://doi.org/10.1080/08098131.2013.780091

Holloway, I., & Wheeler, S. (2002). *Qualitative research in nursing* (2nd ed.). Blackwell.

Jack, D. (1991). *Silencing the self: Depression and women*. Harvard University Press.

Majlesi, A., Nilsson, E., & Ekstrom, A. (2018). Video data as a method to understand nonverbal communication in couples where one person is living with dementia. In J. Keady, L.-C Hyden, A. Johnson, & C. Swarbrick (Eds.), *Social research methods in dementia studies*. Routledge.

Mulhall, A. (2003). In the field: Notes on observation in qualitative research. *Journal of Advanced Nursing, 41*(3), 306–313.

Nakken, H., & Vlaskamp, C. (2007). A need for a taxonomy for profound intellectual and multiple disabilities. *Journal of Policy and Practice in Intellectual Disabilities, 4*(2), 83–87. https://doi.org/10.1111/j.1741-1130.2007.00104.x

Nilsson, L. (2012). Using video methods in grounded theory research. In V. Martin & A. Gynnild (Eds.), *Grounded theory: The philosophy, method and work of Barney Glaser*. Brown Walker Press.

Ollerenshaw, J., & Creswell, J. (2002). Narrative research: A comparison of two restorying data approaches. *Qualitative Inquiry, 8*(3), 329–347. https://doi.org/10.1177/10778004008003008

Polit, D., & Hungler, B. (1999). *Nursing research: Principles and methods*. Lippincott.

Schoenfeld, A. H. (1992). On paradigms and methods: What do you do when the ones you know don't do what you want them to? Issues in the analysis of data in the form of videotapes. *Journal of the Learning Sciences, 2*(2), 179–214. https://doi.org/10.1207/ s15327809jls0202_3

Speziale, H. J. S., & Carpenter, D. R. (2007). *Qualitative research in nursing.* Lippincott.

Strauss, A., & Corbin, J. (1998). *Basics of qualitative research: Grounded theory procedures and techniques* (2nd ed.). Sage Publications.

Zijlstra, H. P., & Vlaskamp, C. (2005). The impact of medical conditions of children with profound intellectual and multiple disabilities. *Journal of Applied Research in Intellectual Disabilities, 18*(2), 151–161. https://doi.org/10.1111/j.1468-3148.2005. 00244.x

Under Observation

Line Drawing as an Investigative Method in Focused Ethnography

Andrew Causey

espite their methodological differences, both psychology and anthropology depend on careful observation when investigating their fields of inquiry. Instructors in these disciplines laboriously teach their students *what* to see in human behavior, but they may simply take for granted that students already know *how* to see. After all, if practitioners have gotten far enough to be engaged in advanced research, surely they must have developed advanced perception abilities as well. The assumption that different practitioners come to their research topics with equivalent visual attention and acuity may be misleading, however, and in the case of focused ethnography (where purview is limited and time is truncated) it may be, in fact, deceptive. This chapter provides an overview of the focused ethnography method, proposes that social scientists must reexamine the assumption that they already know how to see, offers some thoughts on how and why line drawing might be used as a legitimate research method, and then considers what might restrain researchers from drawing.

Portions of this chapter have been adapted and updated from "Using Focused Ethnography in Psychological Research," by L. M. Simonds, P. M. Camic, and A. Causey, in H. Cooper, P. M. Camic, D. L. Long, A. T. Panter, D. Rindskopf, and K. J. Sher (Eds.), *APA Handbook of Research Methods in Psychology: Vol. 2. Quantitative, Qualitative, Neuropsychological, and Biological* (pp. 157–170), 2012, American Psychological Association (https://doi.org/10.1037/13620-010); and from *Drawn to See: Drawing as an Ethnographic Method*, by A. Causey, 2017, University of Toronto Press. Copyright 2017 by University of Toronto Press. Adapted with permission.

https://doi.org/10.1037/0000252-011
Qualitative Research in Psychology: Expanding Perspectives in Methodology and Design, Second Edition, P. M. Camic (Editor)

THE ETHNOGRAPHIC METHOD

What is the aim of ethnographic research? In short, it is to closely examine social experiences and interactions by a particular group of people over a long period of time (many granting agencies offer funds to cover at least a year's worth of fieldwork) and in a defined and described environmental context. This close examination should attend to the perspectives of those who are the focus of the research: The ethnographer is trying to "see" and understand the world from the insiders' viewpoint, taking extensive careful notes, then documenting (publishing or otherwise making public) the observations, often in written form.

To understand and record aspects of human social lives and cultural worlds by investigating actions and motivations, ethnographers use methods that can be both passive and intrusive; they quietly observe but also ask many questions (often speaking dialects and languages imperfectly, sometimes using local translators) that are often difficult to answer. They ponder and guess about what they hear and see, seeking to interpret, translate, then transliterate into written words such things as personal opinions and narratives, folktales, gossip, history, and artful lies. At some point, they weave all of this into a final, permanent document that communicates what may end up being the sole lasting assessment about a single group at a single moment in time from a single perspective. Some might say this endeavor is nearly impossible.

The ethnographic project is a mix of both objective and subjective observations (some would say only the latter) and is, by its very nature, interpretivist (see, e.g., Clifford & Marcus, 1986; Geertz, 1973). For this reason, ethnographers both embrace the subjectivity of their work, by making honest reflexive note of their personal or theoretical assumptions as well as any limitations to their research, while enhancing the scientific aspects of data collection whenever possible, such as verifying information through various means and from multiple viewpoints. To make up for limitations resulting from subjectivity or interpretation, ethnographers try to write reflexively; that is, by taking careful note of themselves as researchers (Denzin, 1997, p. 217) and also to focus on the scope and depth of their observations (see Robben, 2007). Ethnography is less about discovering cultural "truths" than it is about exploring individual behaviors, cultural artifacts, and social relationships. As James Spradley (1980) noted, "Rather than *studying people*, ethnography means *learning from people*" (p. 3, italics in original).

Ethnographers can't capture the entirety of lived cultural worlds, of course, even when they investigate and experience them daily and persistently for an entire year or more, nor even when it is a collaborative effort; every ethnographer knows this, deep down. As Clifford (1988, Introduction) said, "Ethnography, a hybrid activity, thus appears as writing, as collecting, as modernist collage, as imperial power, as subversive critique": It is the production of a "serious fiction" (pp. 10–13). Lived experience with others, when the intent is to understand social interactions, reveals only a modest glimpse of life, of which only traces can be documented. It is unavoidable that these traces will later be edited, selected, forgotten, or lost. From what remains, ethnographers piece together a "quilt" of experiences to present a final product containing some truth, some accuracy, and some honesty. Many ethnographers are content that this is the best we can do.

The ethics of ethnographic research require that researchers always make known their position and intent (Spradley, 1980, pp. 20–25). Although one does not want to unduly influence the ordinary workings in a social setting, neither does one want to obtain data by any but transparent means, and so researchers should follow the human subjects protocols of their discipline (see Roper & Shapira, 2000, pp. 56–61). Privacy and protection of those researched is essential; in some cases, informants should be referred to by pseudonyms, and informed consent forms are almost always appropriate (see Morse & Field, 1995, pp. 54–64).

Ordinarily, of the ethnographer's varied notes (in any media appropriate to the project, whether written, audio-recorded, or visual-recorded), the written ones still have the greatest significance. Analysis and synthesis of the data are often addressed upon the researcher's return home and often aim to situate fieldwork observations within a "grounded theory" (Glaser & Strauss, 1967), that is, an explanatory theory of social interactions based on the data gathered rather than testing a preexisting theory (Morse & Field, 1995).

FOCUSED ETHNOGRAPHY

Focused ethnography (sometimes referred to as applied, or "microethnography"; Spradley, 1980, p. 30) concentrates on the lived experiences of the researcher and specific subsets or segments of a group in limited contexts, usually for limited amounts of time and with a specific predetermined topic in mind (Morse & Field, 1995, p.154). The aim is to gather extensive bodies of data, from a variety of sensory impressions and using different methods, that will be analyzed and interpreted to understand the character of social interactions, often with the broader interest in exposing or explaining an existing problem and ways that it might be addressed (Roper & Shapira, 2000, p. 8). Researchers interested in this methodology would be well served by reading Marjorie Muecke's (1994) *On the Evaluation of Ethnographies* to consider how their work might fare in critical academic arenas before starting their research.

Long-term, in-depth ethnographic projects often contain within them instances of micro-ethnography, and there is no doubt that these provided the foundation for focused ethnographic work as a stand-alone methodology. In such instances, ethnographers might find themselves in a new locale or with an affiliated group or subgroup. Experiences from this temporary interaction are often fleeting yet considered to be potentially valuable to the larger project and so must be intensely observed and recorded in detail.

I conducted my fieldwork with the Toba Bataks of North Sumatra, an Indigenous group whose traditional homeland is Samosir Island, which sits in the midst of Lake Toba, high in the cool central mountains. While my work centered on their interactions with international tourists in the souvenir market-place (Causey, 2003), I also had the opportunity to travel with my carving teacher and his wife several miles inland so he could get metaphysical help for his business from a spiritual healer (*datu*). I only had 6 hours to gather as much information as possible about the practices of a traditional shaman, as well as the life-ways of Bataks living beyond the tourist center, and I used the approach of focused ethnography to do so.

In this instance, because it was an honor to be an outsider-participant, I knew I would have to keep my written note taking to a minimum to avoid distracting from the solemn ritual being performed. For this reason, I brought only a small pocket notebook and pencil with me on our hour-long walk up the mountainside to the datu's rural hamlet. Being unable to take written notes of the event meant that I'd have to depend almost entirely on my memory to record the details.

Once we got settled on the woven mat in the main room of the datu's house, he began the necessary preparations for the ritual that was to come. After an hour of watching him place a white cloth on the mat, then remove small containers of powder and tobacco snuff from a hidden bag, wrapping them up in cotton bolls, and purifying himself and my teacher, I was getting worried that I would be unable to recall everything happening when I would finally be able to type my notes the next day. There was no time to fret, however, for the ritual continued on immediately after the cleansing and prayer preparations.

The datu consulted with my teacher, asking specific questions about why his carving business seemed to be failing. Once he had an idea of what was going on, he pulled a small ancient book of incantations and instructions written in the Batak script down from a dusty shelf. As he consulted it and read the archaic words aloud, it was clear from my teacher's nervous squirming that he did not understand what was being said. While the datu translated the ancient prognostic words into ordinary Batak language, I was able to move myself closer to see the book to "memorize" it (see Exercise 11.2 later in the chapter). He then brought out the flat magical sticks they call *bulu parhalaan* (scorpion bamboos), which are also inscribed with phrases in Batak script, forming them into the shape of an upside-down man on the white cloth. He instructed my teacher to choose one and his wife to choose another for him to read out the instructions written there. We had been with the datu for 4 hours by now, and I was now very worried that I would forget the order of the ceremony, telling myself to take "snapshots" of the objects and to invent mnemonic word-links between them and the actions I witnessed.

After 2 more hours, the ritual was over, and I was invited to go outside to get some fresh air and relieve myself. Behind a small thicket of trees, I took a moment to draw some very quick sketches in my small notebook, knowing they would trigger my memory faster than sloppily written words. It was dark by the time we left the isolated hamlet, and we had missed the afternoon bus and so had to walk for hours to get home.

The following day, I sat at my laptop and tried to focus my memory on the very first thing that happened that day, racing along to remember all the fine points and particularities that were evaporating as quickly as I pictured them, much like a dream dissipates upon recall. Frustrated, I decided stop thinking of my experience via words and instead refer to my quick sketches to draw more careful ones (see Figure 11.1). I was amazed at how details came flooding back the more I drew. Drawing and writing in tandem now enabled me to record two complementary descriptions that provided a very clear accounting of the entire day. I realized that the original sketches, quick as they were, managed to carry a depth of meaning that became magnified as I redrew them carefully, and so brought back sharp "snapshots" that I could then put down in words.

Focused ethnography, such as this brief example, by its very nature truncates aspects of ordinary ethnographic research, whether the limit is of research time spent, topical scope, or social sphere investigated. Because of this more focused interest, the researcher must enhance the intensity of data gathering, not simply of quantity but of quality as well, and does so primarily via documentation of enriched sensory experiences. The researcher's field notes must reflect the more focused nature of the project: They must become a detailed account of all that is sensed, not just the visual and aural (Clifford, 1986, p. 11), realizing that the individuals of the social context will themselves be experiencing expansive environmental situations and circumstances.

Focused ethnographies often address particular "structural questions" when making observations (Spradley, 1980, p. 107); that is, rather than simply observing social interactions in the context of a general subject, they attend to a specific question or problem. Even though the issue is more defined or the time more limited, the researcher should make note of the most wide-ranging sensory experiences to avoid allowing certain aspects—those outside of the structural question—to be ignored precisely because those other aspects may offer the clue to understanding the complexity of the social situation. One should be attentive not simply to what is being said, but also the special jargons and inflections used. A focused ethnography is not created from the amassing of a collection of a predetermined number of rushed interviews performed in a social setting but is built upon diverse impressions, interpretations, interventions, and observations gathered with a variety of methods (Geertz, 1973, pp. 3–30, referred to as "thick description"), and may also make use of methods that expand beyond words and writing (e.g., creating maps, drawings, schematics).

Once a research site has been identified, it is important to document the environment thoroughly and sensitively (Spradley, 1980, p. 55). Because focused ethnographic projects often limit expenditures of time, they must expand sensory experience and the breadth of data collection measures deployed (Marion & Offen, 2009, p. 13). Before designing a focused ethnography project, researchers might reflect on how their ordinary sensory awareness informs their everyday thoughts, reactions and experiences—not just the basic five senses but also ones such as the sense of apprehension, of curiosity, of being watched, of fear, of wonder, of delight; in short, any "sense" that is honestly felt or consciously identified. Acknowledging the full panoply

FIGURE 11.1. Fieldnotes From Work With the Toba Bataks of North Sumatra

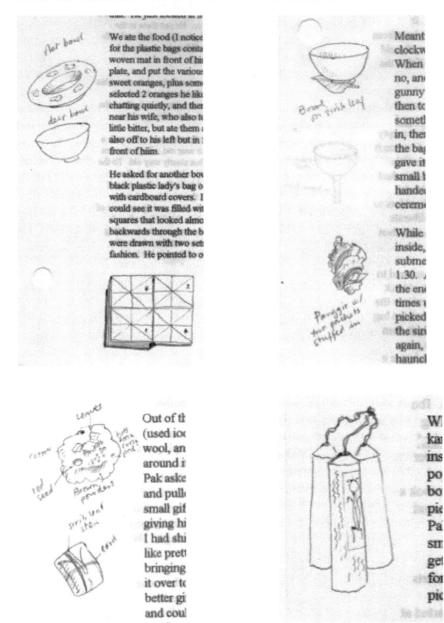

Note. These marginal drawings were recalled as I wrote the fieldnotes about the trip to the *datu* and were added afterward.

of sensory experiences in familiar settings will assist investigations in new socioenvironmental contexts. For many psychologists, this approach may be seen as the antithesis of years of research training that sought to make them objective scientists, and it is because of the positivistic epistemology underlying much of psychological inquiry that sensory and reflective experiences often become discarded and highly suspect (Camic et al., 2003, pp. 4–7).

The ethnographic approach, therefore, requires the researcher to become hyper-aware of the subtleties of existence and attuned to the potentially informative nature of these. For example, is the electric fan's whirr in harmony with the computer's hum? Is the researcher feeling agitated in a given social situation? Is a room's fluorescent light alienating, sterile, or simply illuminating? Does the physical layout of space engender cooperation or defensiveness? The researcher should recognize and record as many sense impressions as possible. Sometimes a researcher is unable to fully document sense impressions in the moment, so experiences must be re-created with words or drawings as soon as possible once returning from the study site. Notes at this preliminary stage of research must be made in as much detail as possible because such first impressions of environment will fade quickly; even quick sketches can help record aspects of the experiences that may not be easily reduced to words.

FOCUSED ETHNOGRAPHY IN PSYCHOLOGICAL RESEARCH

For many psychologists, perhaps even those who situate themselves within what might broadly be termed the qualitative tradition, the focused ethnography methodology might seem alien. So, why might they consider using it? Perhaps the best reason is that this approach might allow the psychologist to gain understanding into human behaviors and experiences that are otherwise difficult to access, potentially allowing insights into a broader range of understandings. Given the truncation of standard ethnographic procedures, the focused approach allows one to address smaller scale issues within limited time frames, making the approach relevant not only for research doctorate students but for those undertaking taught practitioner doctorates. The approach may also appeal to applied psychologists who want to understand the context of their (inter)action in a contextualized and time-effective way. Finally, the focused ethnographic approach could be relevant to psychologists as educators in expanding the skills, repertoire, and critical awareness of students as apprentice researchers. Its methods and epistemology invite curiosity, critique, and rigor and can challenge long-held assumptions. In this respect, if nothing else, focused ethnography encourages an approach that treats the familiar as strange, which increases a sense of engagement with the psychosocial and cultural world and helps to develop a questioning frame of mind.

Not all psychology-focused ethnographies will be successful, of course, and that is why this chapter proposes an approach that is exploratory rather than prescriptive. As always: Data collection methods must be mindfully selected and combined when addressing research questions. Focused ethnography has limits to its application, and it is especially challenging to consider its use in the realm of psychological enquiry generally because its methods are so different to those typically deployed. Although it is true that the central requirements of sustained contact and participant observation limit its range of application, engagement with its possibilities raises the potential of turning our attention toward overlooked areas.

What are focused ethnography's implications if used in psychological research? First, researchers must understand that it is a contextualist epistemology and places situated and constructed real-world contexts (as revealed through such things as action, thought, signs, and symbols) at the forefront. To use this methodology means one accepts that the social world is central in shaping perceptions, attitudes and experiences and that these are developed diachronically and in varied shared spaces. The approach attempts to document how meaning is both inherited and mutually negotiated in social contexts using a range of data collection methods, drawing on diverse modalities, to accumulate a rich corpus of data that is then analyzed and interpreted by the researcher to illuminate patterned behaviors related to the issue at hand and, more importantly, to make unknown issues apparent.

Focused ethnography might seem for many psychologists to be unacceptably subjective and interpretative, despite its use of complementary methods and triangulation of data sources, perhaps because of its diverse, sometimes experimental methods. Use of the subjective position does not mean that careful observation of self and others in the wide social context gives way to ungrounded or imagined personal impressions. Social interactions are dynamic and multifaceted and can only be witnessed and documented partially regardless of which research method is used. It is because of this that the notion that there is a single socially shared "truth" is untenable. To the extent that the methods of focused ethnography require considered use, rigorous application, diligent recording techniques, and grounded data analysis, then this methodology is entirely fitting for psychological research. Focused ethnography allows the researcher to document partial realities with greater depth and breadth precisely because it attempts to access multiple and differing viewpoints. As such, the obvious strength of this approach for psychologists lies in its encouragement of blending a multiplicity of data sources to develop theories grounded in social actions and interactions. Observation and description of the social group's "culture" allows questions to emerge, creating an emphasis on emergent theory generation.

METHODOLOGY OF LINE DRAWING IN ETHNOGRAPHIC RESEARCH

Ethnographic research uses a broad spectrum of qualitative and quantitative methods to gather and record data, the primary one of which is "participant observation" (discussed subsequently). Metaphorically, the varied methods are perhaps better thought of as complementary tools in a toolbox rather than stacked bricks in a foundation: They can be used independently and freely;

they are not necessarily contingent upon each other. This chapter concentrates on a recently emerging method, line drawing, and because of that, we might refer to focused ethnography projects that integrate drawing as having an "ethnographic approach" rather than as an example of "doing ethnography" (Blum Malley & Hawkins, 2010). Each focused ethnography project is unique, so the researcher must carefully examine which aspects of the investigation are being limited to decide which methods are appropriate and useful in obtaining a thorough picture of the circumstances under investigation. The data obtained by any one method is often supported by that derived by other methods. This process of "triangulation" of methods not only creates diversity in the data pool but also helps validate observations (Roper & Shapira, 2000, p. 24).

Method: Participant Observation

As noted earlier, participant observation is perhaps the most fundamental method associated with the ethnographic approach despite the fact that participating in the life of a culture at the same time you are observing it might seem to be a paradox: "It requires of the researcher to be both 'inside' and 'outside' the field of inquiry at one and the same time" (Ingold, 2011, Chapter 1, p. 4). Extensive general information on this method is available (see, e.g., LeCompte & Schensul, 1999; Spradley, 1980), so the goal in this chapter is to address its use in focused ethnographic projects. One of the attractive aspects of this method is its seeming naturalness: One simply "lives" in the social context of interest, experiencing what it is like to be an insider, then produces extensive documentation. Sometimes it is precisely this easy: The researcher locates a cultural setting, integrates within it by finding a social place, creates thorough notes on both personal experiences and observed behaviors, all the while recording details (via written and other means) of the physical environment. More often, however, the researcher's efforts to fit in are stymied, essential observations are hidden from view, and note taking is continuously interrupted. To get the most out of this method, one must be socially, intellectually, and methodologically flexible and must resist the urge to allow the project's outcome to depend exclusively on its written data.

Method: Mapping

Once the first impressions of the field site have been recorded in detail in writing, and recognizing that sensorily rich notes should continue throughout the project, the researcher might consider using line drawing to record observations. A particularly useful such tool is the simple map (Morse & Field, 1995, p. 115), a line drawing of the field site from a bird's-eye view based on the researcher's own experience of space (i.e., not traced from an existing map) and including such things as geographic edges, boundaries, paths, intersections, and "landmarks" (Lynch, 1977). The map can be photocopied and shown to individuals in the research group for corrections and additions, but the researcher should also make a mental note of how the corrections or additions are made (with irritation? in anger?) and what is added; researchers might consider asking respondents to draw their own maps of the area of concern to then use in gaining understanding of the insiders' differing perspectives and uses of the space.

Method: Line Drawing

Psychologists may be more familiar with using drawing as an elicitation or therapy intervention method versus using it as a self-focused investigative technique (e.g., Camic et al., 2014; Drake et al., 2016; Guillemin, 2004; Maycock et al., 2009; Ostrofsky et al., 2017). Using line drawing as a way to document researcher experiences, however, is also well documented (Arnheim, 1954, 1966; Langer, 1951, 1953; Mitchell et al., 2011), and some think this method can "enrich and extend language-based cognitive knowledge" (Roberts & Riley, 2014, p. 294), providing the researcher with novel, insightful data (Finley, 2008; McNiff, 2008, pp. 47–49). Of course, it is a risk to use an arts-informed method in focused ethnography because it does not necessarily "answer" questions. Still, we should consider that doing so might simply be "relinquishing the ties that fetter the imagination," recognizing that it "tells us . . . about our own capacities to experience the affective response to life" (Eisner, 2008, p. 11).

Scrutinous Drawing-Seeing

Line drawing is a novel approach for social scientists, so it may help if two genres are described here. *Representational drawing*, perhaps the first style that comes to mind, encompasses efforts to make a documentary picture that attempts to realistically re-create what is perceived (Massironi, 2002, p. 3). For those who are out of practice drawing and who may have a low frustration level, this genre may actually be the least effective to use in recording visual research data. *Scrutinous drawing*, however, is a closely connected genre and can be one of the most useful forms of research drawing. Here, the point is not to concentrate on the picture created (the product) but rather to focus on using of the act of drawing as a process of perception. Also referred to as drawing-seeing (Causey, 2017), in scrutinous drawing, the researcher focuses on seeing intently; that work is facilitated by actively marking lines on paper. The process (seeing) is a manifestation of the product (drawing), not the other way around, and the product may or may not be of use in the researcher's corpus of data documentation. By practicing the use of drawing as a tool of seeing, the researcher will, over time, develop concentrated visual focus (Exercise 11.1).

Recall Drawing-Seeing

The genre of scrutinous drawing-seeing can powerfully augment the researcher's attention to detail unfolding in a moment, yet there are times when drawing

---

EXERCISE 11.1 | **CONTOUR DRAWING-SEEING**

Place any object on a table several feet in front of your drawing position. With the pencil placed somewhere near the center of the paper, start drawing what you perceive as the edge of the object, allowing your eyes to move very slowly around its perimeter for 3 to 5 minutes. Let your drawing hand become your eyes, following the same direction as they see and marking a single continuous line as evidence. Focus seeing only the object's edge, making sure to concentrate so that your eyes don't "slip" by looking inside or beyond. Try not to glance down at your drawing as you proceed, and if you do, don't judge your work. Remember: You are using drawing to help you focus seeing, not creating a finished artwork. After several minutes, you will probably realize that while your eyes were focused on the edges, your mind was also busy perceiving the object itself and its physical context as well (see Figure 11.2).

---

materials are unavailable or the act of drawing is inappropriate. In such situations, *recall drawing-seeing* can be used (Fernandes et al., 2018). Here, the researcher heightens the senses of total body awareness to memorize a "snapshot" of an experience (an event, an action, or an object) with heightened awareness and clarity to record it in drawing later. In doing this kind of drawing-seeing, many find that keeping the eyes closed helps them maintain visual focus. Here, the researcher will relax with pencil and paper at hand and draw what is "seen" in the darkness of the mind's eye (Manghani, 2013, p. 102; Tchalenko et al., 2014). Although the end result drawing may look preposterous, the act of forcing the mind to recall the event through blind drawing will often bring it back in clear focus in the mind. Another way to use recall (especially useful when dealing with material objects) is to amplify all of the senses to examine something as if it will disappear. When the object is removed, the researcher "re-senses" their varied sensual stimuli and attempts to record them visually with paper and pencil. This aspect of the method can produce remarkable results (Exercise 11.2).

Additional Genres of Drawing-Seeing

Other, more accessible (not to say easier) genres are also worth exploring. In *relational drawing*, the researcher depicts the juxtaposition of visual elements to document distance or position (physical or social) of people or objects (see also Green & Denov, 2019). Distance and placement of elements on the page will assist in seeing how proximity can be recorded more clearly than in writing. *Schematic drawing* attempts to record the interactions of perceived elements of research and can incorporate expansions of Venn diagramming, flow-based note taking, or sketch noting (Rohde, 2013). Like mapping, these genres of drawing allow the researcher free rein in creating the iconic images used to pictorially create data and so may allow the mind to discover connections that words may otherwise restrict.

FIGURE 11.2. Contour Drawing-Seeing Exercise

Note. The contour drawing-seeing exercise demands that the viewer look only at the visible edge of the object, without looking at the lines being made on the paper.

EXERCISE 11.2 | **RECALL DRAWING-SEEING**

Choose a familiar everyday object such as a key-fob and, in a calm, quiet place, examine it with intense concentration for 1 minute (time yourself). Feel its texture, heft its weight, and identify its colors. You might realize that you've never actually seen this mundane thing with care, and its particularities are unknown to you. After 1 minute, remove the object from sight, and with eyes open draw what you experienced with as much detail as possible, trying to convey all the senses in lines. It is gone from sight now, but it is embedded in your visual memory, and that's what you use to make your visual document. Imagine how much more perceptive you would be when visually memorizing something of even greater importance to you (see Figure 11.3).

FIGURE 11.3. Recall Drawing-Seeing Exercise

Note. The result of the recall drawing-seeing exercise shows that an untrained artist can remember many details of an object in just 1 concentrated minute of examination.

To encourage you to experiment with drawing as an investigative method, I offer three suggestions:

1. *Just draw what you see*. Draw what you *actually* see, not what you *think* you see, not what you *accept* as known. We are all enveloped by a swarm of images, from Internet pop-ups to holiday wrapping paper, and we are nearly unable to free ourselves from representations devised by others. This makes it difficult to see the world as *you* want to see it. Before accepting any pre-digested images, find the time to actually see to what they refer. Draw a hand by carefully examining it; don't just draw what you know as "hand." See first, and interpret what you see into lines, but try to avoid, when you can, passive use of hackneyed images.

2. *Stop self-reflecting*. Many of us become hyper-aware of ourselves when we try something new, saying in our mind's voice, "Ok, here I am: a person drawing. . . ." Try to block that introspection when attempting drawing-seeing because it is distracting you from the concentration you need to see. If you are thinking about yourself in order to pass judgment, simply stop. There are no mistakes with this method, just explorations.

3. *Practice*. Here, practice is a kind of engaged repetition. There is no right way to draw when you are exploring, so practice is not affiliated with seeking perfection. Instead, practice here means doing something over and over, each time being attentive to whether the process and product are expanding your understanding of what you see. No one can know that but you. Try to take joy in each repetition for its own sake.

Seeing to Write or Drawing to See?

Ethnographic research can expand your understanding of what "reality" can encompass. When you work with individuals whose perspectives or assumptions are not generally shared, you are exposed to their notions of what's really real, and you'll begin to understand aspects of a different ontology. You'll be introduced to the ways that those new aspects of reality are verified, so you'll also learn something about their epistemology. But how well do we actually see?

Many social scientists make sense of another's perceptions and assumptions by cognitively translating, then articulating, them through language. Once the language-based interpretation is formed, we then document it through writing. In fact, language is so fundamental to our intellectual perception and understanding that some would say that "if you can't say it, you can't see it." Nevertheless, I suspect we've all had experiences when we've come upon something so extraordinary that we have trouble categorizing it, even as we perceive it. This kind of pure perception, which might happen for only a brief and stunned second, is a moment of seeing without words. Interestingly, when we do categorize what we've seen, either by finding the word for it or creating a verbal metaphor, we might then discard it by ignoring or dismissing it, by looking away in disgust, or by rationalizing it as something ordinary. In some cases (especially with the easy access of camera apps on phones), we might take a quick photograph, but usually, as social scientists, we perform the academically appropriate behavior, as noted earlier: We write about it.

Suppose, however, that instead of writing we decide to document our experience with line drawing? In visual documentation, we are making a picture of an image, where "image" refers to a kind of cogitation (or interpretation) of that which we've delimited from all available visual stimuli (that is, our view of reality): The 3D visible world is translated to 2D visible code.

George Lakoff and Mark Johnson (2003) stated that because the brain is housed in the body, the work it does in understanding the environment must be framed within that physicality (217, 255). That is to say, the mind interprets our surroundings in terms of our bodies. This notion of the "embodied mind" suggests that humans are unable to make truly "objective" or "unaffected" observations. We don't ever perceive generally, but always within the boundaries of a body-self, and that varies from person to person and from culture to culture. Although it's true that we can have direct experiences that we need not translate to language (e.g., a sudden electrical shock) to understand those direct experiences, we usually revert to the structure of language—often via analogy—to help us (Stafford, 2001). When we articulate the interpretations of what we perceive using language, we must do so by using linguistic metaphors (Lakoff & Johnson, p. 4). So, our understandings of experiences are filtered through comparisons to what we already know, and our documentation takes the form of writing, which is at best an approximation.

Although all representational methods have their drawbacks, using writing to encode visual experiences is doubly interpretive—not just reducing three dimensions to two but also translating iconic stimuli (the scene) to symbolic translations (words). Often, social science research, particularly in the form of focused ethnography, requires the researcher to see things very clearly but also very quickly: The world is in movement; people gesture; things disappear; events unfold. Perhaps, then, it makes senses to practice a method that uses a single translation, from three to two dimensions: line drawing.

To ask the question "How well do we see?" in a chapter on qualitative methodology is not a digression from the topic but, rather, the very foundation of it. If we social science researchers are unable or unwilling to reflect on the fundamental acts (seeing and writing) that undergird our work in trying to perceive human behavior and its contexts, then we might be limiting our capacity to understand and document it.

Whether we are trying to see something novel or unknown, trying to observe our mundane world with vivid attention, or trying to document something that is no longer before us, the drawing-seeing process will help us perceive with more clarity and understanding. To address the question asked at the beginning of this section, perhaps we can learn something from the book artist Keith A. Smith (1992), who said, succinctly: "When I say, 'I see . . .,' it is not a passing exclamation, but a statement of triumph" (p. 17).

Looking Versus Seeing

As noted earlier, there are numerous ways to use line drawing in social science research, from creating denotative or representational works to recalling memorized images. In my own ethnographic research, I came to depend on drawing as an auxiliary method because I knew I *could* see more than I *had* seen, more than was recorded in my notes, and more than was documented in my photographs. Fieldwork photographs can document the visible characteristics of a moment, but the details are undifferentiated: the photos are visual stews of competing specificities, all weighted the same, visually and semantically. When I tried drawing such a moment, however, I was able to think out the shapes and forms to recreate them—to *see* them—and to concentrate on those that most honestly represented my experience of the place, without translating the moment to words. As an ethnographer, I have drawn what I *think* I see to understand it more accurately, and in doing so have realized that drawing is an integral part of my work because it enables my written notes to be more perceptive.

Before we can approach the notion of drawing what we perceive, some clarification is needed. "Looking" and "seeing" are very different acts: The way I understand it, looking is a kind of scanning and tends to be passive, whereas seeing is a kind of scrutiny and tends to be active.

Guided by the works of a number of visual researchers, I have come to the understanding that in *looking*, our vision floats across the visual terrain without directed engagement, whereas *seeing* interpretively illuminates the visible, in many ways bringing it into being. The more challenging of the two, of course, is seeing—*really* seeing. In my own academic explorations, the struggle to see cannot be performed by the attentive yet passive eye alone. To *see* to document an ethnographic experience denotatively requires active visual engagement. When that active engagement is made manifest by the hand's creation of permanent marks, such as drawn lines that document what the eyes are perceiving, the seeing will be more discerning and more attentive to detail. That's because the marks made with the hand become the actual evidence of visual perception, proof that there is some concurrence between perception and representation. The *scene* (what is perceived) and the *image* (the interpretation of the scene) are recorded by the hand, whose subtle and searching movements are constantly checked and corrected by the seeing eyes, to create the *picture* (the actual document of marks and lines) that represents, to the best of the actor's ability, a product that is an honest and accurate document of what was seen.

Line Drawing as Data

Most humans have an innate tendency to perceive the world in an interpretive way: We see things in our surroundings as named, discrete entities, as having articulating relationships to other things, and as being meaningful. We assume that words naturally attach to the entities, we see connections between them whether they exist or not, and we make judgments or ratings in order to understand them. But really, things simply *are*, whether we are there to perceive them or not.

Charles Saunders Peirce (1887–1888/1998) tried to discuss this paradox (i.e., that there is a "real" out there, with or without humans conceiving of it, yet by calling it "real" we've already defined it in our terms). He used the terms *firstness, secondness,* and *thirdness* (p. 267) to help us find our way out. "The First," he says,

> is that whose being is simply in itself, not referring to anything nor lying behind anything. . . . It precedes all synthesis and all differentiation; it has no unity and no parts. It cannot be articulately thought: assert it, and it has already lost its characteristic innocence; for assertion always implies a denial of something else. Stop to think of it, and it has flown! (p. 248 and pp. 356–357)

In short, The First means "just is."

The Second is our identification of The First, that is, our naming it as a category or thing, and The Third is our sense of the connection between the two: the "is" and the name. The Third in essence, is *us*—as cointerpreters, as interacting mediators, as those who find meaning in the world by using our various codes (primary among them, language) to identify the determinacy (the boundaries, the edges) of all that "is."

Perhaps this is why Peirce's notion of The First is so useful to us here. In drawing to see, we use one of our human codes (a two-dimensional visual one) to depict how we articulate and define the "is." In line drawing, we are interpreting The First—all "that precedes synthesis and differentiation," all the indeterminate—in a kind of code that makes sense to us, a code that may be less interpretive than writing.

There are no "right" or "better" drawings, and there is no single way to see the "is" around us. Our act of drawing, when done seriously and with focus, is evidence that we saw something and manifested it in our own visual form: It is simultaneously a souvenir of your experience, a primary document, an interpretive remembrance, a concocted mnemonic. Oddly, when complete, your drawing-seeing data itself becomes one of The Firsts, and so, as Peirce said, "is a being simply in itself."

Hesitating to Draw

There may be an underlying flaw in my proposal that psychologists (and other social scientists) use line drawing as a way to see: I assume the reader is enthusiastic about trying this method. After many years of teaching students and interacting closely with colleagues, however, I know this not true for everyone.

Betty Edwards (1986), a well-known drawing pedagogue, talked about how educational systems (if they even offer "art" in the classroom) might actually be teaching us that we can't draw (pp. 5–6); many of us have been convinced to believe we have no "talent." Thinking back, some of us might recall that the last time we drew with happiness was when we were about 7 or 8 years of age. After that, teachers may have begun to notice the so-called good drawers and held their work up for all to see, ignoring or perhaps belittling those whose drawings didn't fit the preconceived notion of "good." This kind of subjective judgment can crush the aspirations of those whose works do not fit the criteria, so they stop—sometimes forever. How can we move beyond this hesitation to draw?

First, remember that with this method, the point is not to draw but rather to see: *Drawing is the means of a process of seeing*, not a means to create a product, an image. Realizing that your main goal is to see (not to make a picture) will put your line-work in the same category as your attempts to write down an idea or theory: The characteristics of your peculiar handwriting is entirely irrelevant to the idea you are documenting.

Second, the truth is that all drawings are unique, yet they are often inspired by—and thus derivative of—the work of others. Knowing so should relieve you if your fear is that you must create something "new" when you draw. Recognizing that each image you make is a response to images already made— and that you are merely "in dialog" with them (Bakhtin, 1990, p. 276) will give you confidence that there is no impossible standard by which you will be judged, nor by which you may judge yourself.

Third, don't be afraid to take a gamble in considering use of the drawing-seeing method. This is a safe risk, showing that you are willing to consider taking an inspired and logical jump into the unknown—it is a calculated risk. In trying to draw to see, you are, in fact, daring yourself to perceive the world in a new way when doing your research, and in taking that small risk, you might find out something unexpected, remarkable, or even revolutionary.

Fourth, when you use line drawing to help you see, you are claiming the fundamental right to represent the world around you imagistically. Your act is a direct statement to yourself and others that "This is how I see it." There is no backing down, and no apologies are needed or expected, no matter what others might tell you. It is your right to document your interpreted rendition of the unfolding, emergent world—your fraction of it—and as long as you can stand behind what you create (ethically, morally, intellectually), your work is as much an unassailable statement as any other document you make. When you opt to commit 3D space–time reality to two dimensions using your own unmediated rendition of a visual code, your work is unarguable and irreducible. You are indicating both that you choose to depict your experiences through pictures and that you have permitted yourself to do so. Your interpretation via drawing is not purporting to be the real (how could it be?) but is rather an admission that this is your best effort at depicting in drawn from what you witnessed: to say, in Michael Taussig's (2011) words, "*I swear I saw this!*" (p. 1, italics in original).

For some researchers, however, the hesitation to draw may come from a deeper, more metaphysical source. Once, while doing my fieldwork, I was drawing caricatures to entertain the children grouped around me. A young man standing behind them spoke up: "How do you know where to put the first line?" I said, "Well . . . just anywhere on the page!" This did not satisfy him, so I got a follow-up question, "Okay, how do you know where to put the *second* line?"

This got me to thinking about the nature of marking lines. Is it easier to draw lines once the first one has been made? Perhaps the hardest thing to do is make that initial mark because it states so guilelessly: "I create." To carry the line across the paper is to further state: *This* is not *that*, whether the *that* is one of the sections demarcated by the line, or whether the *that* is the very line itself as it is defined from the space around it. So, it seems to me, each line we make—from its very inception—is a kind of declaration that we have the nerve to create, to depict (see also May, 1975). In this way, perhaps some of us are thinking: "This is the first line of the rest of my life . . . it had better be good!" That's a daunting prospect, but it should not deter you.

So, now to answer the question "Where does the first line go?" Well, perhaps it goes where no one else has put it: in your research notes . . . or in your publication.

CONCLUSION

This kind of "drawing-enhanced seeing" is a balanced interaction between eye and hand, as well as the complex interplay of mind and body: cerebral and muscular, questioning and documenting. It is the active integration of drawing and perceiving that makes this method such so valuable for those wishing to see more deeply.

The world around us is increasingly proliferated with pictures, messages, objects (real and virtual), and many of us have learned to simply shut them out. As we learn to choose which visual stimuli we must attend to, I suspect we also inadvertently edit out much of the environment that surrounds us, either by seeing with inattention or by becoming blind to all but the most pressing cues. In the process, we may be losing the ability to see what we want, so pressured are we to see what we must or to see what we should. It's because of this, I think, that many of us have lost the knack of seeing the expected and the ordinary aspects of our surroundings with clarity and insight. Now, in the interest of enriching our varied forms of research, we need to reawaken our visual curiosity.

As our social science disciplines grow and evolve, it becomes evident that our methodologies of observation and analysis must keep pace. Many of us, it seems, continue to collect cultural "data" primarily by means of written notes (whether handwritten or digitally composed), and when we do use visual means to record information, we tend to rely on photographic technologies (both analog and digital). As a natural outcome of this, the majority of our texts are presented in textual form, with imagery being used secondarily, only to illustrate what is written. I am urging psychologists to embrace all forms of line making, from handwriting to the drawn sketch, to understand the material world as comprising emergent objects, social contexts, behaviors, and actions. I encourage you to draw what you see, to enhance your "visual literacy" (Armstrong, 2007; Elkins, 2007), and perhaps even to use your drawings to convey your primary data.

REFERENCES

Armstrong, A. (2007, Summer). Visual literacy/literary vision. *American Arts Quarterly*, 23–28.

Arnheim, R. (1954). *Art and visual perception: A psychology of the creative eye*. University of California Press.

Arnheim, R. (1966). *Toward a psychology of art*. University of California Press.

Bakhtin, M. M. (1990). *The dialogic imagination: Four essays by M.M. Bakhtin* (M. Holquist, Ed., C. Emerson & M. Holquist, Trans.). University of Texas Press.

Blum Malley, S., & Hawkins, A. (2010). *Translating cultures: Ethnographic writing in the composition classroom*. http://www.engagingcommunities.org

Camic, P. M., Rhodes, J. E., & Yardley, L. (2003). Naming the stars: Integrating qualitative methods into psychological research. In P. M. Camic, J. E. Rhodes, & L. Yardley (Eds.), *Qualitative research in psychology: Expanding perspectives in methodology and design* (pp. 3–15). American Psychological Association. https://doi.org/10.1037/10595-001

Camic, P. M., Tischler, V., & Pearman, C. H. (2014). Viewing and making art together: A multi-session art-gallery-based intervention for people with dementia and their carers. *Aging & Mental Health, 18*(2), 161–168. https://doi.org/10.1080/13607863.2013.818101

Causey, A. (2003). *Hard bargaining in Sumatra: Western travelers and Toba Bataks in the marketplace of souvenirs*. University of Hawaii Press. https://doi.org/10.1515/9780824843557

Causey, A. (2017). *Drawn to see: Drawing as an ethnographic method*. University of Toronto Press.

Clifford, J. (1986). Introduction: partial truths. In J. Clifford & G. E. Marcus (Eds.), *Writing culture: The poetics and politics of ethnography* (pp. 1–26). University of California Press.

Clifford, J. (1988). *The predicament of culture: Twentieth-century ethnography, literature, and art*. Harvard University Press.

Clifford, J., & Marcus, G. E. (1986). *Writing culture: The poetics and politics of ethnography*. University of California Press.

Denzin, N. (1997). *Interpretive ethnography*. Sage Publications.

Drake, J. E., Hastedt, I., & James, C. (2016). Drawing to distract: Examining the psychological benefits of drawing over time. *Psychology of Aesthetics, Creativity, and the Arts, 10*(3), 325–331. https://doi.org/10.1037/aca0000064

Edwards, B. (1986). *Drawing on the artist within*. Simon & Schuster.

Eisner, E. (2008). Art and knowledge. In J. G. Knowles & A. L. Cole (Eds.), *Handbook of the arts in qualitative research* (pp. 3–12). Sage Publications.

Elkins, J. (Ed.). (2007). *Visual literacy*. Routledge.

Fernandes, M. A., Wammes, J. D., & Meade, M. E. (2018). The surprisingly powerful influence of drawing on memory. *Current Directions in Psychological Science, 27*(5), 302–308. https://doi.org/10.1177/0963721418755385

Finley, S. (2008). Arts-based research. In J. G. Knowles & A. L. Cole (Eds.), *Handbook of the arts in qualitative research* (pp. 71–82). Sage Publications.

Geertz, C. (1973). *The interpretation of cultures: Selected essays*. Basic Books.

Glaser, B. G., & Strauss, A. L. (1967). *The discovery of grounded theory: Strategies for qualitative research*. Aldine.

Green, A., & Denov, M. (2019). Mask-making and drawing as method: Arts-based approaches to data collection with war-affected children. *International Journal of Qualitative Methods, 18*: Advance online publication. https://doi.org/10.1177/1609406919832479

Guillemin, M. (2004). Understanding illness: Using drawings as a research method. *Qualitative Health Research, 14*(2), 272–289. https://doi.org/10.1177/1049732303260445

Ingold, T. (Ed.). (2011). *Redrawing anthropology: Materials, movements, lines.* Ashgate Publishing.

Lakoff, G., & Johnson, M. (2003). *Metaphors we live by.* University of Chicago Press. https://doi.org/10.7208/chicago/9780226470993.001.0001

Langer, S. (1951). *Philosophy in a new key: A study in the symbolism of reason, rite, and art.* Mentor Books.

Langer, S. (1953). *Feeling and form: A theory of art.* Charles Scribner.

LeCompte, M. D., & Schensul, J. J. (1999). *Designing and conducting ethnographic research: Part 1. Ethnographer's toolkit.* AltaMira Press.

Lynch, K. (1977). *Image of the city.* MIT Press.

Manghani, S. (2013). *Image studies: Theory and practice.* Routledge.

Marion, J. S., & Offen, J. L. (2009). Translating multisensory experience: An introduction. *Anthropology News, 50*(4), 1–13. https://doi.org/10.1111/j.1556-3502.2009.50413.x

Massironi, M. (2002). *The psychology of graphic images: Seeing, drawing, communicating.* Lawrence Erlbaum Associates.

May, R. (1975). *The courage to create.* Bantam Books.

Maycock, B., Liu, G., & Klein, R. M. (2009). Where to begin? Eye-movement when drawing. *Journal of Research Practice, 5*(2), M3. http://jrp.icaap.org/index.php/jrp/article/view/179/177

McNiff, S. (2008). Art-based research. In J. G. Knowles & A. L. Cole (Eds.), *Handbook of the arts in qualitative research* (pp. 29–40). Sage Publications.

Mitchell, C., Theron, L., Stuart, J., Smith, A., & Campbell, Z. (2011). Drawings as research method. In L. Theron, C. Mitchell, A. Smith, & J. Stuart (Eds.), *Picturing research.* Sense Publishers.

Morse, J. M., & Field, P. A. (1995). *Qualitative research methods for health professionals* (2nd ed.). Sage Publications.

Muecke, M. (1994). On the evaluation of ethnographies. In J. M. Morse (Ed.), *Critical issues in qualitative research methods* (pp. 187–209). Sage Publications.

Ostrofsky, J., Nehl, H., & Mannion, K. (2017). The effect of object interpretation on the appearance of drawings of ambiguous figures. *Psychology of Aesthetics, Creativity, and the Arts, 11*(1), 99–108. https://doi.org/10.1037/aca0000084

Peirce, C. S. (1998). *The essential Peirce: Selected philosophical writings: Vol. 2 (1893–1913)* (The Peirce Edition Project, Eds.). Indiana University Press. (Original work published 1887–1888)

Robben, A. C. G. M. (2007). Introduction. In A. C. G. M. Robben & J. A. Sluka (Eds.), *Ethnographic fieldwork: An anthropological reader* (pp. 51–55). Blackwell.

Roberts, A., & Riley, H. (2014). Drawing and emerging research: The acquisition of experiential knowledge through drawing as a methodological strategy. *Arts and Humanities in Higher Education, 13*(3), 292–302. https://doi.org/10.1177/1474022213514559

Rohde, M. (2013). *The sketchnote handbook: The illustrated guide to visual note taking.* Peachpit Press.

Roper, J. M., & Shapira, J. (2000). *Ethnography in nursing research.* Sage Publications. https://doi.org/10.4135/9781483328294

Simonds, L. M., Camic, P. M., & Causey, A. (2012). Using focused ethnography in psychological research. In H. Cooper, P. M. Camic, D. L. Long, A. T. Panter, D. Rindskopf, & K. J. Sher (Eds.), *APA handbook of research methods in psychology: Vol. 2. Research designs: Quantitative, qualitative, neuropsychological, and biological* (pp. 157–170). American Psychological Association. https://doi.org/10.1037/13620-010

Smith, K. (1992). *Structure of the visual book*. Sigma Foundation.

Spradley, J. P. (1980). *Participant observation*. Wadsworth/Cengage Learning.

Stafford, B. M. (2001). *Visual analogy: Consciousness as the art of connecting*. MIT Press. https://doi.org/10.7551/mitpress/7123.001.0001

Taussig, M. (2011). *I swear I saw this: Drawings in fieldwork notebooks, namely my own*. University of Chicago Press. https://doi.org/10.7208/chicago/9780226789842.001.0001

Tchalenko, J., Nam, S. H., Ladanga, M., & Miall, R. C. (2014). The gaze-shift strategy in drawing. *Psychology of Aesthetics, Creativity, and the Arts, 8*(3), 330–339. https://doi.org/10.1037/a0036132

DEVELOPING AND EXPANDING QUALITATIVE RESEARCH

12

Into the Ordinary

Lessons Learned From a Mixed-Methods Study in the Homes of People Living With Dementia

Emma Harding, Mary Pat Sullivan, Keir X. X. Yong,
and Sebastian J. Crutch

In this chapter, we describe a mixed-methods approach incorporating qualitative case study and focused ethnographic methods as well as quantitative data from neuropsychological tests, self-report questionnaires, and physiological measures. This mixed-methods approach was used in a home-based observational study of people affected by two types of dementia: the more common memory-led Alzheimer's disease (AD) and posterior cortical atrophy (PCA), a rare form of dementia that mostly affects the processing of visual and spatial information (Crutch et al., 2012, 2017; Mendez et al., 2002; Tang-Wai et al., 2004). We first discuss the context for the study and the research questions and design before outlining how the data was collected and integrated for analysis. We then explore some of the methodological issues researchers may face when conducting extended observations in the homes of people with dementia and their care partners, as well as the unique insights that can emerge when integrating mixed methods of data collection. We conclude the chapter with recommendations for other researchers considering dementia research involving mixed approaches in naturalistic settings.

CONTEXT OF THE STUDY: A MIXED-METHODS APPROACH TO OBSERVING PEOPLE WITH DEMENTIA

This home-based observational study of the everyday experiences of people living with two kinds of dementia was a substudy of the interdisciplinary Economic and Social Research Council and National Institute for Health

https://doi.org/10.1037/0000252-012
Qualitative Research in Psychology: Expanding Perspectives in Methodology and Design, Second Edition, P. M. Camic (Editor)

Research–funded "Seeing What They See" project, which explored the impact of dementia-related visual impairment. Complementing neuropsychological investigations and lab-based assessments of functional abilities (e.g., navigational skills, object localization), these home-based observations built on a series of dyadic interviews that were also conducted within the home environment in the first phase of the project. Findings from the dyadic interview study (see Harding et al., 2018) highlighted a series of challenges people with dementia-related visual impairment faced in their interactions with the physical environment, such as reading, navigating between different rooms, and locating and using familiar objects, as well as wide-ranging psychosocial implications associated with this, including feelings of dependence and threats to one's sense of identity. To build on these findings, we embarked on designing a mixed-methods home-based observational study to explore how the challenges in these intersecting environments are navigated in real time and in the social and relational context in which they occur, while also exploring how a variety of data sources might contribute to this understanding.

Encouragingly, there has been a relatively recent increase in mixed-methods studies in the field of dementia research, although much of the published work is on therapeutic interventions as opposed to observational studies, and these are mostly conducted with people with more common, memory-led presentations of dementia (e.g., George et al., 2014; Moyle et al., 2018; Sampson et al., 2008). Mixed-methods research can be used for the purposes of collecting complementary data to build a fuller picture of a concept or for the purposes of triangulation, in which different data sources are integrated and cross-verified against each other to help with validating any findings.

Acknowledging that findings of mixed-methods studies can be rich but also potentially challenging to interpret, Robinson et al. (2011) called for more specification and transparency about the data collection, integration, and analysis procedures. These authors highlighted the particular suitability of mixed methods to capture the complexity of the dementia experience in a more comprehensive way but warned against the uncritical acceptance of such methodological approaches. Robinson and colleagues also argued that this perhaps occurs because of a lack of formal design in mixed-methods research, which they cited as a possible by-product of long-standing tensions among the qualitative and quantitative research traditions. One of their key recommendations to tackle this is the transparent reporting of the analytic process when using mixed-methods data. In this chapter, we discuss the process and challenges of triangulating qualitative observational field notes and video data with quantitative physiological data, neuropsychology assessment scores, and self-report measures.

Existing mixed-methods work has shed important light on some of the potentially pertinent issues and possible insights to be gained. For example, George (2011) collected data using pre- and postintervention psychometric self-report stress scales that suggested stress decreased after participation in an intergenerational workshop, and qualitative data from interviews and participant observations revealed some of the mechanisms by which that had happened (e.g., the workshop fostered a sense of purpose and usefulness and provided opportunities for people living with dementia [PLWD] to develop relationships with others). Conversely, Windle et al. (2018) showed in their longitudinal evaluation of a visual arts program for PLWD some of the possible discrepancies and inconsistencies that can coexist in qualitative and quantitative data within the same study. Although the participants in their study did not report any improvements in their quality of life (QoL) on standardized measures used pre- and postintervention, this contrasted with what participants self-reported in the qualitative interviews. Here they described the program as stimulating to attend and important for fostering their sense of social connectedness, well-being, and feelings of inner strength.

Another relative gap in the existing literature is in home-based observational research involving PLWD. Only a handful of observational studies conducted in people's home or in community settings have been published. The vast majority take place in care-home or health care settings where there is arguably a higher degree of control (e.g., scheduled mealtimes and structured activities) and less variability than in the naturalistic home environment (e.g., home furnishings, floorplan). Observational work conducted in the homes of PLWD has been shown to offer valuable insights. For example, such studies have documented processes such as the routinization of care practices and adaptations made to the physical home environment which enable PLWD to continue to engage in activities that were important to them (Askham et al., 2007; de la Cuesta & Sandelowski, 2005). This builds the case for further empirical investigations that capture the complexity of the real-world, day-to-day experiences of those affected by dementias and residing in their own homes.

DEVELOPING THE MIXED-METHODS RESEARCH DESIGN

This study used mixed methods to better understand the day-to-day impacts of an atypical dementia diagnosis in people's everyday home environments. The design of this study was informed by two methodological approaches— the qualitative case study and focused ethnographic approaches—both of which encourage mixed-methods data collection and analysis. We now briefly introduce these two overarching methodological approaches, as well the rationale for the neuropsychology, self-report, and physiological data, before detailing our own data collection and analysis procedures.

Qualitative Case Study Influence

A qualitative case study approach is considered most fitting for studying and describing complex real-world phenomena that are heavily context dependent, where there are many interrelated variables that cannot be controlled or manipulated and usually asks "how" or "why" questions (e.g., Baxter & Jack, 2008; Stake, 1995; Yin, 2017). Case studies are focused on accurately and richly describing the particular case(s) being studied, and participant observation and guided natural interviews, among others, are key data collection methods (e.g., Baxter & Jack, 2008; Stake, 1995; Yin, 2017). The researcher is required to pay careful attention to the setting and to be an engaged listener while attempting to retain some element of objective distance to reflect on and recognize their impact on the context (Yin, 2017).

As in other qualitative approaches, data analysis is an iterative process that involves breaking down the data into segments and examining, categorizing, combining, and testing the data before constructing an overall interpretation, which gives as accurate an account as possible of the case(s) (Stake, 1995; Yin, 2017). Analysis should be thorough and systematic; researchers should be attending to all evidence and proposing alternative explanations, and a general analytic strategy should be articulated. A helpful part of this process is finding ways to display or organize the data so that patterns, insights, and key concepts can more easily be noticed and interpreted (e.g., tabulating, visualizing, making data matrices, combining qualitative and quantitative data).

Yin (2017) suggested some starting points for "playing" with the data so that the researcher can begin to get a sense of where they may want to focus; we found the following ones particularly helpful:

- juxtaposing data from two people (looking at data from two participants side by side)

- organizing data into different themes and subthemes

- making a matrix of categories and assembling evidence

- creating visual displays such as flow charts and other graphics

- writing memos (all the way through data collection and analysis) about what the researcher thinks they might be observing, which may help consolidate ideas for future ways of exploring or interrogating the data (i.e., "lightbulb moments")

A combination of the following general inductive analytic strategies were adopted in the study reported on in this chapter:

- *Working the data from the ground up.* This involves the researchers immersing themselves in the data to notice key concepts and their possible relationships (Yin, 2017). Coding can help with this process because it encourages the abstraction of data and can make patterns clearer (quantitative data can also help with this).

- *Developing a case description.* This requires organizing the case study data according to a descriptive framework, the headings of which are decided by the researcher, on the basis of the story they are seeing in the data. Deciding these headings and organizing the data accordingly allows any patterns that seem salient and intuitive to be thoroughly considered (Yin, 2017).

- *Categorical aggregation.* This involves intuitively grouping and tallying elements and features of the data to identify meaningful patterns in complex data (Stake, 1995).

- *Direct interpretation.* This requires the researcher to directly interpret meanings that are apparent to them by repeatedly asking themselves, "What did that mean?" (Stake, 1995).

Focused Ethnography Influence

Focused ethnography is a pragmatically derived and time-efficient variation on classic ethnography designed to lead to findings that have some practical application (e.g., Roper & Shapira, 2000; Simonds et al., 2012). It is increasingly used in health care and educational settings where prolonged immersion in the field is perhaps not possible or deemed necessary (e.g., resources, participant burden, reduced "otherness" of the sample; Knoblauch, 2005; Wall, 2014). The method shares many features with classic ethnography, and its central aims are still to learn about the socially constructed meanings and practices of a specific cultural group and how those guide action, via experience and immersion in a real-world context (Knoblauch, 2005). For pragmatic reasons, however, the shorter time period is facilitated by the more focused nature of the research questions (although these can and should still evolve and develop over time) and in the selection of a cultural group who are not completely unfamiliar to the researcher (e.g., Higginbottom et al., 2013; Knoblauch, 2005). Despite the reduced amount of time spent in the field, the intensity and volume of data collected are often enhanced by technological aids (e.g., video/audio recordings; e.g., Mondada, 2006; Pink & Morgan, 2013; Simonds et al., 2012).

Role of the Researcher

The importance of the role of the researcher as the data collection instrument and analyst in ethnographic research cannot be overstated (e.g., Higginbottom et al., 2013; Roper & Shapira, 2000). The trustworthiness and authenticity of the ethnography are seen as inextricably linked to the practical sense of knowing that the researcher gains via their immersion in the field (Guba & Lincoln, 1994). Keeping a detailed research journal reflecting about the potential impact of any researcher-related factors (e.g., emotional burden, existing assumptions, theoretical positioning) on the data collection and interpretation is essential (Roper & Shapira, 2000; Simonds et al., 2012).

The key methods of data collection for use in focused ethnographic research include the following:

- *Participant observation.* Observation is the primary source of data collection and can place significant demands on the researcher in terms of their social, intellectual, and methodological flexibility. The data may be documented in field notes with or without the assistance of supplementary video or audio recording.

- *Informal interviewing*. As well as encouraging authentic responses from participants, interviewing informally aids rapport building by following the natural flow of conversation.

- *Mapping*. The purpose of this is to sketch the field based on the researcher's experience of the physical space and any salient features (e.g., areas of clutter, a participant's preferred chair, any repeated journeys made through the space).

- *Object or photo elicitation*. Physical objects and photos can provide an anchor or prompt for a participant's personal reflection and may be initiated by the researcher or participant (e.g., Morse & Field, 1995; Roper & Shapira, 2000; Simonds et al., 2012; Spradley, 2016).

The richness and volume of data generated by ethnography make organizing and indexing a major priority (Roper & Shapira, 2000), and developing strategies for the selection and transcription of the most relevant data is key. This can varyingly be driven by the data itself or by emergent research questions and supports further familiarity with and immersion in the data. Analysis is a process of breaking up or segmenting the raw data into smaller chunks before rebuilding these into patterns and key concepts (Jorgensen, 2015). Described as cyclical and iterative, the analytic process should encompass identification, classification, categorization, and eventually move toward the formulation of abstract and explanatory patterns (e.g., Angrosino, 2007; Higginbottom et al., 2013).

At a more granular level, analysis begins with coding, requiring the researcher to reduce down and simplify their data segments by assigning meaningful labels to them (Roper & Shapira, 2000). Codes are then combined to make broader and more general categories. Here begins a process of comparing and contrasting to verify any emerging patterns or key themes among the data segments, as well as any points of divergence. This comparing and contrasting is one iteration of the constant comparison (Glaser & Strauss, 1967) that should continue throughout analysis, in which emerging assumptions and analytic ideas about the data and what it means can be tested. The eventual aim is to abstract this enough to develop and articulate a coherent and comprehensive set of themes that fit the data collected and that provide an overarching picture of what has been identified as happening in the data. Data-viewing sessions with colleagues, particularly with video data owing to its real-time representation and multidimensional modality, can encourage the intersubjectivity in interpretations to come to the fore, and this can help with the identification of rival explanations and facilitate the gathering of supportive evidence for any working interpretations (e.g., Knoblauch & Schnettler, 2012; Pink & Morgan, 2013).

Although ethnography is epistemologically aligned with the qualitative paradigm, concerned with capturing multiple perspectives and subjective meaning making, it can include some quantitative data collection. Some combination of descriptive text and numbers can also be helpful during the analysis stages, when presenting data in a variety of matrices and/or tables can help to illuminate patterns and emerging concepts of interest (Angrosino, 2007; Roper & Shapira, 2000). It is recommended, however, that analysis of quantitative data should generally be conducted toward the end of the overall analytic process so as not to overly restrict the researcher in their inductively led focus on areas of (emerging) significance (e.g., Roper & Shapira, 2000).

Both focused ethnographic and qualitative case study approaches are often acknowledged to be methodologically underspecified or flexible, especially in terms of their analytic processes (e.g., Knoblauch, 2005; Roper & Shapira, 2000; Stake, 1995; Wall, 2014). It is acknowledged within both approaches that the analytic strategy needs to be custom built for the needs of each project; there is no one-size-fits-all approach (e.g., Angrosino, 2007; Knoblauch, 2005). Simonds et al. (2012) described the different options of focused ethnographic methods as tools in a toolbox. Along with Roper and Shapira (2000) and Wolcott (1990), they emphasized the importance of choosing the selection of methods most appropriate to the research questions and study sample at hand, and it being the intent of a study, rather than the specific methods used, that ultimately make it ethnographic in nature (i.e., making an ethnographic approach not incompatible with a qualitative case study–inspired design). Similarly, Stake (1995) claimed that case studies are defined by an essential interest in individual case(s) and not necessarily by the methods of enquiry that are used. Nygård and Winblad (2006) and Wall (2014) described the necessary methodological adaptation and innovation that such heavily context-specific research questions can demand, as well as the exciting possibilities such study designs permit for novel analytic approaches.

Both approaches encourage the collection of mixed-methods data, and here we outline the rationale for the quantitative (neuropsychology and self-report) and physiological data that we also collected as part of this project.

Neuropsychology Data

Neuropsychological assessments aim to detect and characterize impairments in cognition through standardized behavioral or cognitive tasks. Tasks are intended to examine particular cognitive functions or domains, including memory, attention, language, and visuospatial and visuoperceptual functioning (Burrell & Piguet, 2015). However, it is worth noting that there is no one-to-one correspondence between tests and cognitive functions, and performance on an individual test may be impaired for a number of reasons. Tests are intended to assess impairment objectively based on a normality threshold defined through an appropriate reference sample (usually the fifth percentile of a group of healthy participants), minimizing the use of subjective and self-reported measures. Scores on such tests are useful in screening, diagnosis, and assessment of the impact of neurodegenerative disease over time and in establishing the extent and specific pattern of cognitive impairment for an individual (Burrell & Piguet, 2015). Neuropsychological assessments may complement clinical interviews and questionnaires to inform consideration of patient needs, appropriate services, and referrals. There can be easily conceived implications of cognitive behavioral tests (e.g., memory and dysexecutive problems; motor, visual, and reading assessment) for functional independence (managing routine and finances, considering home adaptation and referral for driving test).

Examples of the application of neuropsychological measures in research contexts range from validating novel biological markers of neurodegeneration (Frisoni et al., 2017), serving as outcome measures for interventional studies, and understanding how altered function or structure of particular brain regions or networks manifests in cognitive symptoms. In the context of this project, of particular interest is understanding what implications different profiles of cognitive impairment have for functional independence and activity engagement.

Self-Report Scale Data

Self-report data are data that participants report about their own subjective experiences. This type of data is particularly useful when it is an element of a person's subjective experience that is of interest—for example, an individual's sense of their own QoL or mood (e.g., Banerjee et al., 2009; Spreadbury & Kipps, 2019). These data are often made measurable and collected via self-report scales because this allows, for example, for comparison across groups and analysis of statistically significant differences (e.g., across populations, pre- and postintervention; e.g., Perfect et al., 2019; Spreadbury & Kipps, 2019). Many quantified self-report scales are also used for clinical assessment and diagnosis, with the scale element allowing for classification and categorization. Owing to the dominant memory difficulties and common secondary language impairments of PLWD, traditionally many self-report measures for use in dementia populations have been designed to be completed by either family or professional carers. These include those assessing neuropsychiatric symptoms, such as depression, apathy, and delusions, or ability to perform a range of activities of daily living (ADLs; e.g., dressing, cooking), although the contributions that PLWD can make to research are increasingly being recognized (e.g., Brod et al., 1999; Moyle et al., 2007). In the context of this project, of particular interest is understanding how participant self-reported data may (or may not) map onto data obtained from participant observation within a naturalistic setting.

Physiological Data

Adding and in contrast to a self-report approach to data collection, physiological data offer researchers an opportunity to capture something more objective about a person's experience, outside of their conscious awareness or possible self-conscious reporting (e.g., Bourne et al., 2019; Sequeira et al., 2009; Thomas et al., 2018). For example, accelerometer data can offer information about a person's level of physical activity, measurement of electrodermal activity (EDA) offers an indication of emotional and sympathetic response useful for detection of levels of emotional and physiological arousal, and measurement of heart rate can be used to infer indicate excitement, stress, and increased physical activity (e.g., Bourne et al., 2019; Camic et al., 2018; Sequeira et al., 2009).

In being outside of conscious control, and as a result of continual technological advancement, physiological factors can often be measured non-invasively while limiting input or effort from participants, which increases the accessibility of participation for PLWD who may be in the more advanced stages or who are less reliably able to communicate their experiences verbally (e.g., via self-report measures or interviews; e.g., Camic et al., 2018; Thomas et al., 2018). This passive and continual data collection can also offer rich and meaningful baseline data and an understanding of experience "in the moment," as part of a process, as opposed to solely at distinct and discrete time points (Camic et al., 2018). In the context of this project, of particular interest is understanding how objective physiological data regarding, for example, the amount of activity or arousal, may relate to researcher interpretations or participant self-reports of the meaning and experience of activity engagement.

RESEARCH QUESTIONS

The broad study aim to explore the impact(s) of the diagnoses on the intersecting physical and psychosocial environment was gradually refined to the following research questions about engagement in everyday activities:

- Which activities are people taking part in and why? (Who instigates this and how? Are they familiar or new activities? Are they predominantly socially or physically engaging, or both? What does the activity provide?)

- How is participation in activities challenged and/or supported? (Who instigates this? Do physical objects help or hinder with this? How?)

DATA COLLECTION

A mixed-methods approach was selected to build as full a picture as possible of the rich and varied contexts of individual experiences and to permit cross verification and validation of different sources of data relating to both objective physical and physiological properties with standardized measures of cognitive function and participant's subjective self-reporting along with the researcher's subjective interpretation.[1] The data types collected were as follows:

- *Demographics*. Demographic information about participants' health, employment, and relationship status and living situation were collected from informants using questionnaires.

- *Field notes*. Field notes were recorded on time-labeled worksheets to allow these to be aligned with the video data. Knowing the video data would support these notes, they were mostly shorthand key words, and this was helpful for ensuring the researcher was mostly present with the participants and active in the setting, noticing thoughts, feelings, and reactions. The researcher wrote up more detailed field notes as soon as possible once out of the setting, and this included a weighted reassessment of what, on balance by the end of the visit, had seemed to be of particular relevance and significance for the research questions.

- *Video data*. Video recording was selected because of the rich volume of data it could capture and was considered particularly suitable given the interest in observing the interactions of people with PCA with their physical environment. The video was also used to capture audio data, including informal conversations and commentaries participants provided while doing, reflecting on or storytelling about their engagement with activities. Video data were collected via 360-degree (4K; 360-Fly; e.g., Clare et al., 2020) and wearable cameras (Veho HD; Muvi). The 360-degree camera was used to capture the overall and simultaneous total scene level of detail—for example, how participants were using the space, their proximity to each other and objects, and so on. The wearable cameras offered an audiovisual approximation of participants' view of the world from the perspective of their orientation and also offered useful close-up recordings of people's interactions with objects (another key interest in people with PCA given their characteristic cognitive symptom profile).

- *Neuropsychology assessment*. Participants completed a brief neuropsychology test battery and the tests administered and the functions tested are presented in Table 12.1.

- *Self-report questionnaire data*. Three standardized self-report questionnaires were administered to gain a quantified measure of any neuropsychiatric symptoms that may have been additionally impacting on engagement with daily activities (measured using the Neuropsychiatric Inventory; Cummings et al., 1994), participants' levels of functional independence in ADLs (measured using Johnson's ADL Scale; Johnson et al., 2004), and participants' own and informant rated QoL (measured using QoL-AD—Logsdon et al., 1999).

---

[1]Data collection was conducted by the first author, and accordingly there are some first-person accounts in the following sections.

TABLE 12.1. Neuropsychology Tests Administered and Cognitive Functions Tested

Test	Function(s) tested
Mini-Mental Status Exam	Level of cognitive impairment
Short Recognition Memory Test for Words[a]	Episodic memory
Digit span	Working memory
Graded-difficulty naming test[b]	Naming from verbal description
Figure ground discrimination[c]	Early visual processing
Fragmented letters[c]	Visuoperceptual processing
Dot counting[c]	Visuospatial processing

[a]Warrington (1984).
[b]See Crutch et al. (2013).
[c]VOSP: The Visual Object and Space Perception Battery (Warrington & James, 1991).

- *Physiological data.* Passive physiological data (heart rate, three-axis accelerometer data, EDA, and skin temperature) were collected using an Empatica E4 wristband (Empatica, Milan, Italy) on each wrist of participants for the duration of the home visit.

- *Luminance and room dimensions.* Some objective information was collected about the physical properties of the home, including room dimensions, layout, and luminance levels in each room at a minimum of two points during the day.

- *Visual ethnographic mapping.* The researcher drew subjective freehand sketches of the layouts of the main areas of the homes indicating any points of note about how the participant had used the space during the course of the day, for example, if they had a certain chair that they mostly sat in or if they made repeated journeys to a particular area of the home.

DATA ANALYSIS

Here we outline the particular method for data analysis that was informed by the analytic techniques described earlier. The first step in organizing the data once out of the field was digitizing it. This meant uploading and labeling video and audio files and typing up the time logs, end-of-day field notes, and reflexivity notes. Scanning through the video files to label them and typing up the field notes was a helpful reimmersion exercise; it acted as a reminder of passing moments that may have seemed more significant on reflection and generally helped to ensure that the researcher stayed familiar with the whole data set. Qualitative data analysis software Atlas.ti (Version 7) was used to help classify data segments. Field notes were coded to label both what was happening in terms of actions (e.g., "washing up," "reading") and also possible meanings (e.g., "feeling lonely," "blaming diagnosis"). These codes could overlap according to the multiplicities of events and perspectives of different participants and the varied meanings that appeared to be being constructed.

It was during this initial coding that two concepts that went on to be major components of two of the overarching themes, meaningful activity and preservation of self, were solidified as key concepts. However, it began to seem that the coding process itself, which required breaking down moments further and further, meant that the individual and contained "caseness" of the holistic and contextual moments and events in the field were starting to get lost or diluted.

Moving between the whole subunits of analysis (i.e., individual participants) and individual segments (e.g., individual moments, comments) while retaining this sense of caseness can be challenging (e.g., Maxwell & Miller, 2008; Richards & Richards, 1991; Sandelowski, 1995). To facilitate constant comparison across individual subunits of analysis and to assist our efforts to play with new ways of organizing and juxtaposing the data, we developed a set of index cards that contained summary mixed-methods data for each participant (for an example, see Figure 12.1).

This format of data presentation meant that the researcher could easily order the index cards according to dominant symptoms, gender, age, how long participants had lived in their homes, their career history, and so forth.

FIGURE 12.1. Example of Index Card Developed for Data Triangulation Purposes

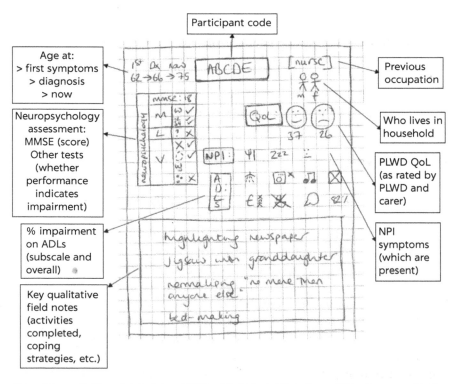

Note. ADL = activities of daily living; MMSE = Mini-Mental State Exam; NPI = Neuropsychiatric Inventory; PLWD = people living with dementia; QoL = quality of life.

This allowed for the identification of patterns and their easy testing among other possible combinations or organizations of the cases and subunits of analysis. It also illuminated negative cases much more easily than initial coding had by breaking the data down beyond the subunit level. Using the quantitative scores from the neuropsychology assessment and self-report scales to inform some of these groupings of the subunits of analysis allowed the creation of data matrices, but as broader patterns began to emerge in the qualitative data, these matrices were put to one side until critical quantitative discussions with the research team were held to ensure the quantitative data did not start to drive the overall analysis. This reflected a bigger epistemological crisis regarding the status of different data sources. White et al. (2009) described a similar predicament regarding their methodological process, and their openness in reporting their justifications and thinking processes was invaluable as the researcher grappled with structuring the analysis and prioritizing of different data streams. The research team did briefly discuss the idea of using the quantitative physiological data to drive the qualitative analysis—for example, looking at the corresponding video data for the four most active or arousing moments of the day for each participant (as determined by their Empatica data). However, it soon became clear that it was too difficult to attend only to selected moments of the qualitative data, having been experientially involved—and therefore familiar—with all of it. This qualitative data driving was also in keeping with the recommendations of both overarching approaches informing the study design. Quantitatively data-driven analysis may offer the most promise for researchers with access to secondary mixed-methods data sets and, in those cases, may permit valuable refined and targeted investigations of predefined areas of interest.

Triangulation of different theoretical frameworks happened throughout the study design, data collection, analysis, and interpretation stages. During the analysis, triangulation of qualitative data sources happened throughout, and triangulation of the mixed-methods data sources occurred toward the end of the analytic process (as recommended) as multiple data sources and the varied interpretations of them were juxtaposed and used to test one another. The quantitative data were used to potentially aid innovative interpretations of the qualitative data, and this process in turn illuminated potential ways that qualitative data could help inform the interpretation of the quantitative, which we provide some examples of subsequently. Examples of the sorts of questions that characterized this triangulation included the following: Is the level of ADL impairment indicated by the self-report questionnaire reflected in the field notes? How do participants' Mini-Mental Status Exam (MMSE) scores relate to their self-rated QoL? Triangulation also occurred among the investigators as interpretations from data segments and themes were reviewed and discussed. Examples of these conversations and the insights they provided are also be discussed subsequently. See Figure 12.2 for a diagrammatic overview of the analytic process.

FIGURE 12.2. Diagrammatic Overview of Analytic Process

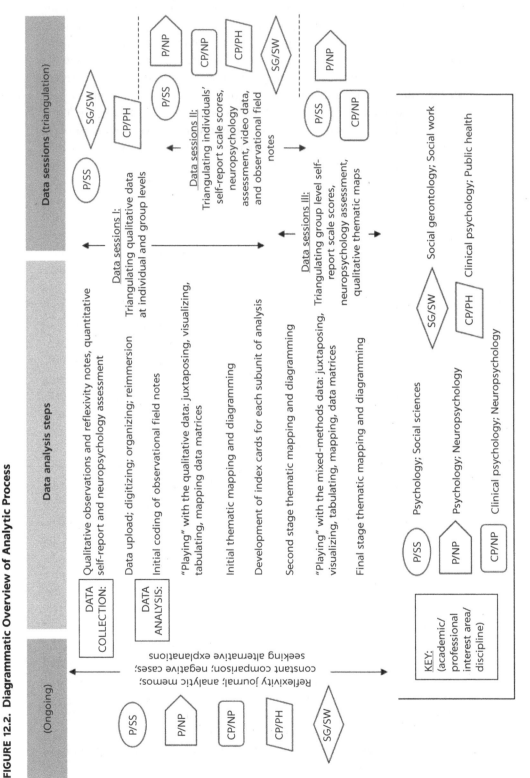

LESSONS LEARNED, PART 1: CONDUCTING EXTENDED OBSERVATIONS IN THE HOMES OF PEOPLE LIVING WITH DEMENTIA

In this section, we describe some of the challenges we faced and the ways these were navigated, as well as some considerations for other researchers planning to conduct home-based observations with PLWD.

Rapport Building: Maintaining Access

Building rapport and trust with participants is key to ensure maintained access to the setting, especially in extended periods of observation such as these. Spending time with people, getting to know them, and making them feel comfortable are essential components of this (e.g., Nygård & Winblad, 2006). This involves elements of empathy, listening well, not being preoccupied with in-the-moment note taking, and being nonjudgmental; an informal interviewing style and flexible or unstructured protocol can help with this (Higginbottom et al., 2013; Pink & Morgan, 2013; Roper & Shapira, 2000). An illustrative example of how rapport-building was achieved was with Mark,[2] who seemed fairly quiet and apprehensive when the researcher arrived. In initial conversations with him and his wife, it became clear that he was having some difficulty talking about his diagnosis, and, taking into account his body language and facial expressions during those early conversations, it seemed that he was uncomfortable with the idea of a day revolving around assessing or exposing his condition. As a result, rapport building was facilitated by enthused and lively conversations about topics unrelated to his dementia diagnosis, such as a family member's recent musical release and his reflections on his own career history. The demands this places on researchers to be perceptive and sensitive are great, but practicing regular reflexive note taking and frequent supervision can both help this process to become more intuitive. Confidence in one's own ability to detect and respond accurately also grows with exposure, although some ability to sit with the discomfort and uncertainty inherent in those early stages of observation proved essential.

Understanding the Researcher's Role

The rapport and relationship that must be developed, even when good, can feel precarious; Briggs et al. (2003) discussed how this can interact with participants' expectations of the researcher's role. Researchers may feel there are expectations on them to provide care, clinical advice, or counseling, for example, and navigating this requires the researcher to reflect on their role and boundaries in real time while in the field (Briggs et al., 2003). Experiences such as this occurred, with examples including participants asking for

---

[2]All names and other identifying details have been changed to preserve participant confidentiality.

practical advice about how they should adapt their home, clinical advice about medication and symptom progression, and expectations that the researcher would take a role of supervising or safeguarding the person with the diagnosis over the course of the day. Linked to this, rapport building and relationship management can be particularly difficult in scenarios where there are multiplicities of accounts. Occasionally participants would expect or ask the researcher to mediate their disagreements or to offer some "expert" advice to resolve them. In all cases, remaining attuned to participants' understandings of the researcher's role throughout the home visits was important so that they felt their concerns and perspectives had been heard and appropriate follow-up support and signposting could be provided where needed. This seemed especially important after such an intensive investment of participants' time and their generosity in openly sharing their experiences.

It's Never Going to Be a "Typical Day" (and That's OK)

Unstructured observations in participants' homes naturally pose challenges because data collection happens in a naturalistic setting with many complex and interacting variables that the researcher cannot control or manipulate. In addition to concerns about how much a researcher will need to consider, there are also documented concerns about what cannot be observed and how this affects validity. Briggs and colleagues (2003) outlined a common criticism that observations cannot be representative because the very presence of the researcher will change the setting and therefore the interactions and activities that happen within it. Briggs et al. attested, however, that although observations may not generalize to a typical day for participants, they often can still offer unique insights into those other, more typical days and wider practices and issues that extend beyond the observation period. One poignant example of this came from Oscar, who saved up his chores for the whole week for the observational visit. Although it was not representative for him to do all those chores in one day, it provided some useful insights into how his PCA was affecting a wide range of familiar tasks. It also (when contextualized within the broader home visit) provided further evidence of the conscientiousness that was characteristic of Oscar—in the same way that he wanted to take on the household chores as a means of contributing to family life since he had had to give up work—and he also wanted to be a conscientious research participant and contribute to the lives of others with the condition. Contrary to initial concerns about these instances posing a challenge for the representativeness of the data, these occurrences in fact facilitated within-setting constant comparison (e.g., why is this unusual, and what does that mean?), as the researcher began to hold in mind the idea that "everything can tell you something."

As with the rapport building, an essential skill in managing these concerns about data quality also seemed to come down to an ability to sit with the discomfort and essentially trust the research process itself. Learning about the day-to-day lives of the populations involved was, for us, as much about learning about how best to learn about them and feeling assured that if the data had been collected, documented, and organized as thoroughly as outlined in this chapter, there was time and space within the process for some flexibility and creativity in the thinking around this.

LESSONS LEARNED, PART 2: INTERESTING INSIGHTS WHEN INTEGRATING MIXED DATA TYPES

Valuable insights emerged when triangulating the qualitative and quantitative data collected in this study. These examples are by no means exhaustive or comprehensive but are a select handful of many interesting instances, and although these often speak at the level of the individual, they offer a glimpse into the possibilities for mixed-methods data from both ends of the qualitative–quantitative spectrum to shed new light and open up new questions or interpretations of the other, and contribute toward useful analytic development more broadly.

Measurement or Meaning of Activities: What Matters?

Juxtaposing the observational field notes with participants' cognitive profiles and an ADL measure of functional impairment proved a helpful part of the analytic process. In doing this, we realized that two of the most severely cognitively and functionally impaired participants were in fact spending a large proportion of their day doing ADL-type activities (more than many of the others). Alan, who had a diagnosis of PCA, an MMSE score of 5 (the lowest of all the participants and indicating severe cognitive impairment), and visuo-perceptual and visuospatial abilities deemed "untestable," spent several hours over the course of the day clearing leaves by hand from the front and back gardens. When talking about this, he explained that he found it satisfying because it was "hands on," before emphatically declaring that he wanted "to do *something*."

This got us as a team thinking about what we measure when we assess functional impairment, factors such as frequency of task completion, efficiency with which things are done, amount of help needed, and how reliably those measurable outcomes may actually be driving activity engagement in people's own homes. For example, Alan's clearing of the leaves was arguably rather inefficient; he had to revisit the same areas of the garden multiple times because of his visual perceptual problems and spent a couple of hours on something that could have been achieved within perhaps 15 minutes using the appropriate tools. Our focus began to shift away from what difficulties people were having with activities with a view to our developing adaptive aids to support them, toward gathering a better understanding of what activities people were motivated to continue doing despite any difficulties they were having and why. These insights contributed to the development of the overarching theme, "The Fun and the Function," about the importance of the experience of activities in making them meaningful for PLWD, often irrespective of the outcomes. The most severely cognitively impaired participant in the memory-led AD group was Helena, who had an MMSE score of 10 (indicating moderately severe cognitive impairment), showed impaired performance on the Graded Difficulty Naming Test, and was deemed "untestable" on the Short Recognition Memory Test for Words. However, Helena completed a wide range of household chores over the course of the visit, including making the beds, folding and hanging laundry, setting the table, and loading and unloading the dishwasher. Once again, we saw what we considered to be a lack of correspondence between her cognitive profile and ADL functioning scores and her actual engagement with those activities in her home environment. This encouraged our thinking along the lines of how Helena's activity engagement was enabled and why, and was significant in shaping one of the overarching themes, "Reciprocities of Care," about the essentials roles of carers in facilitating meaningful activities, and the importance of those which allow the PLWD to provide care for others (e.g., helping with the running of the house) as well as to receive it.

One of the ways we juxtaposed these data sources was by viewing the quantitative data displayed in charts with the data points labeled with participant pseudonyms and their index cards to hand. The bubble chart in Figure 12.3 shows each participant's rating of their QoL and their carer-rated level of functional impairment in ADLs, with the bubble size representing how cognitively impaired they were according to their MMSE score. This chart was helpful after our immersion in the qualitative data because it either validated or challenged some of our observations. For example, it felt fitting that QoL ratings seemed to be relatively unrelated to carer-rated level of impairment in ADL or MMSE, but (as mentioned) it was more surprising that ADL function did not seem to correspond much at all to how engaged with ADLs participants had been over the course of the home visit. Both that which corroborated and that which conflicted proved useful in the development of our analytic interpretations.

Assessing Apathy: Actual or Assumed?

Another important insight that juxtaposing scale data with observational data revealed was regarding levels of apathy and activity engagement. When looking at the Neuropsychiatric Inventory data, the same number of participants in each diagnosis group were rated as displaying apathy by their carers, and in the light of the observational data, this seemed surprising in the first instance because all members of the PCA group had spoken at some length about their varied interests. Looking more closely at the two data sources alongside each other helped to formulate our interpretation that the PCA participants—despite maintaining interest in and motivation to engage in a range of

FIGURE 12.3. Bubble Chart Displaying PLWD Self-Rated QoL, Carer-Rated Percentage of ADL Impairment, and PLWD MMSE Score

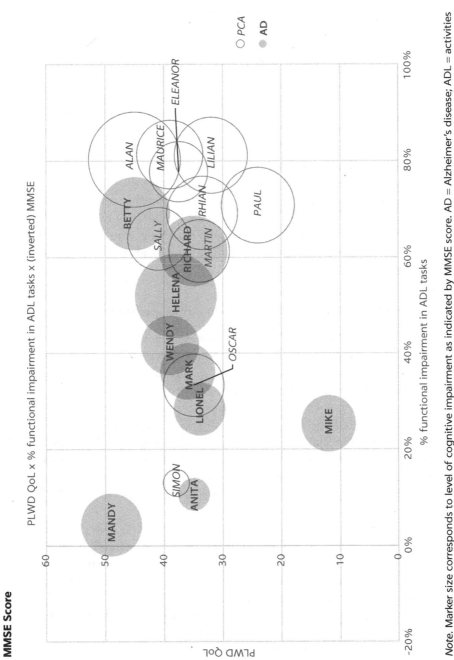

Note. Marker size corresponds to level of cognitive impairment as indicated by MMSE score. AD = Alzheimer's disease; ADL = activities of daily living; MMSE = Mini-Mental State Exam; PCA = posterior cortical atrophy; PLWD = people living with dementia; QoL = quality of life.

activities—were limited very early on in their diagnosis in their abilities to enact or instigate these activities because of their profound visual and spatial processing problems. Maurice, for example, explained that as he could no longer read his computing magazines; he had wanted to donate them to a local IT group but was unable to look one up, use his calendar to plan a date, or navigate himself to a meeting.

Looking at different data streams alongside each other for both groups further developed our understanding of the group-level differences in apparent apathy and how this related to engagement. The memory-led AD group members appeared to demonstrate more apathy in terms of a lack of motivation and interest in initiating activities but were often seemingly happy to be engaged in activities orchestrated and supported by their family carers. Helena's productivity with household chores was always instigated by her husband (although executed by her), and Wendy's craft activities were almost always initiated following her husband's encouragement (although she would, once engaged, appear motivated to continue the activity). This exercise in data juxtaposing was helpful for developing our analytic thinking in terms of not only which activities were done and why they were important to people but also how they came to be completed or challenged, and the diagnostic differences underlying these discrepancies.

Interpreting Physiological Data: Engaged or Exasperated?

Some particularly important insights came from recontextualizing the physiological data within the observational video data. For example, we may assume that the more active someone is according to their accelerometer data the better, but without knowing what this increased exertion corresponds to means our interpretations are at risk of oversimplification. Is someone enjoying playing with the family pet dog or repeatedly looking for their handbag? We would argue that especially in the case of life-limiting conditions like the dementias, that quality of activity is as important as quantity, and mixed methods such as those used in this study can be helpful in building a more nuanced and real-world representative image of how that is experienced in ecologically valid settings.

The same holds true for the electrodermal activity data, which broadly indicates a person's level of arousal. (An important caveat: Here for the purposes of our theoretical discussion, we focus on the *direction* of change in EDA data, as opposed to *magnitude* of change, which is also of critical importance in the interpretation of EDA data but beyond the scope of this chapter; see Andreassi, 2013; Boucsein et al., 2012.) How can we know whether a surge in EDA means someone is pleasantly engaged in an activity or exasperated by it? EDA is often measured in experimentally controlled settings with a stimulus of a certain valence (e.g., a distressing vignette, a smiling face), so that the direction of the arousal measured can be relatively reliably inferred. However, when passively collecting these data in an uncontrolled environment like the home, being able to realign this data with qualitative field notes and video data is of critical importance to allow any meaningful interpretation to be made. For example, Martin showed similar levels of EDA response when dancing around the kitchen with his wife as when struggling to differentiate and correctly transfer from his slippers to his walking shoes.

Another important point about the direction of EDA is that in a naturalistic setting, activities, interactions, and individual responses can be infinitely more complex and multilayered than simply in a positive or negative direction.

Maurice provided an example of this over dinner time, where his EDA data showed a flurry of spikes of activity (see Figure 12.4). Over the course of the dinner, numerous events that could be categorized as either "engaging" or "exasperating" overlapped. As dinner went on, Maurice had increasing difficulty finding the food on his plate because of his dominant visual problems, as there was gradually less and less food there to "see," but this also offered more time for him to engage in animated conversation, which he had done throughout the visit, cracking jokes and sharing funny stories. However, Maurice also had some concurrent word-finding difficulties, so the more storytelling he did, the more he needed to struggle to find the words he was looking for.

It became clear that contrasting the video and physiological data could be useful not only for recontextualizing to clarify but also for demonstration and appreciation of the complexity of the scenarios we were observing and as a reminder of the limitations of any single data source in building a representation of something as variable and individuals as a person's lived experience. Although analyzing these rich and complex moments with multiple data sources did not always mean a clear and undisputable interpretation could be made, the combination of data sources helped toward our understanding of the complexity of the everyday environment, the limitations of the data collection tools, both individually and together, and the potential scope or parameters of the research questions we are able to ask within such settings.

ETHICAL ISSUES IN MIXED-METHODS RESEARCH IN NATURALISTIC SETTINGS

Conducting mixed-methods research involving home-based observations of PLWD raises several ethical issues associated with numerous participant, researcher, study design, and data-related factors. These include ensuring the informed and ongoing consent of participants throughout data collection visits. Home visit protocols that are of an extended duration and include multiple data collection methods bring added complexity in terms of ensuring participants' full understanding of what all elements will involve and in assessing participants' continued awareness of and agreement to the study procedures throughout the visit. Understanding participants' motivations for taking part in the study was also an important consideration given the novel mixed-methods approach and the extended and immersive nature of the data collection, and it offered an added opportunity to ensure participants understood the purpose of the study and assess their eligibility and suitability.

FIGURE 12.4. Physiological Data Collected by Empatica E4 Wristband

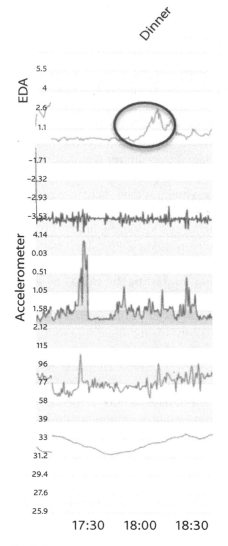

Note. EDA = electrodermal activity.

Describing such a study to participants can be particularly challenging when data collection procedures are mixed method because some quantitative components are likely to be more structured and able to be more clearly specified and communicated (e.g., questionnaires) than some qualitative elements, which may be (necessarily) less well specified and predefined (e.g., unstructured observations of meaningful activities). Unstructured observational data collection also poses ethical issues in that there are numerous, often uncontrollable variations within naturalistic settings such as the home environment and endless possibilities for the different activities that may be undertaken, which all serve to increase the possibility of unanticipated risks arising. This increases the importance of ensuring the researcher's role and responsibilities are well-specified and agreed to before the start of the visit and of there being clearly defined risk-reporting procedures in place before data collection begins. In the study reported here, this included ensuring another researcher was available during the observational period for telephone consultation and support in case a particular situation arose that needed to be carefully negotiated by the observing researcher. Owing to this inability to predict what would occur during the unstructured home-based observational visits, it was also important to offer participants opportunities to request the deletion of any unanticipated data (e.g., video footage of unannounced visitors), which we did during the debrief at the end of the visit and in a follow-up call 1 week later. Taking steps to address these considerations from the beginning stages of the study design and throughout permitted the ethical collection of a rich data set of high social and clinical value.

RECOMMENDATIONS FOR RESEARCH USING MIXED METHODS

For other researchers considering undertaking mixed-methods data collection within a naturalistic setting, we offer the following recommendations.

Extended immersive data collection:

- Keep a detailed reflexivity journal (as part of one's research journal) with frequent and prompt entries (ideally while in the field or very shortly afterward) to ensure that the researcher's responses to and interactions with the data can be acknowledged and factored into the analysis.

- Use data sessions with fellow researchers to develop alternative interpretations and explanations and to address and make explicit any researcher biases and assumptions.

- Ensure regular supervision of researchers throughout immersion in the research setting and in the data during analysis.

- Anticipate and prepare for the emotional intensity of immersive home-based work.

Mixed-methods data integration:

- Encourage epistemological openness and flexibility so that mixed-methods data can be juxtaposed to illuminate new insights (e.g., considering data status explicitly and experimenting with reversing data hierarchies).

- "Play" to find creative ways to display data that allow data to be visualized and processed as a whole or at once in a summarized or reduced format to permit some comparison between the qualitative and quantitative data.

- Although this chapter describes primary data analysis of a primary data set, it is anticipated that for researchers doing a secondary analysis of mixed-methods observational data like this, the option of using quantitative data to help with selecting which moments of the rich qualitative data to analyze could be a helpful tool in data reduction.

CONCLUSION

This chapter's aim was to demonstrate the rich, nuanced insights it is possible to gather from extended immersion in the home environments of PLWD and especially so when combining methods of data collection. Despite the difficulties, finding ways to integrate varied data sources is an essential step toward building a fuller, richer, and more complete picture of the lived experiences of PLWD and their families. In addition to providing useful insights for shaping analytic outcomes, the observed discrepancies among cognitive, functional, and experiential outcomes illustrated here also raise questions for research and practice. Considering the significant role cognitive measures can play in the diagnostic process and in tracking disease progression, which in turn can determine, for example, access to services and support, trial participation, and pharmacological interventions, these discrepancies present a conundrum in terms of how they are interpreted and reconciled (including whether they need to be). This further demonstrates the need for future work that explores how mixed-methods data can be integrated and what different data sources can reveal in each other. In being transparent about some of the tensions and challenges we experienced and navigated, other researchers may feel more equipped to embark on immersive and ecologically valid research that endorses and represents the truly complex picture of life with diagnosis of a dementia. Mostly, however, it is hoped that they too will openly report the trials and tribulations, obstacles, and decisions taken during their own research experiences, which will be essential for the further methodological development in this area of ever-increasing importance (Punch, 1994).

REFERENCES

Andreassi, J. L. (2013). *Psychophysiology: Human behavior and physiological response.* Psychology Press. https://doi.org/10.4324/9781410602817

Angrosino, M. (2007). *Doing ethnographic and observational research.* Sage Publications. https://doi.org/10.4135/9781849208932

Askham, J., Briggs, K., Norman, I., & Redfern, S. (2007). Care at home for people with dementia: As in a total institution? *Ageing and Society, 27*(1), 3–24. https://doi.org/10.1017/S0144686X06005307

Banerjee, S., Samsi, K., Petrie, C. D., Alvir, J., Treglia, M., Schwam, E. M., & del Valle, M. (2009). What do we know about quality of life in dementia? A review of the emerging evidence on the predictive and explanatory value of disease specific measures of health related quality of life in people with dementia. *International Journal of Geriatric Psychiatry, 24*(1), 15–24. https://doi.org/10.1002/gps.2090

Baxter, P., & Jack, S. (2008). Qualitative case study methodology: Study design and implementation for novice researchers. *Qualitative Report, 13*, 544–559. https://nsuworks.nova.edu/tqr/vol13/iss4/2

Boucsein, W., Fowles, D. C., Grimnes, S., Ben-Shakhar, G., Roth, W. T., Dawson, M. E., Filion, D. L., & the Society for Psychophysiological Research Ad Hoc Committee on

Electrodermal Measures. (2012). Publication recommendations for electrodermal measurements. *Psychophysiology*, *49*(8), 1017–1034. https://doi.org/10.1111/j.1469-8986.2012.01384.x

Bourne, P., Camic, P. M., Crutch, S., Hulbert, S., Firth, N., & Harding, E. (2019). Using psychological and physiological measures in arts-based activities in a community sample of people with a dementia and their caregivers: A feasibility and pilot study. *Journal of Aging Studies and Therapies*, *1*, 1–11. 10.16966/jast.102

Briggs, K., Askham, J., Norman, I., & Redfern, S. (2003). Accomplishing care at home for people with dementia: Using observational methodology. *Qualitative Health Research*, *13*(2), 268–280. https://doi.org/10.1177/1049732302239604

Brod, M., Stewart, A. L., Sands, L., & Walton, P. (1999). Conceptualization and measurement of quality of life in dementia: The dementia quality of life instrument (DQoL). *The Gerontologist*, *39*(1), 25–35. https://doi.org/10.1093/geront/39.1.25

Burrell, J. R., & Piguet, O. (2015). Lifting the veil: How to use clinical neuropsychology to assess dementia. *Journal of Neurology, Neurosurgery, and Psychiatry*, *86*(11), 1216–1224. https://doi.org/10.1136/jnnp-2013-307483

Camic, P. M., Crutch, S. J., Murphy, C., Firth, N. C., Harding, E., Harrison, C. R., Howard, S., Strohmaier, S., Van Leewen, J., West, J., Windle, G., Wray, S., & Zeilig, H. (2018). Conceptualising and understanding artistic creativity in the dementias: Interdisciplinary approaches to research and practice. *Frontiers in Psychology*, *9*, 1842. https://doi.org/10.3389/fpsyg.2018.01842

Clare, A., Camic, P. M., Crutch, S. J., West, J., Harding, E., & Brotherhood, E. (2020). Using music to develop a multisensory communicative environment for people with late stage dementia. *The Gerontologist*, *60*(6), 1115–1125.

Crutch, S. J., Lehmann, M., Schott, J. M., Rabinovici, G. D., Rossor, M. N., & Fox, N. C. (2012). Posterior cortical atrophy. *The Lancet Neurology*, *11*(2), 170–178. https://doi.org/10.1016/S1474-4422(11)70289-7

Crutch, S. J., Lehmann, M., Warren, J. D., & Rohrer, J. D. (2013). The language profile of posterior cortical atrophy. *Journal of Neurology, Neurosurgery, and Psychiatry*, *84*(4), 460–466. https://doi.org/10.1136/jnnp-2012-303309

Crutch, S. J., Schott, J. M., Rabinovici, G. D., Murray, M., Snowden, J. S., van der Flier, W. M., Dickerson, B. C., Vandenberghe, R., Ahmed, S., Bak, T. H., Boeve, B. F., Butler, C., Cappa, S. F., Ceccaldi, M., de Souza, L. C., Dubois, B., Felician, O., Galasko, D., Graff-Radford, J., . . . the Alzheimer's Association ISTAART Atypical Alzheimer's Disease and Associated Syndromes Professional Interest Area. (2017). Consensus classification of posterior cortical atrophy. *Alzheimer's & Dementia*, *13*(8), 870–884. https://doi.org/10.1016/j.jalz.2017.01.014

Cummings, J. L., Mega, M., Gray, K., Rosenberg-Thompson, S., Carusi, D. A., & Gornbein, J. (1994). The Neuropsychiatric Inventory: Comprehensive assessment of psychopathology in dementia. *Neurology*, *44*(12), 2308–2314. https://doi.org/10.1212/WNL.44.12.2308

de la Cuesta, C., & Sandelowski, M. (2005). Tenerlos en la Casa: The material world and craft of family caregiving for relatives with dementia. *Journal of Transcultural Nursing*, *16*(3), 218–225. https://doi.org/10.1177/1043659605274979

Frisoni, G. B., Boccardi, M., Barkhof, F., Blennow, K., Cappa, S., Chiotis, K., Démonet, J.-F., Garibotto, V., Giannakopoulos, P., Gietl, A., Hansson, O., Herholz, K., Jack, C. R., Jr., Nobili, F., Nordberg, A., Snyder, H. M., ten Kate, M., Varrone, A., Albanese, E., . . . Winblad, B. (2017). Strategic roadmap for an early diagnosis of Alzheimer's disease based on biomarkers. *The Lancet Neurology*, *16*(8), 661–676. https://doi.org/10.1016/S1474-4422(17)30159-X

George, D. R. (2011). Intergenerational volunteering and quality of life: Mixed methods evaluation of a randomized control trial involving persons with mild to moderate dementia. *Quality of Life Research*, *20*(7), 987–995. https://doi.org/10.1007/s11136-010-9837-8

George, D. R., Stuckey, H. L., & Whitehead, M. M. (2014). How a creative storytelling intervention can improve medical student attitude towards persons with dementia: A mixed methods study. *Dementia, 13*(3), 318–329. https://doi.org/10.1177/1471301212468732

Glaser, B. G., & Strauss, A. L. (1967). *The discovery of grounded theory: Strategies for qualitative research.* Aldine De Gruyter.

Guba, E. G., & Lincoln, Y. S. (1994). Competing paradigms in qualitative research. In N. K. Denzin & Y. S. Lincoln (Eds.), *Handbook of qualitative research* (pp. 105–118). Sage Publications.

Harding, E., Sullivan, M. P., Woodbridge, R., Yong, K. X. X., McIntyre, A., Gilhooly, M. L., Gilhooly, K. J., & Crutch, S. J. (2018). "Because my brain isn't as active as it should be, my eyes don't always see": A qualitative exploration of the stress process for those living with posterior cortical atrophy. *BMJ Open, 8*(2), e018663. https://doi.org/10.1136/bmjopen-2017-018663

Higginbottom, G., Pillay, J. J., & Boadu, N. Y. (2013). Guidance on performing focused ethnographies with an emphasis on healthcare research. *Qualitative Report, 18*, 1–6. https://nsuworks.nova.edu/tqr/vol18/iss9/1

Johnson, N., Barion, A., Rademaker, A., Rehkemper, G., & Weintraub, S. (2004). The Activities of Daily Living Questionnaire: A validation study in patients with dementia. *Alzheimer Disease and Associated Disorders, 18*(4), 223–230. https://pdfs.semanticscholar.org/f022/2a658d3516a7ccef8efbf86799b6e5c8086f.pdf

Jorgensen, D. L. (2015). Participant observation. In R.A. Scott & S.M. Kossly (Eds.), *Emerging trends in the social and behavioral sciences.* Wiley. https://onlinelibrary.wiley.com/doi/abs/10.1002/9781118900772.etrds0247

Knoblauch, H. (2005). Focused ethnography. *Forum Qualitative Sozialforschung/Forum: Qualitative Social Research, 6*(3), Article 44. https://www.qualitative-research.net/index.php/fqs/article/view/20/43

Knoblauch, H., & Schnettler, B. (2012). Videography: Analysing video data as a "focused" ethnographic and hermeneutical exercise. *Qualitative Research, 12*(3), 334–356. https://doi.org/10.1177/1468794111436147

Logsdon, R. G., Gibbons, L. E., McCurry, S. M., & Teri, L. (1999). Quality of life in Alzheimer's disease: Patient and caregiver reports. *Journal of Mental Health and Aging, 5*, 21–32.

Maxwell, J. A., & Miller, B. A. (2008). Categorizing and connecting strategies in qualitative data analysis. In S. N. Hesse-Biber & P. Leavy (Eds.), *Handbook of emergent methods* (pp. 461–479). Guildford Press.

Mendez, M. F., Ghajarania, M., & Perryman, K. M. (2002). Posterior cortical atrophy: Clinical characteristics and differences compared to Alzheimer's disease. *Dementia and Geriatric Cognitive Disorders, 14*(1), 33–40. https://doi.org/10.1159/000058331

Mondada, L. (2006). Video recording as the reflexive preservation and configuration of phenomenal features for analysis. In H. Knoblauch, B. Schnettler, J. Raab, & H. G. Soeffner (Eds.), *Video analysis: Methodology and methods: Qualitative audiovisual data analysis in sociology* (pp. 51–67). Peter Lang.

Morse, J. M., & Field, P. A. (1995). *Qualitative research methods for health professionals* (Vol. 2). Sage Publications.

Moyle, W., Jones, C., Dwan, T., & Petrovich, T. (2018). Effectiveness of a virtual reality forest on people with dementia: A mixed methods pilot study. *The Gerontologist, 58*(3), 478–487. https://doi.org/10.1093/geront/gnw270

Moyle, W., McAllister, M., Venturato, L., & Adams, T. (2007). Quality of life and dementia: The voice of the person with dementia. *Dementia, 6*(2), 175–191. https://doi.org/10.1177/1471301207080362

Nygård, L., & Winblad, B. (2006). Measuring long term effects and changes in the daily activities of people with dementia. *The Journal of Nutrition, Health & Aging, 10*(2), 137–138.

Perfect, D., Griffiths, A. W., Vasconcelos Da Silva, M., Lemos Dekker, N., McDermid, J., & Surr, C. A. (2019). Collecting self-report research data with people with dementia within care home clinical trials: Benefits, challenges and best practice. *Dementia*. Advance online publication. https://doi.org/10.1177/1471301219871168

Pink, S., & Morgan, J. (2013). Short-term ethnography: Intense routes to knowing. *Symbolic Interaction, 36*(3), 351–361. https://doi.org/10.1002/symb.66

Punch, M. (1994). Politics and ethics in qualitative research. In N. K. Denzin & Y. S. Lincoln (Eds.), *Handbook of qualitative research* (pp. 83–97). Sage Publications.

Richards, L., & Richards, T. (1991). Computing in qualitative analysis: A healthy development? *Qualitative Health Research, 1*(2), 234–262. https://doi.org/10.1177/104973239100100205

Robinson, A. L., Emden, C. G., Croft, T. D., Vosper, G. C., Elder, J. A., Stirling, C., & Vickers, J. C. (2011). Mixed methods data collection in dementia research: A "progressive engagement" approach. *Journal of Mixed Methods Research, 5*(4), 330–344. https://doi.org/10.1177/1558689811416940

Roper, J. M., & Shapira, J. (2000). *Ethnography in nursing research* (Vol. 1). Sage Publications. https://doi.org/10.4135/9781483328294

Sampson, E. L., Thuné-Boyle, I., Kukkastenvehmas, R., Jones, L., Tookman, A., King, M., & Blanchard, M. R. (2008). Palliative care in advanced dementia; A mixed methods approach for the development of a complex intervention. *BMC Palliative Care, 7*(1), 8. Advance online publication. https://doi.org/10.1186/1472-684X-7-8

Sandelowski, M. (1995). Qualitative analysis: What it is and how to begin. *Research in Nursing & Health, 18*(4), 371–375. https://doi.org/10.1002/nur.4770180411

Sequeira, H., Hot, P., Silvert, L., & Delplanque, S. (2009). Electrical autonomic correlates of emotion. *International Journal of Psychophysiology, 71*(1), 50–56. https://doi.org/10.1016/j.ijpsycho.2008.07.009

Simonds, L. M., Camic, P. M., & Causey, A. (2012). Using focused ethnography in psychological research. In H. Cooper, P. M. Camic, D. L. Long, A. T. Panter, D. Rindskopf, & K. J. Sher (Eds.), *APA handbook of research methods in psychology: Vol. 2. Research designs: Quantitative, qualitative, neuropsychological, and biological* (pp. 157–170). American Psychological Association. https://doi.org/10.1037/13620-010

Spradley, J. P. (2016). *The ethnographic interview*. Waveland Press.

Spreadbury, J. H., & Kipps, C. M. (2019). Measuring younger onset dementia: A comprehensive literature search of the quantitative psychosocial research. *Dementia (London), 18*(1), 135–156. https://doi.org/10.1177/1471301216661427

Stake, R. (1995). *The art of case study research*. Sage Publications.

Tang-Wai, D. F., Graff-Radford, N. R., Boeve, B. F., Dickson, D. W., Parisi, J. E., Crook, R., Caselli, R. J., Knopman, D. S., & Petersen, R. C. (2004). Clinical, genetic, and neuropathologic characteristics of posterior cortical atrophy. *Neurology, 63*(7), 1168–1174. https://doi.org/10.1212/01.WNL.0000140289.18472.15

Thomas, G. E. C., Crutch, S. J., & Camic, P. M. (2018). Measuring physiological responses to the arts in people with a dementia. *International Journal of Psychophysiology, 123*, 64–73. https://doi.org/10.1016/j.ijpsycho.2017.11.008

Wall, S. (2014). Focused ethnography: A methodological adaption for social research in emerging contexts. *Forum Qualitative Sozialforschung/Forum: Qualitative Social Research, 16*(1). Advance online publication. 10.17169/fqs-16.1.2182

Warrington, E. K. (1984). *Recognition Memory Test: RMT. (Words). Test Booklet 1*. NFER-Nelson.

Warrington, E. K., & James, M. (1991). *VOSP: The Visual Object and Space Perception Battery*. Thames Valley Test Company.

White, J., Drew, S., & Hay, T. (2009). Ethnography versus case study—Positioning research and researchers. *Qualitative Research Journal, 9*(1), 18–27. https://doi.org/10.3316/QRJ0901018

Windle, G., Joling, K. J., Howson-Griffiths, T., Woods, B., Jones, C. H., van de Ven, P. M., Newman, A., & Parkinson, C. (2018). The impact of a visual arts program on quality of life, communication, and well-being of people living with dementia: A mixed-methods longitudinal investigation. *International Psychogeriatrics, 30*(3), 409–423. https://doi.org/10.1017/S1041610217002162

Wolcott, H. (1990). Writing up qualitative research. In *Qualitative research methods* (Vol. 20). Sage Publications.

Yin, R. K. (2017). *Case study research and applications*. Sage Publications.

13

Using Qualitative Research for Intervention Development and Evaluation

Lucy Yardley, Katherine Bradbury, and Leanne Morrison

Qualitative researchers are aware of the value of qualitative methods for exploring and understanding people's experiences of new situations, and so the potential benefits of using qualitative methods to understand people's views and experiences of psychological interventions might seem self-evident. In recent times, the importance of qualitative methods has become explicitly acknowledged in many fields of applied psychological research, particularly fields such as health, clinical, counseling, and educational psychology (Gough & Deatrick, 2015; Hanson et al., 2005; Rohleder & Lyons, 2014). This recognition has included an appreciation of the vital role qualitative methods can play in both the development and the evaluation of psychological and "complex" behavior change interventions (O'Cathain et al., 2019).

Qualitative approaches to exploring and analyzing experiences of behavior change interventions are particularly well suited to understanding the complexity of such interventions (Thirsk & Clark, 2017). Qualitative methods are able to reveal and examine the often unexpected ways in which intervention elements interact and are influenced by the user's context—for example, their lifestyle, environment, and culture. For this reason, qualitative methods are now strongly recommended for process analyses of experiences of implementing and trialing interventions (Moore et al., 2015), to investigate how and why the hypothesized mechanisms of action may or may not have led to the desired behaviors and outcomes. Qualitative methods are now also routinely used in "feasibility trials" of interventions as a means of evaluating the

https://doi.org/10.1037/0000252-013
Qualitative Research in Psychology: Expanding Perspectives in Methodology and Design,
Second Edition, P. M. Camic (Editor)

acceptability and feasibility of intervention and trial procedures and detecting unanticipated deviations from protocol that need to be understood and addressed (O'Cathain et al., 2015).

Although qualitative studies embedded in feasibility trials and process analyses provide invaluable insights into how the intervention operated and was experienced by users, these analyses often reveal problems that could and should have been addressed before implementation and trialing. For this reason, using qualitative methods at the development stage is increasingly advocated as a means of reducing research waste by identifying and correcting problems with accessibility, comprehensibility, acceptability, and feasibility during the intervention design phase (O'Cathain et al., 2019). For this purpose, novel, applied qualitative methods may be needed. For example, the "person-based approach" to intervention development (see Figure 13.1) combines traditional, in-depth qualitative methods from the social sciences with "agile" methods from user-centered design for gaining feedback about user needs and views (Yardley et al., 2015). This novel combination of methods enables intervention developers to rapidly gain an in-depth understanding of user needs and perspectives to ensure that the intervention is not only accessible, usable, and engaging but also successfully modifies the drivers of behavior change, such as beliefs, attitudes, motivations, and skills.

The first part of this chapter considers how qualitative data can inform intervention design. Often there is a relevant preexisting qualitative literature, such as investigations into the values, context or needs of members of the target population, or studies of experiences of other similar interventions. This chapter introduces and illustrates possible approaches to synthesizing relevant qualitative and mixed-methods papers to understand the range of user needs, views and circumstances. This section also outlines a variety of methods of primary qualitative data collection and analysis that can be used if it is necessary to gain new insights into the particular situation of a specific target population or the likely influences on engagement with a novel intervention. The next section describes how qualitative methods can be used to optimize the intervention during its development. Eliciting reactions to intervention elements and materials allows intervention developers to identify problems with the intervention that need to be addressed before the intervention is implemented to maximize uptake, reach, engagement and effectiveness. This chapter then considers how and why qualitative research can be used to evaluate interventions once they are implemented. Qualitative methods can enable researchers to explore experiences of implementing the intervention and reveal unexpected or subtle influences on outcomes that may not be captured by quantitative measures. Mixed-methods process analyses allow intervention developers to examine how the intervention may or may not have worked in practice, which can then feed back into further modification of the intervention in a continuous improvement cycle (Bradbury et al., 2015). Finally, the chapter concludes by discussing future directions for the use of qualitative methods in intervention development and evaluation, including the relationship with stakeholder, patient and public involvement,

FIGURE 13.1. Person-Based Approach to Intervention Development

Stage	Qualitative activities	Research questions	Outputs
Design	Evidence synthesis +/or Inductive primary research	In what contexts will users access the intervention and apply the information and advice provided? What are users' values, needs, and priorities? What are users' prior experiences of engaging in a behavior or using an intervention? What are the likely barriers and facilitators to engaging with a behavior or intervention? How have these been addressed in prior interventions?	Guiding principles
Optimization	Think-aloud, longitudinal qualitative feasibility studies, observation, etc.	What are users' immediate reactions to the intervention content? How do users experience applying the suggested behaviors in their everyday lives? What are the important barriers to engagement? How can these barriers be addressed?	Tabulated feedback on the intervention and prioritized intervention modifications
Evaluation	Inductive primary research as part of a mixed-methods process evaluation	How do users experience applying the intervention content in their everyday lives? What are the likely influences on the observed outcomes?	Contextualized understanding of intervention effects

Refined guiding principles

Further intervention modifications

and the potential value of complementing and triangulating qualitative with quantitative methods.

USING QUALITATIVE METHODS TO INFORM INTERVENTION DESIGN

Qualitative methods enable a rich and deep understanding of the contexts within which individuals, groups, or communities will access a behavior change intervention alongside the challenges they may face when using the advice and support it provides. Interventions are likely to be more engaging if they are designed to acknowledge and address the following: (a) users' needs, values, and priorities; (b) users' past experiences of the target behavior or other intervention; (c) barriers and facilitators that undermine or support engagement with the intervention and target behavior; and (d) priorities of other individuals, organizations, or systems that are needed to support the delivery and implementation of the intervention.

For example, to develop an intervention that supports practitioners to prescribe fewer antibiotics (when clinically appropriate), it would be useful to first explore their current prescribing practice alongside values, beliefs, and any external factors that may influence their practice. Exploring the experiences and beliefs of patients would also be helpful. This means practitioners' concerns, challenges to implementing the advice (e.g., managing patient demands), and potential strategies for facilitating a change to their current practice (e.g., peer advocates to reinforce norm of prudent prescribing practice) can be anticipated and addressed. This detailed understanding of the user context will guide the selection of theory or evidence-based features that will be most relevant and acceptable to users, avoid features that are likely to be off-putting or unnecessary, and identify new ways in which the intervention can support and motivate behavior change that are not yet evidence based.

SYNTHESIZING EXISTING EVIDENCE

Identifying and synthesizing evidence that has examined a particular target behavior or type of intervention is a useful first step in the intervention design process. This will ensure that the intervention provides novel tools and techniques that are optimally relevant to and engaging for the target user, rather than "reinventing the wheel." Taking a qualitative approach to evidence synthesis means that quantitative questions such as "What works?" can be supplemented with process-orientated questions about "how" or "why" interventions work (or do not work). Qualitative approaches also allow individual-level experiences of a behavior or intervention to be explored in more depth. Research questions can explore individuals' prior experiences of a health issue, behavior, or intervention; the barriers and facilitators to engaging with behaviors or interventions and how they have been addressed in other interventions; and the features that appear to be important for enhancing the persuasiveness, acceptability, feasibility, or effectiveness of the intervention. The aim is not necessarily to synthesize only qualitative evidence but rather to draw on qualitative methods to synthesize diverse forms of evidence, where available and appropriate.

There are a range of qualitative approaches to synthesizing research. These can differ in terms of (a) underlying epistemological assumptions, (b) forms of evidence included, (c) selection of evidence for inclusion (e.g., exhaustive vs. purposive sampling), (d) synthesis methods employed and the extent of iteration, and (e) appraisal of study quality (for a critical review, see Barnett-Page & Thomas, 2009). The aim of this chapter is not to provide an exhaustive critical summary of methods but instead to illustrate key approaches that have been used to inform intervention design, health care policy, and practice (e.g., metaethnography, Noblit & Hare, 1988; thematic synthesis, Thomas & Harden, 2008; critical interpretive synthesis [CIS], Dixon-Woods et al., 2006). Metaethnography can be used to derive insights by comparing findings from a set of qualitative papers (see Case Study 1). Metaethnography explores similarities and translates findings from one study to another through *reciprocal translation*, explores differences between study findings through *refutational synthesis*, and integrates comparisons across studies to generate new conceptualizations that extend beyond the findings from individual studies through *lines of argument synthesis*.

CASE STUDY 1

We used a metaethnographic approach to synthesize qualitative studies of patient and practitioner experiences of digital interventions to support self-management of chronic conditions (Morton et al., 2017). Systematic searches identified 30 relevant papers. These were read thoroughly to understand how they related to one other and identify any connections in the key concepts they discussed. Each paper was then compared with all other papers in terms of these key concepts, extracting both first-order constructs (quotes from study participants) and second-order constructs (authors' interpretations of their data). Comparisons were made between papers, which studied particular health conditions and types of digital intervention, while taking into account the contextual details of each study. A line of argument was developed that inductively built a conceptual understanding of patients' and health care professionals' experiences of using self-management digital interventions.

We found that digital interventions offered complementary benefit to both patients and practitioners. Practitioners were able to retain clinical control without undermining patients' motivation to self-manage. Patients could feel empowered to self-manage their condition without undermining their perceptions of feeling cared for. However, potential barriers to the successful integration of digital

(continues)

CASE STUDY 1 (*Continued*)

self-management interventions within a UK primary care context were uncovered. These were used to inform the design of a new intervention to specifically support the self-management of hypertension (see Band et al., 2017). While patients appreciated having practitioner feedback on their self-recorded physiological data, practitioners were concerned about the impact this may have on their workload. It was therefore crucial that procedures for reviewing and responding to patient data be made efficient (e.g., by integrating within existing systems used in UK primary care). Clear guidelines were also needed on how to deliver feedback that facilitated patient empowerment while defining appropriate boundaries so that practitioners did not feel pressured to meet unrealistic expectations of support.

Thematic synthesis can be used to support intervention design by focusing on the needs, context, views, or priorities of target users, as well as factors important for supporting the feasibility of an intervention. Principles of thematic analysis are used to develop initial descriptive themes from which more interpretive analytical themes are generated. Although thematic synthesis is most often used to synthesize qualitative studies, to inform the design of a digital intervention for cancer survivors, we analyzed data based on intervention descriptions, participant quotes, outcome data, and author interpretations from a range of study types, including randomized controlled trials, feasibility studies, and qualitative process evaluations (Corbett et al., 2018). This analysis revealed that although some intervention features showed promise for supporting lifestyle change (e.g., enabling people to set, monitor, and review progress toward diet or physical activity goals), these same features could inadvertently cause distress if individuals felt blamed for their cancer or were not able to see progress.

CIS draws on the principles and techniques used in primary qualitative research to guide an iterative approach to the synthesis of evidence, but also the search and selection of literature. For example, tentative research questions are proposed that evolve throughout the review process, and concepts of purposive and theoretical sampling are applied to select relevant evidence from a wider sampling frame. A specific aim of CIS is to question and critique the assumptions and discourses underlying a body of evidence, not just the findings or methods of individual studies. CIS was recently applied to examine how educational interventions to support the self-management of chronic health conditions combined face-to-face and digital components (see Sangrar et al., 2019). The authors noted that the literature reviewed did not consider the time since or duration of individual diagnoses when designing interventions, nor did it offer explicit descriptions for how self-management or educational theory was selected and used to inform the design of specific intervention features. This meant that existing interventions were not adequately addressing the varied needs of target users and provided limited evidence to understand how and why interventions were successful.

Recent trends in using evidence synthesis to inform intervention design recognize the need to explore the "complexity" of intervention systems, that is, the nuanced ways in which intervention features, users, and the wider systems within which interventions are implemented interact to produce health outcomes (see Petticrew et al., 2019). However, the intervention design process can be constrained by limited time and resources. This may mean that adopting a broad complexity perspective is not possible, particularly those that require significant time and expertise to carry out (Booth et al., 2018). In this case, it may be useful to narrow the focus of the evidence synthesis. For example, when developing an intervention that targets the behavior of individuals, the experiences of those individuals and their immediate social (e.g., family and friends) and practical (e.g., daily routines) context may be more essential than also exploring the broader political or service delivery contexts (see Chapter 9, this volume, for more on this).

CONDUCTING PRIMARY RESEARCH

Sufficient, good-quality evidence may not always be available for synthesis, or further insight specific to a particular intervention context may be needed. Thus, conducting primary qualitative research is often necessary to provide a sufficiently deep understanding of any potential barriers to successful engagement that are directly relevant to a specific type of intervention or setting within which the intervention will be implemented. Typically, this evidence is collected through interviews, focus groups, or observations of behavior.

The person-based approach highlights the advantages of first taking an inductive approach to data collection using open questions that invite participants to describe what is important to them (e.g., "Tell me what it has been like for you to manage X"). This can be followed by additional theory or evidence-driven questions that probe other potentially important aspects of participants' experiences identified a priori (e.g., "How confident do you feel doing Y?"). Stimuli materials can be used to initiate and facilitate discussion. Participants may be invited to reflect on example scenarios that describe a particular behavior or discuss their thoughts about example interventions and features. For example, prompt cards describing potential intervention features (e.g., goal setting, advice on pacing physical activity) were presented to patients with diabetes to explore their positive and negative reactions to the ideas presented and any anticipated problems with using the ideas (see Greenwell et al., 2018).

FORMULATING GUIDING PRINCIPLES FOR INTERVENTION DESIGN

Insights gained from evidence syntheses and primary qualitative research need to be distilled so that they can clearly and easily guide the design of an intervention. This can be done in a variety of ways. "Personas" or "scenarios" have been used to summarize the different needs, motivations, or goals users may have for using an intervention (LeRouge et al., 2013). These personas are referred to regularly throughout the design process to ensure that the evolving intervention will meet the needs and preferences of the varied users that it targets. Within the person-based approach, "guiding principles" are formulated to describe what the intervention must do or include to maximize user engagement with the entire behavior change process, not just the intervention product being designed (Yardley et al., 2015). Specifically, guiding principles comprise the following:

1. intervention design objectives—what the intervention must do to address a challenge or barrier to engagement
2. key intervention features—how the design objectives will be achieved.

Intervention features may refer to the proposed intervention content (e.g., specific tools or messages needed to support and persuade users to engage with the behavior), as well as delivery format (e.g., technological or communication format, delivery through a particular setting; see Case Study 2).

CASE STUDY 2

The person-based approach has been used to design a digital employee well-being intervention within a commercial setting (see Howarth et al., 2019). The developers reflected that strong user involvement was crucial in the design process given that within a commercial workplace context, interventions must be sufficiently personalized to the individual yet feasible to roll out at scale across multiple geographical sites internationally. Employees from a diverse range of backgrounds were invited to contribute to the intervention development. Semistructured interviews and focus groups were used to explore 39 employees' prior experiences of using and implementing other well-being interventions. Positive and negative experiences were used to inform optimization of the intervention. Employees described finding it difficult to engage with other interventions within the workplace setting because they were difficult to understand, required substantial personal investment (i.e., through reading content) within prescribed timeframes, or failed to acknowledge their own personal progress within the intervention. Consequently, a key design objective was "to make participation in the intervention fun and easy." Key features to achieve this were to use informal accessible language, provide access to bite-sized chunks of content at times convenient for the user, and enable users to track personal progress and milestones.

USING QUALITATIVE METHODS FOR DEVELOPING INTERVENTIONS

After completing the intervention planning process, a prototype behavior change intervention can be developed. Optimization of this prototype intervention is essential to ensure that it will be acceptable, persuasive, feasible, and motivating for users and, crucially, that it will change their behavior (Yardley et al., 2015). Qualitative approaches enable optimization by providing in-depth exploration of how users think and feel about a prototype intervention. This feedback allows an understanding of where the intervention is working well, but more important, it enables identification of barriers to engagement, highlighting where the intervention needs to be modified to maximize its likelihood of being effective. Conducting this important qualitative optimization work avoids wasting time and resources evaluating or implementing suboptimal interventions. It is important to note that even very experienced intervention developers who have conducted careful intervention planning find that their prototype intervention requires some modifications during optimization studies (e.g., Bradbury et al., 2019), which highlights how vital this qualitative work really is.

Several different approaches to intervention development involve qualitative methods (for an overview, see O'Cathain et al., 2019). For instance, user-centered design (which originated in the field of human–computer interaction) employs qualitative interviews to understand target users' views of a prototype intervention (Erwin, 2013). The person-based approach (Yardley et al., 2015) also uses qualitative research to gain feedback from target users on a prototype intervention. This approach is based in behavioral science and so focuses strongly on whether an intervention is likely to change behavior, rather than just whether it is usable, acceptable, or engaging—a common focus within other approaches. The person-based approach outlines two types of qualitative interview studies that are especially useful for optimizing behavior change interventions: think-aloud interviews and qualitative feasibility studies. These approaches are discussed next, followed by an overview of how to use participant feedback to inform intervention modifications. To make sure that interventions are as useful as possible for all who might want to use them, sampling in both think-aloud and longitudinal optimization studies needs to include users from a variety of backgrounds. It is especially important to include those who might struggle most with the intervention, such as those with lower health literacy, least motivation to engage, or the most complex health needs.

THINK-ALOUD INTERVIEWS

If a prototype intervention has written content (e.g., a leaflet, booklet, digital intervention such as a website or app), then think-aloud interviews are indispensable to capture how participants respond to the intervention (Van den Haak et al., 2007). In a face-to-face–delivered intervention, the person delivering the intervention can change what they are saying to address concerns based on verbal or nonverbal feedback, which suggests a barrier to engagement is present. In a written intervention, barriers to engagement therefore need to be understood in detail before an intervention is evaluated or implemented, so they can be anticipated and addressed in the written content.

Think-aloud interviews facilitate this by providing detailed feedback on user views of every aspect of the intervention content. Think-aloud interviews can also be useful for optimizing written recruitment materials to maximize uptake either in evaluation studies or real-life implementation (Bradbury et al., 2018). Case Study 3 provides an example of how think-aloud interviews enabled optimization of an intervention for hypertension.

CASE STUDY 3

When developing a web-based intervention for the treatment of hypertension, we sought feedback from people with hypertension to understand how we might need to optimize this prototype intervention (Bradbury et al., 2018). Twelve participants with elevated blood pressure who were taking at least one medication for hypertension were recruited from primary care. Each participant took part in three think-aloud interviews, where they viewed the intervention with a researcher and provided immediate reactions. All positive and negative feedback were tabulated to help the researchers understand which parts of the intervention were working well and which required refinement.

The intervention involved patients monitoring their blood pressure at home for 1 week every month and entering these readings into a website. If the patient's blood pressure readings were too high, the website would inform the general practitioner (GP) because this would indicate a medication change was required. The start of the intervention explained why patients would need to monitor their blood pressure at home. This rationale included explanation that GPs often do not increase people's medication quickly enough when faced with elevated blood pressure readings, meaning that people are left with high blood pressure (a well-documented phenomenon called *clinical inertia*). One of the first patients to view this information noted that although she understood this, "*my GP is different*"—he was a trusted "family doctor" as had treated her for years. This feedback indicated that some people would not want to feel critical of their GP and that this could create a barrier to engagement. In response the rationale was rephrased to instead explain that patients could help their GP to make more accurate treatment decisions if they followed the intervention procedures because this would provide the GP with one week's worth of readings, rather than a one-off reading that their GP usually has to base decisions on. Patients were much more convinced by this argument as it didn't blame their GP or challenge their belief that their GP always provides them with the best treatment.

Think-aloud interviews are straightforward to conduct; they simply ask target users to say aloud exactly what they are thinking while they view the intervention. For example, in the case of a booklet for promoting physical activity, participants may be asked to look through the booklet and say what they are thinking aloud. The interviewer simply repeats statements such as "What are you thinking/feeling now?" or "Why did you choose that option?" using neutral prompts to explore participants' thoughts further (e.g., "That's interesting, can you tell me more about that?"). Thinking aloud is an unusual situation for most participants; it can help them if you acknowledge this at the start and note that most people forget to think-aloud at some point during the interviews, so you will need to remind the participant regularly. A challenge with interpreting think-aloud audio-recorded data is that it can be difficult to know what part of the intervention the participant is referring to when you listen back to the recording; a helpful technique is to say the name of the page, section, or screen that a participant is looking at whenever they move on to the next part to help navigate the interview data later.

Qualitative Feasibility Studies

Qualitative feasibility studies involve a participant using an intervention for a few weeks and then providing feedback on their experiences during an interview. This type of design enables the participant to try behaviors the intervention is asking them to do (e.g., self-monitor their blood pressure at home), to check whether this behavior is likely to be implemented as anticipated and to identify any potential barriers to performing this behavior (Bradbury et al., 2018). Qualitative feasibility studies can also allow identification of potential problems with implementing an intervention in practice, such as delays in scheduling appointments or practitioners not having sufficient time to deliver the intervention in full. Such studies are a useful way of exploring barriers to face-to-face interventions, which cannot easily be assessed by the think-aloud approach. Equally they are a useful addition to follow think-aloud studies for written interventions, as they enable the participant to use the intervention on their own as they normally would when not in the presence of a researcher, which may affect how they respond, for example, by prompting them to engage more than they would if the interviewer was not present (Cotton & Gresty, 2006).

Qualitative feasibility studies involve the patient using the intervention for a few weeks and then taking part in an interview about their experience. The exact timing of the interviews should be determined based on the content of the intervention; for example, a brief intervention may only take a few minutes to deliver, and the patient could then be interviewed after a week or two, once they have had time to try out the behavior that the intervention is asking them to change. In the case of longer interventions (e.g., a 12-week face-to-face CBT intervention) interviews may need to be conducted later, perhaps after the intervention finishes, or after a crucial part. Multiple interviews can be used to capture thoughts and feelings at critical time points, this might be especially important in longer interventions as participant recall is likely to degrade over time. Asking participants to keep a diary of their experiences of the intervention or of carrying out the behavior can be a useful addition to aid recall and this data can then be triangulated with the interview data to provide a fuller picture of the participants' experiences. Other sources of data that can be useful to triangulate against in this kind of study include digital intervention usage data (showing which parts of the intervention participants used) or observations of face-to-face–delivered intervention sessions, which could help identify ways in which the intervention was or was not working well.

USING QUALITATIVE FEEDBACK TO INFORM INTERVENTION MODIFICATIONS

Both think-aloud and qualitative feasibility studies provide crucial user feedback that can identify areas of an intervention that require modification to maximize engagement. Both types of study ideally require an iterative approach whereby data from a few interviews are collected and then analyzed to identify barriers to engagement, modifications designed to overcome identified barriers are implemented, then further interviews are conducted to check whether the modifications are successful and to explore whether there are other important barriers to engagement that need to be addressed (Yardley et al., 2015). This process continues until no new important barriers to engagement are being identified in further interviews, a type of "saturation" (Saunders et al., 2018) unique to intervention optimization (Bradbury et al., 2018).

There is often limited time to develop an intervention, and thus analysis of optimization of study data to inform intervention modifications needs to be conducted quickly, before the next batch of interviews are due to be conducted. An efficient yet systematic and effective approach to analyzing these data is to simply tabulate all positive and negative comments about each particular intervention feature (Bradbury et al., 2018). Tabulation supports discussion of both the feedback and potential modifications that could be made within the intervention development team. Positive feedback highlights where an intervention component is working well, and negative feedback identifies barriers to engagement, suggesting that an intervention modification is needed.

Often qualitative studies identify many possible intervention modifications that could be made. Because most projects have limited time and resources, intervention modifications need to be prioritized and then implemented in order of priority. Table 13.1 provides an overview of criteria that can be used to help choose which intervention modifications to prioritize (Bradbury et al., 2018). The primary focus must be to implement changes that are crucial to helping participants change the targeted behavior. Changes should also be prioritized if they are in line with the intervention's guiding principles (which are based on the evidence, theory, and user feedback from the intervention planning). Changes that are uncontroversial and easy to make (e.g., a grammatical error in a booklet) can often be implemented straightaway. However, sometimes it is not obvious whether a change needs to be made after one or two people comment on a potential barrier, so further data need to be collected. If something is said repeatedly by many people, then it can be very

TABLE 13.1. Criteria for Deciding When to Implement an Intervention Modification

Criterion	Description
Criteria for deciding whether to make modifications	
Important for behavior change	The modification is expected to have an impact on behavior change or a precursor to behavior change (e.g., acceptability, feasibility, persuasiveness, motivation, engagement).
Consistent with guiding principles	The modification is in line with the intervention's guiding principles (which incorporate theory, evidence, and user perspectives).
Uncontroversial and easy	An uncontroversial and easy-to-implement solution that does not involve major design changes (e.g., simplifying a sentence that was misunderstood).
Repeated by several participants	This point was made by more than one participant.
Criteria for prioritizing which modifications to make (MoSCoW)	
Must have	This modification must be made for the intervention to be effective in changing a participant's behavior (given what we know about the evidence base).
Should have	This modification should be made if possible because it may impact effectiveness but may be able to be delivered in a different way or is in some way less critical than a must-have.
Could have	This modification would be useful but may be less critical to behavior change than a should-have and may only be implemented if time and resources are available.
Would like	This modification is not needed to support behavior change but could be useful if time and resources allow.

Note. Adapted from "Using the Person-Based Approach to Optimise a Digital Intervention for the Management of Hypertension," by K. Bradbury, K. Morton, R. Band, A. van Woezik, R. Grist, R. J. McManus, P. Little, and L. Yardley, 2018, *PLOS ONE*, *13*(5), Table 3 (https://doi.org/10.1371/journal.pone.0196868). CC BY 4.0.

obvious that it needs to change. However, if even one user suggests that a feature is very off-putting or raises a significant barrier to behavior change, then a modification should be considered.

PROCESS EVALUATIONS

Randomized controlled trials (RCTs) enable robust evaluation of the effectiveness and cost-effectiveness of interventions, but there is increasing recognition of the importance of process evaluations to aid understanding of how an intervention produces its effects (i.e., what are its mechanisms of action?), under which circumstances an intervention works best (e.g., who does it work best for? In what contexts?), and whether an intervention might cause any harm (Fletcher et al., 2016; Moore et al., 2015). Mixed-methods approaches that triangulate trial findings with quantitative and qualitative process evaluations are best suited to answering these questions (for detailed guidance on combining quantitative and qualitative approaches, including epistemological and technical considerations, see Bishop, 2015; see also Chapter 12, this volume). Quantitative process evaluation data (e.g., questionnaires or objectively measured intervention delivery) can be used to examine mediators or moderators of an intervention's effect and predictors of any harm occurring. Of course, such approaches can only explore what the research team has assumed is important, whereas qualitative process evaluations can explore what is most important to participants and those delivering the intervention, enabling novel, unanticipated findings to be captured. Qualitative process evaluations can therefore help to refine an intervention's "theory of change," which details an intervention's mechanisms of change (Kneale et al., 2015), by suggesting further potential mediators or moderators that are not captured in the quantitative process evaluation.

Qualitative methods are particularly adept at capturing the potential influence of contextual factors on an intervention that are often difficult to measure using quantitative methods. These might include factors such as participants' previous experiences (e.g., experiences of managing a health problem or of prior treatments), family situations, or elements of the system in which the intervention is situated (e.g., staff culture within a hospital). Qualitative methods can unpack the influence of such factors, which may act as barriers or facilitators to participant adherence or implementation of the intervention in practice (Fletcher et al., 2016). Case Study 4 provides an example of triangulating data from quantitative and qualitative process evaluations; the qualitative interviews highlighted an important potential barrier to implementation of a weight loss intervention, which would not have been captured by the quantitative data. Understanding such barriers enables researchers to improve an intervention and thus maximize its chances of success in larger scale implementation.

CASE STUDY 4

In an RCT evaluating the effectiveness of a digital weight loss intervention, POWeR+, health care practitioners provided patients with either remote (phone or email) or face-to-face support to encourage engagement with POWeR+. The quantitative process evaluation suggested that practitioners largely provided support to patients as intended (Smith et al., 2017), and the RCT result showed that both types of support were effective in helping patients to lose weight; however, remote support was cheaper and thus better to implement at scale (Little et al., 2016).

A qualitative process evaluation was also conducted (Smith et al., 2017). This involved semistructured telephone interviews with 13 health care practitioners who had provided support to patients within the RCT. These interviews explored

---

CASE STUDY 4 (*Continued*)

what it was like to provide support to patients within the trial. The interview data were analyzed using thematic analysis. Despite the trial result showing that both types of support were effective, the qualitative process evaluation revealed that the practitioners felt remote support would be less effective than face-to-face support. Without more positive perceptions of the efficacy of remote support, it seemed likely that practitioners might be reluctant to implement remote support in everyday practice. The qualitative process evaluation therefore showed that important changes to the health care practitioner training were needed to try to persuade practitioners that remote support was indeed effective.

Qualitative process evaluations are extremely valuable within pilot and feasibility trials, where they can highlight problems with study procedures, enabling improvements to be made before beginning a larger fully powered trial. Another important function of process evaluations is that they can help to explain why an intervention is found to be ineffective. Triangulating qualitative and quantitative data can highlight whether an intervention failed to produce an effect because the theory on which it was based was incorrect or incomplete (theory failure) or because the intervention components were implemented in a way that was hard to understand, off-putting, unfeasible, or unmotivating (i.e., implementation failure; Cargo et al., 2018). While quantitative process evaluations might be able to examine potential theory failure (assuming the variables of the interventions theorized mechanisms have been measured), they are less likely to uncover implementation failure, which qualitative methods can identify by exploring experiences of the intervention.

ETHICAL ISSUES

The design and conduct of primary qualitative research used to inform intervention development and evaluation must consider and address ethical considerations relevant to any qualitative method. This includes, for example, ensuring informed consent, protecting anonymity of participants, keeping participant data confidential and secure, taking a reflexive approach to data analysis and interpretation, maintaining transparency, and addressing potential for harm (e.g., sensitive questions, using prototype interventions).

Additional ethical considerations are relevant when applying these qualitative methods to other specific activities within the intervention development and evaluation process. Qualitative evidence synthesis requires critical reflection on the contextual and epistemological approach taken by the authors of included papers to determine how the diverse needs, views, or priorities of participants have been represented or interpreted. This should be considered alongside other potential sources of bias and quality appraisal to guide realistic and appropriate conclusions from the data reviewed. Multiple individuals with varied characteristics, skills, and expertise may conduct think-aloud or qualitative process interviews; these individuals can hold dual roles as both interviewer and intervention developer. The impact of this on building rapport with participants and the richness of the data collected should be considered. Acting on feedback provided by participants to optimize an intervention requires development teams to make decisions on what changes will be made to the intervention materials. There is a risk that the participant voice can be misrepresented or that dominant voices in the data are prioritized. The table of changes approach presented earlier in this chapter provides a transparent and rigorous method to address this.

CONCLUSION AND FUTURE DIRECTIONS

This chapter has outlined some of the benefits of using qualitative methods to develop and evaluate complex interventions and has discussed some ways in which qualitative research methods can be used to address the aims of development and evaluation. It is clear from this brief overview that development and evaluation of interventions is not a linear process but naturally forms a set of cycles, whereby evaluation is used to inform adaptations and improvements to the intervention. The further intervention development that arises from qualitative evaluation of the intervention is required to address problems with accessibility, acceptability, feasibility, or effectiveness during the optimization process described in the second part of the chapter. In addition, qualitative evaluation can play an important role in informing how the intervention may need to be adapted for new implementation contexts—whether this is different sectors of the population, related but different behaviors, different countries or cultures, or the changing context created by social or technological change.

Although qualitative research makes a vital contribution to the development–evaluation–adaptation cycle, it is important to acknowledge the limitations of qualitative data for these purposes. Qualitative research can give crucial insights into user perceptions and experiences, but users' accounts of what influences their behavior can be misleading for a variety of reasons. Research participants often politely concur that intervention features could be useful even though they would not actually engage with them (often suggesting other people they could be useful for instead; Yardley et al., 2006). If this problem has been overcome, research participants can accurately report what they like or dislike about an intervention but may not be able to predict correctly the factors that will motivate and support sustained engagement with the intervention or to accurately recall their reasons for engaging or not engaging with the intervention. For these reasons, it may be useful to complement qualitative methods with quantitative methods of objectively recording behavior and contextual influences on behavior (Yardley et al., 2016). For example, digital technology now allows intervention developers to track when and where different behaviors occur in daily life (Naughton et al., 2016), as well as when and how users engage with the digital intervention; triangulating these data with users' accounts of how they engaged with an intervention can provide valuable in-depth insights into real-world engagement with an intervention (Morrison et al., 2014).

Another important issue for qualitative researchers involved in intervention development and evaluation concerns how best to combine qualitative research with public and community involvement and stakeholder codesign (Muller et al., 2019). The rapidly expanding role of public and stakeholder involvement in codesign in interventions is welcome and entirely compatible with the use of qualitative methods; indeed, public contributors and stakeholders often find qualitative research into users' views and experiences particularly relevant and interesting. Codesign with stakeholders can be an efficient and valuable means of ensuring there is substantial input from the target user group throughout development. However, in-depth qualitative research can complement stakeholder input in important ways—for example, by obtaining insights into the perspectives of people less motivated to engage with the intervention. These people can be less likely to volunteer for involvement with codesign but may be persuaded to undertake a single interview in their own home to explore their views of intervention materials in depth. It is vital to access the views of people who are less engaged because they may have motivational or practical barriers to engagement that must be addressed to ensure the intervention is accessible, persuasive, and feasible for all sectors of the population, including people with barriers such as limited time, education, or money.

While this chapter has argued that in-depth qualitative research is crucial to successful intervention development, some developers are concerned about the resources required for this research. When there is not enough time or resources to undertake extensive qualitative research, even small-scale studies can provide extremely useful information. However, given the invaluable insights to be gained into how to overcome barriers to intervention implementation and effectiveness, it is to be hoped that this chapter provides powerful arguments for devoting sufficient resource to be able to achieve an in-depth understanding of users' context and experiences.

REFERENCES

Band, R., Bradbury, K., Morton, K., May, C., Michie, S., Mair, F. S., Murray, E., McManus, R. J., Little, P., & Yardley, L. (2017). Intervention planning for a digital intervention for self-management of hypertension: A theory-, evidence- and person-based approach. *Implementation Science, 12*(1), 25. https://doi.org/10.1186/s13012-017-0553-4

Barnett-Page, E., & Thomas, J. (2009). Methods for the synthesis of qualitative research: A critical review. *BMC Medical Research Methodology, 9*(1), 59. https://doi.org/10.1186/1471-2288-9-59

Bishop, F. L. (2015). Using mixed methods research designs in health psychology: An illustrated discussion from a pragmatist perspective. *British Journal of Health Psychology, 20*(1), 5–20. https://doi.org/10.1111/bjhp.12122

Booth, A., Noyes, J., Flemming, K., Gerhardus, A., Wahlster, P., van der Wilt, G. J., Mozygemba, K., Refolo, P., Sacchini, D., Tummers, M., & Rehfuess, E. (2018). Structured methodology review identified seven (RETREAT) criteria for selecting qualitative evidence synthesis approaches. *Journal of Clinical Epidemiology, 99*, 41–52. https://doi.org/10.1016/j.jclinepi.2018.03.003

Bradbury, K., Dennison, L., Little, P., & Yardley, L. (2015). Using mixed methods to develop and evaluate an online weight management intervention. *British Journal of Health Psychology, 20*(1), 45–55. https://doi.org/10.1111/bjhp.12125

Bradbury, K., Morton, K., Band, R., van Woezik, A., Grist, R., McManus, R. J., Little, P., & Yardley, L. (2018). Using the person-based approach to optimise a digital intervention for the management of hypertension. *PLOS ONE, 13*(5), e0196868. https://doi.org/10.1371/journal.pone.0196868

Bradbury, K., Steele, M., Corbett, T., Geraghty, A. W. A., Krusche, A., Heber, E., Easton, S., Cheetham-Blake, T., Slodkowska-Barabasz, J., Müller, A. M., Smith, K., Wilde, L. J., Payne, L., Singh, K., Bacon, R., Burford, T., Summers, K., Turner, L., Richardson, A., . . . Yardley, L. (2019). Developing a digital intervention for cancer survivors: An evidence-, theory- and person-based approach. *NPJ Digital Medicine, 2*(1), 85. https://doi.org/10.1038/s41746-019-0163-4

Cargo, M., Harris, J., Pantoja, T., Booth, A., Harden, A., Hannes, K., Thomas, J., Flemming, K., Garside, R., & Noyes, J. (2018). Cochrane Qualitative and Implementation Methods Group Guidance Series—Paper 4: Methods for assessing evidence on intervention implementation. *Journal of Clinical Epidemiology, 97*, 59–69. https://doi.org/10.1016/j.jclinepi.2017.11.028

Corbett, T., Singh, K., Payne, L., Bradbury, K., Foster, C., Watson, E., Richardson, A., Little, P., & Yardley, L. (2018). Understanding acceptability of and engagement with web-based interventions aiming to improve quality of life in cancer survivors: A synthesis of current research. *Psycho-Oncology, 27*(1), 22–33. https://doi.org/10.1002/pon.4566

Cotton, D., & Gresty, K. (2006). Reflecting on the think-aloud method for evaluating e-learning. *British Journal of Educational Technology, 37*(1), 45–54. https://doi.org/10.1111/j.1467-8535.2005.00521.x

Dixon-Woods, M., Cavers, D., Agarwal, S., Annandale, E., Arthur, A., Harvey, J., Hsu, R., Katbamna, S., Olsen, R., Smith, L., Riley, R., & Sutton, A. J. (2006). Conducting a critical interpretive synthesis of the literature on access to healthcare by vulnerable groups. *BMC Medical Research Methodology, 6*(1), 35. https://doi.org/10.1186/1471-2288-6-35

Erwin, K. (2013). *Communicating the new: Methods to shape and accelerate innovation.* John Wiley & Sons.

Fletcher, A., Jamal, F., Moore, G., Evans, R. E., Murphy, S., & Bonell, C. (2016). Realist complex intervention science: Applying realist principles across all phases of the Medical Research Council framework for developing and evaluating complex interventions. *Evaluation, 22*(3), 286–303. https://doi.org/10.1177/1356389016652743

Gough, B., & Deatrick, J. A. (2015). Qualitative health psychology research: Diversity, power, and impact. *Health Psychology, 34*(4), 289–292. https://doi.org/10.1037/hea0000206

Greenwell, K., Sivyer, K., Vedhara, K., Yardley, L., Game, F., Chalder, T., Richards, G., Drake, N., Gray, K., Weinman, J., & Bradbury, K. (2018). Intervention planning for the REDUCE maintenance intervention: A digital intervention to reduce reulceration risk among patients with a history of diabetic foot ulcers. *BMJ Open, 8*(5). https://doi.org/10.1136/bmjopen-2017-019865

Hanson, W. E., Creswell, J. W., Clark, V. L. P., Petska, K. S., & Creswell, J. D. (2005). Mixed methods research designs in counseling psychology. *Journal of Counseling Psychology, 52*(2), 224–235. https://doi.org/10.1037/0022-0167.52.2.224

Howarth, A., Quesada, J., Donnelly, T., & Mills, P. R. (2019). The development of 'Make One Small Change': An e-health intervention for the workplace developed using the Person-Based Approach. *Digital Health, 5*, 2055207619852856. https://doi.org/10.1177/2055207619852856

Kneale, D., Thomas, J., & Harris, K. (2015). Developing and optimising the use of logic models in systematic reviews: Exploring practice and good practice in the use of programme theory in reviews. *PLOS ONE, 10*(11), e0142187. https://doi.org/10.1371/journal.pone.0142187

LeRouge, C., Ma, J., Sneha, S., & Tolle, K. (2013). User profiles and personas in the design and development of consumer health technologies. *International Journal of Medical Informatics, 82*(11), e251–e268. https://doi.org/10.1016/j.ijmedinf.2011.03.006

Little, P., Stuart, B., Hobbs, F. R., Kelly, J., Smith, E. R., Bradbury, K. J., Hughes, S., Smith, P. W., Moore, M. V., Lean, M. E., Margetts, B. M., Byrne, C. D., Griffin, S., Davoudianfar, M., Hooper, J., Yao, G., Zhu, S., Raftery, J., & Yardley, L. (2016). An internet-based intervention with brief nurse support to manage obesity in primary care (POWeR+): A pragmatic, parallel-group, randomised controlled trial. *The Lancet Diabetes & Endocrinology, 4*(10), 821–828. https://doi.org/10.1016/S2213-8587(16)30099-7

Moore, G. F., Audrey, S., Barker, M., Bond, L., Bonell, C., Hardeman, W., Moore, L., O'Cathain, A., Tinati, T., Wight, D., & Baird, J. (2015). Process evaluation of complex interventions: Medical Research Council guidance. *British Medical Journal, 350*, Article h1258. https://doi.org/10.1136/bmj.h1258

Morrison, L. G., Hargood, C., Lin, S. X., Dennison, L., Joseph, J., Hughes, S., Michaelides, D. T., Johnston, D., Johnston, M., Michie, S., Little, P., Smith, P. W., Weal, M. J., & Yardley, L. (2014). Understanding usage of a hybrid website and smartphone app for weight management: A mixed-methods study. *Journal of Medical Internet Research, 16*(10), e201. https://doi.org/10.2196/jmir.3579

Morton, K., Dennison, L., May, C., Murray, E., Little, P., McManus, R. J., & Yardley, L. (2017). Using digital interventions for self-management of chronic physical health conditions: A meta-ethnography review of published studies. *Patient Education and Counseling, 100*(4), 616–635. https://doi.org/10.1016/j.pec.2016.10.019

Muller, I., Santer, M., Morrison, L., Morton, K., Roberts, A., Rice, C., Williams, M., & Yardley, L. (2019). Combining qualitative research with PPI: Reflections on using the person-based approach for developing behavioural interventions. *Research Involvement and Engagement, 5*(1), 34. https://doi.org/10.1186/s40900-019-0169-8

Naughton, F., Hopewell, S., Lathia, N., Schalbroeck, R., Brown, C., Mascolo, C., McEwen, A., & Sutton, S. (2016). A context-sensing mobile phone app (Q Sense) for smoking cessation: A mixed-methods study. *JMIR mHealth and uHealth, 4*(3), e106. https://doi.org/10.2196/mhealth.5787

Noblit, G. W., & Hare, R. D. (1988). *Meta-ethnography: Synthesizing qualitative studies*. Sage Publications. https://doi.org/10.4135/9781412985000

O'Cathain, A., Croot, L., Duncan, E., Rousseau, N., Sworn, K., Turner, K. M., Yardley, L., & Hoddinott, P. (2019). Guidance on how to develop complex interventions to improve health and healthcare. *BMJ Open, 9*(8), e029954. https://doi.org/10.1136/bmjopen-2019-029954

O'Cathain, A., Hoddinott, P., Lewin, S., Thomas, K. J., Young, B., Adamson, J., Jansen, Y. J., Mills, N., Moore, G., & Donovan, J. L. (2015, September 7). Maximising the impact of qualitative research in feasibility studies for randomised controlled trials: Guidance for researchers. *Pilot and Feasibility Studies, 1*, 32. https://doi.org/10.1186/s40814-015-0026-y

Petticrew, M., Knai, C., Thomas, J., Rehfuess, E. A., Noyes, J., Gerhardus, A., Grimshaw, J. M., Rutter, H., & McGill, E. (2019). Implications of a complexity perspective for systematic reviews and guideline development in health decision making. *BMJ Global Health, 4*(Suppl. 1), e000899. https://doi.org/10.1136/bmjgh-2018-000899

Rohleder, P., & Lyons, A. (2014). *Qualitative research in clinical and health psychology.* Palgrave Macmillan.

Sangrar, R., Docherty-Skippen, S. M., & Beattie, K. (2019). Blended face-to-face and online/computer-based education approaches in chronic disease self-management: A critical interpretive synthesis. *Patient Education and Counseling, 102*(10), 1822–1832. https://doi.org/10.1016/j.pec.2019.05.009

Saunders, B., Sim, J., Kingstone, T., Baker, S., Waterfield, J., Bartlam, B., Burroughs, H., & Jinks, C. (2018). Saturation in qualitative research: Exploring its conceptualization and operationalization. *Quality & Quantity, 52*(4), 1893–1907. https://doi.org/10.1007/s11135-017-0574-8

Smith, E., Bradbury, K., Scott, L., Steele, M., Little, P., & Yardley, L. (2017). Providing online weight management in primary care: A mixed methods process evaluation of healthcare practitioners' experiences of using and supporting patients using POWeR. *Implementation Science; IS, 12*(1), 69. https://doi.org/10.1186/s13012-017-0596-6

Thirsk, L. M., & Clark, A. M. (2017). Using qualitative research for complex interventions: The contributions of hermeneutics. *International Journal of Qualitative Methods, 16*(1), 1–10. https://doi.org/10.1177/1609406917721068

Thomas, J., & Harden, A. (2008). Methods for the thematic synthesis of qualitative research in systematic reviews. *BMC Medical Research Methodology, 8*(45), 45. https://doi.org/10.1186/1471-2288-8-45

Van den Haak, M. J., De Jong, M. D., & Schellens, P. J. (2007). Evaluation of an informational web site: Three variants of the think-aloud method compared. *Technical Communication, 54,* 58–71.

Yardley, L., Donovan-Hall, M., Francis, K., & Todd, C. (2006). Older people's views of advice about falls prevention: A qualitative study. *Health Education Research, 21*(4), 508–517. https://doi.org/10.1093/her/cyh077

Yardley, L., Morrison, L., Bradbury, K., & Muller, I. (2015). The person-based approach to intervention development: Application to digital health-related behavior change interventions. *Journal of Medical Internet Research, 17*(1), e30. https://doi.org/10.2196/jmir.4055

Yardley, L., Spring, B. J., Riper, H., Morrison, L. G., Crane, D. H., Curtis, K., Merchant, G. C., Naughton, F., & Blandford, A. (2016). Understanding and promoting effective engagement with digital behaviour change interventions. *American Journal of Preventive Medicine, 51*(5), 833–842. https://doi.org/10.1016/j.amepre.2016.06.015

14

Qualitative Meta-Analysis

Issues to Consider in Design and Review

Kathleen M. Collins and Heidi M. Levitt

Qualitative research is on the rise in psychology. It has a long-standing history within psychological research (Wertz, 2014), although only in the past half-century have scholars put forth systematic formulations of these methods. Indeed, it was not until 2003 that the American Psychological Association (APA) published its first textbook on qualitative methods (Camic et al., 2003). Early methods introduced into psychology include phenomenology (Giorgi, 1970) and grounded theory (Glaser & Strauss, 1967), and versions of these and other methods soon followed. Although it still comprises a minority of the psychological research that is conducted, reviews of the literature consistently indicate a strong positive trend, suggesting a striking increase over time (Gelo et al., 2020; Rennie et al., 2002).

Qualitative research is often concentrated in certain areas within psychology that are focused on developing an understanding of the internal experience of a phenomenon as it unfolds within an interpersonal context, such as in education, psychotherapy, and health research. The surge of qualitative research over the past 50 years has led to the development of collections of studies that are focused on certain topics (e.g., Levitt, 2015). The introduction of qualitative meta-analysis—sometimes referred to as metasyntheses, as discussed in more detail throughout the chapter—has advanced these areas by offering methods to identify patterns across these groups of studies, develop new theories and insights, summarize findings, and deepen the understanding of contextual factors. Findings derived from meta-analyses

https://doi.org/10.1037/0000252-014
*Qualitative Research in Psychology: Expanding Perspectives in Methodology and Design,
Second Edition*, P. M. Camic (Editor)

BOX 14.1 | **EXAMPLES OF QUALITATIVE META-ANALYSES**

Lavik, K. O., Frøysa, H., Brattebø, K. F., McLeod, J., & Moltu, C. (2018). The first sessions of psychotherapy: A qualitative meta-analysis of alliance formation processes. *Journal of Psychotherapy Integration*, *28*(3), 348–366. https://doi.org/10.1037/int0000101

Levitt, H. M., Pomerville, A. & Surace, F. I. (2016). A qualitative meta-analysis examining clients' experiences of psychotherapy: A new agenda. *Psychological Bulletin*, *142*(8), 801–830. https://doi.org/10.1037/bul0000057

Minges, K. E., Owen, N., Salmon, J., Chao, A., Dunstan, D. W., & Whittemore, R. (2015). Reducing youth screen time: Qualitative metasynthesis of findings on barriers and facilitators. *Health Psychology*, *34*(4), 381–397. https://doi.org/10.1037/hea0000172

Timulak, L., & McElvaney, R. (2013). Qualitative meta-analysis of insight events in psychotherapy. *Counselling Psychology Quarterly*, *26*(2), 131–150. https://doi.org/10.1080/09515070.2013.792997

Tohidian, N. B., & Quek, K. M. (2017). Processes that inform multicultural supervision: A qualitative meta-analysis. *Journal of Marital and Family Therapy*, *43*(4), 573–590. https://doi.org/10.1111/jmft.12219

---

may have a range of applications as well, including outlining principles for practice, providing methodological direction in an area, or designing measures of theoretical constructs.

Qualitative meta-analytic methods first emerged in fields adjacent to psychology, including nursing, sociology, and education (e.g., Noblit & Hare, 1988; Paterson et al., 2001; Sandelowski et al., 1997). In contrast to quantitative meta-analytic approaches, which use varied methods to average findings across quantitative research studies, qualitative meta-analytic methods assist researchers in aggregating and synthesizing findings from a body of primary qualitative studies on a given topic. Because psychology has been a bit later than these other fields in embracing qualitative research, qualitative meta-analyses are comparatively rare but are becoming more common (for some recent examples, see Box 14.1).

VARIED FORMS AND GOALS OF META-ANALYTIC METHODS

There are many forms of qualitative meta-analytic method, including well-established approaches such as metaethnography (Noblit & Hare, 1988), meta-study (Paterson et al., 2001), and metasummary (Sandelowski & Barroso, 2003). Most of these methods come from outside of psychology, although more recently descriptions have come from within psychology (e.g., Levitt, 2018; Timulak, 2009). These methods vary in both their procedures and the goals of their analysis. Most meta-analytic methods aim to develop new interpretations of findings by identifying patterns in the results of primary studies (e.g., Noblit & Hare, 1988), or by conducting a critical analysis (e.g., feminist, critical queer, multicultural analysis) of studies' findings (Dixon-Woods et al., 2006).

There are a few methods, however, that aim to avoid reinterpretation of primary results and focus on summarizing or organizing findings. For instance, the metasummary approach aims to catalog findings (Sandelowski & Barroso, 2003), and metamethod approaches assess the quality of procedures and designs used in primary qualitative studies (e.g., Paterson et al., 2001). The method of meta-aggregation, put forward in nursing, is focused on developing practice-level theory to develop measurable recommendations to guide policy while avoiding reinterpretation and reconceptualization of the original findings (Lockwood & Pearson, 2013). Although coding in qualitative research can mean systematically identifying and organizing themes and the relationships between themes in the data in a manner that develops new findings, this is not the case in the metasummary approach. Instead, researchers code if data appear to be unsupported, unequivocal, or equivocal; discard the findings found to be supported; and then combine meanings within findings across studies to produce additive findings. For instance, a finding might indicate that health professionals should be kind, warm, considerate, and respectful (terms that came from separate studies) rather than trying to identify a common underlying feature, effect, or function of these traits.

Bergdahl (2019) contended that qualitative meta-aggregation methods are incompatible with the philosophies and ethics of methods of qualitative metasynthesis (a term that researchers sometimes use in place of qualitative meta-analysis but that has the same meaning) and that restraint from conceptual analysis produces findings that are thin and not useful. In her scathing critique, she argued that the focus on developing repeatable and generalizable results contrasts with the intent of metasynthesis to develop results that focus on integrating both commonality and conflict and are embedded in rich contextual cues to aid their local application.

This conflict demonstrates how it can be helpful for researchers to consider why they are selecting a given metamethod and whether the type of data that it produces will advantage the goals of the analysis. For instance, one approach might be more efficient in producing straightforward summaries of findings that aggregate commonalities when a topic is not very complex, whereas another might be advantageous when findings are meant to guide clinical practice, which is often directed by intentions and contextual cues. Depending on the goal of a study, researchers may also choose to develop two (or more) separate meta-analyses with more specific foci (e.g., Paterson et al., 2001), such as a metamethod study that is focused on the methods used in a body of literature and a metasynthesis that describes findings.

Researchers have developed multiple sets of guidelines (Barnett-Page & Thomas, 2009; Levitt, 2018; Timulak, 2013; Timulak & Creaner, 2013) to aid researchers in conducting qualitative meta-analyses. This chapter describes steps for conducting a qualitative meta-analysis by considering how the selection of procedures can be considered in relation to researchers' study questions and goals, as opposed to selecting any one set of procedural guidelines. It retains the term *qualitative meta-analysis* because it is widely recognized in psychological research (Levitt et al., 2018). This argument that procedures should be tailored to the goals and characteristics of a given study is at the heart of framework of methodological integrity.

METHODOLOGICAL INTEGRITY IN QUALITATIVE RESEARCH

The framework of methodological integrity (Levitt et al., 2017) was developed by a task force of APA's Society for Qualitative Inquiry in Psychology in reaction to qualitative researchers' experience that methods were being standardized in ways that did not allow for their attunement to particular study features. The purpose of the framework was to identify the logic that drove the selection of procedures. This process was intended to counter the process of expecting qualitative researchers to rigidly apply methods in the way they were used when they were originated and to encourage the thoughtful adaptation of procedures to best fit the qualities of a given study (e.g., increasing its methodological integrity).

The features of methodological integrity are described in detail in Levitt, Motulsky, et al. (2017) and were recently integrated into the APA journal article reporting standards and the latest edition of the *Publication Manual of the American Psychological Association* (APA, 2020). In this chapter, we describe the two central components of methodological integrity so that we can refer to these concepts throughout the chapter as we consider the rationale for selecting and adapting procedures for meta-analyses.

Fidelity to the subject matter refers to the quality in a study in which the researcher has clearly conveyed the qualities and dynamics that are characteristic of a phenomenon. This quality is not tied to any epistemological perspective. Even if the subject is conceptualized as a socially constructed issue, researchers will want to represent with accuracy the ways it is socially constructed, the ways in which the subject functions socially, and the meanings it holds for people in that setting. The fidelity of a study will be strengthened by researchers collecting data that capture variations in the phenomenon to create a more comprehensive answer to their research question (*data adequacy*); recognizing and being transparent about their own influence on their research and appropriately limiting that influence so it does not unduly shift their data collection (*perspective management in data collection*); considering and reporting on how they either limited the influence of their own experiences, expectations, and ideologies in their analysis or used this influence as a tool within their analytic process (e.g., using a critical feminist lens) to strengthen their perspicacity (*perspective management in data analysis*); and demonstrating how their findings were based in their data (*groundedness*).

Utility in achieving research goals refers to quality of a research study in which its findings usefully further the goals of that study. The aims of qualitative research studies can vary greatly, including hypothesis development, the deepening of understanding, theory generation, social change, clinical guidance, the identification of social practices, and consciousness raising. Researchers act to improve the utility of a study by considering findings and data excerpts in context and providing description of location, time, interpersonal dynamics, and cultural situations (*contextualization of data*); collecting data that are detailed and thorough and can lead to insightful analyses (*catalyst for insight*); developing findings that advance the inquiry related to a phenomenon (*meaningful contributions*); and reconciling findings that appear to be in conflict (*coherence among findings*).

When considering methodological integrity then, fidelity and utility always are understood in relation to the specific study goals, the approaches to inquiry used by investigators (e.g., their epistemological perspectives, worldviews, paradigms; Ponterotto, 2005), and the study characteristics (e.g., the study topic, the researchers, and participants). This relationship means that even when using the same method, procedures may need to be changed to strengthen the fidelity and utility of different studies. When applied to a qualitative meta-analysis, these same considerations hold.

STEPS FOR CONDUCTING A QUALITATIVE META-ANALYSIS

It is beyond the scope of this chapter to review all the procedures used across meta-analytic methods (see Barnett-Page & Thomas, 2009, and Timulak, 2013, for detailed reviews of meta-analytic methods). Instead, we describe the general procedural commonalities that most forms of metasynthesis share. This section outlines general steps for conducting a qualitative metasynthesis and how to adapt analytic procedures using the framework of methodological integrity. To illustrate these procedures, we describe the process using the example of a qualitative meta-analysis on the topic of sexual minority identity development. The goal of the meta-analysis is to identify the key stages and processes of identity development that have been identified in the literature.

Step 1: Identifying an Initial Pool of Primary Studies

The first step is to identify the specific studies the researcher plans to analyze. This process is similar to the process of a quantitative meta-analysis. Typically, researchers will need to use electronic databases (e.g., PsycInfo, PubMed, ScienceDirect) to locate the primary studies. Researchers should take care to use keywords and search terms that will assist them in finding studies that are relevant to their question. For our hypothetical study, we might specify the terms "LGBTQ, gay, lesbian, bisexual, transgender, trans, or queer," "identity development or sexual minority identity," and "qualitative." As the search continues, new terms may be identified for inclusion or exclusion that can help focus the search (e.g., "sexual identity formation"). Researchers might decide to add or move around terms, as needed, to assist in obtaining the relevant literature. For instance, we might include the terms "LGBTQ, gay, lesbian, bisexual, transgender, trans, or queer" as required terms in the title of papers, have the second term required in the abstract and the term "qualitative" be required anywhere in the paper. As a tip, we do not find it helpful to use the PsycInfo advance search tool that specifies the use of qualitative methods because the identification of these methods appears unreliable at this point. At minimum, researchers will wish to report the databases they searched, the time period in which they searched for articles (e.g., article published between 2000–2019), and the language of the studies reviewed. It can be helpful for authors to examine the PRISMA reporting standards because they are expected in many journals (Moher et al., 2009).

Step 2: Selecting Studies for Inclusion

A search of the database(s) will provide an initial pool of literature from which authors can select specific studies for review. Not all of the articles that are initially identified will be appropriate for the goal of a meta-analysis, however. For instance, our search returned articles focused on a wide range of both related and unrelated issues. Researchers will wish to narrow down their search results to select appropriate studies to review, noting how they made decisions to retain or eliminate studies so they can describe that process. Also, they will consider two key factors—the *fit* of the topic of the primary studies to the meta-analytic study question and the *rigor* of the methods.

Considering the Topic

To produce a meaningful analysis, researchers must select studies for inclusion that are an appropriate fit for their meta-analytic research question. In addition to outlining their initial inclusion and exclusion criteria, researchers will want to document the process of selecting articles along with any adaptations they make to their criteria. Reporting this process will make the selection process clear and help readers understand the broader context from which the primary articles were drawn. To do so, researchers will report the number of articles that initially came up from their keyword search, along with how many were eliminated at each wave of review and due to each exclusion factor. Typically, the first wave of review eliminates articles based on a review of their title and abstract. For instance, in our example, studies may be eliminated if they involve LGBTQ+ participants but do not specifically explore the phenomena of sexual identity development (e.g., focusing instead on topics such as spirituality, counseling, and academic success).

Next, a full-text review is conducted to decide whether the remaining articles are appropriate. Following from quantitative meta-analysis, it is common for qualitative meta-analyses to have multiple people from a research team participate in this selection process. Typically, two researchers will review the articles and engage together to reach agreement. The process that they use will be reported in the manuscript (e.g., independent reviews and then a discussion of differences to reach consensus). This process can provide a way for researchers to check their own perspectives by bringing to bear others' opinions for mutual consideration. They may augment this process as well by employing processes that are used in primary qualitative studies to reduce the impact of investigators' perspectives, such as deepening their understanding of their phenomenon, memoing, bracketing, and structuring discussions of perspectives in research teams. If a researcher is conducting a metasynthesis on their own, they will want to create as clear a description as possible on how decisions are made.

When reviewing the full texts and deciding that articles are outside of their scope, researchers will identify the factors that were responsible for excluding articles. For example, we might decide that we want to focus on adult sexual identity development and exclude articles that focus on development in youth. We might decide to exclude others that focus on coming out versus remaining closeted in certain settings but do not talk about the internal process of sexual identity development. When reporting the selection process, we would identify these reasons for excluding studies as well as the number of texts eliminated based on each of these concerns.

During this process, researchers may wish to reevaluate the scope of their research question in relation to the returns of their review. They can evaluate whether there are enough relevant studies available to provide adequate data. When considering a given question, if the number of studies is too small or if they do not include enough diversity, the fidelity of the meta-analysis may be compromised because it will not capture diverse perspectives within the topic (Levitt, Pomerville, et al., 2017). For instance, we may want to evaluate the literature on the interaction between sexual minority identity development and religious identity development, but we might find that the studies in this area are all on Judaism and so we narrow the scope of our meta-analysis to examining the influence of religion in the sexual minority identity development of Jewish people. Or we may want to look at sexual identity development within people with queer identities but, given that there is a dearth of qualitative studies on this relatively new topic, we may either choose to broaden our question to look at a wider selection of sexual minority identities. Researchers will wish to set meta-analytic research questions that they feel confident they can answer with some fidelity and so will review the characteristics of the primary literature with care.

Also, researchers can decide whether their goal is to review an entire literature. This practice makes sense for quantitative meta-analyses because each new study can influence the effect sizes that are identified. Qualitative researchers may also wish to do this when they are interested in describing the practices or findings across a field. In contrast, if the research goal is to come up with a central set of findings that are held up by the literature, researchers may wish to stop analyzing data after they reach saturation (Glaser & Strauss, 1967), which is the moment at which the addition of new data no longer leads to refinements in the results. Either approach can work well so long as it approaches the goals of the research (see Levitt et al., 2016).

Considering Rigor

One major consideration when assessing which studies to exclude from a systematic review is whether to include unpublished work and reports from organizations (e.g., World Health Organization) and institutions (e.g., charities, think tanks), commonly referred to as "gray literature." Some meta-analytic approaches outline their own guidelines for evaluating studies for inclusion (e.g., framework synthesis, thematic narrative analysis, and thematic synthesis). Also, a number of methods have been put forward to assist researchers with determining the quality of research studies. The Critical Appraisal Skills Program (2017), asking basic questions about design, appears to be the most commonly used of these approaches, but we do not recommend its use because virtually all published studies would be expected to meet these criteria. The Joanna Briggs Institute Critical Appraisal Checklist (JBICA; Joanna Briggs Institute, 2007) is much stronger and asks questions that reflect the idea of methodological integrity (e.g., whether there is congruity between design elements, such as the philosophical perspective, research questions, objectives, and design; see Hannes et al., 2010, for a detailed comparison of quality appraisal systems).

Still, we do not see this quality assessment method as useful in psychology because of the page limit problem for qualitative research. Simply put, many journals in psychology do not allow the space required for authors to expound upon the rationale behind their design. Perhaps as more psychology journals shift to allotting qualitative manuscripts, a word limit that is appropriate to those methods (as done by some journals with separate length requirements and as recommended in the APA journal article reporting standards; Levitt et al., 2018), this type of assessment of quality may be more appropriate. At present, qualitative researchers often are forced to make decisions between removing descriptions of their methods or details of their findings to meet page length requirements that were developed for quantitative methods. Because many reviewers and editors still lack the expertise to understand the rationales for selecting qualitative methods, authors may elect to omit that information. The absence of this information then does not indicate a lack of methodological integrity in design. The types of details that would be needed to establish the answers to the JBICA are only rarely reported in psychology manuscripts (see Levitt, Pomerville, et al., 2017, for details on the infrequency of this information).

Instead, we recommend the process of selecting only published qualitative research to increase quality control (see Timulak, 2009), which requires that study meet a standard of rigor during peer review. Even if some of the discussion in the review process was required to be omitted from the final manuscript, having gone through a review process, the authors would have had to prove to reviewers that the study was rigorous enough to meet professional standards. In that process, reviewers should have assessed whether the studies had the methodological integrity to support their publication in an academic journal.

When considering quality, however, it is important to consider the goal of the qualitative meta-analysis at hand and the state of the literature. In our example, the goal is to develop an understanding of the qualitative literature on the topic of sexual minority identity development. In our search, the search engine initially identified more than 150 articles, but in a closer review to select the topic and qualitative methods, we narrowed the studies down to about 25 articles. Because qualitative meta-analyses can be conducted with very few studies (often between seven and 10 studies; McGillivray et al., 2015; Timulak, 2007, 2009), this number seems promising (although meta-analyses also can include many more studies, as in Levitt et al.'s, 2016, omnibus review of the literature on clients' experiences of psychotherapy, which included 109 studies). Our review of the articles indicated that they cover a wide range of topics, including diversity in gender, ethnicity, race, religion, geographic location, and context, so they may help us to develop an understanding of our topic that has good fidelity (i.e., adequacy of data) and be likely to lead to a comprehensive understanding.

However, if we wanted to review the literature on sexual minority identity development for people of color, we might change our decision. Because we could only identify five such articles, we might decide that this small number of studies would not be adequate to obtain a comprehensive understanding of the phenomenon, and so we might decide to include dissertations using qualitative methods as well. Even though they may be of a somewhat lower quality in terms of rigor on whole, they may help us to develop a foundation that will advance our goal of gaining a comprehensive understanding grounded in adequate data. Also, they do include a committee review process that can be similar to peer review. In either case, researchers will wish to be transparent about the procedures used and the rationale to support them.

Step 3: Discerning Meanings in the Primary Study Data

Once the primary literature has been identified, the process of data analysis can begin! This process usually involves creating smaller units of data that then are combined into conceptual categories, with labels that describe the common meanings therein. Depending on the method of meta-analysis in use, researchers may seek to create higher order categories or a central finding from the analysis as well. We consider each of these processes more closely.

Generating Units

Within a meta-analysis the units of data under analysis are the findings from the primary qualitative studies. To render the findings usable, researchers typically first separate the findings from all of the primary articles into smaller units that can be worked with more effectively. This process is similar to the process in phenomenology of creating meaning units (Giorgi, 2009), which each capture a central meaning or finding related to the phenomena under study. These units may vary in size (a sentence, a paragraph, a page from the primary article) and one section of findings in a primary study may generate multiple units if the researchers discern multiple meanings that are relevant to their metastudy questions. Data in the primary studies that are not relevant to the meta-analytic question can be excluded from analysis and not transformed into meaning units because they will not add to the understanding of the phenomenon. Indeed, incorporating all the findings, regardless of their relevance, can muddle the analytic process, lead to confusing findings, and ultimately compromise the fidelity of the study.

To provide an example, in the metastudy of sexual minority identity development, researchers conducted an interesting study on identity development within online fandom communities includes findings relevant to identity development generally and other findings that are focused on fandom activities (McInroy & Craig, 2020). Because the question of the study is on sexual orientation identity development generally, researchers may want to consider how to select findings in a way that their relation to general practices is clear (e.g., instead of creating units that distinguish how specific forms of online media content is used experimentally focusing more generally on process of exploring social roles). By selecting units that are clearly related to the metastudy question, findings between studies can be related to each other more easily.

Generating Labels

Each unit is assigned a label that articulates its meaning and condenses the amount of material with which the meta-analysts work. There are a number of ideas, sometimes competing, that can guide researchers in the process of creating labels for these units.

First, ideally, these labels are grounded in the original researchers' ideas and participants' words to authentically reflect the findings put forth by the primary study. This process can lead to increased fidelity by capturing the diversity of phrasings and meanings in the primary works and by helping the researchers to avoid their own perspectives having undue influence over the data at this early stage. As well, creating labels that are well grounded will have increased utility because they represent their contexts clearly, and so findings can be more easily transferred as readers relate them to their own contexts.

For instance, the following is a segment of text that describes a finding about sexual and gender minority development:

> Online fandom supported the initial phases of SGM [sexual and gender minority] identity development. Fandom "opened so many doors" and helped participants "realize the limitless possibilities" of SGM identities in a variety of ways based on individual activities within communities. One prevalent way comprised the increased opportunities to encounter, interact with, and more fully understand a spectrum of SGM identities through the plethora of SGM media representations found within fandom and fanwork. (McInroy & Craig, 2020, pp. 239)

This text might be assigned a label such as "Initial phases of SGM identity development include seeking opportunities to encounter, interact with, and understand SGM identities via art, media, and community." Using the language from the primary study helps to retain the finding's meaning better than if it were summarized as "SGM seek opportunities to explore SGM identities in community" because it details the processes used.

Second, when the connection to the metastudy research question is not clear and concise in the wording of the primary study finding; however, it can be useful to reframe these labels. For instance, in the assigned label, more general processes were retained that will connect better to the broader scope of the research question (e.g., "community" rather than "fandom" and "art" rather than "fanwork"). It will be easier to form connections with other studies when terms that fit the scope of the question are used, and this can bolster the utility of the eventual findings.

Third, labels ought to articulate an answer to the meta-analytic questions rather than restating the questions. For instance, in the study about sexual identity development, labeling the finding something like "contexts in which sexual orientations are supported" or "processes by which SGM people explore identity" are both correct. The problem with these labels, though, is that they reflect the researchers' questions more than the answers to those questions. For instance, the first label might be rephrased as "In which contexts are sexual orientations supported?" and the second label might be rephrased as "What are the processes by which SGM people explore identity?" Looking at the labels in this way, it is apparent that the labels do little to actually answer the questions that are being explored in the research. Instead, forming nuanced labels that respond to the research questions will improve the fidelity of the metastudy. Compared with conducting a primary study, this process can be much more challenging in a qualitative meta-analysis; however, because the primary studies may have suggested labels for findings that reflect their questions (and so have poor fidelity). In these cases, meta-analysts may be required to carefully read the descriptions of the findings to develop their own labels for each of those findings.

Step 4: Organizing Units Into Thematically Distinct Categories

Once each primary study has been analyzed to generate units that capture a key finding, these units are compared with each other and grouped according to shared themes or meanings. These groups are typically referred to as categories, themes, or findings and sometimes are used interchangeably. As mentioned earlier, some methods will focus only on summarizing or aggregating findings (e.g., Lockwood et al., 2015; Sandelowski & Barroso, 2003), but it is more typical in psychology that researchers engage in identifying patterns in the findings—potentially because of the interest in advancing clinical practice, which is advantaged by identifying common trends in intentional, relational, and contextual features. As a result, we focus our description on these methods.

Creating Initial Categories

By comparing the labels for each of the units to one another, categories of units are created to reflect patterns across the findings of the primary studies. Each category will be assigned its own unique title, which is produced in a similar manner to how unit labels are developed to describe its content. The point of commonality that drives the grouping of the units together becomes articulated as the label for that category of findings. As a general rule, when a larger number of units are grouped together (around six to eight), we tend to consider whether there are nuances in those units that can be combined into subcategories to capture differentiations in meanings. There may not be, but when there is, it often supports the development of a more attuned category title that has greater fidelity to the subject matter.

Strategies in creating category titles are similar to those described for the process of creating the titles for units, with some small additions. First, at this stage, the researcher should draw language from the labels of the units so that the category titles remain grounded in the initial findings from the studies. If there is a particularly evocative phrase that captures the description of a phenomenon, it can be worthwhile to retain it in the category title to bring the finding to life. For instance, a recent study on initial memories of same-sex attractions in young sexual minority women used a direct phrase from the data—"What took you so long?"—to enliven a category title about not recognizing same-sex attractions until later in adolescence (McClelland et al., 2016). Although the quote came from one specific participant, the title draws together multiple units that expressed a similar meaning.

Second, meta-analysts may find that more often it is worthwhile to use their own language to describe commonalities across the studies because the primary studies are focused on their specific data and not on the concepts that bridge studies. The language tends to become somewhat more abstract when developing categories (and upper-level categories), and the researchers may need to remind themselves to remain as specific as possible so that their findings are well contextualized and generate contributions that are meaningful and have utility.

Third, as indicated when describing the labeling of units, researchers will continue to develop titles for categories that reflect the answers to their questions rather than the questions themselves. Because the process of creating categories is naturally more abstract than creating initial categories, it may be more tempting to develop categories that mirror the questions of a study. Keeping in mind the goal of creating labels that have the potential for insight into the phenomenon may assist researchers in developing labels that reflect patterns of responses across the primary studies that have greater fidelity.

Creating Higher Order Categories

In many forms of metastudy (e.g., metagrounded theory, thematic meta-analyses), researchers will continue on to compare their initial categories with one another and to generate higher order categories in much the same way as described in developing initial categories. These higher order categories naturally tend to capture themes at an even higher level of abstraction so researchers will wish to keep questioning whether the titles are developed enough to make a meaningful contribution. For example, in their recent article on the process of transgender identity development, Bradford and Syed (2019) were able to subsume several distinct thematic categories under the higher order categories "Cisnormativity as a Master Narrative" and "Transnormativity as an Alternative Narrative." These titles pull together shared meanings from the various subcategories to articulate two key processes that influence transgender identity development, which can aid psychotherapists in guiding their gender diverse clients by identifying, understanding, and reauthoring their personal narratives of identity development.

One further tip can advance the development of higher order categories. As the analysis develops, it is not unusual for qualitative meta-analysts to find that they have formed categories that express seemingly contradictory perspectives on the same topic. For instance, studies about sexual identity development can be expected to describe diverse experiences; some findings may describe the experience of recognizing one's nonheterosexual orientation early in life in conjunction with gender-nonconforming behaviors, others studies may describe becoming aware of their sexual orientation during adolescence when puberty increased attunement to sexual feelings, and others may describe not feeling inspired to explore the bounds of their sexuality until mid-life. Categories of findings may have been developed to reflect these different sets of findings.

When organizing these initial categories into higher order categories, researchers will seek to reconcile these discrepancies by identifying the factors that underlie them. For instance, an upper-level category such as "some people recognize their sexual identity during childhood and others don't" is not very useful. It loses nuance about the meanings and motivators behind the initial categories and does not synthesize these findings into a coherent experience that will have utility for the reader. Instead, meta-analytic researchers could subsume the commonalities in these findings under labels such as "exploration of sexual identity is spurred by an increased awareness of internal feelings and urges, which may happen in responses to shifts across the lifespan" or "awareness of one's LGBTQ+ identity emerges when people notice a discrepancy in authentic experience and expectations rather than being tied to a uniform developmental stage or process." Instead of aggregating these findings and retaining their contradiction (which may confuse readers and reduce the utility of the findings), this synthesis provides a meaningful understanding for the reader.

Depending on the goals of the researcher, this process may culminate in the generation of a core finding of the analysis that reflects central meanings from the higher order category. The central finding should provide a clear and useful answer to the research questions and may involve suggest practice recommendations or future research directions that are grounded in the specific data from primary studies.

Throughout this process of meta-analysis, researchers will continue to use methods to be aware of their perspectives and to contemplate their influence.

These may include the processes describe previously to help manage perspective within data collection, however, in the analytic phase researchers also may deliberately use their epistemological theories as a tool to guide their analysis. For instance, researchers conducting the metastudy on sexual identity development might use a critical queer lens to identify forms of oppression and privilege in the primary studies and examine how they influence identity formation. The use of these ideological perspectives can help improve researchers' sensitivity to dynamics that may be implicit in the primary studies, improving the fidelity of the review to the phenomenon under study.

IDENTIFYING RESEARCH GOALS AND TAILORING META-ANALYSIS

Through the course of this chapter, we have described how researchers can select procedures to improve the methodological integrity of a metastudy. In the process of achieving fidelity to the subject matter, we have described how researchers will wish to consider factors such as whether the scope of their question would support their having adequate data to conduct a meta-analysis given the state of the relevant literature. In the process of selecting primary research for review we described processes that meta-analysts use to manage their own perspectives and prevent them from imposing on the data collection. We discussed how these processes can be used in data analysis to restrict the influence of researcher perspectives, as well as how researchers may use critical or other ideological approaches (e.g., psychodynamic approaches) to guide their analysis so as to enhance their perspicacity. Finally, we have emphasized the importance of creating units and categories that are grounded in the findings of the primary research articles.

Utility in achieving research goals has been described as being facilitated in a number of ways. These include providing appropriate contexts when labeling units and categories, developing labels for units and categories that are both tied clearly to the research question so that they will lead to insightful data and meaningful contributions to the literature. Also, we discussed the importance of reconciling differences within the categories so that findings will be intelligible and can make sense to readers.

There is one further approach to improving methodological integrity, however, that we have not discussed, is unique to meta-analysis, and is tied to increasing fidelity. It is the process of considering the situation of the primary studies. In this process, researchers go beyond considering their own perspectives and expectations and reflect on and describe the perspectives of authors in the meta-analytic literature. For instance, it may be noted that many of the researchers on sexual minority identity studies are Western, and this may lead to discussion of the perspectives that may be absent in the literature or a warning about the colonialist implications of adopting the findings from the meta-analysis to understand experiences in other regions.

Contrary to the writings of some theorists (e.g., Lockwood & Pearson, 2013), our experience is that most meta-analytic approaches can be recruited to pursue a wide variety of goals (e.g., policy formation, clinical guidance, theoretical development, social change). The challenge for researchers is to be aware of their goal and then to deliberately adopt and adapt procedures that are in synchrony with it. The framework of methodological integrity has been developed to guide researchers in these considerations to produce meta-studies that will advance their goal by providing rationales that can be used to argue for this form of coherence in methods.

CONCLUSION

Qualitative meta-analyses are an exciting method with a range of applications, including developing new theories, summarizing the state of the literature on a given topic, and providing a rationale for methodological advances in a field of study. This method has long been used in fields adjacent to psychology but has only recently begun to gain traction in mainstream psychology. Recent advances have included the development of guidelines for reporting and assessing the methodological integrity of qualitative meta-analyses. We hope that this chapter serves as both a conceptual overview and a practical guide for researchers who aspire to use this rigorous and innovative method.

REFERENCES

American Psychological Association. (2020). *Publication manual of the American Psychological Association: The official guide to APA Style* (7th ed.). American Psychological Association.

Barnett-Page, E., & Thomas, J. (2009). Methods for the synthesis of qualitative research: A critical review. *BMC Medical Research Methodology, 9*(1), 59. https://doi.org/10.1186/1471-2288-9-59

Bergdahl, E. (2019). Is meta-synthesis turning rich descriptions into thin reductions? A criticism of meta-aggregation as a form of qualitative synthesis. *Nursing Inquiry, 26*(1), e12273. https://doi.org/10.1111/nin.12273

Bradford, N. J., & Syed, M. (2019). Transnormativity and transgender identity development: A master narrative approach. *Sex Roles, 81*(5–6), 306–325. https://doi.org/10.1007/s11199-018-0992-7

Camic, P., Rhodes, J., & Yardley, L. (Eds.). (2003). *Qualitative research methodology in psychology: Expanding perspectives in methodology and design*. American Psychological Association.

Critical Appraisal Skills Programme. (2017). *CASP Qualitative Checklist*. http://www.casp-uk.net/checklists

Dixon-Woods, M., Cavers, D., Agarwal, S., Annandale, E., Arthur, A., Harvey, J., Hsu, R., Katbamna, S., Olsen, R., Smith, L., Riley, R., & Sutton, A. J. (2006). Conducting a critical interpretive synthesis of the literature on access to healthcare by vulnerable groups. *BMC Medical Research Methodology, 6*(1), 35–48. https://doi.org/10.1186/1471-2288-6-35

Gelo, O. C. G., Lagetto, G., Dinoi, C., Belfiore, E., Lombi, E., Blasi, S., Aria, M., & Ciavolino, E. (2020). Which methodological practice(s) for psychotherapy science? A systematic review and a proposal. *Integrative Psychological & Behavioral Science, 54*(1), 215–248. https://doi.org/10.1007/s12124-019-09494-3

Giorgi, A. (1970). *Psychology as a human science: A phenomenologically based approach.* Harper & Row.

Giorgi, A. (2009). *The descriptive phenomenological method in psychology: A modified Husserlian approach.* Duquesne University Press.

Glaser, B. G., & Strauss, A. L. (1967). *The discovery of grounded theory: Strategies for qualitative research.* Wiedenfeld and Nicholson.

Hannes, K., Lockwood, C., & Pearson, A. (2010). A comparative analysis of three online appraisal instruments' ability to assess validity in qualitative research. *Qualitative Health Research, 20*(12), 1736–1743. https://doi.org/10.1177/1049732310378656

Joanna Briggs Institute. (2007). *SUMARI: The Joanna Briggs Institute system for the unified management, assessment and review of information.* https://www.jbisumari.org/

Levitt, H. M. (2015). Qualitative psychotherapy research: The journey so far and future directions. *Psychotherapy, 52*(1), 31–37. https://doi.org/10.1037/a0037076

Levitt, H. M. (2018). How to conduct a qualitative meta-analysis: Tailoring methods to enhance methodological integrity. *Psychotherapy Research, 28*(3), 367–378. https://doi.org/10.1080/10503307.2018.1447708

Levitt, H. M., Bamberg, M., Creswell, J. W., Frost, D., Josselson, R., & Suárez-Orozco, C. (2018). Journal article reporting standards for qualitative primary, qualitative meta-analytic, and mixed methods research in psychology: The APA Publications and Communications Board task force report. *American Psychologist, 73*(1), 26–46. https://doi.org/10.1037/amp0000151

Levitt, H. M., Motulsky, S. L., Wertz, F. J., Morrow, S. L., & Ponterotto, J. G. (2017). Recommendations for designing and reviewing qualitative research in psychology: Promoting methodological integrity. *Qualitative Psychology, 4*(1), 1–22. https://doi.org/10.1037/qup0000082

Levitt, H. M., Pomerville, A., & Surace, F. I. (2016). A qualitative meta-analysis examining clients' experiences of psychotherapy: A new agenda. *Psychological Bulletin, 142*(8), 801–830. https://doi.org/10.1037/bul0000057

Levitt, H. M., Pomerville, A., Surace, F. I., & Grabowski, L. M. (2017). Metamethod study of qualitative psychotherapy research on clients' experiences: Review and recommendations. *Journal of Counseling Psychology, 64*(6), 626–644. https://doi.org/10.1037/cou0000222

Lockwood, C., Munn, Z., & Porritt, K. (2015). Qualitative research synthesis: Methodological guidance for systematic reviewers utilizing meta-aggregation. *International Journal of Evidence-Based Healthcare, 13*(3), 179–187. https://doi.org/10.1097/XEB.0000000000000062

Lockwood, C., & Pearson, A. (2013). *Comparison of meta-aggregation and meta-ethnography as qualitative review methods.* Wolters Kluwer.

McClelland, S. I., Rubin, J. D., & Bauermeister, J. A. (2016). "I liked girls and I thought they were pretty": Initial memories of same-sex attraction in young lesbian and bisexual women. *Archives of Sexual Behavior, 45*(6), 1375–1389. https://doi.org/10.1007/s10508-015-0507-3

McGillivray, J., Gurtman, C., Boganin, C., & Sheen, J. (2015). Self-practice and self-reflection in training of psychological interventions and therapist skills development: A qualitative meta-synthesis review. *Australian Psychologist, 50*(6), 434–444. https://doi.org/10.1111/ap.12158

McInroy, L. B., & Craig, S. L. (2020). "It's like a safe haven fantasy world": Online fandom communities and the identity development activities of sexual and gender minority youth. *Psychology of Popular Media Culture, 9*(2), 236–246. https://doi.org/10.1037/ppm0000234

Moher, D., Liberati, A., Tetzlaff, J., Altman, D. G., & the PRISMA Group. (2009). Preferred reporting items for systematic reviews and meta-analyses: The PRISMA statement. *Journal of Clinical Epidemiology, 62*(10), 1006–1012. https://doi.org/10.1016/j.jclinepi.2009.06.005

Noblit, G. W., & Hare, R. D. (1988). *Meta-ethnography: Synthesizing qualitative studies.* Sage Publications. https://doi.org/10.4135/9781412985000

Paterson, B. L., Thorne, S. E., Canam, C., & Jillings, C. (2001). *Meta-study of qualitative health research: A practical guide to meta-analysis and meta-synthesis.* Sage Publications. https://doi.org/10.4135/9781412985017

Ponterotto, J. G. (2005). Qualitative research in counseling psychology: A primer on research paradigms and philosophy of science. *Journal of Counseling Psychology, 52*(2), 126–136. https://doi.org/10.1037/0022-0167.52.2.126

Rennie, D. L., Watson, K. D., & Monteiro, A. M. (2002). The rise of qualitative research in psychology. *Canadian Psychology, 43*(3), 179–189. https://doi.org/10.1037/h0086914

Sandelowski, M., & Barroso, J. (2003). Creating metasummaries of qualitative findings. *Nursing Research, 52*(4), 226–233. https://doi.org/10.1097/00006199-200307000-00004

Sandelowski, M., Docherty, S., & Emden, C. (1997). Focus on qualitative methods. Qualitative metasynthesis: Issues and techniques. *Research in Nursing & Health, 20*(4), 365–371. https://doi.org/10.1002/(SICI)1098-240X(199708)20:4<365::AID-NUR9>3.0.CO;2-E

Timulak, L. (2007). Identifying core categories of client identified impact of helpful events in psychotherapy: A qualitative meta-analysis. *Psychotherapy Research, 17*(3), 305–314. https://doi.org/10.1080/10503300600608116

Timulak, L. (2009). Meta-analysis of qualitative studies: A tool for reviewing qualitative research findings in psychotherapy. *Psychotherapy Research, 19*(4–5), 591–600. https://doi.org/10.1080/10503300802477989

Timulak, L. (2013). Qualitative meta-analysis. In U. Flick (Ed.), *The Sage handbook of qualitative data analysis* (pp. 131–150). Sage Publications.

Timulak, L., & Creaner, M. (2013). Experiences of conducting qualitative meta-analysis. *Counselling Psychology Review, 28*, 94–104. https://shop.bps.org.uk/publications/publication-by-series/counselling-psychology-review.html

Wertz, F. J. (2014). Qualitative inquiry in the history of psychology. *Qualitative Psychology, 1*(1), 4–16. https://doi.org/10.1037/qup0000007

INDEX

A

Abductive analytic strategies, 111, 170
Abstract (narrative element), 110
Abstract positional map, 180–181
Abstract social worlds/arenas map, 177, 178·
Academic research, impact of Changing
    Minds study on, 98
Accelerometer data, 243, 254, 256
Access, for discursive approaches, 132–133
Action
    complicating, 110
    grounded theory study, 205
    in hypothetico-deductive approach, 141
    situated, 129–130, 171
    unexpected, in discursive research, 136
Action orientation of discourse, 129
Action research, 86–87
Activities of daily living (ADLs), 242,
    251–252
Activity engagement, 252, 254, 255
Adequacy of sampling, 77
ADLs (activities of daily living), 242,
    251–252
Adobe Audition, 132
Advocacy brochures, 97
Affect
    impact of college in prison on, 93–94
    language and, 63–64
Affirmative Action, 98
Africa
    HIV/AIDS film script event in, 109
    support for qualitative research in, 4–5
African Americans, 86

AIDS. *See* HIV/AIDS
Aim of study, information power and, 70,
    73, 74
Albion Prison, 97
Alcock, A., 42
Alcoholics Anonymous meetings, 40
Allport, Gordon, 87, 107
Alzheimer's disease, 235. *See also* Home-based
    observational study of dementia
American Jewish Congress, 87
American Psychological Association (APA)
    *Ethical Principles of Psychologists and Code
    of Conduct*, 19
    guidelines for qualitative research, 57–58
    on methodological integrity, 9, 286
    resources for teaching qualitative
        methods from, 21, 283
    support for qualitative research by, 4, 29
Analytic imagination, 183
Anderson, M. E., 106–107
Anonymization of digital records, 132
Antagonists, 10
Anthropology, 211
APA. *See* American Psychological
    Association
Apathy, actual vs. assumed, 252, 254
Appalachia, 85, 87
Apparent apathy, 254
Applied ethnography. *See* Focused
    ethnography
Applied psychologists, focused ethnography
    for, 217

Appointment diaries, 105
Appropriate methodology doctrine, 33
Appropriate sample, 67–69
Archetypes, 110
Archives, narrative data in, 106–107
Arenas of concern, 177. *See also* Social
    worlds/arenas maps
Asia, support for qualitative research in, 4
Asian Qualitative Research Association, 4
Atlas.ti software, 245
Attention category, in grounded theory
    study, 205
Attuning category, in grounded theory
    study, 205
Attuning theory, 14, 203–206
Aubry, Jeffrion, 96
Audience
    for Changing Minds study findings, 94, 96
    for research narrative, 11
Audio data
    in discursive psychology, 132
    in mixed-methods study, 244
    qualitative inquiry using, 188
    from think-aloud interviews, 273
Augoustinos, M., 125
Authentic self, 188
Autobiographic writing, 56
Autobiographies, 105–106
Autoethnographic writing, 56
Awareness, sensory, 215, 221
Axial coding, 189

B

Balanced approach, 17–18
Balmforth, J., 41
Bamberg, M., 58, 113
Band-Winterstein, T., 19
"Ban the Box" campaign, 89
Barker, C., 29, 32, 36
Barkham, M., 41
Baruch, E., 37
Becoming, process of, 149
Bedford Hills Correctional Facility for
    Women, 88–90, 93, 99
Beebe, B., 190
Being category, in grounded theory study, 205
Belfast prison memory archive, 106–107
Berea College, 87
Bergdahl, E., 285
Berger, P. L., 7, 8
Bernard, M., 106
Bezemer, J., 190, 206
Biases, 15, 61
Billig, M., 127, 130
Biographical interviews
    coherence, 103
    focus of, 101, 102
    guidelines for conducting, 102
    narratives from, 56, 57

Black, Puerto Rican, Latino, and Asian
    Legislative Caucus, 96
Black lung disease, 87
Blix, B. H., 113, 114
Blumer, H., 58, 168n1, 183
Boas, Franz, 41
Body activities, video data on, 191
Body of literature, meta-analysis of, 289
Bogdan, R., 40
Bolden, G. B., 135
Borderline cases, 137
Boundaries, of social worlds and arenas of
    concern, 177
Boyatzis, R. E., 39
Bracketing, 28, 59
Bradford, N. J., 295
Braun, V., 39, 111
Breadth, research, 77
Briggs, K., 249, 250
British Psychological Society, 19, 21, 29
Brown, C. J., 150
Bubble charts, 252, 253
Bulu parhalaan, 214
Burck, C., 201

C

Caddick, N., 116
Camera, video, 189–190
Camic, P. M., 97
Campbell, S., 191
Cancer survivors, 268
Carpenter, D. R., 190
Case description, 238
Case studies. *See* Qualitative case study
Catalyst for insight, utility of, 287
Categorical aggregation, 239
Categories
    in constant comparative method, 200, 201
    higher-order, 294–296
    initial, 294
    for meta-analysis data, 293–296
    for situational maps, 173, 174
    for written documentation, 224–225
Causal relationships, video data to identify,
    192, 193
Causal research questions, 135
Causey, A., 214
Center for Justice, 88–89
Center for NuLeadership, 88
Central examples, 137
Change concept, longitudinal research on, 18
Changing Minds (Fine et al.), 97–99
Changing Minds study, 89–99
    intentional diversity of contacts in, 91–92
    policy crisis preceding, 90–91
    political and affective context for college
        in prison, 93–94
    presenting findings of, 94, 96–98
    reflections on, 98–99

relationships and power dynamics in, 92–93

research collaborative for, 91–92

research design and methods, 94, 95

Charmaz, K., 168n1, 189

Charts, framework, 38

Cheeseman, Peter, 106

Childlessness in midlife. *See* Involuntary childlessness in midlife study

Children, impact of mother's college-in-prison experience on, 94, 96

Chronic health conditions, 267–268

CIS (critical interpretive synthesis), 268

Citizenship, for persons in prison, 94

City University of New York (CUNY), 88, 89, 92, 93, 99

Clark, Kenneth, 88

Clarke, A. E., 167, 169, 171, 179n5

Clarke, V., 39, 111

Classic ethnography. *See* Ethnography (method)

Classic grounded theory, 189, 198–199

Clayman, S., 140

Clifford, J., 212

Clinical inertia, 272

Clinical practice, meta-analysis for advancing, 293–294

Clinical trials, power calculations for, 67

Clinton, Bill, 89

Clustering experiential statements, 151–152, 157–162

Coconstruction

in constructivist grounded theory, 189

of narratives, 104

of situational elements, 171

Coda (narrative element), 110

Code of Human Research Ethics (British Psychological Society), 19

Coding

axial, 189

in focused ethnography, 240

for grounded theory approach with video data, 199–201

in metasummary, 285

in mixed-methods study, 246, 247

in qualitative case study, 238

in thematic analysis of narratives, 111–112

Cognitive style, method selection based on, 31, 43

Cognitive tests

activities of daily living and, 251–252

neuropsychology data from, 241–242

Cognitivism, 141

Cohen, R. L., 33

Coherence

of findings, 140, 287

in narrative accounts, 103

of research methodology, 4

Cokal, S., 117

Collaboration

in critical participatory action research, 85, 91–92

in interpretative phenomenological analysis, 147

Collective human elements and actors, 175, 177

Collective Leadership Institute, 98

Collective resistance, 116

College Bound program, 94

College Initiative, 89

College in prison programs

impact of Pell-grant withdrawal on, 89–90

political and affective context for, 93–94

study of. *See* Changing Minds study

Colombia, community-based research in, 87

Columbia University, 89

Combat veterans, masculine performances by, 116

Coming Home program, 89

Coming of Age in Samoa (Mead), 42

Commission on Community Interrelations, 87

Communication

dyadic, 204

help-intended, 41

by individuals with profound intellectual disability, 203–206

nonverbal, 191, 193–198

quality of, 71–72

Community activists, autobiographical accounts of, 106

Community-based research, 86–88, 98

Community psychology, 33

Community self-survey, 87

Comparisons, making, 30

Complete-member ethnography, 61n2

Complete observer stance, 190

Complete participant stance, 190

Complex intervention systems, 263, 269

Complexity, of situational maps, 173

Complex phenomena, holistic analysis of, 13–15

Complicating action (narrative element), 110

Comprehensive process analysis, 41

Comte, Auguste, 34

Conceptual depth, 76, 77

Conciencia (group), 88

Conditional matrix, 171

Confidentiality

in interpretative phenomenological analysis, 152

for participants with profound intellectual disability, 206

in qualitative research, 20–21

Confirmability criterion, 202

Conflicting cultural narratives, 114–115

Conrad, E., 33

Conscientization, 111
Consent
    informed, 132–133, 206, 255
    process, 206
Consistency, of qualitative data, 14
Constant comparative method
    category naming in, 200
    in classic grounded theory, 189, 198–200
    coding process in, 199–200
    in focused ethnography, 240
    memos in, 201
    saturation in, 68, 77–78
    for theory development, 198
Constructionism, 128
Constructionist grounded theory, 168n1
Construction of discourse, 130
Constructive nature of discourse, 130–131
Constructivism
    defined, 35
    synthesis and strict adherence to, 35–36
Constructivist grounded theory
    commonalities of situational analysis
        and, 167–169
    other approaches vs., 189
    situational analysis combined with, 182
Content analysis
    analysis of narrative form or function vs.,
        55, 56
    generalizable and inductive nature of,
        58–59
    as interpersonal level of narrative
        analysis, 110–113
    and other thematic analysis approaches, 38
    reasons for selecting, 44
Context
    in focused ethnography, 218
    for home-based observational study of
        dementia, 235–237
    impact of, on intervention, 263, 276
    for narratives, 54–55
    and situational analysis, 171
    in thick description, 187
Contextualization, utility and, 287
Contingency manipulation, 137, 139–140
Control
    of data, 8
    research participant, 17, 103, 133–134
Convenience sampling, 70–71
Convergence, in IPA data analysis, 161
Conversation analysis
    in discursive psychology, 128–129
    narrative data in, 60
    and other language-based approaches,
        41
    reasons for selecting, 44
    situated action in, 130
Corbett, T., 268
Corbin, J., 171, 189
Core findings, of meta-analyses, 295

Cost–benefit analysis, 95, 96
Counselor education study, 177, 179
Counternarratives, 62, 88, 116
Countertransference, 113–114
CPAR. *See* Critical participatory action
    research
Craig, S. L., 292
Credibility criterion, for qualitative
    research, 202
Criminal justice research, 98
Critical analysis, 285
Critical Appraisal Skills Program, 290
Critical bifocality, 93
Critical interpretive synthesis (CIS), 268
Critical participatory action research
    (CPAR), 85–99
    Changing Minds study, 89–99
    development of relationships in, 93
    epistemic roots of, 88–89
    and history of community-based
        research, 86–88
    relational analysis of personal narratives
        in, 16–17
    and research justice, 98–99
Critical realism, 34
Crossley, M. L., 111
Culturally-embodied practices, 62–64
Cultural pluralism, 32
Culture, in ethnographic approaches,
    41–42, 212–213
CUNY. *See* City University of New York
Curiosity, visual, 229

D

Dasein, 148
Data
    adequacy of, 286
    from line drawings, 226–227
    quality of, 250
    reduction of, 134
    sharing, 134
    viewing, 240
    visualization of, 257
Data analysis
    in discursive psychology, 123–125,
        136–140
    in focused ethnography, 240
    in grounded theory with video data,
        199–203, 206–207
    in home-based observational study of
        dementia, 245–248
    in interpretative phenomenological
        analysis, 151–152, 155–162
    in meta-analyses, 291–293
    perspective management in, 286, 296
    in qualitative case study, 238
    with qualitative methods, 31
    and recording quality, 133

Data collection
  in discursive approaches, 133–134
  in focused ethnography, 217–218,
    239–240
  in home-based observational study of
    dementia, 243–245
  in interpretative phenomenological
    analysis, 151, 154–155
  line drawings for, 213–217
  perspective management in, 286
  in qualitative case study, 237–238
  for situational analysis, 173
  of video data, 189–190
Data management, 134–135
Data matrices, 238, 247
Data sessions, 136, 257
Datu, 214–215
Davies, B., 63
De Barbaro, K., 193
Debates
  on positional maps, 181
  on situational maps, 175
Debriefing, after data collection, 257
De Chungara, Domitila, 106
Deductive analysis of narrative content, 111
Deductive disclosure, 21
Defiance, 125, 138
Delimiting, 198, 203
Dementia. *See also* Home-based
    observational study of dementia
  individuals with visual impairment
    related to, 13, 236, 242
  self-report scale data from participants
    with, 242
  video data for research participants with,
    191
Demographic data and variables
  and interpretative phenomenological
    analysis, 151
  in mixed-methods study, 244
Denzin, Norman, 171
DePaulo, P., 78
Dependability criterion, for qualitative
    research, 202
Depth, conceptual, 76, 77
Descriptive phenomenology, 148
Descriptive studies, 141
Deviant cases, in discursive research, 140
Dewey, John, 11, 170–171, 183, 188
Dewing, J., 206
Diabetic foot ulcer interview study, 69–73
Dialectic, defined, 35
Dialogue
  relational analysis of, 16
  researcher–participant, quality of, 71–74, 77
Diaries. *See also* Journals
  of feasibility study participants, 273
  narrative data from, 104–105
  research, 105

Digital interventions
  for cancer survivors, 268
  for self-management of chronic
    conditions, 267–268
  usage data from, in feasibility studies, 274
  for weight loss, 276–277
Digital storage, of narrative accounts,
    106–107
Digit span test, 245
Dimensions, information power model, 76
Direct interpretation, 239
Disclosures
  deductive, 21
  first-person, 56, 60
Discourse
  key characteristics of, 129–131
  on situational maps, 175
Discourse analysis
  data inconsistency in, 14
  discursive psychology vs., 128
  narrative data in, 57, 113
  and other language-based approaches, 41
  reasons for selecting, 44
  relational analysis in, 16–17
  and situated analysis, 13
  and situational analysis, 179
Discourse repertories, 41
The Discovery of Grounded Theory (Glaser and
    Strauss), 188
Discrepancy reconciliation, for categories, 295
Discursive approaches, 131–141
  access and consent stage, 132–133
  data analysis stage, 136–140
  data collection stage, 133–134
  data management and transcription
    stage, 134–135
  research question development stage,
    135–136
  in societal level of narrative analysis, 115
  validation stage, 140–141
Discursive materials, situational analysis of,
    173, 182, 183
Discursive psychology, 123–142
  as alternative to hypothetico-deductive
    approach, 141–142
  defined, 126
  focus of, 125–126
  general theoretical orientation of,
    129–131
  main strands of work in, 127–129
  relational analysis in, 16
  sample research data from, 123–125
  stages in execution of discursive
    research, 131–141
Dissemination, of Changing Minds study
    findings, 96–97
Dissertations, in meta-analyses, 291
Distance, drawing to document, 221
Distress, during IPA interviews, 152–153

Divergence in IPA data analysis, 161
Diversity of study participants, 91–92
Divine Orthodoxy, problem of the, 133
Documentation
    in focused ethnography, 215–216
    line drawing for, 220
    of participant observation, 219
    visual, 225–226, 229–230
    writing vs. drawing for, 224–226
Documents, narrative data from, 104–108
Dominant culture narratives, 114
Dot counting test, 245
Double hermeneutic, 148, 157
Downey, Geraldine, 89
Drawing-seeing, 229
    contour, 221, 222
    and hesitation to draw, 228
    recall, 220, 221, 223
    relational, 221
    schematic, 221
    scrutinous, 220
    seeing to write vs., 224–226
Du Bois, W. E. B., 86
*Duquesne Studies of Phenomenological
    Psychology*, 39
Duquesne University, 39
Dutt, A., 107, 111–112
Dyadic communication, 204
Dyadic interview study with dementia
    patients, 236

E

Echoes of Incarceration (video), 98
Economic and Social Research Council, 235
Economic elements, on situational maps, 175
EDA (electrodermal activity), 243, 254–256
"Ed Murphy" single-case study, 40
Educational system, drawing in, 227–228
Educators, focused ethnography for, 217
Edwards, Betty, 227
Edwards, D., 131
Eisner, E., 10, 220
Electrodermal activity (EDA), 243, 254–256
Elliott, R., 41
Ellis, Eddie, 88
El Salvador, 87
Embodied mind concept, 225
Emergent themes, identifying, 152,
    156–157
Emotional intensity, of home-based work,
    257
Emotion transportation, 61
Empathy, 61
Empatica E4 wristband, 245, 256
Empirical phenomenology, 39
Empirical research
    criteria for, 11
    sample size for, 71–73

Empiricism, 7, 34
Engagement
    activity, 252, 254, 255
    codesign with participants experiencing
        barriers to, 279
    in grounded theory study, 205
    and looking vs. seeing, 226
Environmental context, in ethnographic
    approaches, 212
Episodic interviews, 102
Epistemology
    defined, 31
    method selection based on, 31–36
    at root of CPAR, 88–89
    at root of situational analysis, 168
    synthesis of epistemological positions,
        35–36
Established theory, use of, 71, 73, 74
Ethical considerations
    with Changing Minds study, 92
    in discursive psychology, 132
    in ethnographic research, 213
    in interpretative phenomenological
        analysis, 152–153
    in intervention development, 277–278
    with method selection, 31
    in mixed-methods approach, 255–257
    in narrative analysis, 117–118
    with participants with profound
        intellectual disability, 206
    in qualitative research, 19–21
*Ethical Principles of Psychologists and Code of
    Conduct* (APA), 19
Ethnographic approaches
    aim of, 212–213
    change-making with, 62
    in CPAR, 88
    defined, 36
    narrative data in, 60, 61
    research questions answered by, 37, 45
    types of, 41–42
    walk-along interview in, 104
Ethnography (method)
    focused ethnography vs. classic, 42, 239
    reasons for selecting, 45
    relational analysis in, 16
    in situational analysis, 173
    temporal considerations in, 18
Europe, support for qualitative research in, 4
Evaluation
    as narrative element, 110
    process, 275–277
    readers', 140–141
    of sample content, 67–68
Events
    defined, 52n1
    narrative data from, 108–109
    selecting, for narratives, 54
Exasperation, with activity, 254, 255

Exclusion factors, meta-analysis, 289
Exhibitions, narrative data in, 108–109
Existentialism, 149
Existing evidence, synthesizing, 266–269
Expectations about researcher's role, 249–250
Experiential statements, 151, 152, 155–157
Exploration
    qualitative research for, 12, 30
    sample size needed for, 76
External factors, in research method
    selection, 43
External validity, 12, 77
Eye expressions, 191

F

Face-to-face interaction, video recordings
    of, 133
Face-to-face interventions, feasibility
    studies for, 273
Facial expressions, 191
Failures, implementation, 277
Fals Borda, Orlando, 87
Familiarization, 116
Families of qualitative approaches, 36–42
    ethnographic, 41–42
    language-based, 40–41
    narrative, 40
    thematic analysis, 37–39
Family mealtimes study, 131–141
    access and consent, 132–133
    data analysis, 136–140
    data collection, 133–134
    data management and transcription,
        134–135
    research question development, 135–136
    sample analysis from, 123–125
    validation of findings, 140–141
Family members, impact of college in
    prison on, 93–94
Feasibility studies
    approaches in, 14
    in intervention development, 273–274
    methods in, 263–264
    process evaluations in, 277
Feedback-based intervention modifications,
    271, 274–275
Felt sense, 149
Feminist psychology, 33
Festinger, L., 29
Fidelity to subject matter
    considering situation to improve,
        296–297
    judging research based on, 8
    for meta-analysis, 289
    in methodological integrity, 9, 286
Field notes
    in focused ethnography, 215, 216
    in mixed-methods study, 244
    video vs. data collection in, 190

Fieldwork, 42, 104
Figure ground discrimination, 245
Fine, M., 93, 97–99
Fine-grained analysis of video data, 190,
    206
Firstness, 227
First-pass transcripts, 134–135
First-person disclosures, 56, 60
First-wave review, for topic fit, 288
Fisher, M. P., 181
Fiske, D. W., 32
Fit
    grounded theory, 203
    topic, for meta-analysis, 288–290
Fitzgerald, F. Scott, 117
Flexibility, in mixed-methods research, 257
Flick, U., 102
Flow-based note-taking, 221
Flowers, Paul, 151
Focus, in recall drawing-seeing, 221
Focused ethnography. *See also* Line drawing
    and classic ethnography, 42, 239
    exploration with, 12
    holistic analysis of, 13
    longitudinal research in, 18
    in mixed-methods study, 239–241
    in psychological research, 217–218
    reasons for selecting, 45
    role of researcher in, 240–241
    temporal considerations in, 18
Focused interviews, 102
Focus group studies, 76, 95
Folkloric research methods, 88
Follow-up interviews, 105
Ford, J., 125
Formal information power calculations, 75
Form of narrative, analyzing, 55, 58
Fortunoff Video Archive for Holocaust
    Testimonies, 107
Foucault, Michel, 93, 170, 179
Fragmented letters test, 245
Framework (method), 38, 43–44
Free association narrative interview
    technique, 102
Freedom, with qualitative methods, 30
Friese, C., 181
Frontier narratives, 115–116
Frosh, S., 112–114
Frye, N., 110
Full range, sample size to ensure, 78
Full-text review, for topic fit, 288–289
Functional independence, 242
Function of narrative, analyzing, 55, 59
Future, letters from, 108

G

Gagnon, M., 181
Gambling practices, 179, 181
Geertz, C., 29, 167, 183, 187

Generalizability
  as criterion for research, 9
  as goal of qualitative meta-analyses, 285
  of narrative research, 58–59, 61–62
General orders, 173
Generic thematic analysis, 39, 43
George, D. R., 236
Gergen, K. J., 29, 110–111
Gergen, M., 110–111
German youth, national identity of, 115
Gestures, 191
Gilbert, Nigel, 127
Giorgi, A., 148
Glaser, B., 38–39, 169, 188, 189, 198, 200,
  201, 203
Gleser, G. C., 38
Global Dialogues, 109
Global Feminisms Project, 107, 111
Goals, of qualitative meta-analyses,
  284–286
Goldblatt, H., 19
"Good informants" concept, 77
"Good" research, 10
Gottschalk, L. A., 38
Gough, B., 15
Grabe, S., 107, 111–112
Graded-difficulty naming test, 245
Graduate education
  focused ethnography in, 217
  qualitative research methods in, 21, 22
Gray literature, 290
Greenhaven Prison, 88
Greenhaven Think Tank, 88
Grieshaber, Janice, 96–97
Griffiths, C., 204, 205
Griffiths, M. D., 164
Groundedness, 286
Grounded theory
  analysis of narrative content in, 58–59
  attuning case example, 203–206
  classic, 189, 198–199
  constructionist, 168n1
  constructivist, 167–169, 182, 189
  defined, 169, 188
  in ethnographic research, 213, 218
  introduction of, 283
  and other thematic analysis approaches,
    38–39
  reasons for selecting, 44
  sample size for studies using, 71
  saturation with, 68, 77–78
  and situational analysis, 167–170
  Straussian, 167–169
  structured approach to, 189
  theory development in, 198–199
  video data analysis for, 199–203
  visual, 12
Ground up, working with data from, 238
Group discussions, 127

Group setting
  life-story protocol adaptation for, 102–103
  participatory analysis of narratives in, 117
Grove, N., 204
Grzanka, P., 181
Guatemala, national truth commission, 108

H

Halkovic, A., 98
Hammack, P. L., 104, 114–115
Hammersley, M., 58
Haraway, Donna, 171
Harding, E., 236
Harré, R., 63, 114
Harrison, A. M., 193
Haslbeck, F. B., 192
Hawthorne effect, 190
Heidegger, M., 148
Help-intended communication, 41
Henwood, K., 29
Hepburn, A., 129, 133, 135, 137
Heritage, J. C., 140
Hermeneutical explication, 148, 149
Hermeneutic circle method, 4, 59
Hermeneutic relationships, 7, 148, 157
Herodotus, 42
Hesitation about line drawing, 227–229
Higher-order categories, meta-analysis,
  294–296
Highlander Folk School/Research and
  Education Center, 87
Historical data, 173, 179n5, 182
Historical discourses, on situational
  maps, 175
Historic research methods, in CPAR, 88
HIV/AIDS
  community-based research on, 86
  counternarratives of patients with, 116
  script-writing event on, 109
  temporal orientations in narratives of
    people with, 111
Hoecker, R., 108
Holding device, situational map as, 173
Holistic analysis, 13–15
Hollway, W., 102, 103, 112
Home-based observational study of
    dementia, 235–255
  challenges in, 249–251
  context for, 235–237
  data analysis methods, 245–248
  data collection methods, 243–245
  insights from triangulation of data in,
    251–255
  research design development, 237–243
  research questions in, 243
Home-based work, emotional intensity
    of, 257
Homogenous sampling, 150–151, 153

Horton, Myles, 87
Huff, J. L., 150
Hughes, C., 33
Humă, B., 125
Humphreys, K., 34, 40
Hunter College, 89
Husserl, E., 148
Hypertension intervention, 272
Hypothesis testing, 31, 55
Hypothetico-deductive approach, 141–142

I

Identity
    narrative and shaping of, 101
    at societal level of narrative analysis,
        115–116
Ideological dilemmas, 127
Idiographic approach, 149, 157, 162
Images
    defined, 226
    documentation in, 225–226
    narrative data from, 108
Implementation failures, identifying, 277
Implicated actors, 175, 182n7
Inclusion criteria, IPA, 150, 153
Independent living movement, 85–86
In-depth interviews, 95, 173
Index card method of data triangulation,
    246–247
Individual human elements and actors, 175
Inductive research
    exploration with, 12
    for intervention development, 269
    with narrative approaches, 58–59, 111
Influence, researcher. *See* Researcher
    influence
Informal interviewing, 240
Information overload, 77
Information power (IP), 67–80
    and appropriate sample for qualitative
        data, 67–69
    arguments against formal calculations
        of, 75
    defined, 69
    diabetic foot ulcer study example, 69–73
    and existing concepts in qualitative
        methodology, 76–77
    items constituting, 70–73
    for qualitative cross-case studies, 73–76
    research practice implications, 79–80
    saturation vs., 77–79
    transferability of, 79
Informed consent
    in discursive approaches, 132–133
    in mixed-methods research, 255
    from participants with profound
        intellectual disability, 206
Ingold, T., 219

Initial categories for meta-analysis, 294
Inmate College Bound Committee, 90
Inner experiencing, 35
Inquiry, matrix of, 171n3
Insights, from IPA, 152
Institutional actors, identifying, 177
Institutionally-situated action, 130
Institutional settings
    access and consent in, 132, 133
    discursive psychology research on, 129
    and hypothetico-deductive approach, 141
Intellectual disabilities, profound
    attuning theory of interaction with
        people having, 203–206
    classic grounded theory approach for
        participants with, 198
    ethical considerations in work with
        participants having, 206
Intelligence tests, 203
Intelligibility, interaction for, 123, 125
Intentional practice, language as, 62–64
Interaction
    for intelligibility, 123, 125
    schematic drawing to document, 221
Interactionist approaches, narrative data
    in, 60
Intergenerational workshops for people
    living with dementia, 236–237
Internal validity, 12, 77, 79
Interpersonal level of narrative analysis,
    113–114
Interpretation
    in IPA note-taking, 155–157
    in line drawing, 227, 228
    in narrative analysis, 117
    of narrative data, 57, 59, 61–62
    perspective of, 8
    of physiological data, 254–255
    from qualitative meta-analyses, 284–285
    in thematic analysis approach, 37
Interpretative narratives, 162
Interpretative phenomenological analysis
    (IPA), 147–165
    discursive psychology vs., 129
    holistic analysis with, 14
    involuntary childlessness in midlife
        study, 153–162
    methodological developments in,
        162–164
    and other thematic analysis approaches, 39
    reasons for selecting, 44
    stages of, 150–153
    theoretical underpinnings of, 148–150
    theory development with, 12
Interpretative repertoires, 127–128
Interpretive turn, 167, 169
Interrogatives, 125
Intersubjectivity, in narrative construction,
    113–114

Intervention design
    conducting primary research for, 269
    guiding principles, 269–270
    qualitative methods to inform, 264, 266
    synthesizing existing evidence on,
        266–269
Intervention development, 263–279
    conducting primary research for, 269
    ethical issues in, 277–278
    feasibility studies in, 273–274
    feedback to inform intervention
        modifications, 274–275
    future research for, 278–279
    guiding design principles, 269–270
    person-based approach to, 264, 265
    process evaluations in, 275–277
    qualitative methods for, 266, 270–271
    synthesizing existing evidence for,
        266–269
    think-aloud interviews in, 271–273
Intervention optimization
    feasibility studies for, 273–274
    feedback to inform modifications for,
        274–275
    qualitative methods for, 270–271
    think-aloud interviews for, 271–273
Interviewer's role, in narrative interviews,
        104
Interview methods
    in Changing Minds study, 94, 95
    of collecting narrative accounts, 103–104
    diabetic foot ulcer interview study, 69–73
    in discursive psychology, 127–128
    dyadic interview study with dementia
        patients, 236
    free association narrative interview
        technique, 102
    in person-based approach, 271
    in qualitative feasibility studies, 273
    research participant control in, 17
    sample size for studies using, 76
Interviews
    biographical, 56, 57, 101–103
    distress during, 152–153
    episodic, 102
    focused/topic, 102
    follow-up, 105
    forms of, 101–103
    in-depth, 95, 173
    informal, 240
    narrative data from, 101–104
    one-on-one, 95
    open-ended, 127
    with open-ended format, 102, 103
    pilot, 91
    sample size and quality of, 74
    semistructured, 151–153
    subjectivity and experiential narratives
        in, 60

    theme-centered, 56, 57
    think-aloud, 271–273
    walk-along, 103–104
Interview schedule, 154
Intimate partner abuse study, 175, 176
Intonation, warning, 137–139
Intrapersonal level narrative analysis,
        110–113
Invitation, actions in response to, 130
Involuntary childlessness in midlife study,
        153–163
    background and research question, 153
    data analysis, 155–162
    data collection, 154–155
    research participants, 153
    writing up, 162
IP. *See* Information power
IPA. *See* Interpretative phenomenological
        analysis
Ireland, 108
Israeli youth, cultural narratives of, 114–115
Issues, on situational maps, 175
Items, in information power model, 75–76
Iterative approach to intervention
        optimization, 274

J

Jack, Dana, 188
Jacobson, Michael, 96
Jahoda, Maria, 86
James, William, 86
JBICA (Joanna Briggs Institute Critical
        Appraisal)Checklist, 290
Jefferson, Gail, 41, 135
Jefferson, T., 102, 112
Jeffersonian transcripts, 135
Jenkins, Laura, 134
Jenna Foundation for Non-Violence, 96
Joanna Briggs Institute Critical Appraisal
        (JBICA) Checklist, 290
Johnson, Mark, 225
Johnson's ADL Scale, 244
Journal of Phenomenological Psychology, 39
Journals. *See also* Diaries
    personal, 104
    research, 239, 257
Juster, Norton, 5, 6, 8
Justice, research, 85–86, 98–99
Juxtaposition, 238

K

Kaiser, K., 21
Kearney, A. J., 105
Kent, Alex, 134
Kenten, C., 105
Key features, intervention, 270
Keyword searches, 287

Khaw, L., 175, 176
Kimura, M., 150
Kirkham, J. A., 162, 164
Kleinfeld, Judith, 115–116
"Knowing subject," 169–170, 179
Knowledge monopoly, 88
Kvale, S., 17

L

Labels, for units of analysis, 292–293
Laboratory settings, naturalistic vs., 9
Labov, W., 110
Lakoff, George, 225
Langdridge, D., 148
Langellier, K. M., 108, 109
Language
    as culturally embodied and intentional
        practice, 62–64
    for narratives, 54
    and written vs. visual documentation,
        224–226
Language-based approaches
    defined, 36
    research questions answered by, 37, 44
    types of, 40–41
Large samples, overly, 77
Larkin, M., 164
Lechner, E., 117
Letters, narrative data from, 107–108
Letters from Jenny (Allport), 107
Levitt, H. M., 9, 286, 291
Lewin, Kurt, 86–87, 89
Lewis, Helen, 87
Liberation psychology, 87
Life-course interviews. *See* Biographical
    interviews
Life history research, 40, 44
Lifespan psychology, 56
Life-story biographies, 56
Life Story Protocol, 102, 104
Line drawing
    for data collection, 213–217
    data from, 226–227
    in focused ethnography, 211–230
    for holistic analysis, 13
    in interpretative phenomenological
        analysis, 163–164
    looking vs. seeing for, 226
    and mapping method, 219–220
    methodology of, 220–224
    overcoming hesitation about, 227–229
    and participant observation method, 219
    writing vs. drawing to document
        experiences, 224–226
Lines of argument synthesis, 267
Linguistic elements, in IPA, 155
Linguistic meaning, 16
Literary analysis, 117

Lived body concept, 149
Lived experiences
    in ethnographic approaches, 212–213
    IPA for investigating, 147–150
Logic, in natural sciences, 7
Lohuis, A. M., 102–103
Longitudinal studies, 18, 271
Long-Termers program, 89
Looking, seeing vs., 226
Luckmann, T., 7, 8
Luminance, 245
Lykes, M. B., 117

M

Madill, A., 15, 41
Magdalene laundries, 108
Majlesi, A., 190
Malinowski, Bronislaw, 41
Mann, E. S., 181
Mannheim, Karl, 171
Maori communities, 85, 127
Maps
    in focused ethnography, 219–220, 240
    positional, 168, 173, 179–182
    relational, 168, 172, 174–176
    situational, 168, 172–174
    in situational analysis, 168, 170,
        172–182
    social worlds/arenas, 168, 172, 176–178
Marginalized populations
    authentic self of, 188
    community-based research with, 86
    ethnography with, 42
    grounded theory method with, 206
    qualitative research giving voice to, 30
    research justice for, 85–86, 98–99
    situational analysis with, 169
Marienthal, Austria, 86
Marquez-Lewis, C., 98
Martín-Baró, Ignacio, 87, 89
Marymount Manhattan College, 90
Masculinity and masculine performances,
    116, 181
Mason, M., 68
Massumi, Brian, 171
Master narratives, 63, 115–116
Master table of themes, 158, 161–162
Matrix of inquiry, 171n3
Mayan women, 117
McAdams, D. P., 102–104
McCabe, R., 41
McInroy, L. B., 292
McWhinney, I. R., 75
Mead, Margaret, 42, 198
Meaning
    of activities of daily living, 251–252
    discerning, of meta-analysis data,
        291–293

in focused ethnography, 218
in higher-order categories, 295
IPA to investigate making of, 147, 150
linguistic, 16
subjective, 15
Meaningful contributions, utility of, 287
Medicalization of counselor education
    study, 177, 179
Memoirs, political, 106
Memories, narratives and, 56, 57
Memos
    in analysis of case study data, 238
    for grounded theory method with video
        data, 200–202
    in situational analysis, 168, 170, 174, 182
Merleau-Ponty, M., 149
Messy situational map, 173, 174
Meta-aggregation, 285
Meta-analyses. *See* Qualitative meta-
    analyses
Metaethnography, 267–268, 284
Metamethod approaches, 285
Metaphors, documentation using, 225
Metastudy, 284
Metasummary, 284, 285
Metasyntheses. *See* Qualitative meta-
    analyses
Methodological integrity
    judging qualitative research based on, 8
    of qualitative meta-analyses, 286–287
    in qualitative research, 8–11
Methodological pluralism, 32–33
Microanalysis of video data, 193–198
Microethnography. *See* Focused
    ethnography
Microsociology, 41
Miller, P. J., 16
Mills, C. Wright, 171, 183
Mini-Mental Status Exam (MMSE), 245,
    251, 252
Minority groups, in discursive psychology,
    131
Mishler, E. G., 109, 118
Mixed-methods approach, 235–258. *See also*
    Home-based observational study of
    dementia
    in Changing Minds study, 90, 94, 95
    in CPAR projects, 85, 88
    in dementia research, 236
    ethical considerations with, 255–257
    holistic analysis with, 13
    methodological pluralism in, 33
    in naturalistic setting, 255–257
    in process analysis, 264, 275–277
    qualitative and quantitative methods in,
        13–14
    research recommendations, 257–258
MMSE. *See* Mini-Mental Status Exam
Modifications, intervention, 271, 274–275

Moffitt, U., 115
Moran, D., 148, 149
Morse, J. M., 77, 78
Moscovici, S., 117
Motulsky, S. L., 286
Moxley, D. P., 108–109
Muecke, Marjorie, 213
Mulkay, Michael, 127
Multimodal IPA designs, 163–164
Multiperspectival designs, IPA, 164
Murdy, T., 179, 181
Murray, M., 105, 109, 111

N

Narrative analysis, 109–118
    holistic analysis with, 14–15
    at interpersonal level, 113–114
    at intrapersonal level, 110–113
    and life history research, 40
    as participatory analysis, 117
    at positional level, 114
    reasons for selecting, 44
    at societal level, 114–117
    temporal considerations in, 18
Narrative approaches, 57–64
    analysis of form, content, or function in,
        55, 58
    defined, 36
    guidelines for, 57–58
    inductive and generalizable research
        with, 58–59
    language as culturally-embodied and
        intentional practice in, 62–64
    real-life implications of insights/findings
        from, 62
    reflection and reflexivity in, 61–62
    research participant control in, 17
    research questions answered by, 37, 44
    subjectivity and participant's experience
        in, 59–60
    types of, 40
Narrative data, 101–109
    from documents, 104–108
    in interviews, 101–104
    theory development from, 198–199
    visual sources of, 108–109
Narrative discourses, on situational maps,
    175
Narrative empathy, 61
Narrative framework, for analyzing video
    data, 191–193
Narrative interviews, 103–104
Narrative practices, 63
Narrative psychology, 11, 40
Narratives, 51–57
    in Changing Minds study, 95
    and core of qualitative research, 101
    counternarratives, 62, 88, 116

defined, 55
dominant culture, 114
frontier, 115–116
from grounded theory, 188
interpretative, 162
from interpretative phenomenological
    analysis, 162
master, 63, 115–116
nonverbal, 188
personal, 16–17 .
in research, 10–11
sequence and story-hood for, 52–54
in situational analysis, 173, 182
as stories in context, 54–55
trauma, 105, 112–113
units of analysis for, 56–57
Narratology, 58
National Institute for Health, 235–236
Naturalistic models of enquiry. *See also*
    Constructivism
described, 35
in discursive psychology, 126, 128
qualitative research in, 30
research question development with,
    135–136
Naturalistic settings. *See also* Home-based
    observational study of dementia
mixed-methods approach in, 255–257
research in laboratory settings vs., 9
unstructured observations in, 250
Natural sciences, logic in, 7
Negotiated ordering framework, 173
Nelson, J., 76, 77
Neuropsychiatric Inventory, 244, 252
Neuropsychiatric symptom assessments, for
    people with dementia, 242
Neuropsychology data, 241–242, 244
New York, NY, 98
New York State Department of Corrections,
    88, 91, 94
New Zealand, 85, 127
Nicaragua, 181
Nilsson, L., 198
Nizza, I. E., 165
Nonhuman elements and actants, 175
Noninvasive measures of physiological
    data, 243
Nonspeaking research participants
comprehending behavior of, 187
video data on communication by, 191, 198
visual grounded theory approach with,
    206
Nonverbal communication, 191, 193–198
Nonverbal narratives, 188
Normality threshold, 241
North America
balanced approach to qualitative and
    quantitative research in, 18
history of qualitative research in, 4
teaching of qualitative research methods
    in, 21
Northern Ireland, 106–107
North Sumatra, 213
Note-taking
in ethnographic approaches, 213
flow-based, 221
in IPA, 151, 155–157
Novice researchers, information power
    for, 74
Nygård, L., 241

O

Object elicitation, 240
Objective observations, 212
Objective reality, 34
Objectives, intervention design, 270
Objectivity, 8–9, 92
Objects, in situational analysis, 170
Object-side descriptions, 131
Observation(s)
in anthropology and psychology, 211
in ethnographic research, 212
objective, 212
participant, 218, 219, 239–240
in situational analysis, 173
subjective, 212
unstructured, 250, 256
Observational studies. *See also* Home-based
    observational study of dementia
information power for, 79
of people living with dementia, 237
sample size for, 76
Observer as participant stance, 190, 204
Öhman, A., 181
O'Mahoney, J., 108
One-on-one interviews, 95
Online narrative accounts, 105–106
On the Evaluation of Ethnographies (Muecke),
    213
Ontological perspective, on phenomenology,
    148
Open-ended interviews
collecting narratives with, 102, 103
in discursive psychology, 127
Ordered situational map, 173, 175
O'Reilly, M., 78
Organizational actors, identifying, 177
Orientation (narrative element), 110
Outsider perspective, 61–62
Overberg, R., 106

P

Palestinian youth, cultural narratives of,
    114–115
Parallel activities, 191
Park, R. E., 182

Parker, N., 78
Participant as observer stance, 190
Participant observation, 218, 219, 239–240
Participants' orientations, in discursive
    research, 140
Participatory action research
    exhibition of, 108–109
    in history of community-based research, 87
    narrative research with, 117
    support for, 98
    temporal considerations in, 18
Participatory contact zone, 91–92
Participatory research, narrative analysis as,
    103, 117
Pataki, George, 96
Pattern emergence
    in meta-analyses, 285
    for theory development, 199
Patton, M. Q., 77
Pavlish, C., 111
PCA (posterior cortical atrophy), 235.
    See also Home-based observational
    study of dementia
Pederson, J. R., 106, 115
Peirce, Charles Saunders, 227
Pell grants, for persons in prison, 89, 90,
    96, 97
People's survey, 87
Peplau, L. A., 33
Perception
    in focused ethnography, 211, 225–226
    in phenomenology, 149
    in scrutinous drawing, 220
Performance elements, of oral narrative, 108
Personal change, 118
Personal construct theory, 36
Personal experiential meanings, 150
Personal journal, 104
Personal narratives, 16–17
Personas, 269–270
Person-based approach to intervention
    development, 264, 265
    feedback in, 271
    guiding principles of, 270
    inductive data collection in, 269
Perspective, of interpretation, 8
Perspective management, 286, 296
Peru, national truth commission, 108
Peruggi, Regina, 90
The Phantom Tollbooth (Juster), 5, 6, 8
Phenomenological reduction, 148
Phenomenology, 28. *See also* Interpretative
    phenomenological analysis (IPA)
    creating meaning units in, 291–292
    defined, 35, 148
    epistemological position of, 35
    introduction of, 283
    language-based approaches vs., 40
    narrative data in, 59–60

The Philadelphia Negro (Du Bois), 86
Photo elicitation, 240
Photographs, 226
Physical disabilities, individuals with,
    85–86
Physiological data
    interpreting, 254–255
    in mixed-methods study, 242–243, 245
Piaget, J., 29
Picture, defined, 226
Pidgeon, N. F., 29
Pilot interviews, 91
Pilot studies, 277
Pinker, Steven, 35
Piot, P., 34
Pistrang, N., 36
Planned behavior change interventions, 14
Plot structure, 110
Plummer, K., 110
Pluralistic approach
    for method selection, 10, 28, 32–33,
    42–43
    in qualitative research, 4
    research questions and methods in, 6–7
The Polish Peasant (Thomas and Znaniecki),
    57
Political context, for college in prison,
    93–94
Political elements, on situational maps,
    175
Political memoirs, 106
Political pluralism, 32
Pomerantz, A. M., 140
Positional level narrative analysis, 114
Positional maps
    defined, 168, 173
    example, 179–182
Positioning analysis, 63
Positioning theory, 113, 114
Positivism
    epistemological position of, 34–35
    and interpretive turn, 167
    quality of research outside of, 8
    research questions and methods in, 6
    role of quantitative research in, 5
    and sensory experience, 217
    and situational analysis, 169
    teaching of methods incompatible
    with, 21
Posterior cortical atrophy (PCA), 235.
    See also Home-based observational
    study of dementia
Poststructuralism, situational analysis and, 170
Posttraumatic stress disorder (PTSD), 116
Pothoulaki, M., 150
Potte, J., 129
Potter, J., 29, 127, 133, 137
Power calculations, 67, 68. *See also*
    Information power (IP)

Power differential
  and Changing Minds study, 92–93
  in positional level of narrative analysis, 114
  in research, 19
POWeR+ intervention, 276–277
Pragmatic approach
  in focused ethnography, 239
  to qualitative method selection, 31–33, 42–43
  sample size needed for, 76
Pragmatism, defined, 27, 32
Precision, of qualitative research, 8
Prescriptive approach to grounded theory method, 39
Presentation of findings, from Changing Minds study, 94, 96–98
Presidential election (2020), 7
Primary research
  discerning meanings of data from, 291–293
  initial pool of, for meta-analysis, 287–288
  for intervention development, 269
  meta-analyses to identify patterns in, 285
Prioritizing intervention modifications, 274, 275, 278
PRISMA reporting standards, 288
Prison
  college in. *See* College in prison programs
  prisoner-run model, 88
  recent CPAR projects in and about, 98
Private stories, 116
Problem-based learning, 22
Process analysis
  and other language-based approaches, 41
  qualitative methods in, 263, 264
  reasons for selecting, 44
Process consent, 206
Process evaluations, in intervention development, 275–277
Progressive temporal structure, 110
Prompt cards, 269
Protagonists, in research narrative, 10–11
PSP (Public Science Project), 88, 89
Psychoanalytic approach
  data consistency in, 14
  interpersonal level of narrative analysis in, 113–114
  narrative data in, 57
  narrative interview method from, 102
  relationship in, 17
  societal level of narrative analysis in, 116–117
Psychodynamic approaches, 57
Psychological matters
  in discursive psychology, 125–126
  in production of discourse, 131

Psychology field
  focused ethnography in, 217–218
  hypothetico-deductive approach in, 141–142
  nature and scope of, 126
  observations in, 211
  positional maps in, 181
  prominence of qualitative research in, 28–29, 283
  qualitative and quantitative divide in, 5–7
  value of research in, 8
Psychology of language, 129
Psychosocial approach, 112
PsycInfo advance search tool, 288
PTSD (posttraumatic stress disorder), 116
Public, in intervention codesign, 279
Publication Manual (APA), 58, 286
Public policy, 90–91, 97
Public Science Project (PSP), 88, 89
Public stories, 116
Published qualitative research, rigor of, 290
Purposive homogenous sampling, 150–151, 153
Puvimanasinghe, T., 112–113

Q

QoL-AD (Quality of Life in Alzheimer's Disease), 244
QoL (quality of life) ratings, 252, 253
Qualitative case study. *See also* Home-based observational study of dementia
  in mixed-methods study, 237–239
  single, information power for, 79
Qualitative cross-case studies
  information power model for, 73–76
  interpretative phenomenological analysis in, 157–162
  sample size in, 68
  sample variation in, 72
Qualitative data
  context and collection of, 54–55
  defining appropriate sample for, 67–69
  as driver of mixed-method study, 247
  grounded theory from, 188–189
  inconsistency in, 14
Qualitative meta-analyses, 283–297
  examples, 284
  forms and goals of, 284–286
  methodological integrity as consideration in, 286–287
  steps for conducting, 287–296
  tailoring, for research goals, 296–297
Qualitative method selection, 10, 27–45
  epistemological considerations, 31–36
  ethical considerations, 31
  example, 43–45

and families of qualitative approaches, 36–42
and methodological integrity, 10
in mixed-method research, 241
pluralistic approach to, 32–33
pragmatic approach to, 33
in qualitative meta-analyses, 286
and reflexivity in qualitative research, 28
top-down reasoning about, 51–52
two-stage process for, 36–37, 42–43
Qualitative research approach(es)
advantages and disadvantages of using, 29–31
for analyzing subjective meaning, 15
APA guidelines for, 57–58
as art and science, 45
and assumptions underlying social reality, 6–8
in balanced approach, 17–18
coherent methodology for, 4
in CPAR, 88
criteria for judging, 8
divide in psychology between quantitative and, 5–7
ethical decision making in, 19–21
for exploration and theory development, 12
families of, 36–42
global support for, 4–5
for holistic analysis of complex phenomena, 13–15
information power and existing concepts in, 76–77
limitations of, for intervention development, 278–279
methodological integrity in, 8–11
narratives and central core of, 101
prominence of, in psychology, 28–29, 283
from realist vs. constructivist position, 36
reflexivity in, 17–18, 28
for relational analysis, 15–17
research bias in, 61
for situated analysis, 12–13
temporal issues in, 18
terminology challenges with, 3–4
Qualitative Research in Psychology (Camic et al.), 97
Qualitative research methods
for intervention development, 270–271
with quantitative methods in mixed-methods approach, 13–14
teaching, 21–22
Qualitative research method selection
for Changing Minds study, 94, 95
for ethnographic approach, 219
Quality of Life in Alzheimer's Disease (QoL-AD), 244
Quality of life (QoL) ratings, 252, 253

Quality standards, methodological pluralism and, 33
Quantitative data
in balanced approach, 17–18
context and collection of, 54–55
in focused ethnography, 241
in mixed-methods study, 247
narrative approach vs. surfacing to create, 52
value of, in psychology, 7
Quantitative meta-analyses, 284
Quantitative process evaluations, 276
Quantitative research approach
advantages and disadvantages of, 29, 30
from constructivist position, 36
in CPAR, 88
differentiation of qualitative research from, 4
divide in psychology between qualitative and, 5–7
information power for, 79
in intervention development, 278–279
and positivist epistemology, 5
power calculations for, 67, 68
and subjective meaning, 15
Quantitative research methods, in mixed-methods approach, 13–14
The Quest of the Silver Fleece (Du Bois), 86

R

Rabinow, P., 167
Randomized controlled trials (RCTs), 275, 276
Rapid ethnography. *See* Focused ethnography
Rappaport, J., 114
Rapport building, 249, 278
RCTs (randomized controlled trials), 275, 276
Readability, of qualitative research accounts, 30
Readers' evaluation, 140–141
Realism, 33–35, 75
Reality
in ethnographic approaches, 224
objective, 34
social, 6–8, 35
Real-life implications, of narrative research, 62
Recall drawing-seeing, 220, 221, 223
Reciprocal translation, 267
Recording quality, in discursive psychology, 133
Recruitment
for discursive psychology research, 132
information power and ease of, 76
and sample specificity, 71

Reflection
    diary entries to promote, 105
    drawing and, 224
    for ethical decision-making, 19–20
    in narrative approaches, 61–62
Reflexivity
    in constructivism, 35
    defined, 19, 28
    in ethnographic research, 212
    in narrative approaches, 61–62, 104
    in qualitative research, 17–18, 28
Reflexivity journal, 257
Refugees
    action research with, 117
    silences and topic avoidance for,
      112–113
    thematic analysis of narratives of, 111
Refutational synthesis, 267
Regressive temporal structure, 110
Reincarceration rate, 95, 96
Relational analysis, 15–17, 174
Relational drawing, 221
Relationalities, in situational mapping, 175
Relational maps
    defined, 168, 172
    example, 174–176
Relationships
    in Changing Minds study, 92–93
    between grounded theory categories,
      201, 202
    researcher–narrator, 116
Relativism, of pluralistic societies, 32
Reliability, of qualitative methods, 8–9
Religious pluralism, 32
Renault, I., 117
Rennie, D. L., 4, 29
Repertoires, discursive psychology,
    127–128
Repetition, to practice drawing, 224
Representational drawing, 220
Representativeness, in mixed-methods
    study, 250–251
Research bias, 61
Research collaboratives, 91–92
Research collaboratories, 85
Research design
    for Changing Minds study, 94, 95
    for home-based observational study of
      dementia, 237–243
    in mixed-methods studies, 236
    situational maps for, 173
Research diary, 105
Researcher influence
    in ethnographic approaches, 213
    in Hawthorne effect, 190
    in qualitative approaches, 30–31
    studying, 17
Researcher–participant dialogue quality,
    71–74, 77

Researcher role
    in focused ethnography, 239–241
    in intervention development, 278
    in mixed-methods study, 249–250
    in situational analysis, 170
Researcher visibility, in video data, 190
Research experience, writing vs. drawing to
    document, 224–226
Research goals, tailoring meta-analyses for,
    296–297
Research journal, 239, 257
Research justice, 85–86, 98–99
*Research Methods in Clinical and Counselling
    Psychology* (Barker et al.), 29
Research Methods in Clinical Psychology, 2nd ed.
    (Barker et al.), 29
Research Methods in Clinical Psychology, 3rd ed.
    (Barker et al.), 29
Research participant control
    in discursive research, 133–134
    in narrative interview, 103
    in research process, 17
Research participants
    data collection by, 133–134
    deductive disclosure by, 21
    ethical interactions with, 20
    in involuntary childlessness in midlife
      study, 153
    nonspeaking, 187, 191, 198, 206
    orientation of, 140
    quality of dialogue between researcher
      and, 71–74, 77
Research participant's experience
    in narrative approaches, 59–60
    self-report scale data for, 242
    as source of knowledge, 7–8
    as window to understanding, 188
Research practice, information power
    implications for, 79–80
Research question(s)
    capacity of sample to answer, 67
    category titles reflecting answers to, 294
    in discursive psychology, 125–126,
      135–136
    families of qualitative approaches based
      on, 37
    in focused ethnography, 215
    in home-based observational study of
      dementia, 243
    in IPA, 150, 153
    labels for units in meta-analysis that
      answer, 293
    meta-analysis study selection based on,
      288–290
    method selection based on, 27, 33,
      42–43, 241
    in qualitative research, 6
Research relationship, 17
Research teams, reflective practice for, 20

Resolution (narrative element), 110
Responsibility, 181
Resurrection Study group, 88
Rhetorically-situated action, 130
Rhetorical psychology, 127
Rhodes, J. E., 150
Richardson, J. T. E., 29
Riessman, C. K., 109
Rigor
    of meta-analysis studies, 290–291
    for theory development, 202–203
Riley, H., 220
Risk-reporting, 256–257
Ritchie, J., 38
Rituals, focused ethnography of, 214–215
Rivera, Melissa, 91
Roberts, A., 220
Roberts, Rosemarie, 91
Robinson, A. L., 236
Room dimensions, 245
Roper, J. M., 241
Rosenberg, C. E., 182n6
Rosenberg Self-Esteem Scale, 29, 30
Rosenthal, G., 102

S

SA. *See* Situational analysis
Sacks, H., 41, 141
Safety, in prison, 96
Sage Companion Website, 173
St. Luke's Roosevelt Hospital, 89
Salazar, M., 181
Sami women, 113, 114
Samosir Island, 213
Sample content, evaluation of, 67–68
Sample size
    and criteria for judging research, 9
    for discursive research, 134
    in interpretative phenomenological
        analysis, 150–151
    in qualitative research, 11
Sample specificity, in information power,
    70–71, 73, 74
Sample variation, in information power,
    72–74
Sampling
    and information power, 76–77
    in interpretative phenomenological
        analysis, 150–151, 153
    for intervention optimization studies, 271
Sandelowski, M., 75
Sangrar, R., 268
Sargeant, S., 114
Sartre, J. P., 149
Saturation
    defined, 68
    in grounded theory, 202, 203
    information power vs., 77–79

in intervention optimization, 274
in qualitative meta-analysis, 289
Saunders, B., 78
Savaş, Ö, 111
Saville Young, L., 112–114
Scenarios, in intervention design,
    269–270
Scene, defined, 226
Schegloff, Emmanuel, 41
Schematic drawing, 221
Schoenfeld, A. H., 207
Schreiner, Olive, 107
Schuschnigg, Kurt, 86
Schütz, A., 7, 10
Scrutinous drawing, 220
Secondary analysis, in mixed-methods
    research, 257–258
Secondness, 227
Seeing. *See also* Drawing-seeing
    drawing what you see, 224
    in ethnographic approaches, 212
    how to see, 211
    looking vs., 226
"Seeing What They See" project, 236
Self, authentic, 188
Self-management of chronic health
    conditions, 267–268
Self-reflection, drawing and, 224
Self-report scale data, 242, 244
Self-survey, 87, 95
Seltiz, Claire, 87
Semistructured interviews, 151–153
Sense-making, in IPA, 155
Sensory awareness, 215, 221
Sensory disabilities, 203
Sensory experience, in focused
    ethnography, 215, 217
Sequence
    and story-hood for narratives, 52–54
    in video analysis, 192–193
Sequential analysis, discursive psychology
    and, 128–129
Sequentially-situated action, 129–130
Serendipitous findings, 30
Series of narrative interviews, 103
Setting
    in grounded theory study, 205
    in narrative framework for video
        analysis, 191
    for video data collection, 189
Seven Neighborhood study, 88
Sexual minority identity development
    meta-analysis, 287–296
    discerning meanings of primary study
        data, 291–293
    identifying initial pool of primary studies
        for, 287–288
    organizing units into thematically
        distinct categories, 293–296

selecting studies for inclusion in, 288–291

Shaming interrogatives, 125

Shapira, J., 241

Short Recognition Memory Test for Words, 245

Shweder, R. A., 6, 32

Silence
 attention to, in narrative analysis, 112–113
 on positional maps, 180, 181

Silent actors and actants, on situational maps, 175

Silverman, David, 133

Similarization, 116

Simonds, L. M., 241

Simple map, in ethnographic approach, 219–220

Simplicity
 in data collection for discursive research, 133–134
 judging qualitative research based on, 8

Simulated patients, 114

Single case studies, 79

Situated action, 129–130, 171

Situated analysis
 in meta-analysis, 296–297
 with qualitative research, 12–13, 55

Situated interventions, 182

Situatedness, studying, 170–171

Situation
 defining, 170–172
 paying attention to objects in, 170
 in thick description, 187

Situational analysis (SA), 167–183
 defining situation in, 170–172
 exploration with, 12
 and grounded theory, 167–170
 temporal considerations in, 18
 unique contribution of, 169–170

Situational maps, 168, 172–174
 defined, 168, 172
 example, 173–174
 understanding of world from, 12–13

Situational matrix, 171, 172

Six-phase approach to thematic analysis, 39

Sketch noting, 221

Smith, Jonathan A., 39, 148, 149, 151–152, 165

Smith, Keith A., 226

Smith, M., 204, 205

Snowball sampling, 78

Social categories, in discursive psychology, 129

Social change, 87, 118

Social constructivism, 71–72, 78

Social Democratic Party, 86

Social experiences, in ethnographic approaches, 212, 218

Socialization process, 138–139

Social reality, 6–8, 35

Social worlds, defined, 176–177

Social worlds/arenas maps
 defined, 168, 172
 example, 176–178
 positional maps vs., 181

Societal level narrative analysis, 114–117

Society for Qualitative Inquiry in Psychology, 286

Sociocultural context, of discourse, 16–17, 114–117

Sociocultural elements, on situational maps, 175

Sociolinguistic processes, 17

Softened compliance, 139

Solidarity, narratives to promote, 117

Sools, A. M., 108

Sorrentino, J., 125

South America, research justice in, 85

Spatial elements, on situational maps, 175

Specification, 137, 236

Specificity of sample, in information power, 70–71, 73, 74

Spencer, L., 38

Speziale, H. J. S., 190

Spradley, J., 77, 212

Squire, C., 103, 104, 116

Stable temporal structure, 110

Stake, R., 241

Stakeholders
 intervention codesign with, 279
 value of qualitative research to, 8

Stanley, L., 107

Star, S. L., 182

The Star of Ethiopia (Du Bois), 86

State University of New York (SUNY), 89

Stepped approaches, 13–14

Stewart, A. J., 111

Stimulus category, in grounded theory study, 205

Story-hood, narrative, 52–54

Story performance and storytelling, 63, 113

Stoudt, B. G., 98

Strauss, A. L., 38–39, 167, 168n1, 169, 171, 177, 179n5, 188, 189, 198, 201, 203

Straussian grounded theory, 167–169

Street Corner Society (Whyte), 42

Strong, T., 177, 179, 181

Strong objectivity, 92

Structural constraints, for narrative, 55

Structural questions, 215

Structure, degree of, 37

Structured approach to grounded theory, 189

Structure of narrative, analyzing, 110–111

Study aim, in information power, 70, 73, 74

Study selection, for qualitative meta-analysis, 288–291

Subjective meaning, 15

Subjective observations, 212
Subjectivity
    in classic grounded theory, 200
    in focused ethnography, 218
    in narrative approaches, 59–60
    in qualitative research, 15
Subject matter fidelity. *See* Fidelity to
        subject matter
Subject position, in discourse analysis,
        41, 44
Subject-side descriptions, 131
Sub-Saharan Africa, 109
Subthemes, IPA, 152, 157–162
Sullivan, W. M., 167
SUNY (State University of New York), 89
Supervision, in mixed-methods research,
        257
Syed, M., 295
Symbolic elements, on situational maps,
        175
Synthesis
    of epistemological positions, 35–36
    ethical issues with, 277–278
    of existing evidence, 266–269
    qualitative meta-analysis for, 284
Systematic analysis, 170

T

Tabulation, 274
Talk, sociolinguistic processes underlying, 17
TAP (Tuition Assistance Program) grants, 96
Target behaviors, for video analysis,
        192–197
Taussig, Michael, 228
Taylor, S., 40
Teachers College, 89
Teaching qualitative methods, 21–22
Temporal elements, on situational maps,
        175
Temporal issues, in qualitative research, 18
Temporality, in phenomenological
        investigation, 148
Temporally-situated action, 130
Temporal sequence of narrative, 54, 55
Temporal structure, narrative analysis of,
        110–111
Tender Is the Night (Fitzgerald), 117
Testimonio, 106
Text data
    confidentiality of, 20
    sample size for studies using, 76
Thematically-distinct categories, for meta-
        analysis data, 293–296
Thematic analysis approaches
    defined, 36
    narrative approaches vs., 52
    for narrative content, 111–112

    with online narrative accounts, 106
    research questions answered by, 37, 43–44
    types of, 37–39
Thematic organization, 238
Thematic synthesis, 268
Theme-centered interviews, 56, 57
Theoretical codes, 201
Theoretical orientation
    of discursive psychology, 129–131
    for interpretive phenomenological
        analysis, 148–150
Theory development
    qualitative research for, 12, 30
    rigor and elegance of theory in, 202–203
    video data for, 198–199
Theory of change, refining intervention's,
        276, 277
Thick analysis, 167, 183
Thick data, 71–72
Thick description, 29, 183, 187, 207, 215
Think-aloud interviews, 271–273
Thirdness, 227
Thomas, Dorothy S., 171
Thomas, W. I., 57–59, 107, 171
Threats, in family mealtimes study,
        137–139, 142
Time frame, for ethnographic approaches,
        212, 213
Time-labeled worksheets, 244
Timing structure, video analysis, 192–193
Titles, of meta-analysis categories, 294
Toba Batak community, 213–216
Toolis, E. E., 104
Top-down reasoning, 51–52
Topic fit, 288–290
Topic interviews, 102
Torre, M. E., 91
Transcription
    in discursive approaches, 133–135
    in interpretative phenomenological
        analysis, 151–152, 155
    of video data in grounded theory
        approach, 192–197, 205–207
Transferability
    of information power concept, 79
    of qualitative research, 8, 202
Transference, 113–114
Translation, reciprocal, 267
Transparency
    about sample size and content, 68
    in ethnographic research, 213
    of language, 63
    in mixed-methods studies, 236
Trauma narratives
    in autobiographies, 105
    silence in, 112–113
Triangulation
    in feasibility studies, 273–274
    in focused ethnography, 218

in home-based observational study of
dementia from, 251–255
index card method to facilitate, 246–247
and methodological pluralism, 33
in mixed-methods research, 236, 247
in qualitative process evaluations, 276,
277
Trustworthiness criterion, for qualitative
research, 202
Tuition Assistance Program (TAP) grants, 96
Two-stage process for qualitative method
selection, 36–37, 42–43

U

UCLA (University of California, Los
Angeles), 29
Ulead Video studio 7 software, 204
Uncertainty acceptance, for theory
development, 198–199
Unconscious processes, narrative analysis
to explore, 112
Undergraduate education, 21, 22
Underserved populations, narrative
research with, 62
Unemployment, 86, 115
Unexpected actions, research questions
based on, 136
United Mine Workers, 87
Units of analysis
for meta-analysis, 291–296
for narratives, 56–57, 63
Unity, of qualitative research, 8
Universidad Centroamericana, 87
University of California, Los Angeles
(UCLA), 29
University of Chicago, 87
University of Vienna, 86
Unstructured conversations, 104
Unstructured observations, 250, 256
User-centered design, 271
Utility, in reaching goals, 8, 9, 286–287

V

Validation of findings, 140–141
Validity
and conceptual depth, 77
external, 12, 77
internal, 12, 77, 79
judging qualitative methods on, 8–9
and sample size, 11
Van Langenhove, L., 114
Venn diagramming, 221
Video data, 187–207
analysis of, 199–203
in archives, 107
attuning theory case example, 203–206
capabilities when using, 190–191

in discursive psychology, 132
microanalysis of, 193–198
in mixed-methods study, 244
narrative framework for analyzing,
191–193
narratives from, 108
obtaining, 189–190
in qualitative research, 14
for theory development, 198–199
Video-editing software, 191
Violence, masculinity, responsibility, and,
181
Violent Crime Control and Law
Enforcement Act, 89
Visibility, researcher, in video data, 190
Visual arts programs, 237
Visual curiosity, 229
Visual data
in analysis of case study, 238
confidentiality issues with, 20–21
in interpretative phenomenological
analysis, 164
narrative, 108–109
qualitative inquiry using, 188
in situational analysis, 173, 182
Visual discourses, on situational maps,
175
Visual documentation, 225–226, 229–230
Visual ethnographic mapping, 245
Visual grounded theory, 12
Visual literacy, 230
Visual research methods, in CPAR, 88
Vocalizations, on video, 191

W

Waletsky, J., 110
Walk-along interview, 103–104
Wall, S., 241
Ward, R., 191
Warning intonation, 137–139
Washburn, R., 181
Washington, O. G. M., 108–109
Waterford Memories project, 108
Weight loss intervention, 276–277
Weis, Lois, 93
Wertz, F. J., 29
Wetherell, M., 29, 127
Wharton, Susan, 86
White, J., 247
White supremacy, 98, 99
Whyte, W. F., 42
Wiggins, S., 128, 140
Williams, E. P., 181
Winblad, B., 241
Windle, G., 237
Winskell, K., 109
Wittgenstein, Ludwig, 126
Wolcott, H., 241

Word limit, for published qualitative
    research, 290
Wormser, Margot, 87
Writing
    documentation by drawing vs., 224–226
    IPA findings, writing up, 152, 162–163
Writings for a Liberation Psychology (Martín-
    Baró), 87
Written content of interventions,
    optimizing, 271–273

Y

Yamazaki, Y., 150
Yardley, L., 11
Yeats, W. B., 118
Yin, R. K., 238

Z

Zimbardo, P., 29
Znaniecki, F., 57–59, 107

ABOUT THE EDITOR

Paul M. Camic, PhD, was trained as a clinical health psychologist and researcher in psychology and public health in the United States and has previously been on the faculty of the University of Chicago and Northwestern University Medical School. Dr. Camic was a professor of psychology and public health and director of research at Canterbury Christ Church University's Salomons Institute for Applied Psychology from 2005 to 2014. He is currently emeritus professor at Canterbury and honorary professor of health psychology at the Dementia Research Centre, University College London, where he undertakes research related to supporting people with rare dementias.

With research interests that include the arts, health, and well-being, Dr. Camic focuses on older people, those with mental health problems, and those with a dementia. He has particular interests in community-based interventions involving art galleries and museums and singing and music. He has also published in the area of the social and emotional role of material objects—the things in our lives—and has contributed to shaping the development of public health policy in arts and health nationally and internationally. He has taught qualitative research methods for more than 25 years and has published widely using a range of quantitative and qualitative methods.

He was founding coeditor of the journal *Arts & Health* from 2009 to 2018, coeditor of the *Oxford Textbook of Creative Arts, Health & Wellbeing* published in 2015, and continues as a professorial fellow of the Royal Society for Public Health. Dr. Camic's research in the use of museums and art galleries to address problems of social isolation and loneliness has won awards from Public Health England, the Royal Society for Public Health, and the Museums and Heritage Award for Best Educational Initiative.